Mary Lou -
Best Wishes & Happi...
Love -
Roe

The Parenting Advisor

THE PARENTING ADVISOR

By The Princeton Center
for Infancy

FRANK CAPLAN

General Editor

1977

Anchor Press/Doubleday
Garden City, New York

Grateful acknowledgment is made to the following:

Photos on pages 17, 18, 20, from *A Baby Is Born,* courtesy of Maternity Center Association, New York.
Photos pages 129 and 423, courtesy of Delacorte Press.
Photo page 90, courtesy of Ken Brown.
Photo page 116, courtesy of Bob Cox.
Illustration by Mel Klapholz, page 136, based on art from American Dental Association.
Illustrations pages 142, 143, 185, 186, by Mel Klapholz.
Photos pages 208 and 365, courtesy of Reich Publishing Co., Ltd., Switzerland.
Photos pages 216 and 459, courtesy of Marie Dutton Brown.
Illustrations on reflexes page 253 through page 258, courtesy of *Exceptional Infants,* Vol. I, *The Normal Infant,* edited by Jerome Hellmuth, courtesy of Brumuer/Mazel.
Photo page 448, courtesy of Josephine Brown Dutton.
Photo page 472, courtesy of American Montessori Society.

Material excerpted from *Infants and Mothers: Individual Differences in Development,* by T. Berry Brazelton, M.D., copyright © 1969 by T. Berry Brazelton, M.D. Reprinted with the permission of Delacorte Press/Seymour Lawrence. From *Understanding Your Child from Birth to Three: A Guide to Your Child's Psychological Development,* by Joseph Church, copyright © 1973 by Joseph Church. Reprinted with the permission of Random House. From *Three Years to Grow,* by Dr. Sara D. Gilbert, copyright © 1972 by Sara D. Gilbert. Reprinted with the permission of Parents' Magazine Press. From *Today's Child,* by Drs. Elizabeth Robertson and Margaret Wood, copyright © 1972 by Pagurian Press Ltd. Reprinted with permission of Charles Scribner's Sons and Pagurian Press Ltd. From *What Every Child Would Like His Parents to Know,* by Dr. Lee Salk, copyright © 1972 by Lee Salk. Reprinted with permission of David McKay Co., Inc. From *Baby and Child Care,* by Benjamin Spock, M.D., copyright © 1945, 1946, 1957, 1968 by Benjamin Spock, M.D. Reprinted with permission of Simon & Schuster, Inc., Pocket Books division.

Library of Congress Cataloging in Publication Data

Princeton Center for Infancy.
The parenting advisor.

Bibliography: p. 543.
Includes index.
1. Infants—Care and hygiene.   2. Child development.
3. Children—Management.   I. Caplan, Frank.   II. Title.
RJ61.P944   1977   649'.1

Acknowledgments

Never has a book been published that has had so many enthusiastic, earnest professionals and paraprofessionals associated with library work, data collection, digesting, writing, reviewing, and editing. It took courage and insight for a publisher and editor to assign the preparation of THE PARENTING ADVISOR, an encyclopedic undertaking, to an organization with only two books to its credit.

We are indebted to Ms. Loretta Barrett, Editor-in-Chief of Anchor Press/Doubleday, for her ongoing faith in the Princeton Center for Infancy. We wish, too, to thank Ms. Angela Iadavaia-Cox, Ms. Barrett's editorial assistant, for her help in finalizing our manuscript. Every project must have a guiding hand and sometimes a strong arm. Choosing the themes and editorial content of this book was shared by the Princeton Center's general editor, Frank Caplan, and associate editor, Myra D. Hochman.

We are greatly indebted to Theresa Caplan, our unflinching rewriter and editor, whose patience and input were beyond measure.

All the Princeton parents who participated in THE PARENTING ADVISOR took home several packets of material, a pile of books, and a PCI point of view that emerged from numerous staff conferences. All of them have our gratitude for helping concretize what at first looked like an impossible undertaking.

Elizabeth Bartholomew	Marcia Grossman	Ann Reitzel
Carolyn Buss	Mary-Kate Heffern	Susan Rich
Lucille Denney	Celia Morris	Laurel Scheeler
Joan Dolan	Pat Mort	Steven & Gail Simon
Camille Duncan	Florence Nathan	Elizabeth Tomkins
Judy Forusz	Barbara Pinkham	Regina Vance
Judy Glass	Jean Preblick	Ellen Yablonsky

Heartfelt thanks go to the child-rearing specialists who carefully reviewed our subject field digests and wrote chapter introductions. They sensed the need for this book and responded with alacrity to our invitation to contribute their considerable expertise:

Frank Caplan, M.A.

Sheldon Cherry, M.D.

Frank Falkner, M.D.

Robert Harmon, M.D., and
Leon Yarrow, Ph.D.

Frances L. Ilg, M.D.

Eric H. Lenneberg, Ph.D.

Lewis P. Lipsitt, Ph.D.

Fredelle Maynard, Ph.D.

Ashley Montagu, Ph.D.

Myrtle B. McGraw, Ph.D.

Belle Parmet and Morris Parmet, M.D.

Myron Winick, M.D.

We hope THE PARENTING ADVISOR meets their high standards—and yours.

THE PRINCETON CENTER FOR INFANCY
Frank Caplan, General Editor
Myra D. Hochman, Associate Editor
Theresa Caplan, Editorial Assistant

Contents

xi

Introduction

Today more than 45 per cent of all mothers are working; other mothers are returning to college for completion of their schooling and many more are entering the professions. Seeds of discontent in young feminists have been sowed by the Women's Lib Movement and as a result, marriage and family life are changing. Motherhood is turning into parenting, with many more men involved in pregnancy, hospital delivery, care of the newborn, daily routines, and childhood development. Sexual freedom has increased, which has created new situations: increased divorce, communal living, single parenthood, more adoptions, etc.

In the thirties and forties, obstetricians and baby doctors were "gods" to new parents. While many offered routine advice that did lead to better physical health care, most ignored the mental, social, and emotional growth of infants. Concentrating on physical health needs to the exclusion of the other disciplines in the critical earliest years created sad and costly problems for the family and society: academic failure, drinking, drug abuse, depression, violence, and crime.

As the standard of living rose, so did the demands for pediatrics, psychiatry, psychological counseling, and parenting education. In an attempt to share their experience and know-how, professionals began to write books in all areas of child rearing. Some of these books are excellent and deserve to be used as a basis for parent education programs, high school or college courses in child development, or career courses for paraprofessionals in day care for infants and toddlers. Other books, however, are outbursts from professionals without sympathetic regard for the parenting problems faced by today's working and non-working mothers and harassed fathers. Most do not help couples adjust to today's changing sexual and social roles and values.

Sympathy is the key word! Much advice was written without consideration for the working mother, feminist feelings, modern-day fathers, etc. Few child-rearing books have given parents reassurance and support that what they are doing is positive and "normal." Dr. Benjamin Spock was one of the early few who understood this problem and in his writing gave parents the support they were seeking.

Today there are others who share their knowledge and the latest research with parents: Dr. T. Berry Brazelton (*Infants and Mothers* and *Toddlers and Parents*), Dr. Richard Feinbloom (contributor to and editor of *Pregnancy, Birth and the Newborn Baby,* and *The Child Health Encyclopedia*), Dr. Hiag Akmakjian (*The Natural Way to Raise a Healthy Child*), to name just a few. They are telling their readers that only parents can provide the personal attention and encouragement babies need to blossom and are regarding mothers and fathers as people who also have rights.

Happily another breed of parent educators has emerged—mothers who write reassuring, informative books for other mothers (Marguerite Kelley and Elia Parson's *The Mother's Almanac;* Jean Marzollo's *9 Months, 1 Day, 1 Year*); as well as groups of mothers who join in co-operative writing projects, such as the Boston Women's Collective (*Our Bodies, Ourselves* and the *New Woman's Survival Catalog*), and the Princeton Center for Infancy (*The First Twelve Months of Life* and now this book). There also are books being written by fathers for fathers (*Father Power* by Henry Biller and Dennis Meredith). All these books are answering many of the questions parents have with regard to organizing their own lives and tackling with understanding and humor the "everyday crises" of child rearing. They are taking seriously parents' ambitions both at home and in the workaday world.

THE PRINCETON CENTER FOR INFANCY

A revolution in child development thinking has forced researchers concerned with the behavioral sciences to shift their target from the preschool years of three to six to the earliest years, from birth to three. The limited success of Head Start programs with academic skills indicated that remediation and intervention must occur earlier to make a difference. Child researchers have discovered that many newborn learning capabilities are amazingly well developed and varied; that sensory stimulation (both human and environmental) is vital to future growth.

Studies in nutrition indicate a correlation between obesity in infancy and a permanent increase in the number of fat cells at adulthood. They reveal, too, the relationship between malnutrition (specifically protein deficiency) in infancy and later retardation. Psychologists and psychiatrists are becoming increasingly outspoken about the beginning of depression in the earliest years and serious emotional disturbances in adulthood.

In 1971, Edcom Systems, Inc., of Princeton, New Jersey, an organization that specialized in infant environmental research and design, financed the collection of data for an information bank on infancy. The independent Princeton Center for Infancy subsequently was formed to accomplish this. It assumed the monumental task of exploring in a multidisciplinary manner all data relevant to the earliest years, acutely aware of just how little is really known.

Setting up a sequential month-by-month, year-by-year data bank was assigned to a researcher and writer and from this base we produced a series of thirteen illustrated thirty-two-page pamphlets and a large colored Growth Chart on the first year of life . . . one of the few publication series approved by the American Academy of Pediatrics. From these booklets a beautiful book, *The First Twelve Months of Life,* was published and has become a best seller by word-of-mouth advertising by parents.

Collecting another data bank by subject fields was undertaken by seasoned early childhood educator-researchers and the resulting material was sorted and filed into hundreds of topics of concern to parents.

THE PARENTING ADVISOR

Never have there been published so many books on child rearing and infant research. Probably this prolific output since 1950 has been due in part to the electronic devices, electrocardiograph, brain wave machine, etc., that have given researchers access to infant powers that formerly were not measurable. Researchers were discovering that newborn babies were not as passive as had been believed and that they could make perceptual choices in response to stimuli. In fact, there are fetal reactions to noise and movement in utero. These findings encouraged others to research what infants can see and hear and how they take in and process information.

With the new knowledge gained from all these stirrings and the vast outpourings of books and magazine articles for parents on every imaginable subject, the need to digest these and to set new ground rules for rearing infants became imperative. There emerged an obvious need for one book that would combine the best and latest theories of child rearing and thus offer a sound guide for parents constantly bombarded with an endless list of alternatives on what to do and not to do for their child.

In 1974, Anchor Press/Doubleday invited Frank Caplan, director of the Princeton Center for Infancy, to do such a book. The task of overseeing the sorting of information from books, original research, magazines, etc., into usable packets to be digested by parent/writers went to Myra D. Hochman, Associate Editor at the Princeton Center for Infancy. Subsequently twenty-two Princeton parent/writers were recruited—another instance of parents talking to other parents in a sympathetic way. In addition, fourteen experts, all well-recognized authorities in the various fields of child rearing (nutrition, personality, language development, etc.) were chosen to critically review for accuracy the material finally presented in this book.

The Parenting Advisor resulted with fourteen chapters covering all aspects of child rearing. Each chapter contains the essence of the thinking of the leading professionals so that parents will be able to formulate their own opinions as to what is best for them and their children. Parents will notice, however, that controversy exists in the professional parenting field. A great many unanswered questions still need to be researched and studied: mother's and father's roles; single, step, foster, and adoptive parents; day-care centers; the working mother; breast versus bottle feeding; infancy and early learning; the impact of prenatal and birth experiences on newborns, etc. In these cases, parents will have to make decisions based on available facts and experiences of others. When controversy exists, opinions are quoted or referred to by name. When all experts agree, as happens with such topics as health, illness, or enrichment, this is also indicated.

Besides offering the salient points of contemporary research, *The Parenting Advisor* contains two additional opinions. The experts who reviewed the contents of this book have written introductions for their own chapters. The introductions represent their individual views, some of which may be disputed by other experts in the subsequent chapter. Once again it is up to the parents to decide for themselves the route they are to take. The PCI parents who prepared the text also have some very strong convictions, intuitions, and prejudices based on their own experiences. The PCI Point of View, which appears frequently throughout each chapter, is their place to "sound off," to present some tips and practical guidelines and share their concerns. The PCI Point of View is always labeled as such so that it will not be confused with other data. Thus this book is truly a compendium of different points of view and attitudes objectively presented. It will introduce readers to many important ideas.

THE PROFESSIONAL PARENT

Increasingly there is a great hue and cry about the low level of parenting in our society and the need for "licensing" and training *all* prospective parents. The concept of a professional parent rests on several tenets: (1) future generations will *choose* to become parents; they will not feel impelled merely to crank out babies; (2) multidisciplinary research dramatically suggests that the first three years of life have far-reaching influences on personality, emotional behavior, and learning styles; (3) data are being generated daily from such diverse fields as nutrition, stimulation, perception, psychology, and medicine that demand attention and, more than that, require application by parents. After all, what good are all the statistical surveys, charts, and graphs in the world if parents unconsciously perpetuate the hoary maxim "it was good enough for my parents so it's good enough for me."

Professional parents are those who attack their child-rearing job like pros. During the months before the baby's birth they read extensively, attend classes, and gradually evolve their own child-rearing approaches. They find out what all babies are like and how they grow so they will be able to provide their infant with the proper surroundings, loving care, and stimulation.

The Princeton Center for Infancy does not believe that there are pat answers to any child-rearing issue. One of our functions is to communicate to parents the most up-to-date information and opinions that pertain to early childhood and present them in an objective format. All our projects are intended to be tools of the trade for the parenting profession.

Good luck and good parenting!

A NOTE ON STYLE

The Princeton Center for Infancy is deeply committed to parents of both sexes assuming the responsibility for their child, as well as to the recognition of the individuality of both male and female babies. We have uniformly used "parents" unless we were referring specifically to only the mother or father. For lack of a more appropriate universal pronoun, we have used "he" and "she" randomly when referring to babies.

1
Childbirth and Early Parenting

INTRODUCTION BY SHELDON CHERRY, M.D.*

Childbirth is one of the most natural and frequently experienced events in life, yet it has been clouded with superstition, fear, and mystique. In this age of modern exploration and atomic energy, scientific knowledge has also advanced to new frontiers. However, ignorance about reproductive biology remains. Folk tales regarding childbirth have passed from generation to generation, many of which have been perpetuated even by the medical profession. Expectant parents have often remained victims of the reproductive process rather than participants.

Over the past decade a revolution in obstetrical care and childbirth has been occurring. A vast amount of new scientific and medical information has become known. Pregnancy has become very safe for the mother and fetal and newborn mortality has been reduced. In addition, the concept of "prepared" childbirth has been established, which proposes that education of the parents regarding the basic facts of pregnancy, birth, and the newborn will decrease fear and make the entire experience more enjoyable, safer, and rewarding.

The purpose of this chapter is to impart this new knowledge to the layperson in simple, non-scientific language.

* Dr. Sheldon Cherry is presently assistant clinical professor at the prestigious Mount Sinai Medical Center and attending physician for the past ten years at the hospital. He is the author of an excellent book, *Understanding Pregnancy and Childbirth*, and of *The Menopause Myth*, and a graduate of Columbia College and the Columbia Medical School. He was a grantee of a National Institute of Health Research Award from 1967 to 1972.

CHOOSING YOUR DOCTORS

The Right Obstetrician for You

Obstetricians vary in temperament, outlook, and bedside manner. In order to find the best doctor for you, you must develop some notions of what you're looking for in a doctor. Do you want a doctor who makes all the decisions? Do you prefer a doctor who encourages you to ask questions and participate in decision making? Do you feel you want to contribute to your childbirth experience? Check into the hospital your prospective doctor is affiliated with and how your doctor feels about natural childbirth or rooming-in, whereby mother and child remain together from the moment of birth.

In her book *Breast Feeding and Natural Child Spacing,* Sheila Kippley repeatedly emphasizes the *parents' responsibility* for communicating their feelings and concerns about childbirth to a prospective obstetrician:

1. It is your right to be selective in choosing an obstetrician; exercise it.

2. Don't be afraid to question or refuse unnecessary treatment.

3. Ask all your questions at the beginning. Don't wait until you're in labor to find out if your doctor is in favor of natural childbirth and breast feeding.

4. Be specific and direct. Find out how long you will stay in the hospital—assuming both you and your baby are healthy.

5. If you have made a mistake and somehow misjudged your physician or yourself, you have the right to terminate the relationship and seek a more compatible one.

Midwife Care

This relatively new approach to childbirth in the United States (traditional practice in England and many other European countries) is catching on in California and making its way to the East Coast. Under *normal* conditions, the midwife replaces the obstetrician. Of course, a doctor is consulted should any emergency occur.

Nurse-midwives are registered nurses who have specialized training and experience in the care of mothers and babies. Midwives do not use drugs, nor do they perform surgery. However, in the event of a rare emergency, they know what to do and where to get immediate help. Midwives can function both in the home or in a hospital. They view childbirth as the natural, normal experience it really is and are decidedly less costly than traditional American methods of childbirth. Check with your local hospital to see if this option is available to you, should you desire it.

PCI Point of View

PCI supports the concept of birth being a condition of health rather than pathology. Not only does the midwife provide encouragement and support throughout an uncomplicated, natural birth process, but she continues to care for the mother and baby after the delivery. The choice of an obstetrician versus a midwife is up to the feelings and needs of each expectant mother and father. Both need to understand the pros and cons of each approach and then decide which one will suit them best.

Baby Doctor

All parents face the problem of selecting the *right* doctor for their baby. The well-prepared parent attends to this before the baby is born so that only a phone call to the chosen doctor is required for the all-important "first visit" after the baby has arrived. This visit marks the beginning of the first intimate, non-family relationship with an adult that your baby experiences, a relationship that will provide medical care, continuity, education, and support for all of you.

Medical doctors agree that a pediatrician, a specialist in caring for children from birth through adolescence, renders the best care for children. Where do you begin to find the pediatrician for you and your baby?

1. Through the department of pediatrics in your local hospital or medical school.

2. Locate the local medical society. Medical societies that maintain offices are listed in the telephone book.

3. Various social service agencies listed in the telephone book—city or county health departments or the Visiting Nurse Association—would be able to refer you.

4. Ask your relatives, friends, or family doctor for referrals.

5. If you are moving, ask your present pediatrician for a referral. There are about 18,000 pediatricians in the U.S. and most of them have some acquaintance with at least one pediatrician in other areas.

6. Use the *Directory of Medical Specialists,* found in the medical or science sections of libraries.

7. It may not be too important where the pediatrician you are considering trained; what is important is whether he teaches. Teaching physicians whether at a hospital or medical school, must keep up with the latest knowledge in the practice of medicine and while doing it become better physicians.

Prenatal Visit

Once you have "zeroed in" on a doctor (a general practitioner or a pediatrician), it is common practice to pay a prenatal visit. Here, in an atmosphere free of pressure, when both parents are available and there is no baby present to cuddle or attend to, parents and doctor may discuss such philosophical concepts as the role of conditioning in child development, breast feeding versus bottle feeding, how long do you let baby cry, the role of the father, etc. It is also a time to explore the mechanics of the doctor's practice: what are his fees; is this a group practice; are there set calling hours; does he make house visits? Some questions that usually are discussed at the first prenatal visit include:

1. Will the baby be healthy? Everyone expects that he will be—99 per cent are, but mothers usually worry, and it is good to be able to talk about it.

2. What is the pediatrician's role at the hospital? He will check the newborn on the first and next-to-last day and will probably visit the mother sometime during the first twenty-four hours. Usually it is the father who notifies him of the birth.

3. How does the pediatrician know the baby is normal? He reviews tests he performs that determine whether the baby is normal, retarded, has defective vision, hearing, etc. Many of a newborn's very normal behaviors appear strange and atypical to the uninformed parent.

4. How often will the doctor see the baby? Most often it is monthly until the sixth month (a date most parents find exhilarating to keep).

5. What is the charge? This is the time for parents to be frank about their financial picture. Some doctors have flexible rates for students, etc., and many will make allowances regarding payment schedules.

6. How does the doctor feel about breast feeding versus bottle feeding? Most doctors today interpret their roles as supporting the mother's decision, whatever it is, since baby usually will thrive either on a bottle or on the breast. If the mother has decided on bottle feeding, she may inquire if the doctor has any choice of formula, what kind of bottles he recommends, and how he feels about equipment sterilization.

7. What is the family's health history? Parents often are concerned about weaknesses in their own history, i.e., allergy, diabetes, etc., or the history of previous children, if there are any. This should be discussed openly. It would be useful, too, to go over the record of diseases, illnesses, or early deaths in the family.

8. What is the mother's present health status? For example, mother's blood type; if she has given birth before, has the baby been born jaundiced; has the mother a tendency to diabetes?

9. Will a nurse be necessary? The possibility of needing help should be considered ahead of time, whether it be in the form of father, grandparents, the Visiting Nurse Association, or a sleep-in nurse.

After the prenatal visit is over, prospective parents must trust themselves to make a judgment about a particular doctor. Did he listen, was he dogmatic, was he open to questions? These are some questions they must consider and then act.

SOME METHODS OF CHILDBIRTH AND HOSPITALIZATION

Today, natural childbirth and rooming-in are becoming more and more popular. Long before the baby is about to be born, you probably will have become very familiar with what each of these means.

Natural Childbirth

The term *natural childbirth* is a misnomer. First, because as Dr. Alan Guttmacher states in *Pregnancy and Birth,* it "connotes that any other way

7

of conducting delivery is unnatural, and by implication wrong" and, second, because it misses the whole point of what childbirth should be—a major experience in a woman's life, one worthy of thought, planning, and preparation. A woman should be able to undergo childbirth without harming herself or her baby. Perhaps the most appropriate term for "natural" childbirth is *prepared childbirth,* as used by the Boston Women's Collective, in *Our Bodies, Ourselves.* They state that "Childbirth preparation means educating ourselves about what is likely to happen to our bodies, our minds, and our lives during the childbirth experience. It also means finding someone—husband, friend, or relative—to share this period with us."

Prepared or natural childbirth in its modern form was introduced by the late Dr. Grantly Dick-Read in 1932. His key concept was that fear causes tension and tension results in pain and difficulty during labor. Based on this concept, his method stresses understanding of pregnancy and the birth process and prescribes a series of breathing and relaxation exercises that are employed during pregnancy, as well as during childbirth. It also requires that someone remain with the woman during her labor. This natural childbirth approach has enjoyed a high measure of success in alleviating pain associated with childbirth. Although still highly regarded, this method has largely been replaced by the Lamaze method, perhaps because the Lamaze method involves the woman with her partner as coach, while in the Dick-Read method, the woman and her obstetrician form a team, with her partner not nearly so involved.

Hypnosis is also used to relieve fear of pain during labor and delivery. Here the woman is trained during pregnancy to enter a state of self-hypnosis during labor and delivery to prevent pain sensation from becoming conscious during the birth process. Hypnosis can be highly successful at times, but it is not suited to every woman and does not allow women to participate actively in the childbirth experience. Because of these drawbacks, hypnosis is not widely used in childbirth.

THE LAMAZE METHOD

The Lamaze method of psychoprophylaxis for childbirth is somewhat more structured than natural childbirth. Developed by Dr. Fernand Lamaze, it is based on Pavlov's work with conditioned responses. Here the emphasis is on breathing techniques and body positions learned in conjunction with a partner, thereby setting up a pattern of coaching appropriate response. The Lamaze-trained woman reacts to labor by using certain techniques when appropriate, facilitating the work of her uterus. This method is opposed to interpreting the uterine contractions as labor pains and experiencing them passively as a painful experience. Preparation for the Lamaze method of childbirth usually involves attending a series of classes, generally beginning about the fifth month of pregnancy, and choosing a doctor and hospital that are familiar with the method and will encourage its application. Almost without exception, women who have experienced the Lamaze method regard it highly.

MENTAL HEALTH AND CHILDBIRTH

In his book *The Feeling Child,* Dr. Arthur Janov urges parents to consider labor and delivery procedures from the mental health point of view. "I believe that these processes frequently add not only quantitatively to neurosis, but produce qualitative leaps in terms of the amount of pain and residual tension implanted in the system." Natural childbirth should be practiced by mothers since it is most comfortable for the fetus. A prolonged labor or a drugged labor creates more tension and pressure on the baby, plus a restricted oxygen supply. Dr. Janov is in complete agreement with Dr. Ashley Montagu when he stresses the critical importance of "compression and massive physical stimulation during birth."

Whatever method of prepared or natural childbirth you are interested in, it may be helpful to remember the following points presented by Elise Fitzpatrick, et al., in *Maternity Nursing:*

1. Fear makes us feel pain more acutely, but this fear and pain may diminish or disappear when one understands the childbearing process.

2. Psychic tension enhances perception of pain—a woman may relax more easily if the atmosphere is calm and relaxed and if good human contacts have been established.

3. Muscular relaxation and a special type of breathing diminish or abolish the pains of labor.

While the implication exists that for childbirth to be a "good" experience, delivery should take place without drugs of any kind, in fact, Dick-Read, Lamaze and other authorities never said that the *judicious* use of drugs was wrong. If medication is indicated, the woman needs to accept the medical necessity for it and be aware that it will enhance her experience by allowing her to remain comfortable and an active participant in her childbearing.

PCI Point of View

PCI believes that it is far better to have women in pain who are undergoing natural childbirth according to their own rhythms than to drug them into delivering foggy babies! No one can promise a "natural" birth. A small percentage of labors poses serious difficulties, and pain-killing drugs or anesthetics may be indicated to ensure the safe delivery

9

of your baby. In these situations, remember that your preparation for a natural delivery will place you in the best possible condition for any type of delivery.

Birth Without Violence

Medical controversy is erupting about the harsh way the newborn is treated soon after emerging from the peaceful womb, also about the hospital practices affecting the mother in those first few days. Dr. Frederick Leboyer, a French obstetrician (who has delivered more than 10,000 babies) has written a book (or rather a 114-page poem), *Birth Without Violence,* which asks why we have to subject a newborn, emerging from darkness and silence in the womb, to a blaze of harsh lights and loud voices; why the questionable and shocking procedure of slapping the infant's buttocks to start breathing; and why is the traumatic separation from the womb followed by instant separation from the mother?

What would Dr. Leboyer do to correct the newborn's suffering?

1. Since a baby has sight ability at birth, why the violent blinding surgical lighting? Dr. Leboyer would extinguish all the lights in the delivery room except a night light. It is better for the mother to discover and communicate with her child by touch and by speaking to her baby quietly. Since newborn infants are *almost* ugly at this time and their features deformed by fear, it is better to wait to see the child when its face "has relaxed into its true features." "Love," Dr. Leboyer says, "comes often in semi-darkness" anyway.

2. Hearing? Dr. Leboyer would cut down all noises; giving orders would be accomplished with inaudible whispers. We must become "aware that babies can hear and realize how sensitive its hearing is and how easily it is harmed" in the delivery room. Low-keyed music is played all the time.

3. Near darkness, silence, and patience. Dr. Leboyer would also teach mothers how to accept the slowness in the birth process and not become frenzied about birth. Everything must be done to protect the child from shock!

4. Immediate contact with mother by placing baby (with umbilical cord left intact) on mother's hollowed belly with its warmth and suppleness and rhythmic breathing. By delaying the cutting of the umbilical cord, Dr. Leboyer claims that we "let the mother accompany her infant's first step into the world of breathing." The mother goes on breathing for both of them until the infant is safely established in its new domain. Gradually, after several minutes, the newborn's lungs and respiratory system will begin to function properly and the umbilical cord will stop puls-

ing. After about five minutes the cord can be cut. The mother's physical handling of her baby is a must and an expression of love.

5. Passage from the state of unity in the womb to the independence of the new world is traumatic. Placing the infant on a hard and cold metal scale is an outrage. Dr. Leboyer would rather place the baby in a bath— a warm ninety-eight degrees, the temperature of the baby's body. Birth is too important an event to be left solely to the obstetrician; the newborn needs a "loving artist's attention, not a highly trained engineer."

His ideas, although simple and convincing, are nonetheless arousing much protest from obstetricians who point to the dangers of infection in delayed cutting of the umbilical cord. Nevertheless, we at PCI believe it makes sense and deserves testing.

Dr. Marshall H. Klaus of Case Western Reserve University Medical School is researching the ways in which hospital practices affect mothers. It is this immediate separation in humans (especially with premature babies) that results in a disruption of the attachment bond between mother and child and father that is so important to the future behavior and learning of the child. Dr. Klaus is studying these problems over an extended period. He claims, in "Human Maternal Behavior at the First Contact with Her Young," an article that appeared in *Pediatrics Magazine,* that it does not seem unreasonable that present obstetrics systems in the hospital "may have to undergo drastic alterations."

Rooming-in

Rooming-in is the type of hospital accommodation whereby you have the hard-earned result of your recent labor tucked snugly in a crib at your bedside most of the time rather than in the nursery. Typically your baby is brought to you in the morning after your breakfast and remains with you until you are ready to go to sleep at night. During the day, nurses teach you how to bathe your baby, care for the diaper area, the navel, ears, eyes, and nose. They help you with feeding and answer your questions.

Rooming-in offers you the opportunity to get acquainted with your baby from the start, to feed at request, to change, dress, bathe, nuzzle, and count toes as often as you wish while your baby has the same chance to get used to you—your voice, the smell and warmth of your skin, and the way you do things. The father, usually the forgotten man in obstetrical matters, will find that rooming-in has decided advantages for him as well. Dressed in hospital gown, he can hold and change baby and enjoy a family feeling from day one.

John Miller, M.D., author of *Childbirth,* answers a few questions that confront the couple considering rooming-in for the first time.

1. *Will caring for my baby interfere with my need for rest?* No. Everything you need will be at your fingertips and the physical exertion involved is minimal. A new baby sleeps a great deal of the time, so you will have ample opportunity to rest. Actually a mother who is apprehensive because she is certain that the baby crying in the nursery is hers rests far less than the mother who can serenely watch over her own.

2. *Is there danger of infection?* No. Visitors are limited in rooming-in and are asked to wear gowns and masks. Rooming-in has actually reduced the number of hospital infections.

3. *Suppose my baby requires special care or equipment?* Of course, your baby will get it. If for any reason your baby's doctor feels that he should remain in the central nursery, be understanding and grateful for this special care. However, many premature babies have done splendidly in rooming-in.

ARGUMENTS IN FAVOR OF ROOMING-IN

A significant number of psychiatrists, psychologists, pediatricians, and obstetricians feel that there are certain psychological advantages in the rooming-in plan. In addition to the obvious physical needs, a baby needs the security that comes from prompt attention to his demands and from holding, fondling, and snuggling. These needs are difficult or impossible to satisfy fully when a baby is kept away from the mother. Unsatisfied emotional needs may lead to some emotional difficulty. Whether or not you accept this hypothesis, it seems logical to suppose that if baby and parents get off to a good, well-adjusted start, the chance of tensions developing later will be reduced.

The easiest and best way to learn baby care skill is to do so under the guidance of experienced teachers. Thus it would appear obvious that the postpartum period in the hospital would be the ideal time and place to learn how to care for your baby. This can best be accomplished with a rooming-in arrangement.

ARGUMENTS AGAINST ROOMING-IN

Dr. Alan Guttmacher, author of *Pregnancy and Birth,* presents both sides of the issue. One disadvantage is that visiting may be restricted to the husband, who must wear a hospital gown and mask, and wash his hands before handling the baby. Rooming-in requires more nursing personnel who are able to teach. The mothers must be carefully supervised at all times. It is more difficult for hospitals to assign accommodations under the dual scheme—rooming-in and rooming-out. Finally, some women, particularly those having other children at home, do not want the inconvenience and disturbance of rest and sleep.

PCI Point of View

We concur with the substantial number of physicians and other professionals who support the premise that close physical and emotional contact (being held, rocking motion, and cuddling in those first critical beginnings of mothering) is strategically important to the newborn's sense of immediate and future security.

Nevertheless, we feel that rooming-in should be entirely optional. While it is ideal for some women, it may be unsuitable for others. The decision to choose a rooming-in arrangement or the central nursery must be a personal one on the mother's part, with husband and doctor consulted. Sift and sort the information and get and use what sounds best for you. Above all, keep in mind that rooming-in is designed to add to your joy and comfort while you are in the hospital.

PREPARING FOR THE HOSPITAL

For nine months you have gone through many discomforts and bodily changes. For nine months you have had to share your body with your fetus. Under the care of your physician or obstetrician, you have changed your eating habits, and your diet had to include enough proteins, minerals, and vitamins to sustain both you and your baby-to-be.

Throughout the nine months you have had time—perhaps too much time—to worry about whether your baby will be healthy, whether you will feel positively toward her or him, and whether you will be able to serve well as woman and mother. To allay your fears and prepare for childbirth, you may have joined others in the Lamaze method (natural childbirth), free Red Cross Mother and Baby Care courses, and such organizations as the La Leche League (promotes breast feeding), and the International Childbirth Association (furthers the education of parents, hospitals, and professionals).

Your hospital experience will be more comfortable and rewarding if you know beforehand what to expect. Make sure to visit the hospital at least a month before your baby is due.

Visiting the Hospital

Avail yourself and your husband of whatever introductory services the hospital of your choice offers. Now is the time for you to find out if your philosophies mesh. Make sure the following questions have been answered to you and your husband's satisfaction:

1. Is the pregnant woman treated like an invalid; wheelchaired to her room?

2. Is the delivery room harshly illuminated or softly lit?

3. If he chooses, will the father-to-be be permitted to stay with his wife throughout labor and delivery (assuming everything develops normally)?

4. Are the nurses friendly or merely efficient?

5. What is the staff's attitude toward parents—co-operative or distant?

6. Has anyone you know used this hospital? If yes, was the experience satisfactory?

7. Will the mother be permitted to give birth to a drug-free baby, if she so chooses?

8. If desired, will the hospital permit rooming-in?

Maternity Ward

Ask to be shown through the maternity unit. You can see typical rooms and perhaps the nursery, labor, and delivery rooms as well. Often hospitals include maternity floor tours in their prenatal course.

Hospital Procedures

In every hospital there is someone available to tell you what you want to know about the building; where to park and which entrance to use, especially at night; admission procedures; the care of maternity patients; and the cost of maternity care.

Fees

Hospital rates are quoted according to the kind of room you get. Some hospitals have rooming-in arrangements. Nearly all hospitals have private rooms that are more expensive than those you share with one, two, or more mothers. The average stay is four to five days. Hospital rates include

14

board, but there are extra charges for use of the delivery room, anesthetics, medicines, and nursing care for you and your baby. Know exactly what each item includes, how payment is to be made, and when payments are due. If you have hospital insurance, reread your policy.

Personnel

You will be cared for during labor by one or more obstetrical nurses and probably by one house doctor. Of course, your doctor will be there, too, part or all of the time you are in labor. Hospital admission varies, but you may expect something like the following: You will be met by a receptionist, who will take you to the maternity wing in a wheelchair. Here you will change your own clothes for a hospital gown and receive your initial preparation for delivery. Your blood pressure will be taken, a specimen of your urine will be examined, and a general check will be made of your stage of labor. Having completed registration, your husband may be allowed to stay with you in the labor room and join you in the delivery room, hospital and doctor permitting.

LABOR

After nine months of wondering and waiting, your child is about to be born. The process known as labor, aptly named because *it is work,* is about to begin. There are several theories related to what makes a pregnant body ready to give birth. While there are no definite answers, there are several clues that labor is beginning.

Labor Begins

You may find your labor starting with a slight backache and minor abdominal cramps. The cramps, or contractions, last approximately ten to forty seconds and will occur ten to thirty minutes apart. If the contractions continue when you change your position (from standing to lying down, to walking, etc.) and remain quite evenly spaced, you are more than likely experiencing true *not* false labor. It is advisable for your husband to time your contractions. When they are five minutes apart for a first child and ten minutes apart for other children, call your doctor.

Another clue may be the "show." This is a slight red or pink mucus discharge passed through the vagina. If you experience this, but do not have hard contractions, the slight discharge could become as heavy as a menstrual period before you reach the hospital. This is nothing to worry about, but you will want to have a sanitary napkin available to you.

A third sign of labor or impending labor is the breaking of the bag of waters. This is a gush of warm water coming from the vagina. It may begin as a trickle, but increases greatly; the flow cannot be controlled. Again you may wish to use a sanitary napkin, but sometimes it is more effective to reach for a turkish towel. This break does not always happen and your doctor may break your bag of waters in the hospital. In either case, this is not at all painful; however, do let your doctor know if this sign does occur. There is a slight chance of infection if contractions do not begin spontaneously.

Ready for the Hospital

When you realize any of the signs of labor, do not eat any solid foods. If anything, drink clear liquids. A full stomach can complicate any anesthesia you may be using later.

When your doctor tells you to go to the hospital, you will probably have to go through admissions. This is not the case in all hospitals. Ask your doctor or call the hospital well in advance so that you will be aware of the admitting procedures when the time arrives.

Once you are in bed in the labor room, a nurse will record your vital signs (pulse, temperature, and blood pressure), time your contractions, shave your pubic area, and administer an enema to cleanse your lower bowel.

Induction of Labor

Occasionally, labor is induced; that means that certain drugs are used that stimulate the uterine muscles into activity. There are several reasons for inducing labor. The commonest medical reason is the presence of one of the high blood pressure toxemias. The commonest obstetrical reasons are maternal diabetes and immunization of the mother to the Rh factor. It has been shown that the babies of diabetic or Rh negative mothers are prone to certain problems. Therefore such women require close supervision and induced labor is used. The patient's convenience and the convenience of the physician are sometimes a consideration. Before a doctor will consent to induce labor for either his or the patient's convenience, everything must be ideal for its performance. The doctor most likely will start induction with a warm, soapy enema and then artificially rupture the membranes and start administering Pitocin (the labor-inducing drug) intravenously.

Stages in Labor

The labor process is really a continuous process, but is usually divided into three parts for easy identification and discussion.

The first stage is the longest and is the step most women have begun when they reach the hospital. During this time the cervix must dilate to the extent that the baby may pass through it. Dilation occurs as the uterus contracts and pushes the baby downward. Contractions at this time are involuntary so there is little the mother can do to help. It is best for her to relax and, if possible, doze between contractions. She will need her energy during labor's second stage.

Labor, First Stage: Uterus contracting; cervix continuing to dilate.

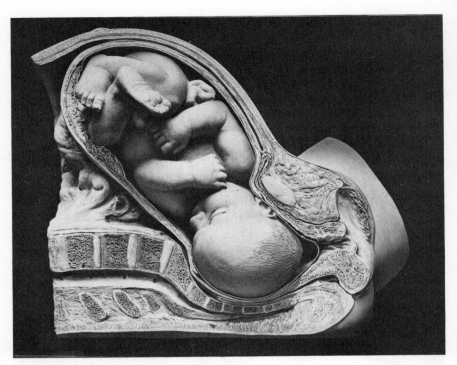

Labor, Second Stage: Head deep in birth canal; pull of uterine contractions draws cervix up.

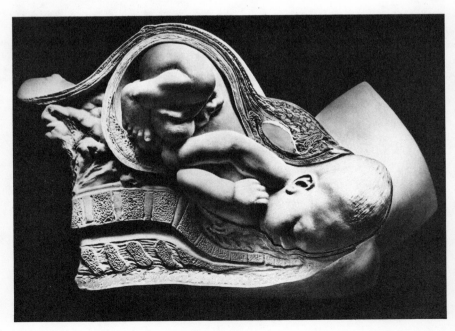

Labor, "Crowning": Head begins to appear; muscles of abdominal wall contract; pelvic floor becomes extremely thin.

The second stage of labor begins when the cervix is fully dilated—ten centimeters, or the approximate equivalent of five fingers held together—and ends when the baby is born. The mother's job at this point is to help push her baby down into the vagina and out into the world.

As you push, the head will become visible. Unless your child is feet first, or breech, the head is the first thing to be seen.

The Father-to-be and Labor

Assuming that the father-to-be remains in the labor room, there are many supportive functions he can assume. If he has been closely involved with his wife's pregnancy from the outset, he most likely will be curious, excited, and quite emotional at this time. These feelings can be translated into useful action: familiarizing himself with the labor room and the hospital bed; changing the bed position; sensing his wife's mood changes and not letting them become bothersome.

DELIVERY

When a rectal or vaginal examination shows the cervix fully dilated and the baby has descended to the vaginal floor, the patient is transferred to the delivery room. Contractions have now become longer in duration and more frequent.

The big moment has arrived. The brightly lighted delivery room looks like a small operating room filled with modern equipment ready to aid in the comfort and safety of both the mother and child.

This second stage of labor, the actual delivery, may vary from five minutes to ninety minutes, depending upon the *type* of delivery your doctor and you have agreed upon.

Episiotomy

The vagina is highly elastic during pregnancy and birth. However, because the tissues at this time may be stretched beyond capacity, an incision called an episiotomy is made in the vaginal wall between the vaginal and rectal openings to prevent tearing or over-stretching. After the delivery, stitches are taken while the mother is still anesthetized.

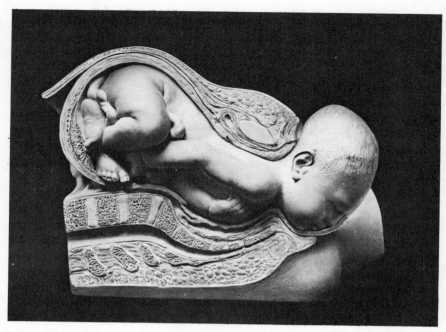

Labor, Second Stage nearly completed: Head turns upward; pelvic floor slips back over face.

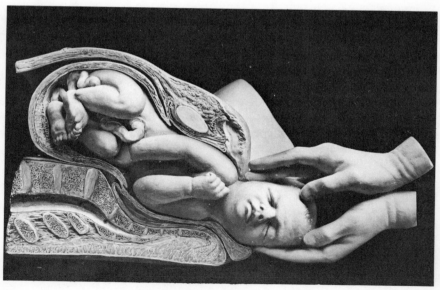

The baby is about to be born!

Anesthetics, Analgesics, and Amnesics

Pain relievers are classified into three groups—analgesia, anesthesia, and amnesia. An analgesic gives relief from pain or discomfort without loss of consciousness. Since the delivering mother is conscious, the analgesics do not prevent her from doing her share of the labor.

An anesthetic is something that produces complete or partial loss of feeling. There are two principal types of anesthetics: *general* and *conduction*. A *general anesthetic* makes one unconscious for a short time. Some are gases inhaled through a mask. Others are solutions injected into a vein. *Conduction anesthesia,* on the other hand, interferes with the conduction of nerve impulses to the brain from the place where it is injected. When the nerves are blocked in this way, there is no feeling in the parts of the body with which they connect. Consciousness is not lost. There are several different kinds of conduction anesthetics. Among them are spinal, caudal, and epidural anesthesia. There are two types of local anesthesia used in obstetrics: the *paracervical* block and the *pudendal* block. The latter affects the external genital organs.

Amnesic drugs allow the patient to remain conscious, but with little or no memory of discomfort. The recipient has no knowledge of what occurs between the time of injection and several hours later when the drugs wear off. Scopolamine is a popular amnesic that usually is given in combination with Demerol.

Most mothers-to-be want very much to be awake when their babies are born and to follow closely what goes on. Others would prefer to be unconscious throughout the delivery. The patient's medical history may play a relevant part in what is decided. The mother-to-be and her physician, after weighing all the facts, can then arrive at the ideal method.

The PCI believes that a normal routine delivery should necessitate very limited, if any, use of anesthetics. Then the baby and/or mother will not have to contend with any possible deleterious side effects.

The Route of the Baby

With each contraction and bearing-down motion, the baby descends farther and farther through the cervix and down the vaginal canal until he is finally born. The normal position is head first, then shoulders, trunk, and finally feet. The doctor grasps the emerged head beneath the jaw and helps to lift the baby into his new world. When the delivery is completed, the baby is held upside down by his heels. Mucus and other residue are

21

quickly aspirated from the mouth and nose. The baby takes the first breath of air into his lungs, perhaps aided by the gentle slap of the doctor. He begins to breathe regularly and then cries. The umbilical cord is then clamped and cut. Nurses swarm around the baby to cleanse him further, weigh and measure him, identify him, and wrap him warmly.

Baby can rest now, but mother's work goes on with the delivery of the placenta. This usually takes just a few minutes. The mother is far too busy thinking of her beautiful new baby to feel much of anything but exhaustion and exhilaration.

The Father-to-be and Delivery

If the father-to-be has decided to be an active part of the experience, then the labor room is behind him. Whether he is permitted into the delivery room is another hurdle to be overcome. Many hospitals currently hold the line at the delivery room door. The standard reasons are presented in Jeanette Sasmor's book *What Every Husband Should Know About Having a Baby:*
1. Fathers will faint in the delivery room.
2. Fathers will increase infection.
3. Delivery is hectic. Fathers will need to be supervised.
4. Fathers will not understand or like what the physician is doing to their wives.
5. Suppose something goes wrong?

The best defense against these concerns is information obtained by education based on high motivation. To put it simply, the informed father-to-be knows what to expect, knows what is going to happen to his wife, and knows what he will do in all circumstances, even the possibility of an emergency.

It cannot be emphasized enough that all of these questions relate to hospital policies. The obstetrician's philosophy and the couple's attitudes should be discussed prior to the selection of a hospital. Driving to the hospital is not the time to decide that you want to share the birth!

Kinds of Birth

At this point, perhaps a note should be made that although approximately 95 per cent of all deliveries are "normal," the other 5 per cent fall into one of the following categories.

Breech birth is a term given when a baby presents herself to the world feet first instead of the usual head first. Such births may require special treatment by the attending physician, but they are usually detected before delivery and can be taken care of with little or no trouble to doctor or mother.

Infrequently a baby encounters difficulty while pushing through the birth canal. There is need then for a *forceps delivery*. The forceps is a tonglike instrument that fits gently on each side of the baby's head and aids in the baby's emergence.

Caesarean birth is a delivery in which an incision is made through the abdominal wall and the uterus of the mother to remove the baby. It is major surgery, but the risks are minimal with modern surgical technique. When the woman's pelvic area is too small for a baby to pass through, or when there is abnormal positioning of the baby, or when other special conditions are noted, the physician and parents decide if this procedure is advisable.

Premature birth (the birth of a less than five-pound infant) occurs in about 10 per cent of all births that go beyond the fifth month. At twenty-eight weeks, a baby's chances of survival are small, but his chances at thirty-six weeks are about the same as those of a full-term baby. Care of the premie is important. The La Leche League cites studies in which early introduction of mother's milk was beneficial for the infants observed.

PCI Point of View

Premature babies should be given an extra amount of love, handling, and rocking to compensate for such loss while in incubators. However, once brought up to normal weight, etc., it is important that they be treated as healthy, normal children and not overprotected.

Some hospitals now have special programs for high-risk babies, including visual, auditory, and tactile stimulation through rocking-heartbeat programs. The premature infant in an incubator is deprived of the stimuli that would have been transmitted by the mother—her fondling, heartbeat, cooing, feeding, handling, etc. To compensate in part, a rocker-bed has been developed that has incorporated in it a continuous tape recording of a heartbeat. Parents are permitted also to gently handle their premature babies while still in incubators.

INFANT MORTALITY

Low birth weight, a shortened period of gestation, and "prematurity" are key factors in infant mortality, and the majority of these deaths occur in the first week of life.

23

Sudden Infant Death Syndrome (SIDS)

Each year 7,500 to 10,000 American families experience the nightmare of sudden infant death (SIDS). They put their apparently normal, healthy baby down in the crib or carriage for a nap or a night's sleep. Hours or perhaps only minutes later, they find the baby dead. No warning, no cry! In 10 to 15 per cent of the cases they find some previously unsuspected disease, but in the other 85 to 90 per cent, no cause is found. In 1974 Congress authorized six million dollars yearly for medical research teams to collect information and for counseling bereaved families.

The medical detectives pursuing this mysterious killer have some clues to follow: the deaths are more common in the winter; many of the babies had runny noses or a minor illness. SIDS strikes infants between two and four months of age. The infant is invariably asleep and this has stymied crib death researchers who have sought to study them when awake. There are all kinds of theories: scurvy, oxygen deprivation, deficiency of vitamins D and E, abnormality of heartbeat, hypersensitivity to bottle milk, blockage in nasal passage, etc. Virus hunters have come up with some inconclusive evidence. One of the hottest clues is apnea during sleep (stopped breathing). However, brief sleep apnea in babies can be normal. The final answers are not yet in, but there are now enough medical scientists who are looking into this most distressing problem.

For the parents of a crib death victim, the aftermath is devastating. They are haunted by guilt that they caused the death. Some families break up soon after the funeral. Even worse, some parents have been jailed because the authorities erroneously accused them of child beating. To help these grief-stricken parents, the National Foundation for Sudden Infant Death, Inc. (at 1501 Broadway, New York, N.Y. 10036) now has forty-three chapters in the United States. Parents can join a chapter nearest them to discuss this shocking situation with others similarly affected. Another group is the International Council for Infant Survival (at 1515 Reisterstown Road, Baltimore, Md. 21208).

Unfortunately for the present, it still appears that nothing can be done to reduce the statistics for the sudden infant death syndrome.

Infant Deaths from Infection or Improper Nutrition

Many infant deaths after the first week and before the first year are the result of infection. *It is possible to reduce this incidence.*

"Breast feeding is one of the most effective ways of overcoming factors related to the lack of resources, such as infection and poor nutrition," according to the report "Key Issues in Infant Mortality" by the National Institute of Child Health and Human Development, but we must also look to better health-care facilities.

This report states, too, that the economically disadvantaged have higher infant mortality rates, a higher ratio of low birth weight babies, and that there is a need to improve the health of girls and young women many years before they become pregnant.

The environment, poverty, poor nutrition, and sanitation, as well as deprived home conditions, are all contributing factors. These babies are born with inferior resistance to infection.

In a recent study of infants who died at birth, 70 per cent had been sick in utero for more than a week prior to birth. This indicates the need to explore the role of the fetus in the initiation of labor.

Family planning also plays a role in infant mortality. "Experience in countries where abortions are readily available suggests that some forms of abortion may increase the risks of prematurity and low birth weights among babies of mothers who have previously had one or more abortions," according to the National Institute of Child Health and Human Development. Some type of consultation service should be provided to help emotionally and nutritionally those mothers who lose their babies.

Indications are that the mother's own utero experience plays a role in the chance of survival of her infant. Mothers born during the great depression had their babies in the fifties, when mortality rates were higher than they are now.

Family planning today can enable a mother to prevent pregnancy until her physical health is ready to undergo the gestation and birth of a child. Statistics show that the principal reason for the majority of unpreventable deaths was that the mother was suffering from a serious medical problem *before* the pregnancy began.

DISCHARGE AND HOMECOMING FROM HOSPITAL

Discharge Procedures

Have the nurse send your insurance policies to be signed by the hospital authorities well in advance of your departure. If your baby is being bottle fed, the hospital may send a twenty-four-hour supply of formula home with you with directions for preparing and using it. Before you leave, the nurse may go over with you the instructions you have been given for your own and your baby's care.

Medical Records

When you are discharged the hospital will provide a medical history of your infant at birth—including sex, blood type, height, weight, Apgar score, and other pertinent information. Save this information and record other data as your baby grows.

Help for You at Home

The excitement of bringing your new baby home from the hospital is second only to the actual birth. Because most mothers are still tired from the delivery or somewhat apprehensive about caring for their baby, most child-care experts suggest that some arrangement be made for help at home.

As Dr. Spock explains, "If you can figure out a way to get someone to help you the first few weeks you are taking care of the baby, by all means do so. If you try to do everything by yourself and get exhausted you may *have* to get help and have it for longer in the end. Besides, getting tired and depressed starts you and the baby off on the wrong foot."

The Practical Nurse

Especially with a first baby, many mothers prefer to hire a practical nurse who is trained to give the baby expert care. Mothers who are timid about handling a newborn baby gain confidence as the practical nurse patiently teaches them how to care for the baby. However, some authorities warn of the occasional practical nurse who acts as if the baby were hers and is not willing to do things your way. Their advice: get rid of her and find another nurse!

To arrange for a practical nurse, call your local health department or social services agency for more information.

Do You Need a Houseworker?

There are some new mothers who want to assume the care of their babies from the very beginning. This is not impossible if a houseworker can be hired to help with the cleaning and cooking. Although houseworkers are often difficult to find, an advertisement placed in a local newspaper often brings good results. If your baby is born in the summer months, do not overlook the possibility of hiring a reliable high school or college student.

What Is a Homemaker?

A homemaker is a mother substitute who is especially trained to keep a home running smoothly when a mother is ill or absent. In communities that have a Homemaker Service, many others find this the perfect answer when they enter the hospital to have their second baby. Since this service is usually partially supported by a community agency, there is generally a sliding scale of fees so you pay only what you can afford. To find out if your town has a Homemaker Service, call your local Community Chest or Council of Social Agencies. (A point to remember: a homemaker is assigned where the need is greatest. Most likely she will only be able to help out for a few days after you bring the new baby home.)

How Long Is Help Needed?

Of course, only you can answer this question. The answer will depend on your finances and how well you are feeling. Each day you should try to get up and do a little more around the house. At the end of two weeks many mothers feel they can resume a normal schedule. If you feel you can get along without help after one week, fine, but if you are still feeling tired after two weeks, do not hesitate to retain your help. It will be cheaper in the long run!

What If You Have No Help?

Fathers and older children are very helpful when the new baby comes home. With a little advance planning, the whole family can pitch in and make the first few weeks at home easier for mother. This, of course, will depend on the ages of the children and the availability of the father. Perhaps if no other help can be found, father can arrange to take a week of his annual vacation at this time.

Start a "New Baby" Club

The *U. S. Government Book of Infant Care* suggests that neighborhood and church groups form clubs to help out when a mother goes into the hospital to have a baby and when she brings the baby home. Club members take care of other children in the family, see that there is enough food in the refrigerator when the mother and baby come home, and sometimes prepare meals for the first few days. Club members might also offer to do shopping or baby-sitting while the new mother recuperates from the birth.

Do Not Forget the Visiting or Public Health Nurse

All child-care experts are unanimous in their praise of the public health or visiting nurse. Most cities have such nurses who will come into your home and show you how to care for your baby. There is usually no charge for this service. To find out if your community has a visiting or public health nurse, call your local health department or ask your doctor.

Limit Visitors at First

One thing you can be sure about: when you bring your baby home from the hospital many people will be calling and wanting to drop over to see the new arrival. Do not feel you have to get up and provide refreshments or entertain guests. Better, explain that you are still rather weak and tired and would prefer to see your friends in a few days. Limit visitors at the start to close relatives. It may be necessary to remind them that the birth process was not easy for baby either and he would prefer not to be picked up or fussed over until he is a little older.

BEING A NEW PARENT

All human beings move through a series of changes that are characterized by pleasures and problems that are specific to each particular stage of one's development. At each and every stage there are countless opportunities for us to succeed and fail, to feel gratification and despair. Becoming a new parent is one such stage. New mothers are supposed to feel jubilant, in ecstasy; the stereotype has them up on a "cloud nine." New fathers traditionally had not been supposed to feel too much since customarily their role was largely down-played or ignored.

Most new parents will feel very deeply and very differently. Parenthood is not a "Yes, I like it," "No, I don't" kind of experience. Complex physiological changes for mother and complex far-reaching changes for the young couple have been initiated through the birth of their baby, changes that will have lasting influences.

On a deep level childbirth awakens in both parents their own semi-

28

conscious childhood memories, when they were totally dependent upon others. Both the past and future are dramatically highlighted by the newborn.

Mother Adjusts to the New Baby

Great variation characterizes how mothers feel at first. There is *fear*. "Am I up to the job?" "The baby is so small and helpless." There is *disappointment*. "All that excitement and not much to show for it." "Everyone is more concerned about baby's well-being than mine." There is *guilt*. "I don't feel anything, except my stitches." There is *pride*. "I really made that perfect human being." There is *affection*. "Look how he nurses from me, how he seems to know it's me." And there is also a *conflict:* "Yes, I want this baby, but he ties me down so. I miss my job."

Changes in Routine Activities

Some of the changes the new mother must adjust to involve routines and activities, both of which will now revolve about baby's behavior. Most babies do establish patterns of crying, eating, sleeping, and current parental practice seems to take baby's disposition into account. What it boils down to is that the mother sleeps or rests when her baby does; she cleans and does the chores in between times. If nursing, then the scheduling is more rigid since the mother—and no substitute—must be available.

Yet a commonsense point of view will permit the mother some privacy and time to get away. Baby-sitters are available and an occasional bottle never ruined a nursing baby. The rule of thumb at first is not to overplan and not to plan too far in advance. Schedules in infancy are changed constantly in order to keep pace with the gigantic growth spurts and rest periods characteristic of infancy.

Expecting everything to be the same as *before baby* is not realistic and can only result in frustration.

Fatigue

As Shirley Ehrlich points out in *Pregnancy, Birth and the Newborn Baby,* in the weeks following childbirth the new mother, whose body is recovering from the enormous physiological tasks of pregnancy and delivery, is more physically dependent. Fatigue results from the new mother's need to be given to and her need to give to the baby. She is committed to meeting all the physical and psychological needs of her baby, but just as definitely requires loving and fondling herself—needs to which new fathers should respond. This fatigue also has a psychological aspect to it. New mothers re-evaluate at this time their relationship with their own mothers, one which could be marked by conflict and ambivalence, thereby creating some emotional strain.

Emotional Adjustments

At first relieved and happy that baby was born healthy, the new mother, after a few days at home, has a vague feeling that something is wrong. She reassures herself that everything is going along just perfectly, but cries with almost no provocation. These or similar symptoms are felt by many women within a few days to a few weeks after giving birth. They are known by many names, including postpartum depression and the "baby blues."

What Are the "Baby Blues"?

Often the symptoms are so mild and go away so quickly that the new mother hesitates to use the term "depression." She may feel discouraged or anxious about her baby. If she is breast feeding, she may be excessively concerned that the baby is not getting enough to eat. She may be worried about her relationship with her husband for no apparent reason. This condition is both common and temporary. (Some child-care experts think it is caused by hormonal or metabolic changes that occur during pregnancy.) Should a new mother experience any of these symptoms, she should know that many women experience them and they normally pass away in a few days or weeks at the most.

Why Some Women Get Depressed

Many authorities point out that psychologically the birth of a first child marks a turning point in many women's lives. Many women expect their girlish figures to return immediately and get depressed when they do not. Nobody has taken the time to tell them that the uterus takes almost six weeks to shrink to its original size.

Without warning, after baby comes home from the hospital, some mothers feel an acute loss of freedom. They are momentarily shocked by the realization that they can no longer do what they want when they feel like doing it. The car may be parked in the garage, but the new mother is no longer free to hop into it and leave for an afternoon of shopping or visiting. She realizes that a hairdresser appointment now involves more than a simple phone call. She can no longer make plans for herself alone; she must also consider her baby.

Other women get depressed because they had an unrealistic expectation of how beautiful their baby would be. Newborns are usually very red and resemble shrunken little old men. Each day they change physically and in a few weeks really do look like the babies in TV advertisements. In the meantime the new mother may admit to mixed feelings of love and resentment toward her baby. This may further depress her if she does not realize that these feelings are commonly shared by most other new mothers.

What to Do About Depression

Knowing that the depression is only temporary will help to some extent, but there are things to do to overcome it more quickly. Most important is to fight that "don't feel like doing anything" feeling. The mother should force herself to get out and visit a friend; take the baby along if a sitter is not available; go to a movie or go shopping—anything to get out of the house. No one is a "bad mother" because she feels she has to get away from her baby now and again. Realize that these feelings are normal and all parents have them from time to time.

Rarely, instead of getting better, the depression seems to get worse. No matter how hard the mother tries to fight it, she cannot seem to shake that "letdown" feeling. If this is the case, the family doctor should be consulted. He may recommend a psychiatrist to help the mother get through this difficult period.

Father Adjusts to the New Baby

The new father's role in the family is currently gaining in respect, so much so that whole volumes are being devoted to it. Several societal themes have influenced this newer role definition: the Women's Liberation Movement; increase of working mothers and de-emphasis on cultural sex stereotyping; current divorce, adoption, and abortion laws; fathers getting custody of children; men adopting children; single-parent families and Men's Liberation—the positive but little publicized phenomenon that advocates a Fathers' Bill of Rights.

Fathers' Bill of Rights

1. Fathers are involved, too. By attending prenatal courses with their

wives, fathers learn about the miracle of birth, the practicalities of caring for a newborn, and adjusting to their pregnant wives' moods.

2. Fathers have feelings. Most new mothers turn to their husbands for additional emotional support at this time and most fathers are able and happy to provide needed help and understanding. At the same time, the new mother is isolating her husband, giving him a minimum of care and attention. Even the most loving husband may experience anxiety, anger, and resentment. The new father also has other worries: will he financially be able to provide? After the demands of the job, will he have enough time to spend with his new child?

3. Fathers are competent. They should be involved in baby routines, such as feeding and changing diapers, from the beginning. Awkwardness and feelings of inadequacy lessen with practice, which translates into bathing, feeding, strolling, and playing with baby.

PCI Point of View

New mothers and new fathers have much in common. Their feelings are at about the same level of intensity. Both parents should recognize and accept each other's feelings and make the necessary adjustments in order to achieve a smooth transition into parenthood.

SHARING RESPONSIBILITIES

Adjusting to Children

At birth, a baby brings much joy, much work, and much worry. Often the parents are not prepared either emotionally or physically to withstand the impact of this demanding albeit exhilarating situation. Even though they have gone through the motions of preparing for the baby—buying clothes, choosing a crib, discussing names, making arrangements for help, going for prenatal checkups faithfully—many parents are jolted when they are alone at home with their infant for the first time, whether it is the first child or the third. This feeling of unease is natural and normal, particularly for first-time parents.

Usually parents are eager to be "good" parents. Anxious to do the right thing, they read books and articles on feeding, schedules, spoiling, and sleeping habits. Nonetheless, because the experience is different and somewhat unpredictable each time, they do become tired, nervous, and irritable. When this occurs, communication and understanding break down between husband and wife and the situation can get out of hand.

Determining Roles and Expectations

Throughout marriage it is helpful for spouses to discuss the sharing of responsibilities. The best time to begin is before marriage. When the first baby arrives is another good time, especially before tensions arise that may make communication difficult. Traditional family roles are undergoing change and this can lead to some confusion in the area of *role expectations*. Although spouses may have worked out a sharing of household tasks and responsibilities while both were working prior to becoming parents, the new role of being a parent may alter this situation.

The husband may expect his wife to assume more (or all) of the household duties if she is home with the baby. Further, although husband and wife may have discussed sharing care of the baby, the husband's unease at handling an infant, coupled with the wife's subconscious attitude that child care is a mother's role, may lead to ambivalence and irritability.

There are many articles concerning changing family roles in magazines and books that deal with the subject of sharing responsibilities. These often include a particular family's solution to its responsibility problems. However, keep in mind that every situation is unique due to the complexity of the people involved. What may work for one family may be unacceptable for another. *Communication* between the spouses and *flexibility* appear to be the essential components for establishing equitable sharing of responsibilities.

Parents' Preferences in Dividing Responsibilities

Within any given family many chores have to be done that are considered by both parents to be tedious, time-consuming and neither fulfilling nor fun. These necessary tasks need to be approached with a sense of fair play. They must be done by someone and they should be shared. One possibility is making daily or weekly lists, although this may be considered by some as a "last resort."

In many cases, the person who is at home most of the time does most of the housework and the other partner helps when at home. This may or may not seem fair. If both work, then the chores may be shared equally, each person picking the chores she or he likes to do first and the disliked ones alternated. In any case, flexibility, sharing, and communication are the prime factors. For a father who has never done housework, these tasks are a radical change in life-style. The wife should be tolerant of her

33

spouse's clumsiness in carrying out these responsibilities. Efficiency requires practice.

The sharing of responsibilities is more important when it is concerned with the raising of children. Children must be fed and clothed, yes, but more importantly they need to be read to, talked to, and played with by *both* parents so they will know, trust, and be comfortable with the mother and the father.

If one parent really dislikes supervising bathtime, the other spouse should take over that part of bedtime procedure. If father resents taking his child to the zoo because he wants to stay home and watch a football game, no one will enjoy the trip to the zoo. Parents should be honest about their feelings to themselves and express them to their mates. They should learn to recognize resentment, isolate the reason, and then work out a solution with their spouses.

When we become parents, we cannot expect to be entirely satisfied with the experience. There is always a gap between one's expectations and one's actual role in family life. We are all people, male or female, who have our own interests, needs, and temperaments. Keeping this in mind, we should strive to meet the needs of the rest of our family.

Children's Needs and Parents' Needs

Children require food, clothing, shelter, physical activity, maintenance of order, and molding of their social characters. They need language stimulation and cognitive encounters with reality; and they need accepting, consistent, and continuous care in order to develop attachment. Parents must provide these things for their children, but who provides for which needs depends on each individual home.

"All parents love their children and want to do what's best for them." We could spend a chapter defending this proposition and qualifying it, but won't since there is enough accuracy in it to move on to the more serious discussion of how so many of us—in the name of love—foster neurosis in our children. The dynamics are surprisingly simple: we do not fulfill their basic needs. According to Dr. Arthur Janov, a parent whose own needs as a child were unmet now has a child whose needs cannot be met either; baby cries (expression of need) are intolerable to the parent who must "suppress the crying and the demand rather than take the time necessary to cater to the child's needs." Thus the message seems to be: fulfill your own needs first, then you'll be emotionally able to fulfill those of your child. The problem with this is the issue of priority; the baby (total dependence and total demand) has no other resources and simply cannot wait. The dilemma then becomes an emotional quagmire for the parent, who must fulfill himself independently rather than using the baby as a scapegoat.

Only a lucky few can project themselves into this emotional relationship prior to parenthood and on the basis of harsh self-knowledge reject or postpone parenthood. For those of us (most parents) who are less fortunate and require intensive "on the job training" there is hope. Growth and insights come rapidly once we become aware of our responsibilities and our own personalities.

The Good Enough Parent

In his book *The Natural Way to Raise a Healthy Child,* psychoanalyst Hiag Akmakjian describes what is needed to be a "good enough parent," a phrase first used by pediatrician-psychologist Dr. O. W. Winnicott to describe parents who do things fairly well—parents who nonetheless are far from perfect. Good enough parents do not panic easily; they are usually relaxed and not guilt-ridden for those shortcomings they do have.

Dr. Akmakjian maintains that good enough parents are "attuned to baby's needs and feel empathy . . . when your child falls and scrapes a knee, you don't say 'Oh come on, now, you're okay' but 'Ow! That must really hurt'—your statement of empathy itself beginning to diminish the pain."

Good enough parents understand that development is a progressive unfolding of what is innate. Writes Dr. Akmakjian, "They are neither intrusive nor aloof. . . . They sense that normal development results largely from letting nature take its course with help from the parents in the form of love, protection, and helping pointers . . . [they] meet the child's emotional needs as they arise."

PCI Point of View

PCI is committed to an "ages and stages" philosophy of child rearing, believing that as a baby increases body control and physical and other abilities mature, he or she constantly faces new elements in a world to master. Competent child rearing in the earliest years calls for parents to know what the normal pattern of emerging skills is and to facilitate and encourage their practice.

2
Behavior Patterns and Routines

INTRODUCTION BY FRANCES L. ILG, M.D.*

What is more exciting and rewarding than the rearing of a child? But to be more successful, parents could profit by being armed with knowledge of how growth patterns unfold. If we know what to expect, we can recognize these predicted patterns of behavior in our own children, enjoy them, and deal with them as we see fit.

As we learn more about the self-regulating mechanism within the child that balances between self-demand and self-adaptation, we can look forward to those stages of equilibrium when the two extremes fuse preparatory to a forward thrust. It is for the parent, the caretaker, and the culture to recognize these swings and to move through them with the child, at times preventing the child from going too far in either direction if the child's own mechanism does not restabilize on its own. Sometimes it is hard to put up with a self-demand style when the infant's ravenous appetite for milk at four to six weeks calls for frequent feedings at once and of prolonged duration. Breast feeding can happily satisfy this demand if the mother has planned her life around her infant.

In the midst of this demand stage, the mother can even now project into the self-adaptive stage at sixteen weeks, when her baby can happily play by himself on waking in the morning for a half hour before demanding his mother's attention. Or let us take a later stage, at two and a half, when a child becomes imperious, demanding right and

* In the 1940s, no new parent could do without Drs. Arnold Gesell's and Frances L. Ilg's *Infant and Child in the Culture of Today*. In those early days, it took great courage to speak out on child care. Very little research existed; pediatrics was in its infancy. At the Yale Medical School, Drs. Gesell and Ilg undertook the task of carefully recording the step-by-step stages of growth of infants and children, with special emphasis on physical and behavior growth patterns. From their painstaking observations (both descriptive and photographic) came a massive body of information that has helped pediatricians, parents, and researchers to evaluate growth and recognize the basic ages and stages of development. Dr. Ilg is now eighty-five years old.

left, pitting his "I" against "you," the other person, with a chasm in between. The parent, the "you," soon learns that life is bearable only if she bows with a "yes, your highness," thus making the child think she is in control, but also knowing that this is the stage when the child responds best to rituals. The parents' consolation as they struggle to keep a sense of humor is that *three* is just around the corner. Then the chasm can be crossed by inevitable growth forces, heralded by the pronoun "we," and the lovely ring of "Let's do this" and "Let's do that." Life can again be lived together, parent and child, child and child.

It is important to realize that each phase of life is as important as the next, that each phase has its own message and growth force. Then the parents can allow life and living to flow as it is meant to flow. The modern return to natural childbirth with new understanding and controls can give both mother and baby a good start, especially if drugs are not resorted to.

Parents need to think of how their child's life can be provided with the expansion experiences he needs, too; from crib to changing table, to lying on the kitchen table surrounded by all the sounds, smells, and movement that he will come to love; to an excursion to the wide expanse of his parents' bed.

Enrichment experiences, of course, extend to other people. The expansion within the family to father and any other members is fairly automatic. It needs to be understood that a child expresses preferences and often shifts his choices. Mother is in many ways the preferred one and the one most needed in times of trouble. Father's feelings should not be hurt if he is rejected, especially by his son and often after he has been preferred. There will come a time when the father–son relationship is or should be well established, possibly by the age of seven. There should also be expansion to other people beyond the family group.

Training and discipline almost take care of themselves if they are considered within the texture of growth. There are marked differences to be sure. Some children are able to express their needs and their satisfactions so that it behooves the parent merely to watch, listen, and respond. Even an older infant can tell you when she's ready for bed by rubbing her eyes or pulling at her ears.

Parents need to give their child preparatory experiences and more supportive handling; above all, to be willing to wait until the child indicates a readiness. Much time can be lost on elimination training when it is started too early. Such a strong resistance may be built up that the child becomes confused in his own growth processes and this is later difficult to reverse. Parents are often too serious. They have taken the fun out of life. A saddle potty that is firm on the floor can be a part of the kitchen equipment used as a toy that the child scoots around on, as well as a training receptacle.

But parents must remember that discipline is after all a learning process and a response to rules and regulations. If parents are geared to the growth process, they will know when their child is ready to respond to rules and regulations. Furthermore, if their actions and reactions are based on love, they are pretty safe in what they do.

Above all, if the mother and father are supported by the three I's of good parenting—intelligence, imagination, and especially ingenuity, they will come through their role gloriously or at least they will sneak through. Their success will give them confidence, and most important trust in themselves, and their children will learn to trust them and steadily to trust themselves more and more.

SLEEP PATTERNS IN THE NEWBORN

Although a baby cannot tell time, he does have an inner biological time clock. Since much of a baby's first three months is devoted to sleeping, it is important for us to learn what we can about sleep and the routines associated with it in order to know what it is that his own biological clock is saying. Understand that your newborn will sleep only as much as he needs, no more and no less.

In a research study conducted by the University of Toronto, the average newborn slept sixteen hours out of every twenty-four. However, the sixteen hours are only an average. Babies, like adults, vary in their sleep requirements.

Most newborns prefer to sleep on their tummies and it is perfectly fine to put your baby down in the position she prefers. Just be sure that your baby gets enough handling and changes of position and scenery when awake and you really need not concern yourself with her sleeping position.

It is best not to bundle or swaddle your newborn *while she sleeps*. Lightweight coverings to suit the season are best. Sleeping bags are deservedly popular. Just be sure your baby is not too warm when wearing one. Set the thermostat at whatever temperature is comfortable for you.

Cradles and bassinets make newborns feel especially secure. Of course, you can give your baby the same safe, secure feeling by placing him crosswise at one end of his crib. Many newborns like to have their heads up against a bumper or other firm surface that also helps them to feel safe and secure. Babies should not have pillows.

Ideally your baby should have a room of his own although a somewhat private area can work just as well. Do not stop making noise just because your newborn is sleeping. He will soon become accustomed to your usual household noises and sleep right through.

A really stressful situation is created by the newborn who mixes up her days and nights, one who sleeps all day and then wakes up raring to go

42

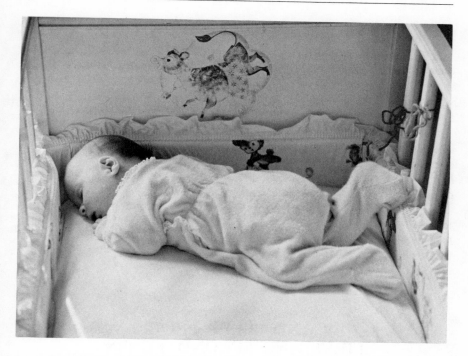

just when you are ready for bed. What can you do about this? Well, some mothers have handled this by keeping their home as stimulating as possible during the day—with music, visitors, by using infant seats and baby swings, and by waking baby for feedings every four hours. At night, they reverse the situation and decrease stimulation by darkening baby's area and responding to her needs in a quiet, calm manner.

Sometimes the above suggestions do not work and you are faced with staying up and comforting a crying baby. Experienced mothers offer these suggestions:

1. You sleep when your baby sleeps. Take enough naps so you get your normal quota of sleep.

2. Make yourself a pot of tea or whatever you prefer, find a comfortable chair for you and baby, put your feet up, turn on the television, and relax.

3. Fortunately, this period will not last forever. Actually, many mothers remember it somewhat fondly. Everyone else is sleeping. At this moment, the entire world consists of you and your baby. It is a perfect time to think beautiful thoughts about the future.

PCI Point of View

PCI believes that sedative-type medications should not be used to induce sleep unless a specific medical problem exists. If your baby has a sleeping problem, remember that he is acting normally for his age and he will outgrow it as he matures. Do what you can to alleviate his distress and then live with it, remembering that his specific problem will pass with time.

For all newborns, PCI recommends the time-tested aids to help baby in sleeping. Playing a soothing music box, gently patting baby's back as she lies in her bed, moving the cradle slowly and rhythmically, or rocking her while singing lullabies. These measures have worked with generations of newborns and will work with your infant, too.

Your newborn will have a great many more resources to assist him in falling asleep as he nears the end of his first year. The age-old comforting measures are especially valuable during the first three months, so use them to the contentment of yourself and your baby.

SLEEP AND SLEEP PROBLEMS: FIRST AND SECOND YEARS

Sleep Positions

When your baby is a couple of months old, you may begin to see his preference for a certain sleeping position either on his tummy or his back. Some mothers try to change this urge in their babies because they may have read that one position may tend to flatten the head or another may not be good for the legs or feet.

Pediatricians think that it is much more important to satisfy the infant's natural urge to repeat a comfortable pattern in sleep than to worry about some of the pros and cons that are presented for each sleep position.

If your baby's head starts to flatten from always keeping it to one particular side, there are various things you can do to get her used to turning her head to both sides. If you put baby to bed where her feet were the time before and there is a particular thing she liked to look at, she will turn her head in that direction part of the time. You may also tie some toys or bright things on the crib in such a way that your baby has to turn her head to look at them. Head flattening will correct itself in time and after your baby learns to roll over, her sleeping position will tend to change.

Sleeping at Night

During the night, infants come to a semiconscious, semi-alert state when they sometimes talk or cry out or move around and then have to get themselves back to sleep again. It is a good idea for you to let your baby do this by himself because if you do not your presence may become a part of his pattern of getting himself back to sleep.

Naps

Around the fifth month, babies are generally taking two or three naps a day. This usually depends on whether your baby is getting a 10 P.M. bottle or not. Some infants have a short morning nap and a long afternoon nap, or vice versa, or two naps morning and afternoon of about the same length of time. Sleep is very individualized and, of course, varies from time to time. Babies may be disturbed by a new tooth coming in, which may make them fretful or wake them up from a nap.

Young children tend to nap better in a room by themselves. They can disturb their parents if they are in their parents' room or the parents can bother them. The same is true of children sharing rooms. All too often they are not on the same schedule and young children especially tend to awaken other sleeping children.

By the time a child is close to a year old, he is going through a transitional period of giving up one of his two daytime naps. You may have to delay the morning nap time by giving your baby an early lunch, then putting him down and upon his waking giving him more lunch. That way he may be able to last until suppertime. (Just having a morning nap tends to make a baby fussy by midafternoon and too tired to eat supper.)

Some children will go to sleep almost immediately after you put them in their cribs, but there are others who seem to have to cry or fret before they can release themselves to sleep. A few others may talk to themselves or bang around in their cribs before they drop off. When you put your child down for a nap, see that she is comfortable and then leave her. It is much better for her to learn to get herself to sleep.

The *U. S. Government Book of Infant Care* says, "It is worth being firm about the importance of going to bed, and staying in bed, from the very beginning. The baby who knows you mean it when you say goodnight is really more comfortable about bed than the one who feels he ought to put up a fuss just to see what you'll do next." Of course, if your baby cries for any length of time, you will want to check him and maybe help him get some gas up or change him again.

As PCI says, in *The Eighth Month of Life,* "The sensitivity of children when they sense a parent's ambivalence or recognize his decisiveness is extraordinary."

Toddler Naps

Most toddlers will take one fairly long afternoon nap every day. If your toddler still wants two naps, that is fine, but you should not insist on it. If conditions are made right for them, children will generally go right off to sleep after their noon meal before they get interested in play and sleep for a couple of hours.

Sometimes children will decide that life is too interesting for them and they have too many things to explore, so they may not want to take a nap. It is a good idea to put them in their crib or bed anyway, perhaps with a toy, and they can amuse themselves quietly even if they do not go to sleep. Many children go back to sleeping again after a period (several days) of staying awake during regular nap time.

Reading or telling a story helps to slow down a child and prepares him to relax before going to sleep. At all times, a kindly but firm attitude on the part of the parent is necessary.

Sleeping with Parents

Children wake up in the middle of the night for various reasons. They might have had a nightmare and be frightened; they may have sleep disturbances because of some problems; or they may have to go to the bathroom and wander into their parents' bedroom. If a child needs comforting and the parents take him into bed with them as the most practical thing to do at the time, chances are it will be a mistake. It turns into a habit that is very hard to break and makes sleeping alone harder to accept. This only creates further sleeping difficulties for your child. It is much better, though harder, to take your child quickly and firmly back to his own bed. You can sit on his bed or by his crib to comfort and reassure him.

Sleep Problems

Growing up is never smooth. At some point, your child will begin to resist taking her nap or going to bed at night. Falling asleep is not usually a problem until about twenty-one months. Awaking during the night can

46

be a problem around fifteen months, however. Babies seem to sense that bedtime is the end of playtime and companionship and do not want to be alone. Often toddlers play happily in their cribs for an hour or more and should be left alone unless their crying is extreme. At about two years of age, they want to snuggle under the covers, which is dramatized in their doll play.

If the child does not fall back into sleep on her own, the parent needs to work out ways that will quiet her and help her return to sleep. Looking out the window at lights is often soothing, or playing in water with any available brush, preferably a toothbrush. When she is ready to go back to bed she will often insist on taking the toothbrush with her and this helps her to release her mother and go back to sleep. The PCI does not recommend a nighttime bottle.

Games Children Play

Throwing Things: A child's favorite stall against sleeping is throwing his stuffed animals or toys over the side of the crib and then crying until someone comes and returns them to him. You have to let him know that you do not consider this a game and be firm in getting him settled down again.

Calling Game: With certainty, at one time or another, your child will call to you after you have put him to bed for a nap or night sleep and have left him. You can call back to him to reassure him that you are close by, but it is better not to go to him unless his cry is frantic and you think something is wrong. Too often the initial calling game develops into "I want a drink of water," and then, "I have to go potty." Of course, you have to follow through on this one, but then you make it quite clear that enough is enough.

Nightmares and Night Terrors

Some children have nightmares. They seem more susceptible to scary dreams because they are more impressionable and less experienced than adults. Dr. Virginia Pomeranz says, in *The First Five Years,* "The child who has had a nightmare will know why he has awakened in a state of fright and will be able to recount his dream experience." It is good for him to do just that. Then you can talk it over with him, reassure him and be sympathetic. Having the light on and holding your youngster for a few moments will comfort him. Presently he will be able to go back to sleep.

Night terrors are different from nightmares and a little less likely to happen, but they are still not uncommon. The child does not waken fully and cannot remember the incident the next day. He often screams, and does not recognize you, and may not know where he is. The "attack" does not last long and the child goes right back to sleep. Your presence and re-assurance are what are needed most. If these so-called "attacks" persist, it is a good idea to talk them over with your doctor, because they sometimes signal some kind of emotional disturbance.

AIRINGS AND SUNBATHS

When Can the Baby Go Outdoors for the First Time?

Most parents look forward to taking their baby outdoors as soon as possible. Although many child-care publications suggest that parents should wait until the baby is at least four to six weeks of age, there are pediatricians who offer alternative advice. They maintain that an eight-pound baby, of whatever age, can go out as long as the temperature is sixty degrees or above—and even when the temperature is below freezing, a twelve-pounder may still be comfortable in a sunny, sheltered spot for an hour or two.

The current viewpoint favors early exposure. Although many women tend to wait a week or so before taking their baby out-of-doors, it is more for their benefit than for the baby's.

The Value of Fresh Air

According to Dr. Spock, cool or cold air improves the appetite, puts color in the baby's cheeks, and gives her more pep. In addition, the infant may be more susceptible to infections when she is constantly left indoors during the cold weather.

Dr. Brazelton, on the other hand, argues that from the baby's standpoint, there is no reason for an airing. Although it may "tone up" the circulatory system, he feels that an open window in the infant's bedroom that changes her temperature will serve the same purpose.

Traditionally, parents have preferred to take their babies out-of-doors for their fresh air. Generally the baby is put outside in her carriage for one of her naps. The carriage is parked in a secluded spot in the yard or on a porch so that it is out of the direct sun and well protected from the wind.

As the baby grows older, she is awake for longer periods and appreciates company more. While she is awake, the baby should not be kept out all by herself. Taking the baby for a walk is good exercise for you, as well as an opportunity to get out of the house for a while. In addition, most babies thoroughly enjoy a walk; the motion of a stroller or carriage is very soothing.

Sunbaths

Since direct sunshine contains ultraviolet rays that actually create vitamin D right in the skin, it seems sensible for babies to be exposed to the sun for at least a reasonable amount of time. There are four precautions, however:

1. To avoid burns, the baby's exposure to the sunshine should be increased very gradually. You should be especially careful when the sun is hot and the air is clear.

2. Even when the baby has been gradually tanned, excessive exposure is probably unwise, because it is harmful to the skin.

3. Since a severe sunburn is just as dangerous as a heat burn, you must try and judge how much sunshine will actually get on your baby's skin. This is especially important when you are putting the baby in a new spot in a season when the sun is bright.

4. Although the baby's body can be exposed to the sun very early in his life, it is advisable to wait longer to expose his face; at least until his eyes are no longer bothered by the bright light. The age varies from baby to baby. Initially, when he is on his back his eyes may be shielded by a peaked cap. When his face is exposed, he should be turned so that the top of his head is toward the sun and in this way his eyebrows will shield his eyes.

At first, the baby should not be left in the direct sunlight for more than a couple of minutes. The exposure should be increased gradually—adding two minutes each day is fast enough. The maximum amount of full exposure is about thirty minutes. On extremely hot days the baby should get his sunbath either very early in the morning or later on in the afternoon. The warmth of your baby's skin can be your criterion as to his comfort. He should feel warm to the touch. It is a good idea to have the baby wear a hat whenever he is in the sun.

When the sunshine is intense, as at the beach, your baby should be in the shade all the time for the first day or two and even then he may get enough reflected glare to give his tender skin a burn. The redness of sunburn does not show up until several hours *after* the damage is done.

49

BATH AND BATH ARTICLES

Bath Articles

A handy tray or basket should contain the following:

bath thermometer (optional)
cake of mild soap
pieces of absorbent cotton in
   a jar with a cover
cotton swabs
alcohol
baby oil (optional)

baby cream or lotion (optional)
baby powder (optional)
diaper pins (plastic heads)
small towel or diaper (to
    put in the bottom of the
    tub to keep the baby from
    sliding on the wet surface)

In addition you will need:

washcloth
bath towel to dry the baby (soft
   flannel, terry cloth, or jersey)
a bath apron to keep your clothes dry
baby's clean clothes: diaper, shirt, nightgown

Bathinette: This is a convenience, not a necessity.

Bath Table and Tub

Since the regular bathtub is hard on your back and legs, a tub may be placed on an ordinary table at which you may sit, or on something higher, like a dresser, at which you may stand. A plastic tub is preferable because it is inexpensive and easy to keep clean. The long, oval shape is favored. Another possibility is using the kitchen sink if it is big enough. It is a handy height and also has good adjacent surface area for drying. Make sure the spigots are turned aside. A turkish towel makes a good sink liner.

How Often and When to Bathe Your Baby

Although it is the custom to give a daily bath, as long as the baby is kept clean in the diapering area and around the mouth and neck, it certainly is not necessary more than once or twice a week. There are some exceptions, however. On excessively hot days, for example, you may give your baby a sponge bath several times a day to keep him comfortable.

Generally, a baby with very dry skin should be bathed much less frequently.

Many mothers are afraid that washing the baby's scalp too often will cause the hair to fall out more rapidly. This is not so. No matter what a mother does some hair will come out, but more will always grow in its place.

Generally, babies are bathed before their feeding. Dr. Spock suggests that in the early months it is usually most convenient to give the bath before the 10 A.M. feeding. However, father may enjoy bathing the baby before the 6 P.M. or 10 P.M. feeding. Dr. Brazelton reports that there are many babies who enjoy their bath after their meal and hate it before. You will have to make the decision.

The Sponge Bath

Until a baby's navel or circumcision is healed, a sponge bath is best. If a baby is particularly tiny and delicate or has dry or irritated skin, the doctor may recommend a sponge bath for the first month or six weeks. Most babies cry when given a bath in the first month, but love the feeling of the water from then on. Part of this may be their motor insecurity, which is made worse by the loose feeling of the water.

Before you begin, assemble everything you will need. Then bring your baby. The temperature of the room should be from seventy-five to eighty degrees and the room should be draft-free. It is unsafe to leave your baby unattended even for an instant while you get forgotten soap, towel, or clean shirt. Even at a few weeks of age, he can fall off of the edge.

To begin, place the baby in your lap or lay him on the bath table. Within easy reach should be a basin of warm water (95° to 100°). The water may be tested with your elbow or your wrist. If you are unsure using this method, try a bath thermometer. No commercial toiletries or softeners should be added to the water. These preparations frequently cause skin irritations and rashes.

Your baby should be in a big towel with the diaper unpinned, but not removed. The diaper and shirt are removed as you go along. Many newborns become upset when they are undressed and free of restraints. Although many parents report that their babies are disturbed by their bath, in reality they are reacting to this exposure.

The face is gently cleaned with a soft cloth dipped in warm water. The baby will hate this, so it is wise to do it as quickly as possible. Twice a week soap your baby's scalp with a lather that you have worked up in your hand. Rub your palm gently over the baby's head and work the soap into the scalp. The soft spot is covered with a tough membrane, so you do not have to worry about it. When it is time to rinse, hold the baby's head and back over the basin with your hand and arm (football carry). Wipe the soapsuds off the scalp with a damp washcloth, going over it twice. If the washcloth is too wet, the soapy water may get into the eyes and sting. (There are shampoos for babies that do not sting the eyes as much as ordinary shampoos.) The head should then be patted dry.

Next, the shirt is removed while the rest of the body is still covered with the towel. The chest, arms, and hands are soaped. Pay special attention to the folds and creases in the skin and then rinse with clean, warm water. Great care should be taken to remove all the soap in order to avoid chafing. The baby is then patted (*not* rubbed) dry with a soft towel.

Now, gently turn your baby over so that you can reach the back side. While supporting his head with your hand, soap and rinse the back area and then dry.

Finally, remove the diaper, wash and rinse the abdomen, genitals, legs, feet, and between the toes. A piece of cotton dipped into warm water is sufficient to clear away the white cheesy material that may collect in the folds of the labia of a girl or around the end of the penis of a boy. Now thoroughly and gently dry your baby.

The Tub Bath

Unless your doctor advises otherwise, by the time your baby's navel and circumcision have healed, he is ready to graduate from a sponge to a tub bath. The procedure is similar to the sponge bath. Until you get the knack of holding the baby securely, use only a small amount of water (two to three inches). This will help your baby become accustomed to the water gradually, too. Nothing really prepares you for dealing with a slippery baby except perhaps the reassurance that comes with practice.

Toiletries Used After the Bath

Before dressing your baby after the bath, especially if his skin is dry, you may wish to apply a lotion or mineral oil. Either the oil or lotion should be applied with a ball of absorbent cotton with all excess wiped away.

Baby powder may be helpful if your baby's skin chafes easily. (*Avoid any powders that contain* zinc stearate *and/or* asbestos.) You must never shake powder directly on your baby, because he may inhale the fine particles that are harmful to the lungs. Instead, dust the powder onto your hands first and then pat it gently onto his skin.

FRETFUL CRYING

All babies cry. The first thing your baby did at birth was to let out a yell and she has not stopped yet. The older the infant, the less she cries. However, you are interested in her crying now. What makes her cry? How can you soothe the fretful cry?

During the first few months of life, an infant cries approximately two hours a day, according to Dr. Marvin Gersh, author of *How to Raise Children at Home in Your Spare Time*. The baby may cry all at one time or throughout the day. When a baby cries constantly, it generally means there is something wrong. Colic, teething, fever, etc., are all specific reasons for crying. We are concerned here with the crying for which there is no apparent reason.

There is a definite contagion or sympathy cry in infants. This may occur when your infant hears a sibling or visiting baby cry. In experiments conducted on newborns by Marvin L. Simner, it was found that an infant's cry does stimulate the same response in newborns. Also female infants reacted more than males to a fellow baby's crying.

By four months of age an infant is well able to cry for attention. She enjoys and recognizes social interaction with parents and siblings.

An infant finds smiling, waving of arms, babbling, etc., much more fun and exciting than being alone in a crib, playpen, or infant seat. More often, she finds these containment devices boring and frustrating.

Parents are not always able to attend to their infant's every whim, nor do they always want to. If your baby is the firstborn, it may be easier to respond to him each time. If not, brothers and sisters are great! Babies love "little people" and a brother's contorted face or a sister's mimicry may be all it will take to quiet and amuse your social baby.

Fussy periods are evident in all infants. They may occur at any time, generally at the same time every day. Your infant may be his fussiest just prior to his feeding times. If this is the case, it will be obvious why he is grumpy. No rattle, friendly voice, or playful brother will keep him content for any length of time. His interest lies in the bottle or breast and the rest of his meal.

Another fussy time of day may be the family's dinner hour. The entire household is usually in an uproar at this time. Your patience is shorter than normal and you are busy. Father is home and tired. Other children are also tired and hungry at day's end. An infant can sense all this and his feelings are not too different from the rest of the family's.

At such a time a mobile may quiet your baby. Bright, bobbling figures will keep his attention for quite a while. He may be content to be alone, to play with his hands, to lie on his stomach and look around, or to listen to music from a radio or phonograph. An occasional pat on the face and a gentle word from mother or father may be adequate also.

Often infants will cry when they see their parents (most often mother) leaving them, even if it is to go into the next room. An infant is used to having you near and feels threatened by your disappearance. He has learned to love you, which should make you feel marvelous.

If you have gone to another part of the house, occasionally call to and talk to your child. Although he cannot see you, he is able to recognize your voice and will feel secure knowing you are near.

When you are going out for the afternoon or an evening and leaving your baby with a relative or a baby-sitter, allow your baby to see the sitter and you together for a time. He will associate the baby-sitter with you and not feel as badly or as strange when left alone.

COLIC

Colic, a catchall term used to explain almost any hard, persistent crying, is unfortunately a common disturbance in infancy. According to reliable studies, as many as 80 per cent of small babies are afflicted. Colic may begin anytime between the second and sixth week, but it gradually disappears by the time the baby is three months old. Due to the regularity of the pattern, it is commonly known as the "three-month colic."

During a classic colic seizure, a baby will stir uncomfortably soon after his evening feeding or even before it is finished. He will shriek for three or four hours with hardly a respite. Neither rocking the baby nor burping him has any effect. Neither a pacifier nor a drink of water will calm him. Finally, at 10 or 11 P.M., he will fall asleep. He may or may not down his 10 P.M. bottle before dropping off. The next morning he is himself again, contented and feeding well, only to repeat the nerve-shattering performance at 6 P.M. It is characteristic of colicky babies that they seem to thrive well and suffer no permanent impairment.

Where one baby may be very regular about his colic, always complaining between 6 P.M. and 10 P.M. or 2 P.M. and 6 P.M., another baby may cry over a longer period of time. This baby may be peaceful in the evening, but disturbed on and off throughout the day. However, this is not as bad as the baby who sleeps all day and wails half the night. Finally, there is the baby who starts out being restless during the day and then gradually shifts to the night or vice versa. Although some babies have just a few attacks scattered throughout the early months, many infants have trouble daily until they become three months old. Occasionally in severe cases the colic lasts up to six months or longer.

Causes

Traditionally, colic has been considered an intestinal disorder. Dr. Spock distinguished between "true colic" and "periodic irritable crying." Dr. Richard Feinbloom, in *Pregnancy, Birth and the Newborn* suggests that this division is no longer acceptable since babies who cry frantically tend to draw in large amounts of air and consequently their abdomens become distended with gas that they may pass by way of the rectum.

Pediatricians now regard the difference between true colic and other more or less regular episodes of crying as merely one of degree. According to Dr. Feinbloom, at this early stage of the baby's development, he may have no other means except crying to relax tensions and let off "emotional steam." Since colic generally disappears by three months of age, a developmental explanation is indicated.

Dr. Brazelton, writing in *Pediatrics,* suggests, "As other ways of discharging tension and of reaching out to the environment become available, there is a constant gradual reduction in the quantity of daily crying . . . Infants gradually seem to replace these crying periods with sociable interaction with their parents or with other activities, such as rolling over, watching their hands or other objects."

When a baby turns colicky, the mother's first reaction is to suspect the feedings. Crying from colic usually begins *after* feeding and in this way can be distinguished from hunger cries that usually occur *before* the feeding. Most mothers instinctively want to feed a baby who is crying violently, but this is hardly advisable in the case of a colicky baby. The problem does not appear to be related to the food itself since colic occurs with feedings of breast milk, cow's milk, and all kinds of formulas.

In *Your Child,* published by the Child Health Centers of America, mothers are warned that crying may result if the baby is swallowing too much air while she is eating. Such crying, unlike colic, may be eliminated by holding the baby with her head higher than her stomach during feeding. In addition, it may be helpful to burp the baby after she takes each ounce of milk. Mothers should also test the milk to make sure it is not too warm.

Pediatricians have often emphasized the relationship between infantile colic and the nervous, inept, insecure mother. Although Dr. Brazelton does not rest all blame on the anxious mother, he does think that she may aggravate the situation considerably.

In a thorough and systematic investigation that covered a period of five years (1963–68) it was found that the "mother's personality, anxiety level, and degree of success in adapting to the maternal role were *not* factors in the development of colic." Further research is still necessary to discover the exact origin of colic.

Treatment

With regard to colic, the tendency is to prescribe for the parents rather than the baby. The important thing is for them to know that the condition is fairly common and it actually does not seem to do the baby any permanent harm. Strange to say, colic occurs most often in babies who are developing well.

SOOTHING TECHNIQUES

Soothing techniques are important tools for you to have in coping with your crying infant. With knowledge of the approaches generally acceptable to infants and sensitivity to which of these are most effective in dealing with your baby, parental frustration resulting from prolonged crying can be avoided. Thus the developing relationship between mother and child can be positively reinforced and enhanced.

In *Three Years to Grow*, Sara Gilbert observes that swaddling is one of the oldest forms of soothing a very young crying baby. Simply placing a baby's arms by his sides and wrapping him snugly in a blanket will often be enough to interrupt the continuous startle reaction (the Moro reflex) that might otherwise keep him crying for prolonged periods. Many doctors question whether a baby should be swaddled routinely as this may retard physical development by restricting free movement of his arms and legs, especially during the first four weeks. By four weeks, the tonic neck reflex is coming in (turning the baby's head toward one side results in the extension of the arm and leg on the jaw side and flection of the limbs on the occiput side), giving the infant a feeling of stability. By eight weeks, he wants to lie freely without clothes on, kicking his feet and waving his arms.

Of course, babies differ in the amount of crying they seem to need, depending upon physical and emotional factors that are not always easily understood. A conscientious mother who has attended to her baby's basic needs should not feel guilty if her baby has crying spells that do not always respond to soothing techniques.

A recent investigation at New York Hospital revealed that mothers who have physical contact with their babies within twenty-four hours of birth tend to hold them on the left side, close to the heart. Mothers who are separated from their infants for twenty-four hours or more after birth tend to reverse the preference, holding the infants on the right side. In further studies it was found that the continuous recorded sound of a human heartbeat in the nursery resulted in babies who cried less and gained more weight than the control group. It may be that the rhythmical heartbeat is associated with the tension-free state in utero and that newborns are thus soothed by the sound of the normal adult heartbeat.

In another study, by Beverly Birns, Marion Blank, and Wagner H. Bridger, some specific stimuli involved in soothing infants were analyzed

57

to determine which are most effective. Continuous noise, a sweetened pacifier, gentle rocking of the bassinet, and immersion of a foot in warm water were the stimuli chosen. The researchers discovered that all the soothing stimuli were more effective than a non-stimulus control period, that from most to least effective stimuli are warm water, pacifier, rocking and sound. Another interesting finding was that some babies soothe more easily than others; that is, an infant easily soothed by one stimulus tends to be easily soothed by all and a baby unresponsive to one soothing stimulus is difficult to soothe with any.

At the Stanford University School of Medicine, Anneliese F. Korner and Rose Grobstein found that picking up a crying infant and putting him to the shoulder frequently induces a state of alertness that may be optimal for the infant's earliest learning. Thus, because a picked-up infant frequently becomes visually alert and scans the environment, he will have more opportunities to learn about his environment than a baby left crying in his crib. Since early stimulation appears necessary for normal human development, the visual experiences given to a crying infant when he is picked up may be an important by-product of this soothing technique.

Harriet L. Rheingold and Helen R. Samuels measured the effect of increased stimulation on the behavior of infants and found that infants fussed when continuously exposed to a non-stimulating environment. Only when toys were introduced did they stop fussing. The researchers concluded that lack of stimulation in the environment can produce fussing and that a change of stimulation maintains positive behavior. A parent has to learn how to read her infant's signals when he is unhappy or bored.

Dr. Lenore D. DeLucia in "Stimulus Preference and Discrimination Learning" found that rocking a baby when she is quiet instead of crying encourages quiet periods and forestalls crying. For any given amount of time, quiet time increased. Grandmother was right when she said that rocking soothes a fussy baby, but the traditional approach of rocking a baby only when she fusses also reinforces fussing!

Fortunately we are coming into closer contact with other societies and especially societies in which slinging is the technique most commonly used for soothing. According to Dr. Frances Ilg, an infant can be slung against her mother's abdomen until she weighs seven pounds. From then on, she is more comfortably slung on mother's back. Slinging devices are readily available and the best designs come from Japan. When the child is able to sit up while supported (seven to eight months), she is more comfortable in a backpack. Mothers know by a certain cry when she "needs to be slung." The baby prefers the parent to move around when she is slung rather than to stand or sit still.

PCI Point of View

PCI believes that the ability to employ successful soothing techniques is an important factor in the parents' relationship with their infant. Since infants differ in their ability to be soothed, a parent should try all of the different techniques available: swaddling, a safely constructed pacifier, change of environment, warmth, and continuous sound, such as music. Highly recommended is swaddling the infant, putting him to the left shoulder, and walking him. The swaddling provides warmth and stroking comfort, putting him to the left shoulder gives him a chance to survey the environment and be close to his parent's heart, and walking adds the rocking comfort that he was accustomed to before he was born.

SECURITY OBJECTS

An early attachment to one object—a toy or stuffed animal, a shoe, a piece of clothing, a diaper or blanket—is common in many young children. There are children who choose their own soft, warm hair as their security object and will stroke or twist a small piece of it when they are frightened or tired. Often thumb-sucking is combined with hair twisting for added pleasure. A "lovey" will be slept with, chewed, hugged, loved, or even "talked to." Removing it for brief periods, even for the best of reasons (like washing) may pose real problems. Cuddly objects, especially stuffed animals, should be chosen with washability in mind. Make sure you, too, can live with it. Pay a little bit more for attractiveness and durability, if need be.

Mother may foster object attachment when she repeatedly includes a particular toy or blanket on a trip to the sitter's or at bedtime. This practice is logical and recommended by most pediatricians. In this manner a familiar object becomes something of a child's known world to take with him into the large and sometimes frightening unknown world.

Attachment to a soft object is quite common. Most babies do not prefer one toy, but some will and you cannot foretell what the favorite will be. One expert believes children's attachments to such objects help in the transition from dependence to independence from mother. The need for a security object is usually outgrown between the ages of two and five. A soft, cuddly object for many young children becomes a "transitional object" that helps them to shift from one type of activity, one situation, or person to another.

In later years people may become security objects; an adolescent may decide not to go to a social gathering because he does not have a friend to go with him or does not know anyone who will be there. Even you may feel hesitant about joining a group of strangers if you are by yourself. A young child cannot always take a friend when he is in a situation threatening to him. Most experts agree that the friend he would like to take is mother. Therefore, he chooses the most familiar, soft, comforting substitute for mother and will drag this security object about with him.

There is less chance of your child needing a security substitute if he receives an adequate amount of the real thing—his mother's physical touch and attention—when he needs it the most. While this does not mean mothers should be on twenty-four-hour duty, it seems there are some particular times when parents are needed the most.

Bedtime seems to be a period when a security object is in greatest demand by children prone to needing such things. Even though the child is in her own bed and her parents are in the house, going to sleep is sometimes frightening for a young child. Singing short, simple songs is also very pleasant to a child. Make up some of your own that include the child's name and names familiar to her.

Almost all the experts are of the opinion that a security object should not be physically removed from a child.

If your child has become dependent on an object, whether it be a night bottle, a worn, fuzzy blanket, or the attachment to the vacuum cleaner, it would be a cruel act to take it away from her. This object represents a stabilizing force in her rapidly changing and constantly challenging world. If you really feel embarrassed by it, you can try limiting the security item to special times—bedtime, tired, bored, or sick periods—and make sure you have given your offspring enough of your physical love in between!

Some security blankets have been successfully cut in half for washing purposes. Other mothers have found an exact match and substituted without the child's knowledge.

THUMB-SUCKING

Thumb-sucking as a Normal Reflex

In a study by the Harvard Pediatrics Department, 86 per cent of the healthy and apparently normal babies who were observed showed that they enjoyed sucking their thumbs even though they were not fatigued, hungry, or uncomfortable. The investigation revealed that finger- or thumb-sucking began between birth and three months, gradually increased in intensity to a peak by seven months and then as motor development occupied the baby more, it decreased. This same period marks the onset of mouthing objects, which most likely contributed to the decline of thumb-sucking. By twelve months, except during periods of stress or tension, most of the babies had entirely ceased sucking their thumbs.

Thumb-sucking is a normal reflex. Dr. Brazelton thinks that finger-sucking is very common among babies who are having a happy time at feedings and is not a reflection of inadequate mothering. "The happiest babies often do the most sucking after feedings."

Dr. David Levy suggests that the main reason a young baby sucks his thumb is that he has not had enough sucking at the breast or bottle to satisfy his sucking need. Apparently babies who are fed every three hours do

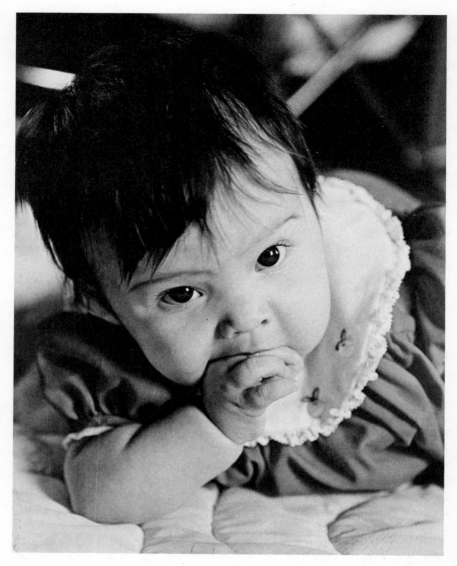

not suck their thumbs as much as babies fed every four hours; and babies who have cut down their nursing time from twenty minutes to ten minutes (because the nipples have become too soft) are more likely to suck their thumbs than babies who still have to work for twenty minutes. In one of a series of experiments, Dr. Levy fed a litter of puppies with a medicine dropper so that there was no opportunity for sucking during their feedings. The animals reacted in the same way as babies who do not get enough chance to suck at feeding time. They sucked their own and each other's paws and skin so hard that the fur came off.

Thumb-sucking in Breast-fed Babies

Some pediatricians believe that a breast-fed baby is less apt to be a thumb-sucker. This is due to the fact that the mother is more inclined to let him continue nursing for as long as he wants to. Since it is impossible for her to know when her breasts are empty, she is forced to rely on the baby. Although the baby gets most milk from the breast within five or six minutes, he may be eager to continue sucking for as long as thirty to forty minutes in order to satisfy this craving to suck. (To go beyond forty minutes is obviously too time-consuming for the mother.) However, one finds great variability in the breast-fed babies who are allowed to nurse for as long as they want. At some feedings they may want as much as forty minutes; other times they may be satisfied with only ten minutes. For this reason breast feeding is particularly adaptable to the baby's individual needs.

Thumb-sucking in Bottle-fed Babies

On the other hand, when the baby finishes a bottle, it is done. She is forced to stop because sucking air is unpleasant or because mother takes away the bottle. Therefore, thumb-sucking is most likely to begin at about the time the baby learns to finish his bottle in ten minutes instead of twenty. This happens because the baby is getting stronger and older, while rubber nipples are getting weaker. One possible solution, of course, is to adjust the nipple holes or buy new nipples.

Teething Versus Thumb-sucking

Quite commonly, around the age of three to four months, the baby may begin to chew on her thumb and fingers. The tendency to extend the arms especially as the head is turned (tonic neck reflex) is now giving way to ease of flection at sixteen weeks, thus allowing fingers or thumbs to be placed in baby's mouth. This is also caused by teething and should not be confused with thumb-sucking per se. During teething periods, the baby who is a thumb-sucker is sucking one minute and chewing another.

Thumb-sucking as a Comforter

In addition to being related to feeding behavior, thumb-sucking is often associated with sleep. Many children suck their thumbs or fingers to comfort themselves as they fall off to sleep. This is quite natural and nothing to worry about. Eventually the baby will stop sucking her thumb.

Handling Thumb-sucking

It is best to ignore this habit, because calling a child's attention to it may prolong the thumb-sucking and turn the habit itself into a psychological problem.

It is generally agreed that using any type of restraint, such as elbow splints or mittens, is a bad idea. Similarly, scolding is of no use; this would only make the child miserable, frustrate him a great deal, and also tend to prolong the habit.

Effect on Teeth

Many parents worry about the effect of thumb-sucking on their baby's jaws and teeth. Granted that thumb-sucking often pushes the upper front baby teeth forward and the lower teeth back, but how much the teeth are displaced depends on how much the child sucks his thumb and even more the particular position in which he holds his thumb. Furthermore, dentists point out that any tilting of the baby teeth has absolutely no effect on the permanent teeth that begin to come in at about six years of age. In other words, if the thumb-sucking is given up by six years of age, and more often by four or five years, as it is in the great majority of cases, there is very little chance of it affecting the permanent teeth.

BOWEL MOVEMENTS AND DIAPERING IN INFANCY

For the first few days of life, a newborn's bowel movements, called meconium, will be greenish black and sticky. During the next month or two, the breast-fed baby will have frequent stools. Some babies will have a movement after each nursing and this is perfectly normal. These stools are usually very soft, loose, or mushy and range in color from light yellow to yellow-orange. Occasionally, the stool may be green and contain curds.

As baby's digestive system matures, his stools will become less frequent. A breast-fed baby may have only one stool in several days and still be perfectly healthy and comfortable. Breast-fed babies often push, grunt, and strain while having a bowel movement.

The newborn who is receiving formula will usually have movements that are pasty or lumpy. Generally, they range in color from pale yellow to tan. The number of movements a day will vary. The formula-fed infant will start off having a movement after each feeding, then taper off and settle down to one to four movements a day. The number of movements each day is not important as long as the consistency of the stool is normal and the baby is doing well.

Parents soon become familiar with the type and frequency of their newborn's bowel movements and are the best judge of anything that seems unusual. If his movements change suddenly in consistency or odor, watch him carefully. One or two different movements may occur now and then, but several abnormal movements are a signal that something is wrong.

Many newborns will have loose stools on occasion. In fact, some babies have loose stools all though infancy. In itself, this is not a cause for alarm and is not considered diarrhea. A sudden change to loose or watery stools that stain the diaper beyond the stool itself is known as diarrhea. Notify your doctor promptly if this occurs. Diarrhea is usually mild and easily treated in newborns, but it can become serious if untreated.

Constipation, or infrequent bowel movements, is not regarded as an illness in the newborn unless it is accompanied by vomiting, abdominal distension, failure to gain weight, pain or excessive difficulty in passing the stool, or a general listlessness or weakness.

Many normal newborns turn red in the face, grunt, and fuss for several minutes when passing a stool. Check with your doctor in helping a constipated baby. Never give a laxative, enema, or suppository to a newborn except on your doctor's advice.

The Diaper Dilemma

Parents have a choice about diapers. You can wash diapers at home, use a diaper service, or use disposable ones.

The following chart lists the merits of each diaper method, as reported to PCI by experienced mothers:

	Cloth Diapers Washed at Home	Cloth Diaper Service	Disposable Diapers
ADVANTAGES	Least expensive—do not forget to include cost of soap and power for washer.	Generally, costs are comparable.	
		Always washed and dried properly—rarely responsible for diaper rash.	Pins not used. Aesthetically pleasing.
	Consider ecological view of increased detergent and power use.	Consider ecological view of increased detergent and power use.	May cause diaper rash
	Can be recycled when no longer needed.		
DISADVANTAGES	Must be washed and dried on schedule.	Your diaper supply depends on reliability of delivery man.	Disposal presents ecological problem.
	Your time and labor are required.	You may receive old, worn-out diapers at times.	

Whatever method you choose, investigate to be sure you are handling the diapers properly. Most baby books provide detailed instructions if you launder your own diapers. Diaper services will tell you how to handle their diapers. For information about disposables, just read the package information or consult your local ecology group.

Changing the Diaper

If you are not sure of how to diaper a baby or if baby's diapers fall off ten minutes after you put them on, get a more experienced mother to demonstrate. This will be far more effective than pictures and words.

A newborn's diaper is usually changed before and after a feeding, after a bowel movement, and at any other time she seems uncomfortable due to a wet diaper. Do not change a sleeping baby unless she has a severe diaper rash—her sleep is more important.

The diaper area must be thoroughly cleaned after each bowel movement. You do not have to clean baby after urinating unless she has a diaper rash. A convenient setup for cleaning your baby when changing her diaper would include three glass jars kept near you, but away from baby. One jar holds cotton balls, one baby oil, and the other holds warm water. After a bowel movement, wipe baby's bottom with the clean part of the diaper, then wash the area using cotton balls and water. Do not forget to dry her. At this age, baby oil will remove any trace of feces. Later you will need soap and water for this. Then powder or apply cornstarch and your baby is ready for a clean diaper.

Diaper rash can be a problem for the newborn. Most rashes will clear up by incorporating these suggestions into your routine:

1. Do not use plastic pants. If you use disposable diapers, remove the plastic covering.

2. Change the diaper as soon as baby is wet or soiled.

3. Clean diaper area *thoroughly* whenever you change baby. Then apply a protective ointment and powder—aids in removal of ointment at next diaper change.

4. Allow baby to be diaper-free for long periods so that the air may get to the diaper area if it is inflamed.

PCI Point of View

Most newborns are not bothered by bowel movements. Problems arise when mothers expect their newborns to fit preconceived notions. Avoid this. Take cues from your baby and become an expert on what is *normal for him.*

POTTY-CHAIR AND BOWEL TRAINING

Conditions for Bowel Control

It is understood by all the writers surveyed that bowel training is accomplished when a child is able to take himself regularly to the toilet for elimination. This is a process that cannot occur until the child is physically ready; that is, his neuromuscular control over his sphincter muscles is sufficiently developed. This occurs sometime after the first year, perhaps as late as age two and a half to three.

Learning bowel control is not easy. The child must learn to withhold his previously involuntary defecation response and indicate his needs (verbally or otherwise) so that he may receive help from an adult. Ultimately he must learn to recognize the need to eliminate and perform the act totally by himself in the proper place.

Potty-chair

Virtually all authorities concur that it is best to provide a special seat or potty-chair for the learning child. Many do not differentiate between a seat that fits the regular toilet and a separate potty-chair, but a few prefer a small, separate chair. They point out that a regular toilet is too high for a child to have her feet firmly on the ground and may have a hole large enough for the child to fall in, thus making her fearful of the training process. A child using a potty-chair can mount it by herself with the resultant sense of self-achievement. A potty-chair is movable.

Also the bowel movement may be retained in the pot until after the child has left the room. It is felt that a child is likely to feel possessive about her movements at first, regarding them as gifts to the parent, and may not want to see them thrown away. In addition, she may be frightened by the process of a flushing toilet—the noise, disappearance of contents, etc.

Dr. Fitzhugh Dodson, in *How to Parent,* adds the suggestion that after initial training the child should learn to use a variety of toilets so that there is no problem when she is in a new place.

How to Bowel Train

Training will proceed most easily when the child is fairly regular with at least one of his daily movements and has learned to understand and/or verbalize about what he is doing. This usually occurs between two and a half and three years, but may be as early as eighteen months. Thus a typical procedure would be for the parent to notice that the child is having a bowel movement and to tell him what he is doing in whatever words the parent wishes to use. In a later stage of training, the parent would try to get the child to the potty-chair before the movement was made. Selma Fraiberg notes that some tact is necessary on the part of the parent while whisking the child away from a pleasurable activity to use the potty.

It is expected that at some point the child must learn to associate the verbalization of the act with the action itself. Although initially the bowel movement may be "caught" by a watchful mother, the child will eventually gain full control over his bowel behavior.

Imitation of older siblings and/or parents is a positive factor in training.

Early Training—Positive and Negative Aspects

There is some controversy over the usefulness of starting to put one's child on a potty-chair at a very early age, i.e., before one year. Most child experts today feel that this serves mainly to train the mother to catch her child's bowel movement, but is not very useful in later training of the child. In any case, it only works with a very regular baby or a very watchful mother.

Drs. Elizabeth Robertson and Margaret Wood, authors of *Today's Child,* believe that such early "conditioning" may be helpful later and real training may be begun as early as one year. However, if the child is balky at that age, it is best to wait until between eighteen and twenty-four months before trying again.

The critics of starting very early say that at best it conditions the child to be aware of the process of elimination (although he still has no conscious control of it); at worst it causes a relapse in training and later psychological damage to the child. Dr. Dodson is the most emphatic critic of early training, saying that later problems (bed-wetting, for example) are almost inevitable. Dr. Salk says of children trained under fifteen months, "Because their muscular control is not quite adequate, they are extremely prone to accidents, which may make them feel like failures since they cannot always comply with your expectations. They fear you will withhold love and affection for their failure."

Problems in Bowel Training

It is generally agreed that shame, punishment, or anger from the parent are out of place and will only prolong the training and cause difficulties in the child–parent relationship.

The parent should give moderate praise at the correct achievement, but very little negative reaction to a lack of success or an accident. Fitzhugh Dodson and Selma Fraiberg emphasize that a child is willing to learn bowel control largely because he wishes to please his parents and to have a feeling of accomplishment.

Overpraise may cause the child to have a distorted view of her achievement and a desire to retain her bowel movement for release at her will. A child who feels too much is expected of her may become directly defiant of the process or may manifest her defiance in other disturbed behavior patterns.

PCI Point of View

The process of bowel training may take as long as a year and usually will not be complete until after the child is two or two and one half, regardless of when started. Even then occasional relapses are not unlikely, especially when a child is faced with new, unusual, and/or upsetting circumstances. The parent must be sensitive to the child's feelings regarding toilet training and should not pressure him. Quietly rewarding him for cooperation is a better way.

BLADDER TRAINING

Maturation of the Bladder

In tracing the development of bladder control, you will see that a newborn up to the age of six weeks may cry when his diaper is wet and become quiet when he is changed. At twenty-eight weeks, a baby urinates frequently and quite excessively. Girls may be dry as long as one or two hours. By nine months, your baby may be dry after a nap and may cry to be changed in the middle of the night. This fussing when wet even during the day is very often true of year-old babies.

By two years of age, your child can usually hold his urine one and a half to two hours. Between 5 P.M. and 8 P.M., there is often an increased frequency of urinating; he is more frequently dry than wet after napping. Night dryness is quite variable, with girls achieving dryness considerably ahead of boys, but most children are still wet in the morning. From this brief description, you can see that the muscles that control the bladder are not mature enough before the age of two for a child to be able to control them. You may think your child is ready to be trained due to his dryness at certain times or his fussing over a wet diaper, but his bladder is still not mature enough. No matter what methods you may use, you *cannot* train a child until his body is ready and he is willing to co-operate.

The control of the bladder function is an involuntary mechanism that is made voluntary by a slow process, whereby, according to Drs. Gesell and Ilg, "the vegetative nervous system and the higher brain centers are co-ordinated to bring about this control. An extremely elaborate network of nerve cell connections must be built up during the first five years of life. Even then the controls are not perfected; growth continues through adolescence."

When you hear stories of babies being "trained" at nine, twelve, or fifteen months of age, you can be certain it is the mother who is "trained." The babies have not been trained to take care of their toileting. They are only responding to their mothers, who have trained themselves to take care of their babies' needs. Doctors and psychologists are familiar with childhood emotional problems that develop as a result of too early toilet training. In other words, you may have a toilet-trained infant only to see him become a six-year-old bed wetter.

The later the training begins the shorter time it takes. In one study involving twins, one was started on training at seven months of age and training was almost complete at two years of age. The other twin was started at two years of age and almost immediately was at the same level of achievement as his twin. From this study and others, it is evident that *after* the age of *two* is the best time for beginning any efforts to toilet train your child.

First Attempts

Parents who are aware that it is sensible to wait until the child is *ready* to be toilet trained should know what to do when the time occurs. After two years of age, many children have a desire to use the toilet like others in the family. You can encourage this readiness because toddlers are usually ready and willing to try to co-operate with a mother's wishes. On the other hand, many two-year-olds are independent and "negative" and may resist your toilet-training advances. If this is the case, relax and forget about toilet training for a few more months.

You will have to give your child a name for urine (whether it be urine or some other word) so that he can signal you when he has to urinate. At first he will tell you *after* he has urinated. This is most certainly a sign of readiness. His timing may be a little off, but it shows that he is beginning to realize he should have voided in the toilet and probably indicates a growing preference for dry pants. The toddler may hold himself or tug at his diaper when he has to urinate. This is a good time to put your child in training pants. Express satisfaction that now he is through with diapers. You should also tell him to try and tell you the next time he has to go and then he can use the toilet. Before success is constant, be prepared to tell this to your child often and with *understanding*.

When she stays dry for as long as two hours, you can take her to the bathroom at two-hour intervals and before and after naps and meals. Even after remaining dry for two or three hours, she still may lack the muscular control to hold her urine even a second longer once her bladder is full. It takes time for her to develop this control. She has to learn how to let you know when she has to go. Bladder training requires both physical and mental development.

It is natural for a boy to stand up to urinate. A small stool should be available to stand on so that he is at a proper height. Watching father urinate is probably the best teacher for a little boy. However, if he wants to sit down, let him. Conversely, your little girl may want to stand to urinate like daddy. Let her try. After several attempts she usually can be convinced to try sitting down.

Night Dryness

Sleeping control over the bladder can be established only when two conditions have been met. First, the child must have learned through daytime control to respond to tension in his bladder by tightening his sphincter muscles. Second, he must keep his sphincters closed without waking up.

What should the parent do to establish nighttime control? Nothing! The natural maturing of your child's bladder, plus the fact that he has learned from his daytime control that urine goes into the toilet will sooner or later take care of the situation.

Remember to praise your child's successes and accept his failures. Years from now it will make negligible difference how long his toilet training took, but a great deal of difference whether it was accomplished agreeably or otherwise.

BED-WETTING

Many psychologists have accused American middle-class mothers of being overly concerned with cleanliness in their children, constantly reminding them to wash their hands, brush their teeth, and wipe their noses. All this has been done in the name of health. A clean child is less likely to get ill than a dirty one. This is a supposition that is difficult to prove, but being dirty is definitely "not nice."

One thing for sure is that if a child is not toilet trained during the day or wets at night by the time he is two and a half or three years old, parents begin to worry. They often blame the child or themselves. Much of the concern about how to toilet train and when is related to the publicity given the subject by Dr. Sigmund Freud, who postulated that personality characteristics such as orderliness, cleanliness, and miserliness are related to bowel training.

Toilet-training practices vary according to the country, educational background of the parents, and age of the child, but by the age of five if a child is not trained or is wet at night, he is subject to great parental pressure.

In *Children Under Five,* by J. M. Blomfield and J. W. B. Douglas, we find that 60 per cent of English mothers start to "pot" their infants during the first two weeks of life, an age at which voluntary control of the anal sphincters is impossible. Neurologists generally consider that six months of age is the earliest possible time to begin toilet training (though not desirable). Blomfield and Douglas attempted to relate early toilet training to later bed-wetting. The results they found were that bed-wetting becomes a problem *after* the age of four years; a larger proportion of the children of manual workers than of non-manual workers wet their beds; among the more prosperous families, boys more often than girls wet their beds; jealousy of a younger sibling did not seem to influence bed-wetting. It was also found that a low standard of maternal care was associated with bed-wetting. The better the maternal care (assessment was based on the management of the child and of his cleanliness and that of the home), the lower the incidence of bed-wetting.

Even the Doctors Do Not Agree

Research concerning the causes of bed-wetting varies greatly. Dr. Marvin Gersh tells us that enuresis (bed-wetting) is not usually caused by psychological problems. A pamphlet recently published by Johns Hopkins University states that most bed-wetting is caused by small bladder capacity rather than psychological problems.

Dr. Neil Henderson and Rudolf Dreikurs maintain that bed-wetting due to physical abnormalities is rare; bed-wetting is usually caused by tensions and emotional problems.

What to Do

If you were a nineteenth-century parent of a bed wetter, you might have forced your child to eat the testicles of a rabbit or the petals of a chrysanthemum. Modern parents have other methods. They consult a doctor to make sure no urinary infection is present and ask his opinion on what course to pursue.

If your child is three and you are concerned about bed-wetting, put your child in training pants and rubber pants and leave a night light on in his room so he can see should he have to get up to go to the bathroom. Do not scold him for a wet bed; always calmly praise him for a dry one. Try to be as indifferent to the problem as possible. Do not allow your child to escape a wet bed by climbing into bed with you. If the wet bed is troublesome, change the sheets. Make clear to your child what is expected of him.

By four years, other remedies are suggested for bed-wetting. Most doctors feel that the bed wetter sleeps so deeply that she cannot feel the discomfort of a full bladder and that medication may be helpful. Dragging a child, half-asleep, to the bathroom in the middle of the night is not recommended by the authorities, although many mothers find this at least keeps the bed dry. Restricting fluids after dinner has not proved to be successful and may result in upsetting arguments between mother and child before bedtime. Do make sure the child voids before going to bed.

Dr. Gersh recommends increasing the capacity of the child's bladder so the child can make it through the night. Approximately ten to twelve ounces of urine collect in the bladder overnight. Most children urinate when three to six ounces collect. Consequently the bed is wet after three to six ounces collect in the bladder at night. To increase the capacity of your child's bladder, Dr. Gersh's advice is to encourage rather than discourage drinking. Suggest that the child try to hold his urine as long as he can so as to stretch his bladder. Make it a game. Ask him to hold his urine as long as possible during the day and measure the amount daily. He will try to improve his score until he reaches ten ounces.

Accidents during the day may occur when a child is very excited, he is outside playing, or he cannot get his pants down fast enough, or when a new baby arrives. *Understanding is necessary.* These types of accidents are quite common. Only when daytime wetting is consistent is there a problem requiring professional guidance. If a child loses bladder control and must urinate more than usual (and especially if there are burning sensations around the genitals), a doctor should be consulted.

Most doctors agree on the following facts about bed-wetting:

1. Male children wet the bed more often than female children.

2. Bed wetters appear to sleep more soundly than children who do not wet the bed.

3. Although bed-wetting may be a symptom of such diseases as diabetes or kidney infection, most of the time the problem is small bladder capacity.

4. Bed-wetting can be due to nervousness, insecurity, jealousy, or other emotional problems. However, in most instances, nervousness in a

bed-wetting child is caused by the criticism he gets and his own feelings of frustration.

5. Bed-wetting appears to be unrelated to intelligence, birth weight, size of family, position of the child in the family, speech disorders, or whether the child is right-handed or left-handed.

Keep in mind that bed-wetting is not something a child wants to do and *no child should be punished for wetting the bed.*

3
Feeding and Nutrition

INTRODUCTION BY MYRON WINICK, M.D.*

It is becoming more and more evident that nutrition at critical times during the life cycle will not only stamp its mark on the organism, but also may leave a permanent legacy in times to come. Certainly infancy and early childhood are extremely critical times in this regard. Studies have shown that severe undernutrition early in life may result in permanent retardation in brain growth. The number of brain cells may be reduced, the insulation around the nerve fibers may be thinner than normal, the number of connections between nerves may be fewer, and the chemical milieu in which nerve impulses are delivered may be disturbed. The changes that result unquestionably contribute to the retarded development seen in children who have been severely malnourished in early infancy. Such children may have severe learning disabilities later in life.

Conversely, overnutrition early in life may result in the development of too many fat cells. This can result in a type of obseity that persists into adult life and is extremely difficult to control. We have learned then that we do not feed our children only for today; how we feed them as young infants certainly will have an effect on their health and well-being tomorrow. Fortunately, there is a "happy medium" between these two extremes that will allow us to reach our goal, the proper growth and development of our children. There are a number of ways that this goal can be obtained. We do not have to set up rigid rules and guidelines. We can use our own judgment and often rely on the infant's instincts. For example, early in life the breast-fed infant will

* Dr. Myron Winick is the R. R. Williams Professor of Nutrition, Professor of Pediatrics, and Director of the Institute of Human Nutrition at Columbia University College of Physicians and Surgeons. He was a participant at the White House Conference on Nutrition in 1969, and in 1970 he received an E. Mead Johnson Award in Pediatric Research. Dr. Winick is the editor of a series of books entitled *Current Concepts in Nutrition* and the author of over eighty scientific articles. He is one of the top men in the field of nutrition.

determine by himself how much milk to take. Usually it will be just the right amount for him to gain adequate weight, but not to grow too large.

This should not be surprising; it happens in every animal in the mammalian kingdom. They all control their own intake and grow properly. In most developed countries infants can be adequately fed either by breast or by bottle. Formulas are sterile, nutritious, and simple to prepare. If we use formulas we must avoid our own overzealous tendency to "empty the bottle" into the infant. More chubby infants are bottle fed than breast fed and this can create problems of obesity later in life.

The introduction of solid foods presents parents with another choice. They can use commercially prepared "baby foods" or blended "table foods." Either can be successful. The kind of food given is more important than its form. For example, some parents introduce cereal early because it contains iron, which is not present in cow's or human milk; however, many infant formulas contain added iron. If such a formula is being used, cereal need not be the first solid food. As solid foods become a greater proportion of the diet, our concern is to present to the toddler a nutritionally balanced package containing adequate amounts of protein for growth, but certainly some carbohydrate for energy and some fat for storage. Too much of any one of these nutrients is not healthy—all are needed. Fortunately, this mix of nutrients can be obtained in many ways.

The best indication that you are using the right mix is a well-developing, healthy, alert youngster. The body has an amazing capacity to store nutrients and to regulate its activities depending on its nutrient supply. Therefore, we do not need to eat a perfectly balanced diet at every meal or even every day. What we aim for is balanced and nutritious patterns of eating over long periods of time. Again, the infant period is extremely critical. This is when long-term patterns are established. This is when "likes and dislikes" are formed. Parents must guide the patterns and mold these likes and dislikes. In many ways our culture is becoming one in which outside forces, advertising and "salesmanship," are telling our children, even our very young children, how to eat. The children then tell us what they want. This practice can be extremely dangerous not only to the child, but to his whole attitude toward food.

It is important to note that while nutrition is extremely important, food and the process of feeding encompass much more than nutrition alone. Eating is a social event; it is a time when the family is together. It should be so for the child even from the beginning. There is ample evidence to demonstrate that young animals or children reared in an isolated environment develop poorly even if they are well fed.

During the past few years, we have come to realize that there is a complex interaction between nutrition and environment that controls subsequent development. Malnourished children returned to the social conditions that caused the malnutrition develop poorly even if subsequent nutrition is adequate. Conversely, in those few situations where malnourished children have entered a different environment, one that has much more stimulation, their development has approached normal. Thus parents need to supply both good nutrition and an enriched environment. This can be done in one effective way by delivering the nutrients in an effective manner.

Do not prop the bottle and leave the infant to "survive." Holding the baby, cuddling and playing with him is a way of enriching his environment. The same is true with older children. Make eating an enjoyable experience. This will help both in providing better nutrition and stimulating your child.

Certainly there is no one way to feed an infant; nor would any book that has a rigid approach to feeding be appropriate to a majority of parents. On the other hand, there are certain concepts that are important to remember:

1. Breast milk is a nearly complete food for the newborn infant. It is still the best form of nutrition that we can supply.

2. Prepared formulas that simulate breast milk are also excellent and while they are more expensive than other means of infant feeding, they are very convenient.

3. Formulas prepared from whole or evaporated milk can be made to approach human milk and can be used successfully in infant feeding.

4. Solid foods are introduced at first to supply specific nutrients and not for either their calorie or protein content. In this regard, iron is probably most important and can be gotten from cereals (that usually are enriched) or meats.

5. Solid foods should be introduced gradually and one at a time so that if a food disagrees with the infant, it can easily be identified and subsequently avoided. Do not introduce "mixed dinners" until each of the ingredients has been tried separately.

6. During very early infancy a vitamin preparation containing A, C, and D should be used in required amounts. Once a variety of solid foods has been introduced, this is no longer necessary.

7. During the latter part of the first year, solid foods gradually replace milk as the major source of calories and protein. They should, therefore, be chosen wisely. The aim is to create a diet adequate in calories, about 30 per cent of which come from protein, another 30 per cent from carbohydrate, and the rest from fat. Some pediatricians feel that the amount of saturated fat (found mostly in milk and milk products and meat) should be limited. This can be achieved by using partly skimmed milk preparations and foods containing vegetable oils. At present, it is also thought that even in infancy too much cholesterol in the diet may not be good. Reduction of cholesterol intake in most children can best be achieved by limiting the amount of egg yolks consumed.

8. There is mounting concern about the amount of refined carbohydrate, especially sucrose, in the American diet. At present, we do not know of any detrimental effects in the young infant. Some people have theorized that feeding sweetened foods will create a "sweet tooth" that will remain into later life. At present, there is no real evidence that this occurs.

9. During the childhood years, a balanced diet containing adequate protein for growth is essential. This can be achieved in a variety of ways.

10. Between-meal snacks are acceptable but care should be taken not to allow frequent ingestion of "sticky"-type candies rich in sugar. These appear to increase the incidence of caries.

These principles combined with our own common sense will help us achieve our most important goal as parents: healthy, normally growing and developing children. It is our responsibility as parents to create the proper environment for our children to attain that goal. Since good nutrition is an important part of that environment, parents must take the time to learn about nutrition for their children. Advertising and commercials rarely teach good nutrition. They try to sell products. There are other sources to which a parent can turn. This book is one of them. It takes a simple straightforward approach to infant nutrition. It is not rigid, yet it attemps to set some guidelines that should be of practical value to parents.

SHOULD I BREAST OR BOTTLE FEED?

Providing nourishment for her newborn child is one of a mother's most important responsibilities after she has given birth. During the nine months prior to delivery she thought about many things, made many plans, and reached many decisions.

One decision that requires careful consideration is the manner in which she will feed her new infant. There are two basic choices: baby can be fed with milk from the mother's body or with a specially prepared formula that is composed of ingredients that approximate human milk. The expectant mother has to consider the relative merits of breast and bottle feeding so that she can decide which method will be best in her case.

Perhaps the first thought that comes to mind when one is considering whether to breast feed or bottle feed a baby is the matter of which kind of milk is most nutritious. Some experts believe that on the basis of nutrition alone there is no conclusive evidence that one method is superior to the other. However, many others are strongly convinced that breast milk is generally superior to any formula.

According to Dr. Niles Anne Newton, who has described infant feeding extensively in her book *Family Book of Child Care,* "Both breast feeding and bottle feeding can produce fine babies who are both emotionally and physically healthy. However, there are certain differences between them which you will want to know."

The Case for Breast Feeding

1. Availability: some formulas must be prepared and warmed. Newborns scream with hunger because their tiny bodies cannot tolerate the necessary preparations that precede bottle feeding. Breast feeding requires no preparation.

2. Nutritionally: breast milk contains the most complete nutritional

package, according to Dr. Winick. It is raw, fresh, and sterile. All formulas simulate breast milk; however, processing may destroy certain nutrients. There are many nutrients that are added to formulas, but there are others that may be unknown, which precludes their being added to formulas.

3. Digestibility: breast milk digests easily and rapidly; certain formulas digest more slowly. Babies fed entirely on breast milk do not get constipated. Breast feeding also promotes the growth of desirable bacteria in the baby's digestive system; therefore, breast-fed babies are less likely to have digestive disorders.

4. Simplicity: the baby is always in control; her sucking regulates the amount of milk she drinks and mother can be assured that baby is "getting enough." Dr. Winick points out that in the U.S.A. breast-fed babies tend to be less chubby than their bottle-fed friends and this, too, may be advantageous.

5. Economical: breast feeding is less costly.

6. Facility: breast feeding requires no special equipment or devices, whereas mixing formula does require very specific utensils, sterile conditions, and appropriate storage.

7. Nurturing: mother, free from the chore of sterilizing and bottling formula, can concentrate on nursing, during which a unique bond develops between her and her baby based on shared satisfaction and intimate physical relatedness.

The Case for Bottle Feeding

There are, of course, some definite advantages to bottle feeding. If an infant is being bottle fed, any member of the family or a baby-sitter can be in charge of the feeding. This releases the mother from complete responsibility for the child's nourishment. It allows her more freedom than if she were nursing. Fathers, in particular, can share in the feeding of their newborn infant, and this can help alleviate feelings of being "left out." During the postnatal period, new mothers can get more rest if others are sharing in the feeding responsibilities and mothers who are bottle feeding enjoy taking turns with their co-operative husbands for the middle-of-the-night feeding!

Some women tend to become anxious when they do not know exactly how much milk their infant is consuming. When a baby is nursing, the mother does not know precisely how many ounces of milk her infant is drinking at any one feeding. To the mother who is bottle feeding her baby, this is no worry. She knows accurately how much milk her baby drinks according to the amount that is left in the bottle when a feeding is over.

There are many other uncertainties that may plague an expectant mother as she contemplates her decision regarding the feeding of her newborn. If she decides to try breast feeding, she may wonder if she will know *how* to nurse her infant or if she will be able to count on someone else to show her how. She may fear that her milk supply will be insufficient in quality or amount. She may wonder how to go about nursing her baby in a public place. She may be concerned that her husband or other relatives and friends may have definite opinions as to the desirability of one method over another and that her ultimate choice will have to include a consideration of their opinions, particularly her husband's feelings.

The mother who decides to breast feed should be prepared to encounter some skepticism or negative reactions from nurses or other mothers in the hospital and even from her obstetrician or pediatrician.

La Leche League

It is important to discuss these issues with knowledgeable individuals. When prospective parents meet with their obstetrician or when they visit the maternity wing of the hospial prior to delivery, they should be prepared to ask questions about the feeding regimen for their new baby. A flexible feeding schedule is ideal for the mother who chooses breast feeding.

Should mothers want to know about the techniques of breast feeding, they should consult the La Leche League International, Inc. This group has national headquarters at 9616 Minneapolis Avenue, Franklin Park, Ill. 60131. There are local chapters in many areas. The La Leche League provides excellent literature for parents who desire information about breast feeding. They have published a helpful book, *The Womanly Art of Breast Feeding*. The La Leche League believes that with proper guidance virtually every mother can successfully nurse her baby.

PCI Point of View

If you are undecided about which feeding technique is right for you, why choose at all? Many mothers consider the combination of breast feeding and an occasional bottle to be the best approach. Regardless of the technique used, you should feel happy and secure when you are feeding your infant. It is much more important that a feeling of confidence and contentment be conveyed to the newly born human being by the one who is caring for him rather than where the milk is coming from.

HOW TO BOTTLE FEED

You are home from the hospital and about to begin bottle feeding your new baby. Excited? Of course! A bit apprehensive? Maybe. You thought you would be a "pro" at giving the bottle during your brief postpartum stay, but now you are not so confident. You would like to take a refresher course in Bottle Feeding 101.

Tender, loving care (plus a few practical pointers) is what it is all about. A U. S. Government booklet on infant care states it simply and well: "Getting enough to eat and feeling safe and warm are about all a new baby needs. Food and love are about equally necessary, and when both are freely available, he can thrive. It is fortunate that both can be given at once."

Having a bottle prepared and choosing a comfortable chair beforehand help make the experience relaxed and unrushed. You will find after a few feedings that your baby fits naturally in the cradle of your arm, his head held somewhat higher than the tummy. If your baby is not alert for the whole feeding and you find yourself getting restless, a book or magazine may keep you from becoming impatient or tense.

Feedings should be close, emotionally satisfying times for you and your baby. They should be times for getting to know one another; times for plenty of snuggling and cuddling, smiling and cooing.

It is mainly for the foregoing and not the much-exaggerated warnings about choking that bottle propping is discouraged in infancy. Dr. Virginia Pomeranz, in *The First Five Years,* says that "the possibility [of choking] exists, if the nipple is unusually fast flowing because it has too large a hole; otherwise there is not much likelihood of such a disaster. . . . But to be on the safe side, I advise against bottle-propping under the age of six months—for quite another reason . . . His earliest pleasurable experiences revolve around this dual sensation of being physically fed [and] held securely in someone's arms."

You will not want to deprive your baby of this vital intimacy, nor will you want to dismiss some bottle-feeding basics.

Techniques

Hold the bottle so that the neck of the bottle is always filled with milk. This keeps baby from sucking in air that could make her feel full before she has taken in enough milk. Some types of bottles have disposable liners designed to prevent air induction. You might want to investigate these and other types and decide for yourself. Air bubbles can cause your baby pain or colic if allowed to pass through her system. *Burp your baby at least once during the feeding and once afterward.* You can either (1) place baby on your shoulder and gently rub her back or (2) sit baby on your lap while supporting her head with one hand and rubbing her on the back with the other. Some babies burp the minute they are straightened up, while others need a lot of coaxing to bring up a bubble.

Hiccoughs

Hiccoughs are normal, being set off by bubbles returning. Do not be surprised if they appear regularly after meals during your baby's first few

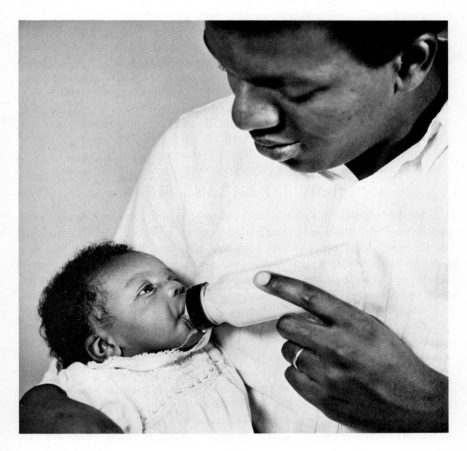

months. They often seem to clear up spontaneously, but can be stopped by offering the baby a drink of warm water.

Check the Size of the Nipple Hole

This probably is the most important bottle-feeding basic because the flow of milk should correspond to the sucking-swallowing rhythm of the baby. The size of the nipple hole will determine how fast or how slow the milk comes from the bottle. If it is *too small,* babies will get air for all their sucking efforts. They may get tired before they get enough milk and become uncomfortable or even throw up. They may also become colicky from all the air swallowed. If the hole is *too large,* the formula will come out too rapidly and could cause indigestion or choking in extreme cases. It will also cut down on adequate sucking time.

According to Dr. Spock, for most babies this is "when the bottle takes about 20 minutes of straight sucking time." A good way to test the rate of milk flow is to hold the bottle upside down without shaking it. Slow, steady drops (about one every second)—not a continuous stream—should come out. Nipple holes may be enlarged by puncturing with a hot needle. Stick the sharp point into the nipple and pull out quickly. Repeat if hole is still too small. The only solution for too-large nipple holes is to *replace the nipples.*

HOW TO BREAST FEED

First of all, relax! You have chosen to feed your newborn in the most natural way and both of you will enjoy a very intimate, special, and personal relationship. You can feel confident that your milk will be *just perfect* for your infant. You will have no worries about allergies, digestive upsets, or formula preparation and sterilization. You will have plenty of milk and plenty of time to relax and enjoy your baby knowing you are giving him the best possible start!

During pregnancy your breasts have probably become larger and your nipples darker in natural preparation for breast feeding. You need not worry about sterility. Sweat mixed with the oily secretions of the skin has an anti-bacterial action; the nipples, having the largest sweat glands of all, are partially sterile. Newly secreted human milk is said to have an anti-bacterial action. Therefore, the nipples are ready for sucking whenever the baby needs to be fed. While general cleanliness of the mother is understood, no special cleaning before or after nursing is really necessary. In fact, too much washing can cause your nipples to become dry and you may then need to use a special cream to keep them soft.

Some doctors recommend regular, gentle massage of the nipples during the last month of pregnancy to toughen them. For a large majority of women this is probably not necessary. Your nipples may be slightly tender during the first feeding or two just from the suction your baby applies to receive the milk. This discomfort seldom continues, particularly as you learn to relax and your milk flows readily.

During the eighth month of pregnancy or perhaps earlier in some mothers, and in the first four to five days after delivery, there is a considerable amount of secretion from the breast that is known as *colostrum*. This colostrum is a nutritional powerhouse for your baby and it is most advantageous for him to nurse frequently (on demand) at this time. Your baby's nursing will stimulate your milk to come in.

Procedure

Ideally while in the hospital you will have a flexible feeding schedule and encouraging, co-operative, and supportive nurses to help you get started and you can begin nursing your newborn whenever she is hungry. This is important in stimulating your milk production.

In order to feed your baby efficiently you need to have considerably more of your breast in her mouth than just the nipple. Your baby has an instinctive reaction to turn toward whatever is touching her cheek and open her mouth. She will become confused and annoyed if you try forcefully to move her head toward your breast. However, if you lightly stroke her cheek (with your finger or your nipple) she will turn her head, and with your thumb and forefinger you can direct as much of the dark area (areola) and nipple into baby's mouth as she can comfortably hold. Baby will receive your milk by compressing between her gums, tongue, and palate the middle and outer parts of the dark areola, under which the milk ducts and small milk sacs are located. She will not get her milk as easily with only the nipple in her mouth and this hold would tend to make your nipples become sore, too.

The normal flow of milk is regulated by the baby's demand; that is to say that the mother makes just enough milk for her baby's needs.

On rare occasions, a surplus is produced. When the baby starts to suck she may receive so much milk that she chokes. In order to avoid this, the mother should gently squeeze her breast, thereby reducing the flow to one manageable for baby.

89

Positions

Positions for nursing vary with each mother. The most important thing is to be comfortable so that you can completely relax. Some mothers prefer lying down, which has the practical advantage of providing a little rest as well. If you are about to feed baby from your right breast, prop up your head, right shoulder, and upper back with a couple of pillows. Then lay your baby on his left side on the crook of your right arm. As you stroke baby's left cheek, he will instinctively turn toward the breast that you will help him take. In this position be especially careful not to let the breast you are feeding him with block his nose passages. If you are unaware that this is happening, you will be obstructing his breathing and might condition him to the point where your baby will not want the breast. You can use your fingers to depress your breast next to baby's nose if this seems to be a problem, particularly if your breasts are especially full.

Some mothers prefer to sit when nursing their infants. A comfortable chair with supportive armrests and a footstool are helpful. You may find a rocking chair with comfortable armrests and back support particularly suitable.

Supplementary Bottle

Let us suppose that in the hospital your baby was receiving both breasts and was apparently not getting enough. Your doctor decided that baby needed formula in addition to the breasts. You are going along with this, but are concerned about losing even more milk by substituting a formula. This concern is justified because milk production is in direct response to demand. In this case you must deliberately cut down on the formula and count on your baby's increased hunger to give more stimulation to the breasts and as a result build the breast milk supply. Cutting down the formula will probably make your baby hungry earlier. This becomes an example of demand feeding. You nurse baby when he becomes hungry whether it is after four hours or even two hours. This will seem difficult at first. However, you are hoping that the frequent stimulation of your breasts will increase your milk supply and eventually increase your baby's satisfaction.

Your pediatrician may recommend that you give your baby a bottle once or twice a week even if your nursing is going along well. This is to ensure that your baby will take nourishment from a bottle in the event that it becomes necessary, and should not adversely affect your milk supply. Do not be surprised, however, if your baby balks at the bottle—formula is not nearly as tasty as mother's milk!

PCI Point of View

Above all, as a new nursing mother, relax! It is a very natural function, as natural as giving birth. You will have plenty of milk if you feed your baby when she is hungry. Eat nutritionally, drink plenty of liquids, especially milk or milk products. There is no need to gain weight while you are nursing even though you will require about 1,000 more calories a day than you did before. Just maximize nutritional intake and cut down on "empty calories." Rest as often as you can and enjoy the deep emotional satisfaction and pleasure you will receive from nursing your own "little miracle."

FORMULA

What Is Formula?

Formula is simply a mixture of cow's milk (or artificial milk), water, and sugar. One may think of formula as a recipe for modifying cow's milk to a better approximation of human breast milk. Cow's milk differs from human milk in having a higher concentration of salts and proteins. Since the higher concentration of these substances in undiluted cow's milk can have an undesirable effect on the infant, the milk is diluted with water to reduce the concentration. This dilution cuts the caloric content so that it becomes necessary to restore the proportion by adding sugar of some kind. The final result is a product much closer to human milk than to the original cow's milk.

The Formula

Although one may prepare formula using the specific milk and sugar in the proportions designated by pediatricians, many mothers today seem to prefer one of the commercially prepared formulas selected with their pediatricians' approval. These formulas are available in ready-to-feed form, liquid form requiring dilution, and dried form that must be constituted with water. All of these products usually contain all the vitamins in amounts required by the baby; some also include iron. Store-bought formulas are a little more expensive than the homemade formulas, but have the advantages of convenience, uniformity of composition, and controlled sterility and quality.

Preparation of Formula

Sterility is the key factor. The equipment needed to prepare sterile formula includes nursing bottles, nipples, bottle caps, measuring pitcher, measuring spoon, long-handled mixing spoon, punch-type can opener, funnel and tongs, bottle and nipple brush, jar for storing extra nipples, sterilizer, deep saucepan, or disposable nurser set.

Disposable bottle set: This is a very convenient method. Follow manufacturer's directions. There are several brands on the market.

Terminal heat method: This method is so called because there is no chance for the formula to be contaminated after it has been heated. With this method, the formula is mixed in clean utensils, poured into clean bottles, and then heated.

Preliminary sterilization method: The formula is boiled and then put into bottles that have been boiled.

Each method has advantages and disadvantages. Your choice of method may depend on your doctor's recommendations, convenience, or your prior experience.

Special Formulas

The formulas discussed above have a cow's milk base. Occasionally an infant shows sensitivity to cow's milk. Infants may also show sensitivity to one of the sugars by developing a rash, or eczema, frequent, loose stools, or upper respiratory symptoms. When physicians suspect an allergic reaction, they usually prescribe one of the special formula preparations. Soybean milk (Isomil, Prosobee, Neo-mull-soy) or meat-base milk (beef and lamb) may be recommended. Citrus or lactic acid formulas may also be prescribed.

Concentration of the Formula

This will be determined by the physicians, who take into account each infant's age, weight, and condition. They may want you to add more or less water.

Temperature of the Formula

One study done in 1962 with premature infants revealed that when comparisons of warmed and cold feedings were studied, there were negligible differences in sleep patterns, vocalization, and motility. There were no observable differences in the intake of food or fluid, weight gain, and regurgitation of food. Thus it would appear that the temperature of the formula does not make too much difference. You might want to take the chill off the formula in the wintertime, but do not over-heat the milk so that the infant perspires while taking it in the summertime.

How Much Milk per Feeding?

This will depend on the infant's size and age. The pediatrician will probably recommend one-half ounce per pound.

FEEDING SCHEDULES

Scheduled Versus Demand Feeding

Each child is a unique individual with his own internal time clock for hunger. Therefore, it is absurd to devise a schedule; i.e., an external time clock to suit all babies. Not only is each baby different from every other one, but even his own hunger is likely to vary from day to day.

However, it took many years before doctors dared to begin experimenting with flexible schedules. In the early 1940s, the first experiment was conducted on what was termed "self-demand feeding." Researchers wanted to find out what kind of schedule a baby would establish if she were breast fed whenever she seemed hungry. They discovered that in the first few days the baby awakened rather infrequently. Then in the second half of the first week, from just about the time the milk began to come in, the baby woke surprisingly often—about ten times a day; and by the age of two weeks she had settled down to six or seven feedings a day, although they were at rather irregular intervals. Finally, by ten weeks she had arrived at approximately a four-hour schedule.

Further investigation demonstrated that flexibility did not lead to diarrhea or indigestion, nor did it result in spoiling, as many had feared. On the contrary, many feeding problems were eliminated.

Demand Feeding

"Demand" or "self-regulating" feeding is the most sensible and flexible approach to an infant's rapidly changing requirements. It does not mean that you will *never* awaken your baby for a feeding after three or four hours of sleep; for example, if it is more convenient for you. Nor does it mean that you will *always* do it. However, it will permit you greater freedom in exercising your own judgment than did earlier, stricter approaches to infant care.

Even more important are the trust and self-confidence babies experience when their needs are met on their terms. Since babies seem to know instinctively when they have had enough, be careful not to push or force them to *finish* their bottles. This can only hurt healthy appetites. Depending on how long they have slept since their last feeding (and other factors), babies are the best judges of how much they need at a particular feeding.

Supplementing feedings with water, especially in hot weather, can calm a fussy, *thirsty* baby, too. Remember, babies are not always *hungry!*

The Schedule in the Hospital

Although many hospitals have incorporated the "rooming-in" plan and can accommodate the mother who prefers demand feeding, newborns are usually in a hospital nursery and fed by the clock. Full-sized babies are taken to the mother every four hours day and night—6 A.M., 10 A.M., 2 P.M., 6 P.M., 10 P.M., 2 A.M.—resulting in six feedings every twenty-four hours. Small babies (five pounds) may be put temporarily on a three-hour schedule by day and a four-hour schedule at night, resulting in seven feedings in twenty-four hours.

The Schedule at Home

Babies tend gradually to lengthen the interval between feedings as they grow bigger and older. Because of the way a young baby's digestive system works, the average baby of six to nine pounds will last about four hours with an ample feeding at the breast or bottle. It seems reasonable to suppose that with more frequent feedings the baby would eat less each time, his stomach would empty more quickly, and emptiness would stimulate fresh hunger sooner. Hence a vicious cycle develops. Therefore, if a young baby becomes hungry more often than every two hours and keeps it up over several successive feedings, it may be desirable to stretch the time between feedings.

Dr. Richard Feinbloom of the Boston Children's Medical Center suggests that the mother might try a pacifier, holding and rocking the baby, or giving a few sips of water (not more than an ounce) to take the edge off the hunger. He argues that if the feeding could be held off for forty-five minutes or an hour, the baby would eat more, his stomach would then take longer to empty, and the hunger pangs would be postponed.

Late Night Feeding

The 10 P.M., or evening, feeding is the one that parents can most easily time to their own convenience. By the time the baby is a few weeks old, he is perfectly willing to wait until 11 P.M. or even midnight for it.

The late night feeding (2 A.M.) is usually given up by the end of the first or second month. One night when the baby is between two and six weeks old, he will sleep through until 3 or 3:30 A.M. This is to be treated

95

as a 2 A.M. feeding. The next night he may sleep until 4:30 or 5 A.M., but this should be counted as the 6 A.M. feeding since the baby will generally not wake again until 10 A.M.

Parents should not let their babies sleep through the 10 P.M. or 11 P.M. feeding even though they may be willing. By waking the baby at this time, the day is at least ended on schedule and this helps to avoid a feeding between midnight and 4 A.M. and tends to start baby off somewhere between 5 and 6 A.M. each morning. When the baby is ready to give up one of the night feedings, the mother will want him to give up the 2 A.M. feeding first in order that her sleep will not be interrupted.

Warning Against Feeding Entirely on Demand

Dr. T. Berry Brazelton cautions against feeding a baby entirely on a demand basis. With a restless, fretful baby, it may lead to a great many feedings and, so, very little rest for the parents. Also, it may encourage the baby to continue with night feedings indefinitely.

According to Dr. Spock, if a bottle-fed baby is draining every one and regularly waking early, the pediatrician should be consulted about increasing the formula. However, if the baby wakes an hour or so after his last feeding and has finished his usual bottle at that feeding, chances are against his being hungry again so soon. Instead, it is more likely he has been awakened by indigestion or colic. Try burping your baby again or seeing whether he will be comforted by some water. Do not rush to feed your baby again.

Hunger is not always indicated when your baby tries to eat her hand or starts to take the bottle eagerly. A colicky baby will indulge in both of these activities. It seems that the baby cannot distinguish between colic pains and hunger pains. In other words, *do not always feed a baby when she cries. If she is crying at the wrong times, study the situation and perhaps consult her pediatrician.*

PCI Point of View

Flexible scheduling is desirable for both baby and parent. It encourages parents to watch and listen sensitively to their babies for clues regarding hunger and other stressful states. Arbitrary scheduling defies reason and ignores the rights of both parties. Flexible scheduling can only encourage relaxed personality formation and a happy experience for everyone concerned.

96

VITAMINS AND MINERALS

Vitamins are complex organic substances that occur naturally in foods and are essential in small amounts for the maintenance of good health. The vitamins required in the diet of the infant that may be lacking in his feedings are primarily A, D, and C. It is generally believed that both human milk and cow's milk contain sufficient B vitamins to prevent deficiencies.

Indications for Vitamin Supplementation

It is generally recommended that an infant's diet be supplemented with vitamins two to three weeks after birth. However, your doctor should be the one to indicate the choice of vitamins to be administered, whether it be a single or multi-vitamin preparation, and the dosage.

An infant who is breast fed receives a sufficient amount of vitamin C if the mother's diet is rich in citrus fruits or if she consumes fifty milligrams of vitamin C daily. It is essential that the breast-fed baby be supplied with a vitamin D supplement.

A bottle-fed infant who is taking vitamin D-fortified evaporated or homogenized milk would be receiving adequate amounts of vitamin D only if a quart of this milk were consumed daily. Many infants do not drink this much milk during the first few months of life. This diet must also be supplemented with vitamin C until the infant is receiving two ounces of fresh, frozen, or bottled orange juice. This is not likely to be given to the baby during the first several months because many doctors feel that there is a high incidence of allergy to orange juice.

A bottle-fed infant who is taking a commercial formula, such as Similac, Enfamil, etc., does not require a vitamin supplement. These formulas contain added vitamins.

Method of Giving Vitamins

Vitamin preparations for the infant are supplied in liquid form and are given with a medicine dropper that is marked with lines to indicate the proper dosage. Although it does not matter what time of the day they are given, it is a good idea to give them at the beginning of one particular feeding so that they are not forgotten. Most infants will readily suck on the dropper when it is placed in the mouth. The liquid should be gently released from the dropper against the cheek or tongue. In order to avoid the baby choking or gagging, do not squirt the vitamins directly into the back of the mouth.

Iron Supplements

Adequate amounts of iron must be present in the diet to ensure proper formation of the red blood cells in the body and to prevent anemia. Although most babies are born with adequate supplies of iron to last several months, this supply will be rapidly used up as the infant starts to grow if iron-rich foods are not added to the diet. Human milk and non-fortified formulas are a poor source of iron. However, foods containing iron, such as cereal, eggs, and meats, are usually added to the diet by the third or fourth month. If your doctor feels that your baby is not getting an adequate supply of iron or if anemia is indicated, iron drops may be recommended.

ADDING SOLID FOODS

Feeding a baby solid food is something to which every new parent looks forward. Why? Probably because this is a sign that baby is developing normally and beginning to make the transition from infant feeding behavior (breast or bottle) to that of the child or adult (solid food). Perhaps this explains why parents sometimes want to rush feeding solids; it is a visible sign that all is well.

When we speak of solids as related to infant feeding, we are actually referring to semiliquid, mushy foods, including commercially prepared baby foods and table foods puréed in a blender, mashed, or put through a strainer.

Fifty years ago babies received only milk for the first year of life. Today both doctors and nutritionists believe that the gradual introduction of solid foods, beginning sometime in the first six months of life, is essential for optimum growth and development. Specifically, solid foods can provide a good source of iron, introduce a baby to eating with a spoon, and give you the opportunity to accustom baby to a wide variety of tastes and textures. Dr. Mavis Gunther, in *Infant Feeding,* states that this is the main safeguard against dietary deficiencies in later life.

The specific age at which solids should first be given is controversial. Some parents feel that the early introduction of solids (as early as two weeks in some cases) assists the baby in sleeping through the night. However, this belief has been disproved by research. A study conducted by the Child Research Council of the University of Colorado School of Medicine reveals that there is no connection between feeding solids and sleeping through the night. In fact, if your baby is hungry, the formula or breast feeding will be as satisfying as solid food.

One reason for delaying the introduction of solid foods is to allow your baby's digestive system to mature sufficiently to handle foods other than milk. Studies have showed that babies are not able to digest complex foods, such as cereals containing starch, until two and a half months.

But most parents and doctors agree that by the time babies' teeth are in, they should begin to take solid foods. Start at three months depending upon the "readiness" of your infant to take foods from a spoon. Offer cereal at the 10 A.M. and 6 P.M. feedings with some rice cereal (a few spoonfuls) diluted with your own formula or ordinary milk. Sugar and the sweeteners should be avoided. If the baby continues to take the rice cereal, experiment with oatmeal and barley. Although the order does not have to be rigidly followed, it is common practice to begin fruits and vegetables at four and five months, meat at five months, and eggs at six months.

An important reason for introducing solids slowly and carefully at a relatively later age is to prevent or diminish allergic reactions. The older a baby is when he receives a new food, the less apt he is to develop an allergy.

Of course, feeding a baby is much easier when the mother understands what to do. To aid you in feeling comfortable about starting your baby on solids, PCI offers the following guidelines:

1. If you find it more convenient than your lap, place your baby in an infant seat on a table in front of you (always hold onto the infant seat when it is on a table or other high surface).

2. Use a baby-sized, long-handled feeding spoon rather than a teaspoon. This can be obtained quite inexpensively in most stores that sell baby supplies.

3. Keep a box of tissues near you. These are used to wipe food off baby, you, etc.

4. An infant hot plate with a suction base is convenient although not essential.

5. Start each feeding with breast or bottle to satisfy your baby's hunger. You will be able to give solids first after your baby has learned that these also satisfy hunger.

6. Generally the first solid food given is cereal. Choose a whole-grain cereal, such as rice, oatmeal, or barley. Do not give *wheat* cereal first as this has a tendency to cause allergic reactions. Use either home-cooked cereal that has been strained or one of the packaged baby cereals. Put a teaspoon of cereal in a dish and mix it up with formula or whole milk,

adding just enough milk so the cereal is a soupy mixture. Give your baby just a small taste at first. If she seems interested, even though all you put in seems to come out on her chin, give her another taste. Scrape the cereal off baby's chin and reinsert into mouth as necessary. Be patient—swallowing is a different process from sucking and can only be mastered as your baby matures.

7. You can feed your baby one teaspoon of dry cereal twice a day, increasing the amount in line with her appetite (unless your doctor advises otherwise). Feed cereal and other solids at times most convenient for you.

8. Do not add cereal to your baby's bottle. This avoids the whole issue of teaching baby to swallow.

9. Cereal is not a magic food. Other foods that can serve equally well as first foods include mashed bananas, applesauce, potatoes, or even liver.

10. If your baby seems uninterested in or opposed to the whole idea of solids, simply wait and try again in a week or two. Never try to force your baby to eat. He will eat only when he is hungry and ready for solid feedings. While giving solids, you can assume your baby has had enough when he turns his head away or shuts his mouth.

11. Stay calm and relaxed. Your baby will copy your attitude about eating.

PCI Point of View

Essentially, PCI feels that introducing your baby to solids should be a gradual process most often begun by offering your baby cereal and undertaken when you and your doctor feel it is appropriate. Your baby has a lifetime ahead to enjoy eating. You can anticipate it, but do not rush it.

MAKING YOUR OWN BABY FOOD

Today we are becoming more and more skeptical about the foods we buy. We are more aware of the nutritional lack in many processed foods and are looking for alternatives. While it is necessary that you feel secure about the quality of food you give your baby, do not let yourself become overly concerned. Infant cereals and baby foods are manufactured under controlled conditions to ensure safety and wholesomeness and to guarantee the nutritional values required in these products.

There are nevertheless a great many benefits to be derived from preparing your own baby foods, not the least of which is economic. In examining processed baby foods, parents should compare their cost in both money and convenience with other ways of feeding babies. With a minimum of effort parents can prepare a safe, high-quality food for their infant at an economical price. Using their imagination, parents can and will come up with ideas peculiar to their kitchen and will be able to save time, effort, and money. One of the satisfactions of homemade baby food is that you are creating something special for your baby according to his tastes—and your tastes as well.

Supplies

A good food blender is a necessity. There are blenders that also have mini blender jars for mixing small quantities and for easy storage. While blenders are expensive, they are long-lasting and are useful for many things in addition to the preparation of baby food.

There is a table model food grinder, the Happy Baby Food Grinder, that is very useful. The food can be ground immediately after cooking and served at once or the food can be ground raw. This hand-sized grinder is convenient for travel, too. You can use it for preparing your baby's food on the table at restaurants, while visiting, or even on a picnic table. It makes several tablespoons at a time and can be purchased in department stores and some supermarkets and health food stores. The Happy Baby Food Grinder is made by the Bowland-Jacobs Manufacturing Co., 8 Oakdale Road, Spring Valley, Ill. 61362.

Plastic ice cube trays, the kind you pop out one at a time, simplify storage. A collection of small jars and plastic containers are convenient to have on hand. If you are also using commercial baby food, save the jars.

In addition to or instead of cooking for just the baby, you can purée in the blender whatever you are having for lunch or dinner.

Fruits

Some babies love fruit; others find it hard to digest. Some pediatricians recommend stewing all fruits (other than bananas) for young babies, but most feel that if raw fruit agrees with your baby, it is excellent. Strawberries are usually not given to babies.

Vegetables

In preparing cooked vegetables for your baby, shorten the cooking time until they are just tender; then use blender or grinder. In some health food cookery, the vegetable stock takes the place of meat stock. You can use fresh, frozen, or canned vegetables, whatever the family is eating.

Potatoes, in addition to being a good source of starch, contain appreciable amounts of salts and some vitamin C, so they have real food value. For babies, they can be baked or boiled and then mashed with milk or put into a blender or grinder. Boiled rice can be a substitute for potatoes.

Cereal

There is some dispute about the nourishment value in commercial cereals for infants. Mostly they are fillers. In health food stores or a special section of your supermarket, you may find whole-grain nut cereals that are suitable for infants, to which you can add yogurt and fruit.

As your baby grows you can alter the consistency of the foods you prepare so they are coarser. Carrot and celery sticks and apple pieces are good substitutes for teething biscuits that are largely carbohydrates and sugar and become very messy. Soon you will be feeding your child regular table food.

Dr. Spock and Miriam E. Lowenberg, a nutritionist, have put together a collection of recipes for children in *Feeding Your Baby and Child. Making Your Own Baby Food,* by Mary Turner and James Turner, includes excellent recipes and suggestions for healthy feeding. For parents interested in organic and health food cookery, *The Natural Baby Food Cookbook* by Kenda and Williams will be of interest. From the number of baby food cookbooks on bookstore shelves, you will find that an increasing number of parents are making food at home for their babies.

Selecting Commercially Prepared Foods

Cereals: Use instant, dry baby cereals (iron-enriched): best buy, if used frequently, is the large box, not the one-ounce box.

Fruits: Use plain baby fruits without sugar added, if you can find them. The "fruit desserts" and puddings are high in calories, low in nutrition.

Vegetables: Use *plain* baby vegetables. Avoid those in cream or with added carbohydrates (creamed corn, etc.). Sugar is usually added for the mother's taste buds. Infants can take or leave sugar.

Meats: Buy *plain* baby meats. Mixed dinners provide only small amounts of meat, combined with vegetables, etc.

Read the labels of all baby foods to ascertain contents. The first ingredient listed is the major ingredient, etc.

FEEDING PROBLEMS

When a baby begins eating semisolid foods, such as cereal or puréed fruits, vegetables, or meats, what should be a pleasant and satisfying experience for baby and parent sometimes is not. Frustrating problems may arise that usually can be dealt with promptly. The important thing is to be aware of some of the feeding difficulties that may arise, recognize them, deal with them, and then proceed to make mealtime relaxing and enjoyable for all.

Hiccoughing

One of the first feeding problems to occur is hiccoughing—to be expected and eased by offering the baby some water.

Gagging

When you first introduce a solid food to your baby's diet, you may find that as you spoon it into her mouth, most of it drools back out and lands on her chin. She may even gag from time to time. Dr. Spock says that babies sometimes object to the pasty consistency of some solid food by gagging. This can be overcome by diluting the food with a little milk or water and spooning it more slowly into the baby's mouth.

Spitting

Babies may also resist the introduction of solid foods by spitting. Try to determine if they are attempting to develop the skill of managing solid food or if they simply do not like the taste of a particular food. When in doubt, wait a week before offering them the food again and concentrate on the foods they seem to enjoy.

Sneezing

There undoubtedly will come a time when babies come out with a hearty sneeze accompanied by a mouthful of food. This is a messy business. It is even messier when they proceed to put their hands into their mouths, in their hair, and on you. It makes sense to bib babies and even more sense to apron yourself generously.

Lack of Appetite During Illness

In the case of a fever, a baby often will suffer a temporary loss of appetite. Pediatricians suggest that infants not be offered any new liquid during an illness unless prescribed by a physician. Formula and juice may be diluted. Do not forget plain water.

They also suggest that when a baby develops diarrhea, eliminate solid foods and fruit juices until you have checked with your doctor. If the baby spurns the formula, dilute it by adding one-third water.

When children vomit due to illness, rest their stomachs for at least an hour before introducing gradually bits of chipped ice or small amounts of water.

After children recover from an illness, do not force them to eat, because they might still be slightly nauseated and, therefore, disgusted by food. This could promote a long-lasting feeding problem. Instead, offer the children small amounts of food without any urging until their appetites return to normal.

Failure to Thrive

A steady weight gain is the most obvious evidence that a baby is thriving. If your baby does not eat well or gain weight, consult your physician.

Of course, a decrease in appetite may be due to teething or simply a slowing down in weight gaining. This normally occurs at about five or six months.

Eating Slowly

No matter how conscientiously you try to provide a pleasant mealtime experience, there are times when your baby eats so slowly that it becomes very exasperating. Try feeding your baby in a quiet room away from the distractions of everyday family life.

Rudolf Dreikurs, in *Coping with Children's Misbehavior,* claims that "no child will become a feeding problem if his parents do not try to make him eat." Being urged to eat, whether mildly or forcefully, can disturb a baby's willingness or even ability to accept food. It also paves the way to resistance in general, a behavior problem to be avoided if at all possible.

Pediatricians warn parents against establishing a tense atmosphere at eating time by forcing a child to eat more than he really wants or needs. In order to gain parental approval, a child may be establishing eating habits that could change the cute chubbiness of infancy to ugly obesity later on.

PCI Point of View

Worrying about what your child eats or does not eat will only make you and your child nervous. It will also adversely affect your child's appetite and digestion.

Problems such as hiccoughing and gagging are relatively minor and easily solved. However, the aftermath of a severe illness and its effect on your baby's appetite and well-being require a doctor's advice.

ARE WE OVERFEEDING OUR CHILDREN?

Chubby babies have long been adored. Chubby babies are cute. Chubby babies, however, sometimes turn into fat, unattractive adults. Recent studies show that a young child's physiological make-up can actually be changed if he is fed excessively. The importance of cutting down the weight of fat children to avoid their becoming fat adults is now being stressed.

Dr. Jerome Knittle, of the Mount Sinai School of Medicine, working with Dr. Fredda Ginsberg-Fellner, studied two hundred obese children between the ages of two and eighteen. The doctors examined a small sample of fat (removed with a special syringe) and found that the number of fat cells in the obese children's tissue was very much higher than that of children of normal weight. In some cases, children as young as five or six years had a higher number of fat cells than average-weight adults. Additionally, there was reason to believe that if their diet were not restricted, these children's fat cells would continue to increase in size and number until some time after puberty.

Speaking at the annual meeting of the American Academy of Pediatrics in the Palmer House in Chicago recently, Dr. Ginsberg-Fellner cited her study of twenty children, ages two to ten, whose weight was almost double for age and height. All had been obese before age one. All were put on a severe reducing diet; then on a 1,200-calorie diet for up to four and a half years. One obese two-and-a-half-year-old boy, who had 15 billion fat cells in his body, was reduced to normal weight by diet and has maintained it for more than a year. On the other hand, an obese seven-year-old girl, who had 43 billion fat cells (about one and a half times as many as the average adult) rapidly regained the weight she lost by diet and now weighs more than she did before dieting. It is likely she will continue to retain this excess number of fat cells throughout life.

105

Fortunately, Dr. Ginsberg-Fellner believes that children who are reduced before they have produced a large number of fat cells have a fairly good chance to maintain their ideal weight.

The implication of these studies can be most valuable to those of you whose child is developing his first eating patterns. For example, Dr. Brazelton criticizes parents who offer teething biscuits or cookies to their babies in a conscious effort to keep them quiet. This is the worst thing to do for it establishes an association between eating and relief of discomfort.

You should *not* try to get your baby to take "just one more mouthful" so that she will finish up the jar of baby food. Instead of feeding your baby more and more, you might encourage other forms of activity, such as singing to her. Expecting children to "clean your plates" can establish attitudes that stay with them for the rest of their lives. Telling children that they cannot have dessert until vegetables are finished implies that they prefer the sweets. Perhaps it is really the parent who prefers the sweets?

There has been a rethinking of the old idea that "a fat baby is a healthy one." With understanding that overweight begins in infancy, we can begin to establish better eating habits for our children and produce healthier children as a result.

OVERWEIGHT VERSUS UNDERWEIGHT

It is safe to say that some children are genetically predisposed to being thin. They are neither physically ill nor emotionally disturbed. Even though they have always been offered plenty to eat, they just never seem to want to eat a great deal and they especially avoid the rich foods. To ensure that a thin child is healthy, however, he should have frequent medical checkups.

According to Dr. Spock, "If your child doesn't seem to be any kind of problem, has been slender since infancy, but gains a reasonable amount of weight every year, relax and let him alone. He is probably meant to be that way." This seems to be a very sensible approach, particularly in view of the new theories regarding obesity.

Food has different meaning for different people. For some mothers, feeding is a form of love, a form of protection, or trying to fulfill an unhappiness within herself. Some mothers feel an infant should be fed each time she cries and this attitude can result in overfeeding. Other mothers continue waking their baby for feeding well beyond the time the night feeding usually is eliminated. Others still feed according to a rigid time schedule whether or not baby wants or needs food. All these things can contribute to the overfeeding problem.

Some researchers believe that babies may become "hooked" or addicted to foods that they are eating daily. Infants and young children are fed many of the same foodstuffs several times each day. As time goes by, they become accustomed to getting these foods regularly and perhaps they get "hooked." Consequently, when they do not get the foods they are addicted to, they become nervous and irritable and to relieve these unpleasant feelings, resort to eating. An addiction of this kind seems to sneak up on an individual (whether adult or child) without full awareness. Unfortunately, once she is "hooked," regardless of how strong her will power, the body will crave the substance she is addicted to. Whether this theory is accurate still remains to be proved. Nonetheless, it is interesting and offers some additional insight into the problem of obesity.

It is surprising that sometimes, under normal circumstances, thin babies consume more calories than fat ones. The customary explanation is that thin babies are very active and "burn up" the calories more readily while the chubby babies tend to be lethargic, thereby converting more of their caloric intake into fat.

It appears that bigger children have this special problem. Even as early as four to six months of age, their excess weight may begin to immobilize them. They stop exercising their muscles sufficiently and this inactivity results in more fat being laid down. Furthermore, as they become frustrated by their inability to move, they eat more or must be fed more to keep them quiet. Consequently an excess of fat cells is produced and these become a permanent part of the body.

The idea of preventing adult heart disease by controlling diet and weight in infancy is so new that nutritional guidelines are still hazy. A paper examining this idea is being readied by the Committee on Nutrition of the American Academy of Pediatrics.

Thus parental guidance is the key factor in controlling overfeeding and its resultant childhood obesity. By offering nutritious meals, discouraging the use of sweets, keeping calories down, establishing good eating habits ourselves, and realizing that the fat baby is not always the most healthy, we can be on the way to raising healthier children.

Too Much Sugar Is No Good

In our country today, sugar represents 20–25 per cent of the calories and 50 per cent of the carbohydrates in our diet that are hidden in such products as baby foods, frozen vegetables, and yogurt, in addition to sweet baked desserts and sodas. There has been a growing controversy surrounding the long-range effects of sugar in our diets: how it affects the development of a "sweet tooth" in youngsters, tooth decay, and certain diseases. Most professionals, including Dr. Myron Winick, advise parents to provide a *balanced* diet for their children.

Dr. Jean Mayer, professor of nutrition at Harvard from 1950 to 1976, and presently president of Tufts University, has finally taken a definite position on the use of sugar in the diet. In reviewing the evidence in an article that appeared in the New York *Times Magazine* on June 20, 1976, Dr. Mayer concludes that the habitual consumption of large amounts of sugar *is* a menace to health. *Sugar and dental caries:* 98 per cent of American children have some tooth decay and by age fifty-five about half of our population has *no* teeth. A recent governmental study suggests that sugar consumption is positively related to tooth decay. *Sugar and overweight:* Current statistics indicate that 10–20 per cent of all U.S. children and 35–50 per cent of middle-aged Americans are overweight. Too much sugar in the diet in the form of "empty" calories (no nutrients) is a major factor. *Sugar and other diseases:* Overweight in general and too much sugar specifically have been found to be related to hypertension and the onset of diabetes in adults. Dr. Mayer urges parents to decrease sugar consumption. Do not buy "junk" foods! Use other sources of carbohydrates; dry beans, unbleached flour, whole-grain cereals, and milk. Brush or rinse your teeth after eating, especially after consuming products packed with sugar.

PCI Point of View

We believe that parents are entitled to the latest and all data relevant to child rearing, especially when there are discrepancies in outlook. It seems safe to conclude on the basis of the most current evidence that sugar should be used sparingly.

WEANING

Readiness

Weaning usually means the process of transferring your baby from breast milk to cow's milk, but it can also mean going from milk in a bottle to milk in a cup.

There are no age limits as to when a baby must be weaned, so you should be relaxed about it. *When* is not nearly as important as *how*. Weaning always should be done gradually. If a family crisis is anticipated, delay the weaning.

There are three major time lags in an infant's interest in breast feeding. The first one is associated with the sudden widening, visual interest in his surroundings. The second accompanies the tremendous motor spurt of seven months. The third occurs between nine and twelve months. It is appropriate in our culture to wean the baby when he begins to lose interest in breast feeding. By the time a baby is six months old, breast feeding will have served its psychological and nutritional functions. It is the age when babies start to get their teeth, which for many women is a good reason for weaning. Every mother must decide for herself and her baby when and how to wean.

Weaning from the Breast

It is possible to wean your baby in a week, if you want to, but there are several good reasons why it is best to wean gradually. This gives everyone time to adjust to the new and different situation; it is more comfortable for you; if done suddenly, weaning very often can be traumatic for the mother. If it is done too quickly a version of postpartum depression may occur due to hormonal changes.

Often a baby's diminished interest in nursing is a clue to the mother to begin the procedure. As baby forgets about an occasional feeding, mother similarly "forgets" about it. Sometimes mother is too busy to feed; other times baby is not interested. Gradually nursing diminishes until there is only one regular feeding a day and eventually none. By this time the mother's milk supply also has diminished, naturally.

During the time that a baby is being weaned it is to his advantage to be cuddled and comforted and given more attention than usual. Some babies seem ready to give up suckling as early as six months. (Even bottle-fed babies sometimes get bored with their bottles at this time). A few have had it with nursing by ten months and more by a year. The suckling urge varies considerably in babies. Those who enjoy it very much are not too interested in semisolid food and they may lengthen the weaning process. Those who enjoy their semisolid food very much are less interested in the breast or bottle.

Begin the weaning process by omitting the daily breast feeding your baby is least interested in and substituting for it either the bottle or the cup, according to age. Then after a week or ten days, substitute another nursing with bottle or cup and so on until the changeover is complete. If the weather is hot or your baby comes down with a cold, you may want to postpone things for a little while. Even teething may make him unwilling. Baby's own inclination is your guide, so do not force him if he does not want to be rushed.

Theoretically, if you wean from the breast to the cup, you can save an extra step by going immediately to it, but in practice this is something else. Most mothers introduce a bottle occasionally to get the baby used to something other than the breast, just in case they cannot be present for a particular feeding. This occasional bottle can be orange juice or water and helps in weaning later on because it is not something "new."

Avoiding a Bedtime Bottle

Sara Gilbert says, "Bedtime bottles have long been a bugaboo and it is probably best for the long term if you do not start your baby on the habit of taking a bottle to bed. It may, in time, prove a mixed blessing." A strong security factor enters here and some children will not give up the bottle until the age of two or three. Many babies enjoy falling asleep with a bottle because it is a source of comfort to them. There is no real harm in this, only inconvenience for parents. If you and your baby do develop the bedtime bottle habit, offer him non-sweet fluids to minimize possible ill effects.

Weaning from Breast or Bottle to Cup

Somewhere around four, five, or six months, begin showing your baby how to use a cup. What you are doing is showing him that there is more than one way of taking liquids. If your baby is on the bottle or breast and has his sucking urge gratified, and you teach him to drink from a cup also, weaning will be easier.

Babies find it hard to manage milk in amounts larger than what they get by sucking on a nipple. To help with this there are special kinds of cups designed for weaning babies. Some have a lid with a flat spout that keeps the milk from spilling; others have a weighted base and two handles that make it easier for a baby to hold. Either kind helps the baby to gain skill in drinking. As you gradually increase the amount in the cup, you can put less and less in the bottle, especially if you give your baby a cup at every meal. This is about the time baby derives most of his calories and nutritional needs from solid food. The need for a large amount of milk is not as necessary as it was when he was younger.

APPETITE AND DIET

By six months a baby's diet can be as varied and interesting as that of the rest of the family provided the texture of her food is easy for her to handle. Few babies have teeth at this stage and chewing is still beyond them, but they can learn to like a wide range of foods.

The late Adelle Davis, controversial nutritionist and author of several books on this subject, conducted an experiment some years ago to determine what children would eat if left to their own desires and given a variety of wholesome foods to choose from. She did not start with older children for fear they would have already developed prejudices about food. She observed eighteen orphans, all six months old, who had never had anything to eat but milk. At each meal a nurse would place before them six or eight serving dishes containing a variety of wholesome, unrefined foods that included vegetables, fruits, eggs, cereals, meats, whole-grain bread, milk, water, and fruit juices. The nurse was instructed to wait until the babies indicated what they wanted before giving any assistance whatsoever.

She found that over a period of time every baby chose a well-balanced diet. All the leading authorities seem to agree with Adelle Davis that if given a free choice, children will eat what they require and round out their own diets over a short period of time, as long as there is no environmental pressure to confound the child's free choice.

Loss of Appetite

Dr. Spock warns that an infant may take solids eagerly for the first few months, but between three and nine months he may rather suddenly lose his appetite. "One reason may be that at this age period he is meant to slow down in his weight gaining. In his first 3 months he has probably gained close to 2 pounds a month. By 6 months he is apt to be down to a pound a month. Otherwise he would become too fat. Also he may be bothered by teething."

Pediatricians encourage parents to avoid pressuring children to eat. They suggest instead that sugar gradually be removed from the baby's formula. In the early months, while the infant was on a diluted formula, sugar was necessary to provide enough calories. When the infant begins eating a good helping of solid food three times a day, he no longer needs these calories.

You might also change from a four-hour feeding schedule during the

111

daytime (6 A.M., 10 A.M., 2 P.M., 6 P.M.) to a three-meals-a-day schedule (7 A.M., 12 noon, 5 P.M.), regardless of whether the infant is still on an evening feeding. If neither of these suggestions revives the child's appetite, the pediatrician should be consulted.

Calories

Dr. Feinbloom (in the *Child Health Encyclopedia*) has this to say about calories: by twelve months, the average child should be consuming 1,000 calories a day. For each year thereafter add about 100 calories more. In adolescence, provision must be made for rapid growth; girls should be getting 2,400 to 2,700; boys, 3,100 to 3,600.

PCI Point of View

The main points of research on the diet of infants indicate that it is important to offer the baby almost everything the family eats in tiny quantities and to keep the emotions surrounding food at a low level. Six months is an ideal time to introduce a baby to high-protein foods—fish, cottage cheese, soybean foods. Once baby develops a taste for these she will eat them throughout her life. A baby tends to choose an adequate diet if she has the chance, and will eat when hungry.

To keep widening children's choice of food, it is a good idea to offer them less-liked foods at their hungriest so that they will give these foods a chance. Since all the solids you will offer them are nutritious foods and as pure as possible, their tastes can hardly go wrong.

SELF-FEEDING

By the sixth month you and your baby have probably settled into a pleasant mealtime routine. Your baby eats eagerly, opening his mouth for more almost as soon as he swallows the previous mouthful. He finishes everything you offer, you wipe off his mouth, pick him up, hug him, and that's it until the next time. This is great and it is tempting to leave mealtime just the way it is.

At about this age, however, your baby may begin to develop very different ideas as she progresses on the road toward eventual independence. She becomes interested in grabbing at the spoon and putting everything she can get into her mouth—food or not. Dr. Brazelton tells of the baby who flings his head, shuts his mouth, and grabs for his dish and spoon, and Sara Gilbert describes the baby who may simply refuse to be spoon fed. These are signals for you to begin to provide opportunities for your baby to experiment with some finger foods.

How the parent handles the beginning attempts at self-feeding is very important. When your baby begins grabbing at the spoon, give him one to experiment with as you continue to feed him your own way. In fact, the more babies are permitted to help at mealtime, the faster they will learn to eat on their own. Giving them finger foods they can handle and refraining from making derogatory comments about their messiness will contribute to the ease with which they make the transition to complete self-feeding.

Spoon feeding, which starts at about a year, needs plenty of opportunity for practice. At about six months, babies are able to hold their own zwieback, and how they progress from this stage depends largely upon the parents' attitude. Babies make an unbelievable mess with a zwieback and the mess increases as they move through the finger-food stage and attempt to develop skill with a spoon. You just have to put up with the mess and not cringe as they remove food from their mouths and reinsert it. Admire their progress, put a plastic drop cloth under the high chair, and relax, bearing in mind that mealtimes are ideally meant to be pleasant for babies, as well as parents.

Some Suggested Finger Foods

It takes some ingenuity to select foods that your baby is capable of eating and that are nutritionally valuable. There are lots of foods from the family menu that your baby can probably handle quite well and enjoy experimenting with. Here is a list of some suggestions to be offered in very small quantities:

dry cereals	potatoes
almost any fruit	rice
crumbled hamburger	spaghetti and noodles
egg	peas with skins split
cheese	cooked carrot pieces
crackers	bits of soft toast
peanut butter and	graham crackers
jelly sandwich	

Age Levels in Self-feeding

The following guide for self-feeding, which was developed by Dr. Feinbloom, is not a rigid timetable. It is designed to reassure mothers.

113

Feeding is a learned experience that begins with sucking on the first day. Some babies express readiness earlier than others. Among the many things an infant has to learn is not to suck solids, to chew, and to swallow—skills that most parents seem to take for granted. To teach your baby good food habits, be consistent, flexible, and emotionally detached.

Self-Feeding: Average Age Levels

6–9 months   Holds, sucks, and bites finger foods.

9 months–   Holds own bottle (or may have given up bottle by now); en-
1 year   joys finger foods; eats most table foods; drinks from cup with
help; will hold and lick spoon after it is dipped into food.

15 months   Begins to use spoon, turns it before it reaches mouth; may
no longer need bottle; may hold cup; likely to tilt cup rather
than head, spilling contents.

114

1½ years	Eats with spoon, often spilling; turns spoon in mouth; requires assistance; holds glass with both hands; size of glass is important.
2 years	Puts spoon in mouth correctly, occasionally spilling; holds glass with one hand; distinguishes between food and inedible materials; plays with food.
2–3 years	Feeds self entirely, with occasional spilling; uses fork; pours from pitcher; can obtain drink of water from faucet by self.

Of course, if your baby consistently gags, chokes, or vomits any of these finger foods, discontinue the culprit for a few weeks.

Pediatricians understand the worry shared by many parents that a baby simply will not be getting a balanced diet on finger foods. They hasten to reassure parents that a baby's nutritional needs can easily be met by several cups of milk (or the equivalent in cheese and pudding), some whole-grain cereal or toast with butter, a little meat or fish, a few bits of vegetable, and some fruit and juice. If, however, a parent is seriously concerned about a baby's nutrition, a vitamin preparation can be prescribed by the pediatrician.

PCI Point of View

PCI wishes to emphasize again the need for a relaxed, happy atmosphere at mealtime. "Be calm and patient" is a basic rule for all mealtime situations regarding the undereater, the overeater, and the messy eater. Parental concern is always transmitted to a baby. Getting the food into baby in any way possible is merely asking for difficulty and resistance later on.

We know that a particular style of feeding babies is related to later behavior. Parents who space feedings to their babies' wishes, respond promptly to their signals of hunger and satisfaction, and allow them to participate in the feeding enjoy smooth, mutually satisfying relations with their children.

COMMON PITFALLS OF FEEDING

At one year, most babies are eating eagerly a full and varied diet. What commonly is construed as a "feeding problem" sometimes arises at this time due to parental expectations. Children's appetites diminish during the second year. Consequently, height-and-weight-gain curves slow considerably after the first year. The parent prepared for this normal lowered in-

take of food will avoid potential feeding problems that develop out of parental over-urging and anxiety.

"Me Do" and the Dawdles

It generally is a good idea to let the child take over her own feeding at this time. It will certainly be messy for a while, but with practice and encouragement most babies manage very creditably. (They also are proud of their achievement.) As toddlers increase their independence in all spheres they naturally also desire autonomy in eating.

It is important to keep the mealtime atmosphere cheerful and relaxed because a toddler is quick to balk at coaxing or scolding. Force-feeding can quickly turn mealtime into an anxious battleground instead of an eagerly awaited period of enjoyment. Many toddlers will dawdle and play with their food if they sense that this disturbs their parents. A reasonable length of time should be given for a meal. (Some children always eat quickly and then want to get down, while others seem to savor each morsel slowly.) Then the child can be taken from the high chair. If she seriously wants to continue the meal, she will let you know! Give her one more chance, then clear the tray and assume agreeably that she has had enough to eat. No child has ever starved herself under these circumstances.

A Balanced Diet

Unlike the infant of a few months before who voraciously ate anything on a spoon, the year-old often develops sudden likes and dislikes that seem to appear capriciously to torment the parents. They lovingly prepare the child's favorite meal only to have it pushed aside with a disdainful and determined "no want." This is indeed irritating, but nothing positive will be gained by making an issue of these occasions.

The parents should by no means become slaves to the young tyrant. However, it is understandable that a small child, like an adult, will vary in appetite and interest from day to day. These denials and demands demonstrate that the baby has learned and remembered differences among foods. She has expectations and is able to anticipate and express preferences. All are impressive developments.

Many parents are worried that the toddler who consistently rejects vegetables or who refuses to drink his milk is not receiving an adequately balanced diet. If the child is getting milk in some form, eating fruit, meat, or eggs, and taking vitamins, there is no cause for concern. *It is not necessary for children to eat foods from each of the groupings every day.* They may devour peas for three days straight and then want to concentrate on meats. This will not harm them in any way. Just continue to offer a variety of foods and let their natural appetite lead the way. Coaxing will only make them ornery.

Parents need to design family diets and menus that favor high-protein foods (soybeans, cottage cheese, lean meats, and fish) and play down sweets and fat-producing carbohydrates. An infant's taste for foods is shaped early by the mother's attitude. Parents have to learn to prepare balanced foods that are attractive and palatable to the entire family. Since feeding habits are formed by two years and are carried over to adolescence and adulthood, parents have a very short period in which to accomplish this vital dietary habit.

"I Hate Vegetables"

Children do not need vegetables if they are eating fruit. If they seem to care for only a few vegetables, let them eat those and then slowly introduce others. Some children who refuse small pieces of vegetables will eat them mashed with potatoes. You also can try giving children just a small plate of mixed vegetables at the beginning of the meal. They will pick out what appeals while they are hungriest.

117

If nothing works and they refuse all vegetables in any form, do not despair. Let them give vegetables up for a while, offer them an extra portion of fruit, and then very slowly bring back the vegetables. It should be noted that many adults do not care for most vegetables (perhaps they were pushed too often). Try not to express food preferences in front of your toddler.

Milk—Too Much or Too Little

If your baby is drinking from a bottle and loving it, she may be drinking so much that her already diminished appetite is dulled. A baby who is drinking more than twenty ounces of milk a day might be put on low-fat or skim milk. Most doctors recommend limiting milk consumption at about six months to about twenty-four ounces daily. Check with your doctor.

When an infant switches from bottle to cup, milk consumption usually drops sharply. This can be alarming, especially if baby persistently refuses to drink more than a sip or two over an extended period of time. However, she will receive most of the benefits in milk in an otherwise well-balanced diet. Calcium, the only mineral that will be missing, should be provided in some other form. Try some of these substitutes and "tricks," remembering that if there are a few ounces of milk in each, the calcium adds up over the day: soups prepared with milk, potatoes mashed with milk, scrambled eggs with milk and cheese, grilled cheese, cubes of cheese, cottage cheese, yogurt, and simple puddings. The milk in cereal counts, too. If your child still is not getting between four and eight ounces daily in some form, check with your doctor, who may recommend a calcium supplement.

How Much Milk?

Assuming your child is eating a mixed diet of meat, puddings, cereals, etc., she will require far less milk than you might think.

Age/Years	Amount of Milk Per Day
1–2	16 oz. or 1 pt.
2–3	18 oz.
3–4	18 oz.
4–6	18 oz.
6–8	20 oz.
8–10	24 oz.

Snacking

Common sense is probably the best approach in this area. If the child is eating well at mealtimes, he certainly should be given a nutritious snack if he wants it. It generally is wise to establish a time (midmorning or after nap) and a place for the snack to avoid continuous wails for snacks and to minimize food being eaten all over the house.

Although snacks usually are given more than an hour before a meal, some children seem to need a quick pick-up just before they eat or they become cranky and irritable. A small glass of juice often helps such a child to relax and eat better.

Now, what of the child who is not eating well at meals and yet constantly requests food between meals? Most pediatricians agree that this usually is the case of a child who is made anxious during meals by over-urging and pushing. The tension makes it impossible for the child to eat. The answer is not to withhold food between meals, but to make mealtime an enjoyable experience.

4

The Healthy Baby

INTRODUCTION BY FRANK FALKNER, M.D.*

In the last decade, two things have occurred in the Western hemisphere that have led to better health of our children: first, parents are better informed and are better educated concerning child health in general; second, there has been a greater emphasis on prevention of disease and the maintenance of good health. We need to keep our babies and children well and although this is an admirable aim, it is so much better if we keep them, in addition, safe.

It is important for parents to have straightforward and clear information on the growth and development of their children. Without this, it is difficult to be alert to lack of progress, to things starting to go wrong, and to know when a seemingly abnormal happening needs in fact be of no concern. This chapter deals with such basic knowledge.

How to keep our well babies and children safe? There simply has to be a balance kept in families between gross overprotection and gross negligence—and it's difficult. Children need to be active, and they will break bones, and they will fall off things and out of trees, and require mending. And we should not be constantly telling them to be

* As a doctor, researcher, teacher, writer, and administrator, Frank Falkner has devoted over thirty years to improving the health of infants and young children.

He is presently Fels Professor of Pediatrics and Professor of Obstetrics and Gynecology at the University of Cincinnati College of Medicine. Dr. Falkner is also director of the Fels Research Institute, one of the first research centers in the United States to study human development. As consultant to both the National Institute of Health Office of International Research relating to Nutrition and the Department of Health, Education, and Welfare Maternal and Child Health Services, International Division, and as chairman of the International Union of Nutritional Sciences, Dr. Falkner pioneers international studies relating to infancy, nutrition, and genetics. In addition to teaching and directing research, he has authored over eighty-five publications.

careful and restraining them from vigorous activities. But if we understand and know some of the proven hazards and are alert to behind-the-scenes protection of our children, then this alone will reduce the overall accident rate and tragedies in the child population and in our own children, too.

WELL-BABY CHECKUPS

The best way to make sure your new baby is thriving is to have him regularly checked by a doctor. Leading baby specialists today are in agreement as to the recommended timetable: as noted earlier, for the first six months, monthly visits; for the second six months, monthly or bimonthly visits; for the second year, visits at three-month intervals.

The most important friend a baby and his parents have is his doctor. Regular visits to his office are enlightening for everyone concerned. For the parents, they offer a routine source of security, an opportunity to find out what new foods may be added to the baby's diet and what new abilities he is working on. Each month parents learn their baby's weight gain, making it unnecessary to buy or rent baby scales. Monthly visits also enable parents to relieve themselves of any worries that have been building up throughout the month, somehow "too insignificant" to "bother" the doctor with on the phone. It is a good idea to keep a notebook handy at home for writing down questions when they come to mind and also for noting new developments, such as teething, the appearance of a rash, etc.

Parents can keep their own record of baby's growth and development, including such items as height and weight, inoculation schedule, etc. Such record books can be bought commercially. If your family moves, if you change doctors, or if only for your own reference, keeping a family record is a good habit to get into, especially on the question of inoculations given or needed. The doctor, via this procedure, is building up a medical picture of your baby also.

The doctor's guidance and opinions, however, may be elicited on many aspects of child rearing that transcend medical ones.

Example: Parents of a firstborn might be overly anxious about normal behavioral manifestations. Baby's doctor can easily pick this up and reassure them.

The baby, "star" member in the case, reaps many benefits from this

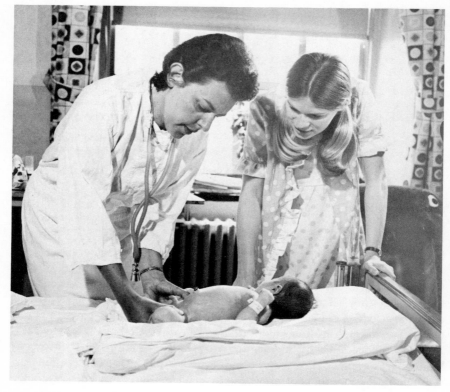

Dr. Virginia Pomeranz examining a baby.

ongoing relationship, depending in part upon how he is prepared for it. Children are not born afraid of doctors; in fact, at first they may be fascinated by them. When they are quite young, a trip to the doctor's office means many new and interesting things to see, hear, and touch.

Nevertheless, a child learns very quickly to be apprehensive about his doctor. The doctor starts to do unpleasant things to him. Strange instruments are stuck into his ears, eyes, nose, and mouth. Once this aspect of the visit is appreciated from the baby's point of view, everyone concerned can help mitigate unnecessary stress.

Parents should accept the feelings of discomfort or even the cries of distress that their baby expresses while at the same time communicating that this is a necessary part of life. Parents need not concern themselves that the doctor thinks their baby is rowdy. He is well aware of such reactions and encounters them daily.

A baby up to about a year and a half simply cannot be prepared for a visit to the doctor. Unable to understand the doctor's function, he reacts to what is done to him. If it is pleasant, he likes it; if it is unpleasant, he dislikes it. Dr. Lee Salk advises parents to hold and cuddle their baby whenever possible when he is unhappy, talk to him, and sympathize with him. Distract him whenever possible. Doctors utilize the same techniques.

IMMUNIZATION SCHEDULE

A common immunization routine is followed by all pediatricians. Dr. Frank Falkner recommends one he considers an optimal guideline from birth to two years. It may need to be adapted or altered to suit individual needs.

Age	Name of Inoculation	Name of Disease To Be Resisted
2 months	DPT	Diphtheria, Tetanus, Pertussis (Whooping Cough)
	Oral Polio Vaccine	Poliomyelitis
3 months	DPT	
4 months	DPT Oral Polio Vaccine	
6 months	Oral Polio Vaccine	
12 months	Live Measles Vaccine Rubella Vaccine* Mumps Vaccine* Tuberculin Test	"Red" Measles German Measles Mumps
18 months	DPT Booster Oral Polio Vaccine	
5 years	DPT Booster Oral Polio Vaccine	

* If given at this time, may be combined with red measles as a combined vaccine.

Dr. Falkner suggests that parents understand this program and help with it. Record the date and type of inoculation or test the baby received. Also note the place and name of the doctor who administered the inoculations, an extremely important suggestion in the light of the high mobility rate in the U.S.A.

The principles underlying immunization are simple. All babies are born with some natural immunities; they manufacture protective substances called *antigens* against certain diseases. In addition, all babies receive from their mothers specific *antibodies* against certain diseases. This natural immunity is encouraged through breast feeding, but is limited to the first few months of life.

All babies exhibit from birth some *allergy* or sensitivity to certain aspects of the environment. Upon birth, babies are immediately exposed to a whole host of allergens, whereupon they are set the task of manufacturing antigens against them. Any immunization is a deliberate stimulation of the body's defenses against a specific harmful germ. A vaccine is injected into the body, the body produces antibodies specifically against that foreign body, and the antibodies are now available in the event of future invasion —the body has become *immune*.

Sometimes more than a single injection of a particular vaccine is necessary for the body to maintain what is called a *protective level*. Then a *booster shot* or several booster shots are administered.

Specifics of Immunization and Other Tests

PHENYLKETONURIA (PKU)

PKU is a rare disease (approximately one in ten thousand babies are affected) that can cause mental retardation and seizures. It is a *hereditary* deficiency that is diagnosed through a urine test (in PKU the urine contains a chemical substance called phenylpyruvic acid. Because an essential enzyme is lacking, the basic amino acid phenylalanine cannot be processed). Treatment, usually dietary, is fully effective for this metabolism disorder. All babies in the United States are now tested for this disease at birth.

DPT

The DPT injection is a mixture containing diphtheria, tetanus, and pertussis (whooping cough). Diphtheria is a contagious disease and can produce heart complications when untreated. Tetanus (lockjaw) is a serious infection. The tetanus germ itself grows most commonly in soil and

128

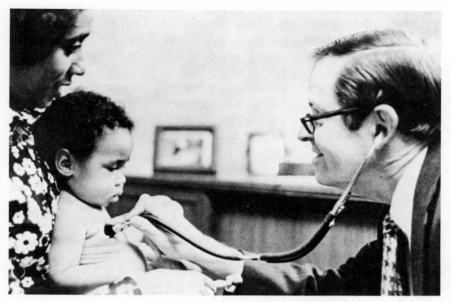

Dr. T. Berry Brazelton examining a young child.

other places where cow and horse manure have been. A wound, if deep enough, is liable to be infected with tetanus. A deep puncture from a nail is risky. Contrary to popular opinion, it is not the rust, but where the nail has been that determines infection. Pertussis (whooping cough) can be extremely serious in small infants; vaccinations prove highly successful.

POLIO (POLIOMYELITIS OR INFANTILE PARALYSIS)

Can be a crippling disease. There are three types of viruses that cause polio and three types of vaccine are given to ensure protection.

MEASLES ("RED" MEASLES)

The illness itself is usually harmless. However, it may include very serious complications, such as ear infection, pneumonia, encephalitis, even permanent brain damage. Measles vaccine producing a lifetime immunity is a "must." Some children—about 10 per cent—do react to the vaccine with fever as high as 103° beginning a week after inoculation and lasting one to five days, and/or a mild rash.

129

GERMAN MEASLES (MEDICALLY CALLED RUBELLA)

A contagious disease that lasts from five to seven days. Fairly mild in children, *extremely dangerous* in pregnant women. A difficult disease to diagnose correctly, rubella begins after a two- to three-week incubation period with a slight headache and other diverse symptoms, such as cold symptoms, slight fever, splotchy rash, and pain in the joints. In 1970, a vaccine was developed that produces lifelong immunity. (Non-pregnant women may be vaccinated, as well as infants and children.)

MUMPS

A contagious disease that may involve serious complications, mumps is rare in children under age five. Its symptoms include inflammation and swelling of the glands. It lasts for about one week to ten days. A vaccine ensures lifetime protection.

SMALLPOX

Public health authorities do not routinely require or recommend vaccination against smallpox. It has been found that the risks (although very small) of complications due to the vaccination are greater than contracting the disease itself. Only in specific instances (e.g., travel to countries where smallpox is present, or epidemics) is it recommended. If it is needed, the vaccine should *not* be administered if the child has eczema, other rashes, is sickly, or if the weather is extremely hot. A drop of serum is placed on the upper arm or thigh and then the skin is pricked through it. A normal reaction includes formation of a red pimple with a whitish blister, followed by reddening of the entire area. Eventually a scab forms and falls off. The entire process lasts several weeks. Parents are urged (1) to keep the area dry during the blister stage; avoid tub baths; (2) leave area uncovered to increase air flow around it; (3) use Band-Aids or gauze pads *only* to avoid child's scratching it. The immunization lasts about five to six years.

TUBERCULOSIS (TB)

The tuberculin "tine" test consists of four tiny prongs that make little red prints no bigger than pinpoints on the skin. If no redness occurs within forty-eight hours, the test is negative. This signifies that the child has not been infected with the tubercle bacillus and does not have TB—or has an old, healed infection. If the tuberculin test is positive, the child is infected with tuberculosis. A careful examination is then necessary to find out where the infection is located and whether active or healed.

130

THE IMPORTANCE OF RECORD KEEPING

The ideal time to start a family health record is when you begin your family. Accuracy is essential, and can be obtained best by recording data and medical observations when they occur and can be verified promptly by the family doctor.

These records not only assist you, the parent, when, for example, years later you are asked to remember the date of your child's polio shot, but also any deviations set down in writing can be useful to future generations. Our genes and chromosomes play a role in the make-up of our grandchildren. Accurate family medical history can be the key that will provide diagnosis without hours of detective work. For instance, if your grandmother had glaucoma (a disease causing blindness and easily controlled by daily use of prescribed eye drops), then your chances of having glaucoma are very high. The significance of treating it before permanent damage is done cannot be stressed enough.

To keep precise records, you can use a variety of baby books sold on the market or create your own. (A book that is comprehensive and inclusive is now in preparation, *This Is Your Early Life,* developed by the Princeton Center for Infancy.) You may use a photo album or a simple manila file folder will serve the same purpose. You will want to include your family tree, recording dates and places of births and deaths of grandparents, parents, aunts, uncles, and other close kin. A record of the mother's health, especially during pregnancy, is important. The type of delivery can affect the child and should be noted. Also, the mother's description of how she felt during her pregnancy and how active her fetus was are pertinent data. Several researchers suggest that a highly active fetus becomes a baby who walks earlier and speaks sooner.

Next, it is a good idea to obtain a copy of your child's birth certificate. This can be done by photostating the original. A certified copy can be obtained from the vital statistics department of the city in which your baby was born. The original birth certificate should be kept in a fireproof place, such as a safety-deposit box. Not only will you need to present it upon your child's admission to school, but it is necessary for obtaining a passport and other documents in later life.

For a neonate (newborn), it is important to obtain from your physician the Apgar score, taken one minute after birth, which rates newborns on a scale of zero to ten. It rates respiration, muscle tone, heartbeat, and reflexes, and is a quick check that tells the attending physician if the baby needs help in the delivery room. It can be a vital clue to possible problems developing later in life. Include your child's blood type here, too. It is of paramount importance to keep precise data concerning immunizations. However, for the mother who occasionally slips up, missing information can be obtained from her family doctor. The mother should note periodic medical findings, because it is important to know when the child has been healthy, as well as sick.

Allergies and problems requiring special medication, such as insulin for diabetes, should be noted, along with the name of your pharmacy. (Federal law requires pharmacies to keep records of family prescription needs.) This information can be crucial in an emergency and may be helpful in a routine consultation; i.e., allergies to antibiotics, etc.

No record is complete without regular notations of your baby's height and weight. These readings are never uniform, but show spurts of growth. This is why your family physician will often check a sick child's weight before prescribing medication; dosage level is based on the child's weight.

In keeping tallies on your baby, remember that the average baby in this country crawls at seven months, but some begin at five months, while others wait to ten months. Some babies crawl—when ready, they walk! Behaviors occur at certain optimum time periods, but they are most favorable with respect to a baby's own learning readiness, not his peers' down the street.

It is not only fun, but important to note when your baby took her first steps or said her first words. These are all factors in her development and indicate how she is using her potential, and how good her motor control is.

According to the late Eric H. Lenneberg, in "On Explaining Language," an article in 1973 in *Science* magazine, "Since motor development is one of the most important indices of maturation, it is not unreasonable to assume that language development, too, is related to physical growth and development. It is also interesting that language development correlates better with motor development than it does with chronological age."

Any injuries should be recorded in your permanent file at the time they happen, as well as the remarks made by the attending physician. For instance, a fall, damaging a baby tooth, could have lasting repercussions on the permanent tooth.

Mementos are a part of your life and your child's as well. Therefore, you will want to include in your file not only snapshots and maybe a lock of hair from your child's first haircut, but also the picture he made in nursery school or the first birthday card he made for you. This is also a good place to preserve report cards, commendations, and awards won.

A behavior profile at various ages should be included in a comprehensive record-keeping program. We are finding that many emotional problems that we confront as adults stem from handling and interpersonal relations between parent and child in the first three years of life. Here are areas that deserve to be recorded:

Aggressiveness or passiveness.

Ego and self-image.

Fears and phobias, jealousies, sibling rivalry.

Social relations: father and child, mother and child, grandparent–child; who was the consistent caretaker?

Early reading. (If child was an early reader at three or four, how was it accomplished by the family?)

Fantasy or reality—favorite playthings.

Learning difficulties, if any.

History of schooling (dates, school reports, etc.).

PCI Point of View

What better present could you give your infant-grown-to-adult than his very own personal history from birth? Even toddlers enjoy this type of reminiscing and most parents we know delight in their role as participating recorders.

FORMATION OF THE TEETH

Tooth formation begins in the early months of pregnancy. A good, nutritious diet, including lots of green leafy vegetables, calcium, and phosphorous are prerequisites for good, strong, healthy teeth. The first two teeth to erupt are usually the lower incisors. The average baby is six months old when she gets her first tooth.

Teething can cause crankiness and irritability. The baby wants to bite on any and all objects that she can find. The gums may be sore and soothing them with a patented medicine, if your doctor approves, or an ice cube wrapped in a damp cloth, may ease the pain. Babies also like to chew on raw apples, carrots, celery, and dry toast, as well as chilled hard rubber teething rings. Doctors today do not recommend paregoric, the traditional remedy, because it contains a narcotic.

Many teething babies drool and have diarrhea. The diarrhea is caused by the added production of saliva that over-digests the baby's food. The baby should be given plenty of fluids to counteract any loss from dehydration that diarrhea can cause.

A child's first teeth help to shape his or her jaw and determine the size of the mouth. They are space savers for permanent teeth and, therefore, should be well taken care of to prevent premature loss. Unfortunately, newly erupted teeth are especially susceptible to decay.

Permanent teeth will appear at about six years of age, although they are already being formed after a few months of life. Dr. Spock says, "The permanent incisors, pushing up underneath, destroy the roots of the baby teeth, which get loose and then fall out." Sometimes teeth that come in crooked later have a tendency to straighten out. Often the permanent teeth are behind the baby teeth and later move forward.

Most babies grind their teeth as soon as they have them. This usually occurs when asleep or preoccupied. This makes a terrible sound and parents fear that their child is ruining his teeth. This is not true. It relieves the baby's tension. Usually he will outgrow it.

Thumb-sucking can push the upper front baby teeth forward and the lower front baby teeth backward. However, it will have no effect on the permanent teeth, provided the child has stopped sucking his thumb by the time he is six years old.

Antibiotics, particularly tetracyclines, can affect developing teeth that have not yet erupted. Dr. Neil C. Henderson writes that "if babies have received certain antibiotics early in life, their baby teeth may be stained brown." According to the American Dental Association, "permanent tooth buds are present at 4–6 months of age, and so tetracyclines should not be given to children from then up to 8 years if discoloration of the permanent teeth is to be avoided."

Fluoride treatment is a controversial subject. However, all the official medical, dental, and public health associations recommend the addition of fluoride to drinking water unless it occurs naturally. It has been found that less tooth decay occurs in regions where fluoride appears naturally in the water.

Today fluoride is added to many water supplies as a preventive measure. In places that do not add it or in the case of people who have their own well, the dentist can prescribe tablets containing fluoride and/or paint the teeth with a fluoride solution. This is usually done once a year for ten years (between the ages of three and thirteen). Toothpastes that contain fluoride reduce cavities by almost 20 per cent.

Unfortunately, not all fluoride dentifrices prevent decay. Those which have been *proven* to prevent dental caries, carry the seal of the ADA's Council of Dental Therapeutics.

Drs. Robertson and Wood indicate that "the tiny amount of fluoride apparently makes the outer layer (the enamel) of the crowns (the visible parts) of the teeth harder and so less easily eroded (eaten away) by the acid produced by the mouth bacteria, which initiate decay."

Some experts claim that the baby born to a pregnant woman drinking fluoridated water will have 40 per cent fewer cavities than a fetus not exposed to water containing fluoride. The American Dental Association claims that several studies failed to find any difference but it has been proven that children who drink fluoridated water from birth can have up to 65 per cent fewer cavities than their non-fluoridated contemporaries.

If your child falls on a hard surface and bangs a baby tooth, take him to the pediatrician for an examination. The baby tooth may darken, become loose, or develop an abscess and require medical attention to prevent damage to the permanent tooth.

CARE OF THE TEETH

The care of your child's teeth is an important responsibility. It is up to you to teach your child the proper home care and to provide the necessary professional treatment.

Home Care

The American Dental Association recommends that you start brushing your child's teeth after her first incisors (front teeth) have erupted and as soon as she will accept brushing. By the time she has most of her first teeth, somewhere around the age of two, she will be able to do some of the brushing herself. Most children at this age readily try to copy the activities of their parents. Although she will certainly not be performing an efficient job at first, your encouragement and help will teach her to develop the necessary skill.

Brushing and Flossing

The American Dental Association has recently updated the traditional method of brushing teeth. Whereas the former methods of brushing and rinsing made for a clean mouth, brighter teeth, and fresh breath, the new reason for brushing teeth is to eliminate disease-forming plaque.

What is plaque? It is the sticky colorless layer of harmful bacteria which is constantly forming on the teeth. Plaque is now recognized as the cause of the two most common dental diseases:

1. Dental caries (tooth decay), the major cause of tooth loss in children

2. Periodontal or gum disease (pyorrhea), the major cause of tooth loss in adults

If you don't remove the plaque daily, it will accumulate and turn into a hard deposit called tartar that can be removed only by your dentist or a dental hygienist.

Since plaque is hard to find, it helps to color the teeth periodically with a special red dental tablet (that you can chew, then spit out) which reveals where the plaque is that needs *flossing and brushing*. A gentle back-and-forth brushing to remove the plaque is recommended. For the front teeth, brush the inside front surface of the teeth with several gentle up-and-down strokes over the teeth and gums. Consult your dentist on correct brushing to remove plaque. For a free and well-done booklet on "Cleaning Your Teeth and Gums," write to the American Dental Association, 211 East Chicago Avenue, Chicago, Ill. 60611 (include fifteen cents for handling and postage).

Brushing does not do anything for the hard-to-get places between teeth. The point of brushing is to remove the plaque, not just the sugar or

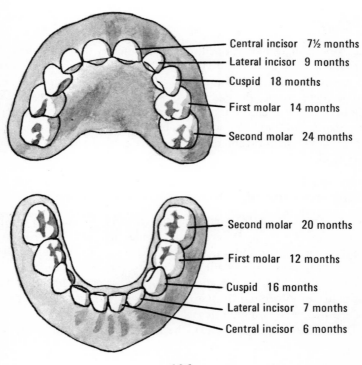

Central incisor 7½ months
Lateral incisor 9 months
Cuspid 18 months
First molar 14 months
Second molar 24 months

Second molar 20 months
First molar 12 months
Cuspid 16 months
Lateral incisor 7 months
Central incisor 6 months

food debris. The use of dental floss should be taught by parents. Parents must set an example by using floss themselves. With the very young child, the child's mouth may also be cleaned out with warm water and a gauze pad or clean washcloth.

The best time for your child to brush his teeth is after meals. This cleansing will help to remove the food debris that can lead to tooth decay and irritation of the gums.

If you are in the habit of putting your child to bed for naps and at night with a bottle filled with milk or other sugar-containing liquids, he may develop a condition known as "nursing bottle mouth." Many of the child's teeth may become badly decayed or permanently damaged. The most important brushing of the day is after the child's last meal, so that his teeth are clean during the long night period.

The toothbrush that you select for your child should be small enough to reach all areas of the mouth. The ADA recommends "a child-sized toothbrush with a small straight head containing soft bristles. The head of the brush should be small enough to reach every tooth." After each use, the brush should be cleaned and hung to dry.

Professional Care

The selection of a dentist for your child is an important decision. If you do not have a family dentist or if your dentist does not treat children, there are several intelligent methods for choosing a reputable dentist.

You can contact your local dental society or the chief of dental service of an accredited hospital for the names of several qualified dentists. You can also ask your physician for a recommendation. It should also be kept in mind that the services of a pedodontist (a dentist who specializes in children) are available in some areas.

Your child's first visit to the dentist should be made when he is between two and three years of age, since a survey has shown that 50 per cent of all two-year-olds in this country have one or more decayed teeth. The only indication for an earlier visit would be in the event of a dental accident, symptoms of pain, or if you noticed some irregularities in his teeth. Hopefully your first visit will be a routine one, so that your child's experience will be pleasant and friendly. This is important in influencing his feelings toward the dentist in the years to come.

At the first examination, the dentist will examine your child's mouth and teeth. He may also clean the teeth. In addition, he may take X-ray photographs to locate the source of any hidden decay if he feels this is necessary.

Following this initial visit, routine examinations of your child's teeth should be made. In most cases, dental visits are recommended every six months.

It is important to remember that the home and professional care of your child's baby teeth will have a direct bearing on his total development. The primary teeth provide him with the ability to chew his food thoroughly. They also preserve the space needed for the permanent teeth that come in several years later. If he were to lose them because of decay, the surrounding teeth might drift into the space and as a result the permanent teeth might grow in irregularly. The ability of your child to talk is partly dependent on a full set of healthy teeth. Lastly, your child's facial appearance will be attractive only if his teeth are clean and healthy.

EYES AND EYE CARE

The eyes of neonates born in the hospital are treated with either a solution of jelly of silver nitrate or antibiotic to counteract possible infection acquired as the infant passes through the birth canal of the mother. (This treatment has been made mandatory because gonorrheal conjunctivitis was a frequent disease leading to severe eye damage. Then it became rare, but with the new sexual freedom it has once again become a problem, particularly in young women and adolescent girls who bear children.)

Silver nitrate can be irritating. The eyes may appear inflamed and puslike material may flow out of them for a day or two, sometimes longer. Usually the eyes will clear up without treatment or you can bathe them with a mild solution of salt water.

Eye Conditions

Viral conjunctivitis is an infection caused by a virus that has recently been identified. The eyes look very much as they do in gonorrheal conjunctivitis except that the viral infection occurs about seven days after birth. Gonorrheal infection and silver nitrate irritation occur right after birth.

Viral conjunctivitis is quite contagious and can spread through a nursery. It usually corrects itself, but occasionally it can become a chronic infection and hang on for months. Antibiotics are effective against bacteria that might complicate the original infection, but not against the virus itself.

The *nasolacrimal duct* is the duct that handles the discharge of tears and normal secretions from the eyes. When this duct is partly plugged, tears are not drained off as fast as they form. They well up in the eye and run down the cheek. A massage a few times a day may re-establish proper drainage. This massage is done using gentle pressure starting at the inside corner of the eye, working toward the bridge of the nose and then down along the side of the nose. Your doctor can show you how to do this.

If massage does not re-establish proper drainage within a month or two, the duct may have to be opened by the doctor.

During a baby's first two or three months, his eyes are not well co-or-dinated (they tend to wander a bit). Usually they will straighten themselves out by the age of three months (six months at the latest). However, if from the very beginning, you notice that your baby's eyes turn in (or out) regularly or most of the time, consult your doctor.

Sometimes a mother thinks her child's eyes are crossed when they are really straight. This is because his nose is wider and more spread out than in an older person, so that a larger amount of white shows on the outer side (toward the ear) than shows on the inner side (toward the nose).

If your child appears to be cross-eyed, it is *extremely* important that you have his eyes examined promptly by the doctor. *Strabismus* (or squint-eyes) is a condition that will not cure itself and it is important that treatment be started early.

With normal eyesight, a person looking at an object sees almost identical images with both eyes and his brain can fuse the images. A person with squint or crossed eyes sees two different images and it is impossible for his brain to fuse the two. The result is that he sees double (a condition called *diplopia*), which is confusing and uncomfortable for him. As a result he learns to suppress the image sent to his brain by the crossed eye and stops using his crossed eye for seeing. If this goes on for too long, it will become impossible ever to bring back vision in that eye.

Ophthalmologists have a number of methods they use to make the "lazy eye" work. They may patch the good eye so that the child is forced to use his crossed eye to see. They may use glasses to correct the vision in the crossed eye or an operation may be performed to straighten the crossed eye. These operations are occasionally performed as early as six months, but more often when the baby is ten to twelve months old.

Be sure to keep your baby's fingernails cut short so that he is not in danger of scratching the cornea of his eye. A corneal scratch can be very painful and takes a long time to heal.

FOOT AND LEG PROBLEMS

Improper development of the feet and legs in young children is dependent on many conditions: fetal position, presence of rickets (soft bones from low vitamin D levels), and injury. Pediatricians are quick to recognize improper development and, in many instances, early treatment will correct the problem simply and quickly.

Knock-knees

It is not unusual for a three- or four-year-old child to have knock-knees as his limbs adapt to carrying the body weight around. Neil Henderson, in *How to Understand and Treat Your Child's Symptoms,* states that the condition does not need treatment; that it will disappear as the child gets older. *Your Child: Keeping Him Healthy,* published by the Child Health Centers of America cites studies showing that corrective shoes, braces, and other appliances are not necessary. If the condition is severe, other factors, such as rickets or an injury, might be involved and the physician may recommend X-rays.

Bowed Legs

Bowed legs are rather common from infancy to about three years of age. This condition does not usually require treatment and will correct itself.

Flatfeet

A newborn baby—and even an older child—can have flatfeet. A child's feet are wider and have a fat pad at the base of the arch for support until the bones harden and the muscles develop. Most authorities believe that flatfeet are perfectly normal at these early ages. Henderson states that "a flat foot is a better functioning foot than one which has an extremely high arch where the weight is not evenly distributed."

Beware of the shoe salesman attempting to sell you on corrective shoes without a physician's recommendation. In certain cases, a physician might prescribe corrective shoes, especially when the degree of flat-footedness is marked.

There are conflicting opinions among specialists as to the effectiveness of corrective shoes for flat feet. Some European pediatricians recommend a toe strap attached to a flat sole to encourage development of the foot muscles.

Your Child: Keeping Him Healthy suggests the following foot exercises to develop the arches: (1) more walking; (2) walking on tiptoes; (3) walking on the outer borders of bare feet with toes curled in; (4) toe-flexing exercises, including standing on a book and curling the toes over the edge until the count of six, then relaxing them; and picking up marbles with the toes and transferring them to a pail.

Parents are encouraged to do the exercises with their young children.

Hips—Congenital Dislocation

The long bone in the upper part of the leg (femur) fits the pelvis as a ball-and-socket joint. Occasionally a congenital dislocation occurs when the socket in the pelvis is not properly developed. The ball at the femur end tends to slip out of the socket. The joint can be completely dislocated, but partial dislocation is more common. It is important that diagnosis be made early so that the condition does not become worse and perhaps irreversible.

When the newborn baby has her examination, the physician holds her legs and "frogs them out." The legs are pushed back to the belly and out to the side, creating a ninety-degree angle. If there is a dislocation, there will be a snap and resistance when the legs are pushed back. The fold of skin in the thighs will not be symmetrical. One leg may appear shorter. X-rays will confirm the diagnosis. It must be stressed again that early treatment is imperative. If correction is not begun before three years of age, surgery will be recommended.

Early treatment is prescribed by the Boston Children's Medical Center. If a partial dislocation exists, several thick diapers are used to keep the thighs apart. If there is total dislocation, a body cast may be necessary for several days to a few weeks. The younger the infant, the more rapid and satisfactory are the results.

Toeing In and Toeing Out

When an infant's foot or both feet toe in, the problem may be due to one of several conditions.

Metatarsus varus simply means that the child's foot curves inward like a comma. Quite often the other foot is turned out. This toeing in is present at birth and probably results from the fetal position. If the problem is not severe, a Denis Browne splint is recommended by the physician. If the infant is three to six months old, correction can result in a matter of weeks. At this age, the infant usually reacts well to the splint. In *Childhood Illness,* Dr. Jack Shiller suggests reversing shoes if the child is not walking. If the condition is severe, a cast may be necessary. Once metatarsus varus is corrected, it usually does not recur.

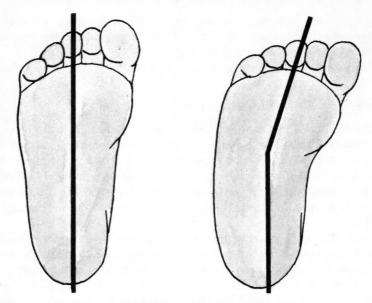

Left, normal position. Right, Metatarsus varus.

Tibial torsion occurs when the main bone of the leg (tibia) is twisted and the foot points inward. The opposite leg usually rotates outward. It is not to be confused with bowed legs. Dr. H. C. Kingsbery, in "Torsion of the Legs in Young Children," describes the condition as the child sitting on his feet and legs with his toes pointed inward. The Denis Browne splint is recommended at an early age.

Femoral torsion results from the thigh bone (femur) being twisted. Dr. James C. Lanier, in "The Intoeing Child," states that this condition, in which the feet are toed in, is not as common in infants as it is in older children. Dr. Lanier mentions that there may be several causes. The child may consistently sit on his buttocks with his thighs turned inward and feet pointed away from his body. Another cause might be the child sleeping with hips inward and his toes touching.

Although Dr. Lanier recommends the Denis Browne splint for femoral torsion, Dr. Shiller and Dr. H. Lee and Violet Broadribb, authors of *The Modern Parents' Guide to Baby and Child Care,* do not. They believe that femoral torsion is a self-correcting condition and that no mechanical device is effective. There appears to be a difference of opinion as to the effectiveness of corrective shoes, splints, and other apparatus for the toe-

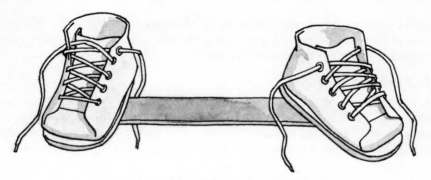

Denis Browne splint.

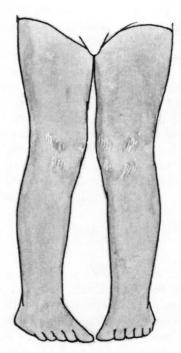

Femoral torsion.

ing-in problem. Many specialists are emphatic as to the necessity of early correction while others are not. It is advisable to consult with your own physician if you are faced with this problem.

PCI Point of View

The causes of femoral torsion and many other leg conditions are not clear-cut. Parents should be aware of any unusual sitting, standing, or sleeping position their children assume. The earlier these conditions are brought to a doctor's attention, the easier and quicker their remediation.

SCREENING OF HEARING

A child is never too young for a hearing test. If there is a hearing problem, the sooner rehabilitation begins, the more beneficial to the patient. Auditory screening programs are being implemented in hospital nurseries across the United States. This test not only tells if a child is deaf, but also gives a quantitative indication whether he is hard of hearing.

It is estimated that one out of every thousand babies born has a hearing problem. The early detection of hearing loss and resulting positive rehabilitation steps are important because they mean no hearing impairment for the infant. A hearing defect will not only affect a child's speech development, but also his emotional security. The normal child must hear words in order to differentiate sounds; this is how he learns to speak. Without speech a child faces a language barrier. Hearing means communication. The aurally handicapped child feels left out and unwanted.

There are two types of deafness. The first, caused by problems in the outer and middle ear, is referred to as "conductive." Conductive deafness can usually be treated medically. The second type is due to a malfunction of the inner ear or to nerve problems. This is called sensory-neural and is not yet curable. If both conditions exist, it is then called a "mixed" hearing loss.

Testing

One reliable way to test a hearing problem in a newborn is to present an auditory stimulus at regular intervals. Use a squeaky toy to see if the child can tell where the noise is coming from. The infant reacts to the stimulus with an accelerated heartbeat. If you think that your baby has a hearing problem, seek medical attention from an otologist. A simple test that can be performed at home is to take a spoon and tap it gently against a crystal glass or vase, then watch your baby's reaction to the tinkly sounds produced. If after several trials at different times there is no response, you may suspect a hearing problem.

Heredity

Heredity plays a significant role in predicting congenital deafness. About 10 per cent of all congenital deafness is blamed on *autosomal* dominant genes. This means that each time an affected adult has a child, each child stands a fifty-fifty chance of developing the disease. If both parents are deaf, they can produce a child with normal hearing, but that child will probably carry a recessive gene that might possibly produce deafness in a later generation. Today medical authorities recommend that if one or both parents are deaf or if there is a history of deafness in the family, they should undergo a gene study before contemplating having children.

Disease

The most common cause of infant deafness is maternal rubella (German measles), but other diseases during the mother's pregnancy can produce hearing loss, such as Asian influenza, infectious mononucleosis, syphilis, and diabetes mellitus. (Syphilis in the mother will cause deafness in 5 per cent of her offspring.) Deafness can result from Rh and other blood group incompatibilities and certain birth injuries, such as anoxic damage, in which the infant is deprived of oxygen during the delivery.

Drugs

A wide variety of drugs taken during the first trimester of pregnancy can affect the child's hearing, including aspirin and other pain relievers containing salicylates. Quinine, certain antibiotics, various aniline dyes, carbon disulfide, carbon monoxide and, of course, thalidomide—all have some type of deleterious effects on normal ear development.

Permanent hearing loss may result from the newborn being given certain antibiotics during the first few days of life. This can also happen if the baby contracts measles.

What to Do?

The parent of a baby with hearing impairment of any type should seek medical help at the earliest possible date. Even infants less than a year old can be fitted with a hearing aid. It is necessary to cultivate all of a child's residual hearing. The deafer the child, the more he needs stimulation around him to use his voice. Therefore, the need to talk to the child cannot be stresssed enough.

It is sometimes advisable for parents of a deaf child to seek counseling. Upon learning that they have a deaf child these parents begin to grieve as if they were in mourning. They must work through their feelings before they can be of constructive help to their child.

Techniques for teaching children with hearing problems have so improved that if a child is enrolled soon enough in a preschool program, she has a good chance of attending an elementary and high school for normal students. It has been found that deaf children are much quieter in a school for the deaf than in a regular school environment. More than other students, they need full opportunity to talk and practice their speech and to learn to read lips if they are to be participating members of the community. Until recently the education of most deaf children ended at the eighth grade.

The Alexander Graham Bell Association for the Deaf, 3417 Volta Place, N.W., Washington, D.C. 20007, is working constantly to alert parents of deaf children to the help that is available for them. Write for their publication list and consider their very fine periodical—*The Volta Review*. They want to make Dr. Bell's dream a reality: "That no deaf child should grow up without the maximum opportunity to learn to speak."

PCI Point of View

Early education is the key that unlocks the silence in the deaf child's world. The child is better off learning to live in an orally communicating society than one limited to the hand language commonly associated with deaf people. However, for the child who cannot learn to speak, manual language is his only hope of communication at all. Also, sign language allows the child to learn concepts with his peers that he might not otherwise understand because of his hearing loss.

CARE OF THE GENITALS

Female Genitals

Because some of the mother's hormones may have crossed into the unborn baby, it is not uncommon for a female infant to have a whitish or blood-tinged vaginal discharge. At the toddler age, however, this condition may be indicative of a mild or serious infection that should be checked by a doctor.

The vulva should be cleansed with a bland soap and warm water. In order to prevent a vaginal or urinary tract infection due to fecal contact, it is best to wipe from front to back, using a different section of the washcloth each time. Disposable premoistened towelettes are now on the market for cleaning the genitals during the diaper stage.

Male Genitals

The penis may be erect at times, indicating a full bladder or irritation, with no sexual connotation.

The size of the opening of the urinary canal should be large enough for him to urinate without difficulty. The scrotum should contain two firm kernels and a small amount of fluid to protect the testicles.

Circumcision—Male

To circumcise or not is a matter of choice or religious preference. Circumcision is the surgical removal of the foreskin at the tip of the penis. It is performed to facilitate the discharge of urine and to make the area easier to clean, thus helping to prevent infection.

Uncircumcised—retract the foreskin gently only as far as it will go without pressure. Cleanse gently and return foreskin to its normal position to prevent constriction and swelling.

Circumcised—the foreskin may adhere to the base of the head of the penis. If so, retract it gently and cleanse with soap and water. Vaseline applied to the cut edge of a newly circumcised penis is adequate to prevent the wound from sticking to the diaper.

Male Abnormalities

A child who holds back his urine and cries when the stream of urine begins usually has an infection or sore near the opening of the urethra. Placing the child in a warm tub usually soothes the area of the urethral opening and relaxes the child so he will urinate.

Reddened ulcers on the head of the penis are due to ammonia burns from the urine or diaper irritation. This should be treated immediately to prevent scarring. Scar tissue can decrease the size of the urinary opening, causing more complications in later life. Preventative measures include:

1. Change diapers frequently (even during the night).

2. Use powder, such as cornstarch, to absorb ammonia.

3. Expose inflamed penis to air—*no rubber pants.*

4. Apply protective ointment, such as Vaseline or antibiotic cream, to tip of penis.

5. Boil diapers with anti-ammonia rinses and *no* detergents. Throwaway diapers are an advantage.

If ulcerations persist, call your doctor.

Hydrocele and Hernias

It is common for baby boys to have excess fluid in the scrotum, causing it to be enlarged. This is called a hydrocele. It is nothing to worry about. Usually the fluid diminishes by the time the infant is a year old. Occasionally the fluid remains and the presence of a hernia should be considered. It is up to your doctor to make the final diagnosis and initiate treatment.

Hernias do not disappear spontaneously. There is always the danger of a portion of the bowel becoming caught in the sac of the hernia and strangulating. A truss offers no help. Therefore, surgery is always indicated regardless of age.

Undescended Testicles

In some boys, one or both testicles are not in the scrotal sac, but are farther up in the groin or inside the abdomen, from whence they normally descend. If the testicles do not descend soon after birth, they may descend by puberty, average age thirteen. If they do not, hormonal treatment and/or surgery may be indicated.

The testicles have a built-in safety device against trauma or injury. They have muscles attached to them that can pull them up into the groin or even the abdomen. Chilling of the skin from being undressed may be enough to make the testicles disappear. A good way to check their descent is to observe the child without handling him while he is in a warm tub.

If one testicle is undescended, there is no cause for great concern, because one is enough for proper development and fathering. The accepted procedure is to operate before the onset of puberty.

If *two* testicles are undescended, which is rare, the boy will have all the normal secondary sex characteristics, but if not repaired, sterility results. With two undescended testicles, the procedure is to repair one in infancy and the other by age five or six, thus giving the second testicle a span of years to descend on its own.

Emotional aspects of undescended testicles are important. Do not worry yourself and do not worry your son. Anxieties are contagious. Frequent exams will not make them appear, but will only develop a self-conscious boy who may feel inferior and malformed. After surgery, if one testicle is absent or removed, plastic surgery can be performed so your child will resemble other boys, thereby allaying psychological problems.

Handling of Genitals

Masturbation will not result in insanity or criminality. Environment plays a large role in either prolonging or diverting this exploration. A stimulating environment will direct interests to other things in time without provocation by parents or producing guilt feelings in the child.

TONSILS AND ADENOIDS

The tonsils and adenoids are spongy masses of lymphoid tissues located in the back of the throat and nose. This lymphoid tissue traps bacteria that are carried to it by the lymph in the lymph vessels. This tissue also produces white blood cells, some of which can produce antibodies, thus helping to develop normal immunity. Because children have to combat so many infections, tonsils and adenoids are normally quite large during childhood and shrink by adolescence.

Tonsillitis

Tonsillitis is an inflammation of the tonsils causing them to appear red and swollen. White patches of pus may also appear. Fever is often present and the patient may experience headaches, vomiting, abdominal cramps, sore throat, and swollen glands in the neck. If tonsillitis is caused by a virus, an antibiotic is of no value. In the case of a bacterial infection, an appropriate antibiotic is prescribed. High fever, difficulty in swallowing, and a bad breath odor are usually present. If no antibiotic treatment is given for a streptococcal infection, nephritis and rheumatic fever may occur as complications.

Adenoiditis

Adenoiditis is an infection of the adenoids that causes fever, sore throat, foul mouth odor, and occasionally an ear infection. The treatment for adenoiditis is the same as for tonsillitis.

Enlargement of the Tonsils and Adenoids

Tonsils gradually enlarge until the age of about nine and most doctors attach no special importance to their size. Enlarged adenoids do not necessarily mean that infection is present; however, they may cause snoring and mouth breathing. They may also press on the eustachian tube, causing recurrent ear infections and deafness. Antihistamines are sometimes given to shrink the size of the adenoids but, according to Dr. Falkner, using antihistamines is not effective. The tonsils and adenoids naturally shrink with the passage of time and are less likely to cause trouble.

Indications for the Removal of Tonsils and Adenoids

Dr. Jack Shiller, in *Childhood Illness,* reports that about fifty years ago tonsillectomies and adenoidectomies were performed on virtually every child whose parents could afford to give them what was then thought to be the best possible medical advantage. He believes that tonsillectomies and adenoidectomies should be performed *only* when the most stringent criteria are met and the child's condition is serious enough to warrant the surgery.

Criteria for the removal of the tonsils include repeated attacks of tonsillitis (that most physicians define as six or more attacks per year); enlarged tonsils that obstruct the airway and interfere with breathing; enlarged tonsils that interfere with the quality of speech; history of tonsillitis in spite of repeated antibiotic treatment; history of more than three ear infections in a year.

In the case of obstruction of the eustachian tube, causing recurrent ear infections that do not respond to therapy, doctors report that the adenoids are often removed and the tonsils left.

It appears that an adenoidectomy is often indicated in the case of partial deafness or mouth breathing caused by enlarged adenoids. A consensus of current thinking appears to be that tonsils need to be removed only rarely and certainly not just because they are large.

Risks in Removing the Tonsils and Adenoids

Your physician should be notified immediately if during convalescence your child experiences vomiting of fresh or old blood, constant ear pain, temperature above 102°, or unusually dark bowel movements indicating possible blood in the stool.

The removal of the tonsils and adenoids will eliminate a normal area of defense against disease and infections may occur more frequently elsewhere in the body.

PCI Point of View

Children normally fear the loss of a part of their bodies. Performing a tonsillectomy or adenoidectomy will reinforce this fear; and these operations cause postoperative pain. Children need special care and understanding when an operation is indicated.

CHOKING AND DROWNING

It is unlikely that you will be one of the lucky few parents who escapes confrontation with a choking child. If and when you do face this situation, try to stay calm and act quickly.

With older children the offending object usually is a piece of unchewed meat. With infants and toddlers beware of buttons, parts of stuffed animals and dolls, sucking candies, the plug of a squeeze toy; they are just the right size for a child's windpipe. In most instances the baby will cough up the object and feel perfectly fine. If more than a few seconds go by and baby is still choking (not just gagging or coughing), then she may, if not treated, turn blue, become limp and unconscious. *You must act.*

Dr. Falkner disclaims the centuries-old treatment of "rib-thumping and finger sticking." Instead, "Turn the baby upside down, and *do not* pat her rib cage; this might cause a dangerous gasping inhalation that would suck the foreign body further in." The spasm most likely will relax and then the foreign body will be coughed up. If the baby is still choking and no phone is available, send someone (do not leave the baby alone) for emergency help.

If your baby stops breathing for any unexplainable reason (we are not referring to the baby who, in a fit of temper, holds his breath), quickly administer mouth-to-mouth artificial respiration. The U. S. Government pamphlet *Infant Care* explains this method in eight easy-to-follow steps.

Mouth-to-mouth Respiration

1. Place baby on his back on any flat surface.
2. With your fingers, quickly clear his mouth and throat of any mucus, food, or other obstruction, if you can.
3. Tilt his head back, with his chin up. Bring his lower jaw forward.
4. Pinch his nose shut.

5. Put your lips to his and blow gently.

6. Release his nostrils and listen for the return of his breathing.

7. Take a breath yourself.

8. Repeat the process. Close your baby's nostrils, breathe into his mouth, release his nostrils, count to three slowly, and repeat again. Continue doing this about fifteen to twenty times per minute until your baby breathes again. Keep your movements slow and gentle. Do not give up too soon.

(With a small infant, you may be able to seal both mouth and nose with your mouth instead of pinching the nostrils shut.)

Never try to give artificial respiration to a child who is breathing.

An airway tube (resuscitation tube) is a valuable first aid tool and available at most drugstores. One end of this tube is put over the child's tongue, the other end you blow into. Directions must be followed *very carefully* or more harm may be done than good.

Swallowing a Small Object

Many times a baby will accidentally swallow a small, smooth object, like a button or fruit seed. If your baby is not choking, crying, or vomiting, just check his bowel movements for the next few days to make sure that it has passed through his body. If your baby swallows a pin or any other sharp object, take him to the doctor *immediately*.

Never give a laxative to a baby who has swallowed an object. It cannot help, but may do harm.

It is entirely possible for the doctor not to be able to find any traces of a sharp object, even though the child complains of still feeling it in the throat. This is because although the object is no longer visible, it has left a scratch on the throat that causes the child discomfort.

Safety Precautions

If you follow a few simple safety precautions, many choking and suffocation problems could be easily avoided. The National Safety Council has set small objects standards for infants. Toys should be

. . . washable, large enough not to fit in a mouth, ear or nose, but light enough not to cause injury if the child drops the toy on himself. The toy should be made of nonbrittle material (never glass). The eyes of a teddy bear or cloth stuffed animal should be sewn on—not attached with pins. Embroidered eyes are safest.

152

Parents should avoid toys with internal spikes or wire. Easily broken rattles are hazards because the beads inside could be swallowed. You need to be sure that tot toys will not break easily, have no parts that can catch fingers, and are labeled *non-toxic*.

Keep plastic bags, especially those used in dry cleaning, away from babies and children. To be absolutely safe, cut the bags up before throwing them away. Never use a thin plastic covering on a mattress. The plastic can stick to the baby's nose and smother her.

Never tie a baby in her crib or place a crib within reaching distance of venetian blind cords.

Avoid clothing that ties around the neck. Do not give a baby any toy that is smaller than her mouth or that has removable parts.

If possible, avoid giving your baby balloons. If you must, blow a balloon up and watch your baby carefully as she handles it. Never let your baby play with a collapsed balloon. It can be sucked into the throat and choked on.

Do not force your baby to take an oily medicine. Oily particles, if inhaled from choking, can cause lung damage.

If your baby vomits, do not pick her up. Lift her hips slightly to let the liquid flow out of her mouth.

Check gas fixtures periodically for leakage. Use rigid metal connections instead of rubber tubing that may wear and crack.

To prevent choking, do not give a child under the age of five any popcorn, raw vegetables, or crisp bacon. Remove bones from fish and chicken for all children under three.

Dr. Brazelton describes a case in which a nursing infant was literally being choked by sucking too much milk at too fast a rate. The baby started sucking, made choking sounds, burped loudly, and spit up milk. This was followed by ten to fifteen minutes of hiccoughing. To prevent such a choking problem, a nursing mother might gently squeeze the large flow of milk from her breast until it just drips. The baby will then have an easier feeding time.

Drowning

At all times watch your baby while he is in the tub. Do not leave a child under two *alone* in a tub for even a second and not even alone in a room where there is a large tub of water (filled even one or two inches high).

Remember to cover small plastic wading pools when not in use and, of course, all wells and cesspools need to be firmly covered.

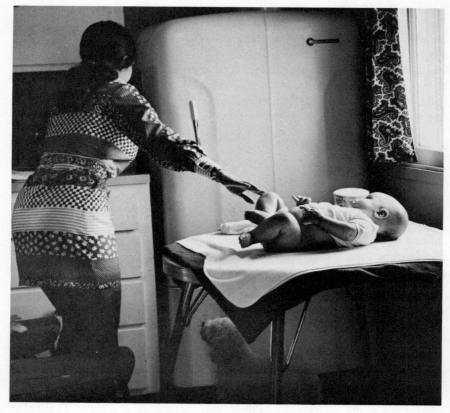

Never, never leave baby alone.

PCI Point of View

Safety in child rearing is an extremely important subject. Many accidents can be prevented by informed parents who purchase only those toys, clothing, and equipment that are safe, fireproof, and appropriate to their growing child's physical abilities and needs. See chapters on play, clothing, and equipment for helpful guidelines.

FALLS, CONCUSSIONS, AND HEAD INJURIES

Falls are a part of childhood. Indeed, Dr. Spock states that if a child is so carefully watched that he *never* has an accident, he is being fussed over too much—bones may be saved, but his character will be ruined.

Actually from the time babies can turn over until they are well on the way to adulthood, falls will have to be dealt with. The only thing parents really can do about falls is to take the necessary safety precautions appropriate to their children's age and then instill safety habits in them when they are old enough for this. After a fall, parents can assess the damage and handle it accordingly.

Complications and Treatment of Falls

A *hematoma* is a lump that forms on a child's skull or other body surface shortly after a fall. It is caused by a broken blood vessel just under the skin and is not anything to be concerned about unless there are other symptoms. A hematoma is not treated specifically. Putting something cold on the lump right after the fall will reduce the swelling and tenderness. If after a fall on the head, a baby stops crying within fifteen minutes, retains his normal coloring, and does not throw up, there is little chance that he has injured his brain. He can resume his normal routine. Some authorities feel that vomiting soon after an accident is normal and may simply be a sign that the child was really shaken up. They stress that what you need to watch for is persistent and/or delayed vomiting, because this may be a sign of head injury.

Everyone speaks of *concussions,* but no one really knows what happens to the brain in this condition. It is probable that the whole brain inside its fluid-containing envelope gets jolted and banged up as it is suddenly forced up against the skull walls. Here a fall or other injury to the head results in a period of unconsciousness, usually fleeting, without any signs of brain damage. The signs and symptoms of a concussion include headache, drowsiness, confusion, paleness (loss of color), vomiting, dizziness, loss of memory after fall, loss of consciousness to some degree (this may be a passing feeling of being dazed, or the child may not respond for a period of minutes or even hours). All of the above need not be present in every concussion.

If your child shows any symptoms of a concussion, you should call your doctor or take him to the emergency room of your nearest hospital. If the doctor feels that your child can be safely cared for at home, you will most likely receive specific instructions. Generally you will be advised to keep your child as quiet as possible for two to three days and to report any new symptoms immediately. Contrary to old wives' tales, it is perfectly okay to let your child sleep. However, it is a good idea to rouse your child twice during the first night to make sure that he is not unconscious.

A *fractured skull* simply means that the skull bone has a crack in it. Most skull fractures are uncomplicated and heal perfectly well by themselves. The important factor is whether or not there is underlying damage to the brain. If this is the case, surgery will be necessary. Even if a skull fracture is uncomplicated, the child will be hospitalized for observation.

Safety Precautions

Here are some safety measures to help prevent falls, adapted from the *U. S. Government Book of Infant Care*:

1. Keep the stairs and landings free of clutter. Hold onto the banister.
2. Place a folding gate at the top and bottom of stairs.
3. Keep a harness or safety strap on an active baby in carriage or stroller. Never leave an active baby unattended in a carriage or on a bed.
4. Buy a high chair with a broad space between the legs so it will not tip over or select a low table-type one.

A basic precaution is *always* to keep your hand on your baby when he is on a table or bed and you have to turn to do something.

All children fall once in a while. Some falls are serious; luckily most are not. The important point to remember is that falls are a part of childhood. Sensible safety precautions, encouragement, and reassurance are called for, not maudlin sympathy or unnecessary restrictions.

ACCIDENTS: BROKEN BONES, SPRAINS, BRUISES, ELECTRIC SHOCK, NOSEBLEEDS

In any accident, it is essential to act at once but without haste or excitement. Speak softly and calmly to instill confidence and allay fear.

Fractures (Broken Bones)

Broken bones are a common mishap for children. They are usually the result of falls, automobile accidents, and blows. Fractures seldom are emergencies and rarely are there serious results. After an accident, examine your child for all injuries. Suspect a fracture if there is pain when moving the injured part, swelling, numbness, black-and-blue discoloration, or deformity. *The injury should be evaluated by a physician.* Keep your child from moving that part of his body where you suspect the fracture and do not move it yourself while you get him to a doctor or hospital. The object is to prevent movement at the broken ends.

156

Arm or Leg

Perhaps the best way temporarily to immobilize an arm or leg is to tie it with strips of gauze or cloth in several places to a rigid splint (a rolled magazine, small pillow, bath towel, or smooth board; a long-handled wooden spoon will work). The splint should extend above and below the adjacent joints. After the splint is in place, take your child to the doctor.

Neck and Back

If you suspect a back or neck injury, do not try to move your child unless absolutely necessary. If you must move him, roll him onto a blanket and try to place him in a firm supporting carrier. Move slowly and avoid jarring his body.

Finger Bones

These are often broken or chipped when a ball is caught on the end of finger. Splint the finger to an adjacent finger, a pencil, or small stick.

Broken toes or small bones of the foot may be painful and have no outward signs. An X-ray is often the only way to be sure.

Fractures of wrists and ankles can also be deceiving and require an X-ray. If there is no deformity, no splints are needed. For the wrist, a sling is sufficient until you get to your physician.

A *vertebra* (bone in the spine) is sometimes crushed in falls on the behind. There are no outward signs, but there is pain when your child bends forward or when he runs and jumps. Suspect a fracture if pain in the limb continues, if there is swelling, or if a black-and-blue mark appears.

Collarbone (Clavicle)

Fractures of the clavicle usually result from breaking a fall with an outstretched hand. There is pain in the shoulder and upper arm and your child will be unable to raise his hand above shoulder level. (You can make a sling out of a large triangle of cloth and tie it behind his neck so that it supports the lower arm across his chest.) Your doctor will apply a figure-eight elastic bandage for about a three-week period. Results are excellent and there will be no permanent damage.

Sprains

A sprain is a pulling of a muscle, a ligament, or the tissue surrounding a joint. Sprains are likely to be accompanied by pain and swelling and sometimes discoloration. Frequently it is difficult to distinguish between a sprain and a fracture. Move the affected area as little as possible. Elevate it to keep the swelling to a minimum. Apply an ice bag, five minutes on and five minutes off. If swelling and pain persist, consult your physician. Many sprains can be eased by correct bandaging or splints. Many sprains and partial fractures are numb for an hour or so and then become painful.

A *sprained knee* needs to be seen and treated by a physician. A knee sprain with injured cartilage that goes untreated may not heal properly and be troublesome for years.

Bruises

Bruises are caused by small blood vessels that break under the skin. The bruise is first red; then black and blue. You can apply cold packs for the first twenty-four hours to keep down any slight swelling. After that, warm compresses will hasten the disappearance of the swelling and discoloration. Minor bruises need no attention unless the bruise is on the abdomen and there is the possibility of internal bleeding.

Electric Shock

Your child might suffer electric shock from a high-tension wire, third rail, faulty electric equipment, or lightning. The shock might be slight, or the child may lose consciousness, or develop painful electric burns.

Immediately break the contact without endangering yourself. Do not touch the child's skin or damp clothes with your bare hands or you will become part of the circuit. Throw off the switch using such non-conductors as rubber gloves or rubber boots. If this fails, knock the wire down with a dry wooden object. Pull your child away with a dry rope of handkerchief looped over his foot, or cover your hands with rubber gloves and pull, or use a wooden board to push him away. Stand on dry wood, cement, or another non-conductor.

Clear his nostrils and mouth of froth. If he has stopped breathing, start artificial respiration and continue until breathing is restored. Massage his arms and legs to stimulate circulation. Immediately take your child to the nearest hospital.

Nosebleeds

Nosebleeds are common in children. Frequently they occur after a cold or a runny nose, especially in the wintertime, when the air in the house is dry.

Pressure is the simplest treatment. Sit your child up and pinch both nostrils with your thumb and forefinger. Hold the nostrils pinched for twenty minutes without checking to see if it is still bleeding.

Some physicians recommend that you have your child blow his nose vigorously to get rid of clots and then irrigate his nostrils with several droppers of 3 per cent hydrogen peroxide or plain water. Next, use nose drops to constrict the blood vessels. Apply ice to the back of his neck and over his nose. Sometimes an ice cube against the upper lip for a minute works. You can also pack the nostrils with cotton.

If it is the same side that bleeds all the time, your physician may be able to find the bleeding vessel and cauterize it, which will end the problem. Any nosebleed that cannot be stopped after an hour should be seen by a physician.

5

The Sick Baby

INTRODUCTION BY FRANK FALKNER, M.D.

In the previous chapter, we stressed the necessity of keeping our children healthy, protected from diseases, and safe—the emphasis being fundamentally one of prevention.

However good we are as parents or guardians, children will get sick. It is, therefore, important for parents to have overall knowledge of sickness in babies. No one expects them to nor should they ever play doctor, but the sick baby will get better more quickly if his parents are informed. This is largely because they will be alert and call for skilled help promptly. They will know, too, how to be of greatest benefit to the sick baby.

Pediatricians have a harder time if the parents of a sick child are ignorant about what is happening. Parents who "go to pieces" when a degree of fever occurs in their child are equally unhelpful. This chapter is intended to outline general knowledge of the main areas of sickness found in babies.

There is a very good rule for parents to follow. If you are in any *doubt* about any aspect of your child's health, acute or chronic, call your doctor. So you will many times find you had no need to call him. So your doctor will laugh at you or be irritated. Won't he? No, he won't! He has to have special skills when dealing with the very young because he cannot get helpful information directly from his patient; and he knows, too, how rapidly a child can become sick, and just as rapidly, better. Therefore, he needs to be called when there is any doubt, so he can rule out illness or treat it promptly and well.

Another reminder. Many doctors have young children of their own. It is surprising how often that is forgotten. When their own children show possible signs of sickness, many of them (this physician included) become much worse than the most overanxious parent!

This section will in general terms show parents how they can help their sick child during this time in the area of their relationship. And as an aside, particularly when a child is sick, it rings the bells of heaven quite loudly if we tell him the truth.

Keeping a child healthy and caring for him when he is sick require teamwork. There are two key members of the team—parent and physician. Above all, there's only one reason for the team to be in existence and striving and that is for the team's core—the child.

EQUIPPING THE MEDICINE CABINET AND BASIC PROBLEMS

The everyday care you give your baby will go a long way toward keeping him healthy. Yet in the normal course of events, your baby will become fussy, acquire bites, cuts, and scratches, and a variety of little aches and pains. For these occasions, you will want to have a few standard items on hand.

The basic danger in giving children any drug, including the over-the-counter, non-prescription products that are discussed here, is that children are not little adults from the standpoint of disease. Therefore, giving young children fractions of adult doses, except in the simplest of conditions, is not treating children safely and adequately. When choosing a drug product for your child, do not casually assume that less of an adult dose is fine for a child. In most instances, it is wise to select those products specifically formulated for children's use. When in doubt, consult your physician or pharmacist.

To Reduce Fever

For fever, aspirin is still the most desirable remedy. Children's aspirin contains one and a quarter grains of aspirin per tablet and is one quarter the strength of regular aspirin tablets. They are convenient to administer since there is no need to break regular tablets. Inasmuch as they usually are flavored, they probably evoke less resistance on the part of the child. The normal dosage is one tablet of children's aspirin for babies under a year; two children's aspirin tablets for children between one and five years; three tablets for six- to eight-year-olds; four children's aspirins (or one adult size) for children nine or older. Aspirin is excreted slowly from the body and thus frequent repeated doses will build up, causing potentially dangerous high levels of aspirin in the bloodstream. Avoidance of continued dosage is very important.

Other analgesics and fever reducers are *Acetaminophen* and *salicylamide*. These are used when a child cannot tolerate aspirin or you prefer a liquid dosage form. When using these products instead of—*not in addition to*—aspirin, follow the detailed dose schedule on the labels. All good brands are comparable and one is as reliable as another.

Cough Mixtures

Only those adult preparations that carry a dosage for children should be used. There are two types of cough mixtures: cough suppressants and cough expectorants. Consult your physician or pharmacist to determine which type you want.

Anti-diarrheals

Diarrhea may be a serious condition in children. It could be fatal in infants if not treated. Since diarrhea may produce loss of essential salts and water and can dehydrate a child more quickly than an adult, a physician should be consulted.

Poison Treatment

No matter how many precautions a parent takes, a child may eat a poisonous substance. More poisoning is reported in very young children than in any other age group. Children one to four years old account for 63 per cent of all poisonings reported in this country. For that reason, your medicine chest should contain two items: *syrup of ipecac* and *powdered activated charcoal*. This does *not* mean that poisonings can be treated at home. The *first* thing to do in poisoning is to call a doctor or poison control center. Then, if you are told to use ipecac or charcoal, you will have it on hand.

Syrup of ipecac induces vomiting. It is available in most drugstores and can be purchased in a ready-to-use form, so that no measuring is necessary at a time of crisis. Powdered activated charcoal does not induce vomiting; it is given *after* vomiting. Its function is to pick up any remaining poison in the stomach. It is given by thoroughly mixing two teaspoonful of powdered charcoal with about a quarter glass of water.

These products should be prominently located in the medicine chest and both parents should familiarize themselves with their use *before* they are needed. To search for a preparation to combat poisoning when it is needed is too late!

Cuts and Surface Wounds and Remedies

The sooner you look after these the better. If they are neglected, there is the danger of infection that may lead to serious trouble. Wash the cut or surface wound thoroughly with soap and water; rinse well; then apply a painless antiseptic recommended by your doctor. *Avoid iodine* since it can burn the skin. Place a piece of sterilized gauze over the area and bandage firmly. If a cut is small, a Band-Aid is sufficient. For large cuts that gape open, consult your doctor. Large splinters need to be removed promptly with a sterilized needle; smaller ones will be rejected or absorbed by the body.

Products for the Medicine Chest—Children's Drugs

The following guide to children's drugs and drug manufacturers is gleaned from *Without Prescription* by Erwin DiCyan, Ph.D., and Lawrence Hessman, M.D. Items listed are suggestions for parents to choose from:

FOR POISONING
Powdered activated charcoal (Requa)
Syrup of Ipecac (Alliance)

FOR TREATMENT OF COLD SYMPTOMS
Aspirin for children (St. Joseph, Bayer, etc.)

DECONGESTANTS
Children's Bufferin (Bristol-Myers)
Children's Romilar cough syrup (Hoffmann-La Roche)—cough suppressant
Coricidin Demilets tablets (Schering)—decongestant
Liquiprin (Thayer)—salicylamide
Romilar Chewable cough tablets for children (Hoffmann-La Roche)—cough suppressant
St. Joseph Cough Syrup for children (Plough)—cough suppressant

167

CHEST RUBS

Mentholatum (Mentholatum)
Musterole (Plough)
VapoRub (Vick)

FOR DIARRHEA

Kaopectate (Upjohn)

In addition, having the following items on hand will enable you to deal with most situations you may have to face:

SUPPLIES

gauze bandage rolls—1″ and 2″
absorbant cotton
sterilized gauze pads
facial tissues
adhesive tape—1″
Band-Aids
painless antiseptic
rubbing alcohol
petroleum jelly
baking soda
rectal thermometer
tweezers
rubber nose syringe (for clearing baby's nose during a cold)
nose drops
hot water bottle

HOW TO ADMINISTER MEDICATION

In spite of the good care you give your children, they are going to get sick at some time. Most of their illnesses will be minor, but some will be serious. Keep your child in bed if there is a fever and call the doctor. Do not give any kind of medicine until directed by the physician.

Your Attitude Toward Drugs

It is wise to avoid asking your doctor for drugs. Parents who are alert to new developments in drug therapy often besiege their doctor with appeals for the latest discovery whether or not it is appropriate for their child. Allow your doctor to use his own judgment in determining medication. Why? Because some drugs are toxic and all drugs can have harmful side effects. That is why they are put on prescription.

A hyperactive child or one with colic may be a terrible drain on you during the early months of life. However, it is questionable if putting the baby on tranquilizers or relaxants is the best course of action. First of all, there is the danger of unnecessary side effects; secondly, some children may react quite the opposite to the intended purpose of the drug. (A toddler given phenobarbital to induce sleep on a long trip may first become restless, then hyperactive, and finally hysterical before falling off to sleep.)

Antibiotics occasionally cause allergic reactions and an individual may become sensitive to a specific antibiotic. The parent who wants the doctor to prescribe antibiotics for every ailment will be sorry later. If antibiotics are given frequently, bacteria can build up such resistance to them that these drugs are no longer effective when needed. Therefore, medication should only be given when the doctor has decided that the danger from the disease and the likelihood of benefit from the medication outweigh the risk of treatment.

Once the doctor has prescribed medication, follow the instructions exactly. If the prescription says "as necessary," use the medication *only as necessary*. Otherwise finish the prescribed amount. This is especially important in the administration of antibiotics. Too often a parent stops the course of treatment as soon as the child appears well. Yet the infection may not have been eliminated and the child may later have a recurrence of the same infection. If the instructions are not clear, find out exactly how much medicine to give, how often, and for how long.

How to Administer Medicine to Children

Giving medicine to children is often quite a trick. A good approach is to slip it into them in a matter-of-fact way as if it never occurred to you that they would not take it. Children will comply once they have learned it is their only alternative.

One convenient way to give liquid medicines to infants and toddlers is to use a medicine dropper. They are available in plastic and in a variety of sizes (some pharmaceutical companies provide them with medication). Several doctors also suggest the use of plastic injection syringes with the needles removed because they squirt so well. Most physicians use plastic disposable syringes. Ask yours to let you have one. Squirt the medicine into the inside of your child's cheek.

Your toddler may enjoy taking his medicine from a very handy test tube-like gadget with a spoon-shaped top calibrated to measure half-teaspoon, one-teaspoon, and two-teaspoon doses. This is one of the easiest ways to administer liquid medication and your child will enjoy the novelty, too. This device (called a *Flexidose spoon*) is packaged with some medications or may be purchased from your pharmacist.

Do not expect your child to be able to swallow a tablet or capsule for some time. Tablets that do not dissolve can be crushed to a fine powder and mixed with a good-tasting food; applesauce, for example. A capsule may be put in something lumpy, like a banana, and followed quickly with a favorite drink.

Eye, ear, or nose drops present different problems. Rather than use nose drops per se, ask your pharmacist to dispense the medication in a plastic spray bottle. Turned upside down, it does dispense drops and unlike a bottle with a dropper, it can be administered with one hand.

Ear drops may be difficult to administer if there is external pain; otherwise your child will probably be co-operative. It is helpful to warm ear drops slightly by holding the bottle under the hot water tap before administering the medication.

Eye drops may be administered while the child sleeps; otherwise it is definitely a two-person job, at least at first. Once one person has immobilized the child, the other puts the medication in as instructed, holding the eye wide open with the other hand. Drop it into the lower lid, pulling the lid down as far as you can.

Suppositories may be prescribed when judged the most appropriate route for the medication. Keep the suppositories in the refrigerator in a clearly labeled container. Remove them, one at a time as needed, about an hour before insertion. Remove the foil wrapper and dip the suppository in petroleum jelly to make for easy insertion. When you insert the suppository, guide it as far up into the rectum as you can by giving it a firm push with your finger. Then squeeze the child's buttocks together and hold them that way for five minutes since as many as three to five minutes are needed for the suppository to melt fully.

Exercise extreme caution when giving any medication and follow these basic rules:

Read the label and instructions beforehand.

Never give medicine from an unlabeled bottle.

Shake liquid medicines thoroughly before measuring.

Never give medicine in the dark. You may make a serious error.

Do not renew an old prescription for a new illness without consulting your doctor.

Do not give leftover medications, especially antibiotics, to your child. Such treatment rarely works and may seriously harm.

Always empty any unused medication down the drain and rinse container before placing it in the trash.

SIGNS AND SYMPTOMS OF ILLNESS

It would be nice to consult with a Sherlock Holmes at those nerve-racking moments when you suspect that your infant might be sick. There is often no direct way for you to make a judgment since babies cannot tell you what hurts them, and when very young they might not even be conscious of their pain or discomfort as being part of them. The older child does have communicative language ability of an imprecise nature. The child complains of a "stomachache" or a "headache" because these are familiar words he has heard others use to express discomfort; yet each may be entirely inappropriate in his case. Anyone who has ever seen a three-year-old hold his throat while insisting that his stomach aches when really his throat is sore can attest to this.

Another problem to contend with when young children get ill is that they get ill quickly and suddenly (but they do get well quickly, too).

Diagnosis and treatment are usually beyond the scope of the average parent. You *can* become professional at recognizing symptoms, however, some of which are subtle, others very apparent.

Following are some signs and symptoms to be used in assessing a sick child:

Are there some unusual elements to your baby's behavior? "He's just not himself" is the observant parent's rule of thumb. When a good eater stops eating for several feedings, when an "always into it" toddler falls asleep during playtime, when usually sweet-tempered baby becomes obnoxious and hard to please, something *is* wrong.

Is your baby acting very atypically in comparison to others her age? Most babies are playful; most preschoolers are physically active.

Is your child having trouble breathing? Continuously cranky?

Is his color pale or bluish?

Is he vomiting?

Does he have diarrhea? Is there blood in his bowels or vomitus?

Does your child have abdominal pain? Is it upper, lower, dull, sharp, crampy in nature?

Is there persistent sneezing or dry hacking coughing, hoarseness or sore throat?

Is your child having chills or is he flushed?

171

Does your child have generalized muscular aches; an earache, dizziness and a headache?

Does he have fever?

If, upon screening your child for illness according to this checklist, he shows one or two symptoms, watch him. Have him rest. Take his temperature. Whenever you are in doubt telephone your doctor. It is wise to let the doctor be the final judge.

Fever

Temperatures vary according to the time of day, temperature of the environment, and degree of activity just before the temperature is taken. Not every normal person registers 98.6° all of the time and a reading of say 97° should not cause concern. A temperature of 101° usually means illness.

Significance of Fever

Fever is a sign that the body is reacting well against an illness, usually an infection. When evaluating the significance of fever, the initial observation of its presence is of less importance than its progression. A fever that begins to climb several days after the start of the infection often indicates that the disease is becoming more serious or may have developed complications. This holds true in respiratory infections, during which a rise in the temperature curve raises the question of whether the cold or sore throat has spread to another site and has set up a secondary infection, in the ears, perhaps, or in the bronchial tubes (where bronchitis or pneumonia can easily develop). A fever that goes up or returns after two or three days is likely to indicate that what started as a common cold is no longer what it seemed when its first symptoms appeared.

Treatment of Fever

Fever caused by bacterial infection, e.g., streptococcus, pneumonia, etc., will usually respond to antibiotic treatment. Fever caused by a viral infection, e.g., flu and grippe symptoms, will not respond to antibiotics, but will have to run its course (three to five days or longer). Aspirin, *plenty of liquids* (to prevent dehydration), and bed rest are helpful. Some pediatricians believe that 75–90 per cent of all childhood respiratory illnesses are viral infections.

172

Prescribing antibiotics for viral infections may make the disease worse or cause side effects that could mask the progression of an illness and the symptoms that the doctor would need to observe. The important element is not the fever, but the other present or occurring symptoms.

Emergency Treatment

When the fever itself becomes a problem, one must take steps to lower it. It is best to try to keep the temperature under 104° because otherwise a small child may have convulsions. When the temperature is 103°–104°, sponge the baby with tepid water, rubbing his body. A wet rub will cause evaporation on the surface of the skin and cool it. As your child's temperature goes up, the amount of clothing and covers should go down. A baby with 104° should have just a diaper and a light cover. Care must be taken to see that the baby will not be in a draft or a room with poor temperature control. A tepid bath for ten minutes or so may lower the fever. Baby aspirin or Tylenol will help reduce the fever, but do not exceed the recommended dosage; a larger amount could make the baby sicker. It is vital that the baby gets adequate fluids in his diet—milk, soda, broth, gelatin, sugared water, etc.—all will help keep him properly hydrated.

The Thermometer

There are two types of thermometers, oral and rectal, and the only difference is in the shape of the bulb. The markings are the same. The oral tip is long and thin so that the mercury can be warmed faster; the rectal bulb is round so that it will not be sharp against the walls of the rectum.

Taking the Temperature

Take the temperature after your baby has been quiet for one hour or more. There are three ways to take the temperature: *oral* (takes two to three minutes in the mouth to register the correct temperature—normal is 98.6° F.); *rectal* (registers well enough in a minute—normal is 99.6°); *axillary* (this is under the armpit—registers in four minutes—normal is 97.6° F.).

When reporting fever, always tell the doctor the exact thermometer reading and where the temperature was taken rather than try to make the conversions yourself.

Most pediatricians recommend taking rectal temperatures for children

173

under eight because the armpit method is less reliable. The oral method accomplishes little since most children have upper respiratory infections and their noses are stuffed. This forces them to breathe through their mouths and makes the oral reading unreliable.

Fever tells the mother that her baby is sick, even if he cannot verbalize it. It is a symptom, part of a total picture of the child's state of being. Fever can be viewed from a positive viewpoint: it means that the child's defensive mechanisms are at work fighting infection.

CARING FOR THE SICK CHILD AT HOME

"Let the child lead just as normal a life as is possible under the circumstances, expect reasonable behavior from him toward the rest of the family, and avoid worried talk, looks, and thoughts," is Dr. Spock's advice to parents taking care of a sick child at home. There will, of course, be changes in the normal routine as you follow medical instructions and try to make your child feel more comfortable. Demands on the parents for comfort and attention will increase during an illness. Do not be afraid of "spoiling" your child with the extra measure of contact that may be needed at special intervals. Keep in mind that this period is short; 90 per cent of children's illnesses are on the way to recovery within a few days.

As the child begins to recover, normal interest in the surroundings will return and the demands for attention should diminish. Some authorities feel that a child can learn to enjoy being sick if it is made too attractive. A child may possibly pretend to be ill after he has recovered if he finds it rewarding.

To avoid such problems, resume normal relations with your sick child as soon as possible. Maintain a friendly, matter-of-fact attitude, because a continued atmosphere of overconcern may have a bad effect on his spirits. Avoid bargaining with and kowtowing to your child when he is unreasonable. Have regular times during which he can depend on your company, as well as times when he knows you will be busy elsewhere.

Diet

When a child is sick, she usually is not hungry. Whole milk may upset her stomach. If a youngster has vomited, wait an hour or so to let her stomach settle and then offer her only one or two ounces of fluid at a time. A sick child's appetite is more quickly ruined by pushing and forcing than a well child's. Keep strictly away from urging unless specified by your doctor. When you find out by experience what your child feels like eating, serve it to her casually.

Rest

Before you panic at the thought of "plenty of rest" for a child who will rarely sit still, Dr. Virginia Pomeranz, in *The First Five Years,* reminds parents that rest does not necessarily mean bed rest. "Most common childhood ills do not require bed rest, although a good deal depends on how the child feels. Ask your doctor to spell out what duration and degree of rest are necessary."

Must the child lie quietly or are sit-up activities permitted? How about the living room couch for a change of scene or the lounge on the porch on a hot, stuffy day?

No one is suggesting that rest is not important, but often rest can be made more acceptable to a child who is allowed to be up and about. The sick child needs to be kept quiet and the best place for her is wherever this can best be accomplished.

Activities

Once you have established the degree and duration of activity restriction, you can cope with the situation accordingly. A child who must be confined to bed needs and deserves more parental time than one who can be more active.

There are a variety of things for a child with acute illness or disability to watch. Birds can be attracted to the windowsill with feeders; goldfish also provide visual interest. Swishy streamers, balloons, and paper windmills can be fastened outside the window. Mobiles can be hung from the ceiling. If the child is able to hold a flashlight, he can have fun switching it on and off. Binoculars and magnifying glasses will give new and exciting perspectives on the most ordinary objects.

A child who is less restricted can take part in his usual pastimes. Try to present him with new projects and materials that are fun, but not overly challenging or exhausting. A very special "surprise and comfort bag" of toys and activities he sees only when ill is suggested for a sick child in *What to Do When There Is Nothing to Do* by the Boston Children's Medical Center and Elizabeth Gregg. To make one, fill a shopping bag, old handbag, or plastic tote bag with an interesting assortment of "junk" and basic materials—keys, jewelry, playing cards, small boxes with lids, walnut shells, buttons, small notebook, gummed stickers, holiday stamps, magazines, Sears, Roebuck catalogues, and so on.

VOMITING

Many of us tend to confuse terms associated with vomiting. Here are definitions of these terms as they are used by professionals in the health field:

> vomiting—feeding or stomach contents are returned accompanied by body spasms
>
> projectile vomiting—vomiting so forceful that the stomach contents will fly through the air and land a few feet away
>
> spitting up—same as regurgitation; here the semi-digested curdlike milk just rolls out of the baby's mouth

Now that we have defined the basic terms, let us discuss upchucking and some related conditions as they affect babies during the first year of life.

Spitting up is a common occurrence in the early months of life. It can be due to baby taking feedings too rapidly or in too great an amount. Another explanation is that the sphincter muscle on top of baby's stomach that controls the passage of milk to and from the stomach has not developed fully. Usually regurgitation is not significant and is not related to the baby's health in any way, although it is definitely a nuisance that must be coped with. Regurgitation decreases naturally as the baby grows and generally stops by the ninth month of life.

Pyloric stenosis (narrowing of the diameter of the part of the stomach from which the intestine leads) is characterized by projectile vomiting after feedings. It can be serious, but can be corrected early by surgery. Because of this, projectile vomiting that occurs after more than two or three feedings or that occurs once or twice a day for several days requires your doctor's attention.

Feeding problems can cause vomiting. Overfeeding, not bubbling baby, too large holes in nipples, or a tense and anxious feeding situation can be the culprits. A good rule of thumb to remember is that vomiting related to feeding problems almost always occurs immediately after a feeding. If you think the upchucking may be related to the way you feed your baby, it may be a good idea to ask a more experienced person to show you how she does it.

Specific food allergies, as well as a formula that just does not agree with your baby can also cause vomiting. Your doctor's guidance will be needed to pinpoint the exact cause and remedy the situation.

Vomiting and diarrhea may result from an inflammation of the stomach and intestinal walls caused by a bacterial or viral infection. Fever, chills, and a general progressive weakness may develop also. Dr. Karelitz, in *When Your Child Is Ill,* stresses that the younger the child the more dangerous this condition may be. An infant may become very ill in less than a day. He advises immediate medical attention.

Do a little investigating before you report vomiting to your doctor. You might ask yourself the following questions:

1. Is baby feeding with vigor or have I had to force him to take his milk?

2. Did he take in a good volume of fluid and spit up only the last ounce or did he take in a small amount and spit up most of it?

3. Does he vomit at every feeding or just once or twice a day?

4. How is baby functioning otherwise? Is he alert, moving about? Are his bowel movements typical and the stools of "good" color?

5. Does he look pale, seem lethargic or unusually irritable?

Continued vomiting can lead to dehydration (dryness or loss of fluids from the body) that can be a severe medical problem in babies. If you are unsure, it is better to check with your baby's doctor rather than wait it out.

Treatment of upchucking depends upon the cause, and for all but sporadic minor upsets you will undoubtedly be working right along with your baby's doctor. Regardless of the cause, one of the major principles of treatment is to rest the digestive system. If your child is vomiting stop all feeding; *give nothing by mouth* for an hour or two (or longer, if your child keeps vomiting); then try ice chips, sips of water, or a carbonated beverage (some doctors recommend cola syrup) every ten minutes for an hour or so.

If your child continues to vomit, your doctor may prescribe medicine. If he holds down the sips of water and does not vomit for two or three hours, offer him small amounts (up to a tablespoon) of any of the following liquids: water, clear liquids, cold tea, cold carbonated drinks, clear broth soups, fruit juice, Jell-O (either liquid or congealed). If your child keeps these liquids down, does not throw up for four to six hours, and is hungry, offer him in the first twenty-four hours: more clear liquids (two to four ounces at a time), soda crackers or dry toast, mashed-up ripe banana, strained canned pears or applesauce, cooked oatmeal cereal. In the second twenty-four hours offer: strained stewed chicken (or other lean meat), mashed baked potato, skim milk (if your doctor recommends it). *Do not give aspirin.* It seems to irritate the stomach and may increase your child's chances of upchucking.

177

DEHYDRATION—DIARRHEA

Loose bowel movements are common during the first year of life. It is perfectly normal for infants and small children to have loose stools a few times a day. Keeping this in mind, let us discuss what constitutes diarrhea and what can be done about it when it occurs.

Bowel movements of healthy babies can vary quite a bit and still be considered normal. Babies who are breast fed may have a loose bowel movement after every feeding. Babies taking formula will usually have stools that are semisolid in consistency. In fact, if a baby's movements are always just a little loose, it can be ignored, provided the baby is comfortable, gaining well, and the doctor finds nothing wrong.

Diarrhea in a baby under one year of age exists when she passes liquid, completely unformed, or watery stools. Other signs of diarrhea often seen in a baby's stools include changes in color (frequently to green) and changes in odor. The stools may contain mucus and be more frequent than usual. Sometimes a baby with severe diarrhea will pass as many as twenty to forty stools a day.

Doctors are usually more concerned about changes in the consistency and odor of a baby's stools than changes in the number and color of movements. Diarrhea in babies may also be accompanied by fever and vomiting.

With mild diarrhea the stool changes are not that great and can be caused by a formula or food intolerance or allergy, teething, treatment with antibiotics, or by a mild bacterial or viral infection. Severe diarrhea is almost always due to an infection, either bacterial or viral.

If a breast-fed baby develops diarrhea, the first thing to do is to check your diet and eliminate laxatives, fruits, or other foods that might be causing the diarrhea. Generally, this will clear up the problem.

Diarrhea related to teething is generally not treated specifically. It will usually be mild and stop as soon as the teething episode is over.

Treating a baby with antibiotics for several days may result in diarrhea. If this happens, you can easily remedy the situation by giving either plain or flavored yogurt. Let the baby have as much as she wants two or three times a day.

Diarrhea due to formula or food intolerance or allergy is treated by eliminating the offending substance. This is not always as easy as it sounds. Patience and persistence are often needed until the offending substance is identified.

Some authorities suggest changing baby's diet in an attempt to alleviate the diarrhea before calling the doctor. They advocate such things as adding more water to the formula, giving water-salt-sugar solution, giving apple juice, stopping all milk.

PCI Point of View

PCI does not agree with this advice. The objection is that time is needed to institute and evaluate these measures. If you try one suggestion and it does not work, no progress has been made in treating the diarrhea and time has been lost. Dr. Spock says that "even for a mild diarrhea you ought to get in touch with the doctor promptly because the sooner treatment is started, the lighter the disease will be and the quicker over."

Diarrhea due to infection is generally treated by a combination of medication and dietary restrictions. Of course, how diarrhea is treated depends on both cause and severity. One general principle is to rest the baby's digestive system.

One word of advice. You may sometimes find the treatment of diarrhea hard to accept. For example, if your baby is crying for his bottle, it is hard to follow your doctor's orders only to moisten his lips with a wet cloth. Remember that your baby cannot judge what is best *in this situation*. The best thing you can do for your baby is to follow your doctor's orders exactly. Better an unhappy baby than a seriously sick one.

Dehydration

Dehydration occurs when fluid output exceeds fluid intake. In mild form, it is a common complication of vomiting and diarrhea. Signs of dehydration include infrequent urination, urine darker than usual, generalized weakness, listlessness, an increased desire to sleep, and skin that feels dry to the touch.

Essentially dehydration is corrected by treating the vomiting and/or diarrhea that caused it. The most important aspect of prevention is to *replace the fluids lost*. If the baby will not take sufficient fluids orally or vomits whatever he takes in, it may be necessary to hospitalize him so he can be treated with intravenous fluids (fluids injected into a vein).

Dehydration can be very serious in babies. Its alleviation depends upon how promptly vomiting and diarrhea are treated and controlled. This is why it is necessary to obtain *prompt* treatment for these conditions.

CONSTIPATION

Constipation refers to the character of the stool rather than the frequency of the bowel movement. Remember that the frequency of movements is an individual matter. When a baby is constipated, the stools will be hard, dry, and either smaller or larger than usual. Passing them will be uncomfortable or even painful.

Sometimes you may see a streak of bright red blood on a constipated stool. This is nothing to worry about. All it means is that a tiny blood vessel near the anus broke from straining while the baby was having a bowel movement. You can take care of this problem by relieving the constipation. Darker blood mixed in with the stool is a sign of difficulty in the digestive system and should be reported to your doctor.

In rare cases, constipation may be accompanied by vomiting, a marked abdominal distension, failure to gain weight, or general listlessness or weakness. When these signs occur, remember that the constipation is merely a part of a total picture and seek your doctor's advice.

Constipation seems to be pretty much of an "occupational hazard" during the first year of life. Most babies do become constipated at one time or another and appear to be especially susceptible when making the transition from breast milk to cow's milk and when an illness is developing.

It is advisable to keep your baby's stools soft by adding whatever is necessary to her diet. This is to prevent her from feeling pain while passing a hard stool. Babies who have painful bowel movements will hold back their movements to avoid pain, thus setting up a circular pattern of holding back, increased constipation, and more pain. Constipation should be treated before this cycle becomes established.

Constipation in babies is usually treated by changing the diet. If your baby has not started taking solids yet, you can change the formula to one made with a more laxative sugar, such as dark corn syrup or brown sugar, or you can add malt soup extract to her bottles. Malt soup extract is a natural preparation and can be used for a baby of any age. If your baby is taking solids, you can give raw fruits, vegetables, and whole-grain cereals and breads. For a constipated baby of any age, it is always a good idea to increase the fluid intake.

Mothers tend to panic the first time their baby gets constipated, because no mother likes to see her baby uncomfortable or in pain. However, after you have handled one episode of constipation successfully, you will become a "pro" at this, and find that you can set up a routine of extra fruit, malt powder, or whatever else works for your baby, and use these measures when indicated to prevent constipation.

In the past well-meaning parents gave laxatives to "correct" patterns of elimination that were perfectly normal. Some children normally have two to three movements a day; for others, every five to seven days is normal.

Only in severe and stubborn cases of constipation, and then *only* when advised by your baby's doctor, should you use laxatives, suppositories, or enemas. Although these measures work, they are harsh, traumatic, and also uncomfortable for your baby. It is much better to use dietary measures if at all possible.

THE COMMON COLD

The most frequent cause of illness among children, as well as adults, is the common cold. Some physicians use the term URI (upper respiratory infection). Most children have from two to six colds a year. A cold is always caused by a virus and thus far 113 distinct viruses have been found that cause colds. Contrary to popular belief, infants have no resistance to colds.

A cold produces swelling of the mucus membrane of the upper respiratory tract. This swelling is accompanied by an increased outpouring of mucus. Forward secretions from the nose are obvious; backward secretions run down the throat and irritate, frequently producing a cough. Sometimes swallowing too much mucus causes vomiting.

Swollen nasal passages make breathing difficult and may close tear ducts, causing watery, runny eyes. If your baby's nose is obstructed with thick mucus, he will have to breathe through his mouth. Unfortunately, babies seem unable to do this. They become irritable, have difficulty nursing, and are unable to sleep.

Common cold fevers in children are usually low-grade (100°– 102° F.), but may be higher in infants and toddlers.

Treating a Cold

Since a cold is a viral infection, it will not respond to antibiotics. The treatment is symptomatic, aimed at relieving the sneezing, nasal discharge and congestion, cough and fever.

181

It is important to keep your baby's nasal passages clear since he cannot breath through his mouth. You do this with a one-ounce infant syringe and/or nose drops. In using the syringe, compress the bulb and fit the syringe tightly to your baby's nostril. As you release the bulb, the suction pulls the mucus from the nose. Your baby will not like this and will fuss, but it can be done safely to the tiniest of infants and will provide immediate relief.

While some physicians do not recommend nose drops, many do. Neo-Synephrine ¼% (0.25 per cent) is most frequently mentioned. It can be purchased without a prescription and may be used for children *older* than three months. If your baby is three to twelve months old, the dose is one to two drops three to four times daily. Children over one year can take two to three drops in each nostril three to four times daily. Nose drops should *not* be used more than three consecutive days.

A third way of clearing the nasal passages is using an antihistamine. Many of these can be purchased without a prescription. Triaminic Syrup and Novahistine Elixir are two frequently recommended. For babies under six months of age, the dosage is an eighth of a teaspoon four times a day. From six months to twelve months, give half a teaspoon four times a day. Antihistamines sometimes cause drowsiness. Frequently after prolonged use your child may develop a resistance to a particular antihistamine. Trying another brand will prove satisfactory.

A certain amount of coughing with a cold is desirable. It is a reflex that clears the respiratory tract of mucus. In most cases, it is not necessary to give your child cough medicine. The most effective treatment for coughs is vapor therapy. Cool vapor is preferred to hot and it is agreed that adding medication to the water is absolutely unnecessary. For concentrated vapor, steam from the shower is ideal. Close the shower curtain and turn on the hot water. Take your baby's clothes off, sit her on the toilet, and allow the hot water to run about ten minutes. *Do not* put the baby into the shower. Then stay an additional ten minutes to cool her off. A simple home remedy cough medicine is equal parts of honey, lemon juice, and whiskey mixed together. One half to one teaspoon, depending on the size of your child, is a good dosage.

Aspirin can be used if your child has a fever or is fussy and irritable. (Refer to the section in this chapter on *Equipping the Medicine Cabinet* for instructions on how to administer aspirin.)

If your baby does not seem to want milk, substitute sugar and water, vitaminized baby juices, diluted sweetened orange juice, or ginger ale. Milk produces more mucus and you may find she needs the sweetened drinks for a day or two before tolerating feedings.

Prevention

The theory that large amounts of vitamin C will prevent or cure the common cold is not believed by most physicians. There is no satisfactory prevention for colds. The immunity that a child develops afterward lasts for no more than a month.

A cool room does not give a baby a cold if he is warmly dressed. A baby who is kept too warm frequently develops more infections. While you need not prevent visitors with colds from coming into the house, it is a good idea to keep them away from your baby. Colds are caught from people with colds.

If you should catch a cold, it is wise to wash your hands well with soap after blowing your nose and often betweentimes as well. There is some research that shows that some viruses are passed on to others through hand contact. Wearing a mask will not help as the cold virus is so very tiny that it will filter through.

Complications

Complications due to secondary bacterial infection are common. The cold virus lowers your body's resistance to bacterial infections, causing swollen glands, bronchitis, pneumonia, sinusitis, and ear infections. If your baby's fever suddenly rises, or his cough gets worse, or he seems suddenly fussier when his cold symptoms are just about over, you should suspect a secondary infection and consult your physician. The eustachian canals running from the throat to the middle ear are shorter and straighter in a baby, so he is more likely than older children to develop an ear infection with a cold.

Colds in older children generally last several days to a week. In babies and toddlers, a cold may not dry up for two weeks and should not cause worry if it does not seem to be getting worse. However, a cold that is chronic or constant is probably not a common cold, but an allergy.

ALLERGY

An allergy is an individual's response to foreign substances (medically called allergens) that gain access to the body. Allergy always includes a definite immunological reaction. An allergic or "sensitive" person reacts to substances that are ordinarily harmless to others.

Allergens enter the body in a number of ways:

1. Foods or medicines taken by mouth.
2. Inhaled through the nose (pollen, dust, molds).
3. Through the skin by contact (cosmetics, wool, poison ivy, insect venom). Allergies can also be reactions to extremes of heat and cold.
4. By injection (penicillin).

There are a wide range of reactions to these substances; included are skin rash, eczema, hives, hay fever, asthma, sneezing, runny or stuffy nose, tearful eyes, "sinus trouble," and digestive disturbances. In 1971, the Department of Health, Education, and Welfare estimated that there were over 30 million allergic conditions in the United States, of which approximately 4 million were in children.

Allergies vary with age groups. Allergic infants are usually allergic to what they eat, toddlers to what infects them, and older children to what they inhale.

A Family Tendency

How can you tell if your baby will be allergic? Look at your family history, because the tendency to allergy is usually hereditary. If one parent has a major allergy (hay fever, asthma), the child may or may not be allergic. The chances of his being allergic are one in four. If both parents are allergic, chances are that most of their children will be, and their allergies will develop at an earlier age. Even if the family history is positive, it does not necessarily follow that allergies will develop. Adopt a wait-and-see attitude.

Here are a number of suggestions for dealing with the problem of allergy in babies. Make a special effort to breast feed the baby since allergy to breast milk is all but unknown. Watch for small signs of allergy that can develop in an infant—eczema (in irritated patches that occur on the cheeks rather than in the creases of the elbows and knees as in older children) and mild to moderate intestinal upsets.

Introduce new foods one at a time so that you will be able to pinpoint the offender. Be on the lookout for chronic stuffy nose and chest congestion in an infant who is not around people with colds.

Once it is established or strongly suspected that your infant is allergic, put him on a diet free from *wheat, cow's milk,* and *eggs* since these are the most likely troublemakers.

There are several good pamphlets available to assist parents in caring for allergic babies. Write to: Ross Laboratories, 625 Cleveland Ave., Columbus, Ohio 43215, and for the U. S. Department of Agriculture Bul-

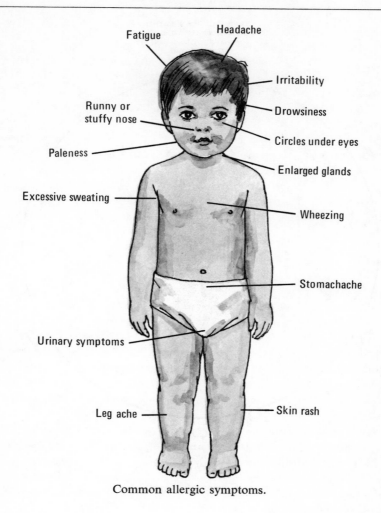

Common allergic symptoms.

letin No. 147, to the U. S. Government Printing Office, Washington, D.C. 20402.

If you have an allergic infant, it is wise to look ahead and make plans for controlling the environment in which he lives. There are four major aspects of the environment that may have to be controlled: (1) humidity, (2) cleanliness, (3) exposure to wool, and (4) contact with pets.

An allergic child should live in an atomsphere with year-round humidification. This can be provided by a humidifier attached to a hot air

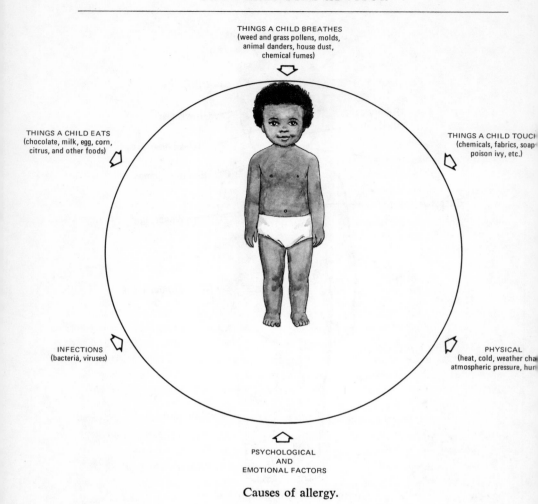

THINGS A CHILD BREATHES
(weed and grass pollens, molds,
animal danders, house dust,
chemical fumes)

THINGS A CHILD EATS
(chocolate, milk, egg, corn,
citrus, and other foods)

THINGS A CHILD TOUCH
(chemicals, fabrics, soap
poison ivy, etc.)

INFECTIONS
(bacteria, viruses)

PHYSICAL
(heat, cold, weather cha
atmospheric pressure, hur

PSYCHOLOGICAL
AND
EMOTIONAL FACTORS

Causes of allergy.

furnace or by a portable humidifier. Vaporizers should be used during any respiratory illness. To keep the air dust free, clean with a vacuum rather than a broom or carpet sweeper. Change the filters in a hot air furnace or air conditioner often.

A useful device is the electronic precipitator; installed in a hot air furnace, it takes the place of mechanical filters. If the house does not have circulating hot air heat, a portable precipitator can be rented or bought and installed in the child's room.

186

Avoid dust collectors in your child's room—venetian blinds, shag rugs or carpets, fuzzy stuffed animals, bookshelves, etc.

Keep your child away from contact with wool; substitute synthetic fibers in clothing, floor coverings, and so forth.

If you have any suspicion that your child is allergic, do not get a cat or a dog. If you do, you may find yourself facing a difficult set of alternatives—keep your child and his pet separated or get rid of the pet. Cats are the worst offenders. There are *no* non-allergenic cats. Long-haired dogs cause almost as much allergy as cats.

A certain amount of allergy can be tolerated without treatment, e.g., dry skin and occasional stuffy nose. Other symptoms frequently can be managed by avoiding the stimulus and by controlling the environment. A child should only go through allergy testing and desensitizing injections if his symptoms and the restrictions they impose on his life are worse than the treatment.

Food Intolerance

Many pediatricians have recognized that food intolerance can cause symptoms that mimic many other medical conditions. They call this the *allergic tension-fatigue syndrome.* The symptoms can include fatigue, irritability and other nervous system symptoms, pale color, circles under the eyes, stuffy nose, headache, stomachache, leg ache, bed-wetting or other urinary symptoms, bowel disorders, or even behavior and learning problems.

The foods most commonly responsible for these symptoms are milk, chocolate, corn, citrus fruits, and eggs. However, any food may be involved, as may pollens, chemical fumes, and other allergens.

If a medical examination does not come up with any other cause for a child's symptoms, the allergic tension-fatigue syndrome should be considered.

What Are Some Allergic Diseases?

Hay Fever: the most common allergy in the United States, its victims suffer from varying degrees of cold symptoms—sneezing, congestion of the eyes, itching ears, and wheezing. The most common form is seasonal, occurring in the spring, summer, and fall.

Asthma: the most serious allergic disease, its symptoms include difficult breathing, coughing, and wheezing. Some youngsters may outgrow the condition by adolescence, but untreated asthma usually gets worse.

187

There is still much to be discovered about allergic diseases. The Allergy Foundation of America is a voluntary health agency whose ultimate goal is to wipe out these sicknesses and whose immediate goal is to prevent their occurrence and ensure that victims receive the best possible medical care and treatment. For information and pamphlets on specific allergic diseases write to the Allergy Foundation of America, 801 Second Ave., New York, N.Y. 10017.

COMMUNICABLE CHILDHOOD DISEASES

Communicable diseases spread from one person to another and contracting some of them is usually inevitable. Some common childhood diseases are chicken pox, scarlet fever, mumps, measles (rubeola), German measles (rubella), diphtheria, whooping cough, and polio (poliomyelitis). Chicken pox and scarlet fever are actually the two we need to be most concerned about, because there are vaccines for the others. However, if your baby's inoculations are kept up to date, it is unlikely that you need worry about the communicable childhood diseases.

In the following discussion, the "incubation period" refers to that period between the acquisition of the infecting agent of the disease and the development of the symptoms of that infection.

Chicken Pox

The most common cause of sudden spots is chicken pox, a virus infection. Some children may be out of sorts and run a low-grade fever *before its onset,* which usually goes unnoticed. This disease is so highly contagious that your child can contact it by passing someone in the supermarket who has it.

What is not commonly known is that children can pick up chicken pox from adults with shingles. The reverse is also true; elderly people in particular can pick up shingles from children with chicken pox. The reason for this is that both conditions are caused by the same virus. Children rarely get shingles. So warn the grandparents!

The incubation period for chicken pox is usually eleven to twenty-one days after exposure. The rash appears as small red bumps or pimples mostly on the trunk, back, and face. The base of the pimple and surrounding skin are reddened. Little water blisters then appear on the bumps and later these become scabs. Several crops of bumps continue to appear for two to five days. The pox may involve the mouth and throat, resulting in complaints of a sore throat. They may also appear in the vagina in girls. A fever usually accompanies the rash. Some children never feel sick and

188

never have a temperature above 101°. Others feel quite sick and have high fever. Itching is a prominent symptom.

What to do for chicken pox. See your doctor to confirm the diagnosis. Some pediatricians recommend that you keep your child in bed; others see no reason to do this if she wants to be up. A bath once or twice a day with an antiseptic soap will prevent infection and the addition of cornstarch (enough to make it cloudy) or bicarbonate of soda (one to two cupsful) may reduce the itching. Most physicians recommend a cool rather than a hot bath because the former helps reduce fever and hot water intensifies itching. *Do not rub off the scabs.* Calamine lotion should be applied and if itching is intense, aspirin or an antihistamine may be helpful. Cut your child's nails short to prevent scratching. Antibiotics are of no value, because chicken pox is a viral infection.

Your child is contagious from *one day before* the onset of the rash until all the pox have scabbed and are dry, usually five to seven days after the first pox appears. Then she can go out even though the crusts will last for about two weeks. People are not carriers of chicken pox, so you or your other children can go out. It is all right to have baby-sitters if they have had chicken pox. One attack usually builds up lifetime immunity. It is rarely contracted twice.

To date, there is no vaccine available by which children can be made immune to chicken pox. Yet it appears likely that within a very few years this will no longer be true—as researchers finalize their present evaluations of a vaccine. The best protection available presently is ZIG (Zoster Immune Globulin) which is not all that effective and is only recommended for pregnant women in early months of pregnancy and other high-risk groups.

Scarlet Fever

Scarlet fever is a streptococcal sore throat accompanied by a rash. There is no medical justification for being more upset by scarlet fever than by a strep throat. Years ago, before it was known to be a form of strep, it was dreaded and the child was quarantined for weeks. Because so many of today's parents and grandparents remember the panic of scarlet fever, many physicians refer to it as scarletina or strep rash. It most frequently affects children between two and eight years of age.

Scarlet fever is not very contagious. When it does develop it is usually within a week after exposure to it or to strep throat. Communicability starts with the first symptoms and lasts until the strepococci are gone. Unfortunately a child can have scarlet fever more than once.

189

WHEN VACCINATIONS ARE AVAILABLE

Although preventive vaccines are available for the following childhood diseases, there are still parents who neglect to have their babies inoculated and so these diseases continue to appear. For example, in the United States in the first 9 months of 1973, there were 118 cases of diphtheria, 54,810 cases of mumps, 25,845 cases of German measles, and 23,951 cases of measles.

Mumps

The mumps virus has been isolated and a vaccine is available. Some physicians vaccinate all children; some only boys; others, boys nearing puberty.

Mumps is a viral infection involving the salivary glands found at the angle of the jaw and the floor of the mouth. It usually starts with swelling just behind the earlobe and extending down over the jawbone. One side swells first and one, two, or more days later the other side may become affected. Fever, headaches, and abdominal pain are common.

Because it is viral, antibiotics are not given. While there is no specific treatment, aspirin for relief of pain or fever can be helpful. Wet compresses, cold or warm, relieve the discomfort of swelling. Liquid foods are easier since swallowing may be difficult. Frequently citrus juices and spices are aggravating and should be avoided.

Mumps is most common between ages five and fifteen. It is spread through direct contact. A child is mildly contagious a few days before the swelling until the swelling disappears, usually in a week to ten days. The incubation period is fourteen to twenty-four days. Most physicians agree that a child can have mumps only once.

Complications are uncommon in children. However, in men and boys who have reached puberty, mumps can spread to the testicles. While this very rarely causes sterility, it can, and that is why most physicians recommend the vaccine for boys. According to Dr. Falkner, "Because the vaccine is available combined with measles and German measles vaccines, it can be considered at twelve months of age. Otherwise its use alone is mainly to protect susceptible children approaching puberty, adolescents, and particularly males with no evidence of having had mumps." Many physicians suggest that adult men who did not have mumps in childhood also be given mumps vaccine. In adult females, the ovaries can be affected, causing pain and some tissue damage.

190

Measles (Rubeola)

The measles virus has been isolated and a preventative vaccine is available. It is now routine for babies to be immunized against measles at about one year of age.

Early stages of measles are like those of a bad cold: sneezing, coughing, red and watery eyes, and fever. Three or four days later the rash appears, usually starting behind the ears along the hairline. At first there are distinct dark red spots. These spread downward over the body and run together, giving the skin a blotchy appearance. A doglike barking cough is very common.

While measles is a viral infection and not affected by antibiotics, a doctor should examine your child for complications. These complications may be ear infections, bronchitis, or pneumonia that *are* treated with antibiotics. While measles does not damage the eyes, frequently the room should be darkened because bright light is irritating to congested eyes.

The incubation period is ten to twelve days. Measles is communicable four days *before* the rash appears to five days *after* the rash is present. Second attacks of measles are practically unknown.

German Measles (Rubella)

The only thing measles and German measles have in common is the name. *They are different viruses.* In rubella there are no cold symptoms and not always fever. Usually the first symptom is the rash that starts as pink or red spots on the face and then covers the body within the day. The second day they may run together and fade so the body looks flushed. This is sometimes confused with scarlet fever or measles.

Occasionally, swollen and tender glands appear behind the ears and at the back of the neck. The rash is gone by the third or fourth day, thus it is frequently called the three-day measles. The swollen glands may remain a while longer. Your child need not be kept in bed.

German measles develops twelve to twenty-one days after exposure and the period of greatest contagion is a few days before the rash appears. It is rarely more than a mild disease and treatment is unnecessary. Second attacks are rare. There are no complications.

Unfortunately, a pregnant woman who catches German measles in her first trimester may give birth to a baby with serious congenital defects. There is now a vaccine to prevent German measles. It should be given to all children, to all non-pregnant women of childbearing age, and to all fe-

191

males who cannot and will not become pregnant for three months after inoculation. This is advised since it is not known at this time whether a fetus might become infected following inoculation of the mother.

Diphtheria

Diphtheria is rare today because of immunization, but when epidemics are threatening, it is frightening to find out just how many susceptible children have *not* been immunized. For the first three months, your baby is protected by antibodies received from your blood.

Diphtheria is a serious bacterial disease requiring hospitalization and large doses of antibiotic. Early symptoms are sore throat and fever. White or gray patches appear on the throat and tonsils. Sometimes this disease begins in the larynx, causing hoarseness, coughing, and difficult breathing.

The disease develops within a week after exposure. Its period of communicability lasts until negative nose and throat cultures are obtained, sometimes up to four weeks. Not only is the patient contagious, but persons and articles he has been in contact with are carriers.

Complications can involve heart damage and nephritis. Nerve involvement may cause paralysis of the back of the throat, deviation of the eye, dilation of the pupil, or drooping eyelids. Nerve paralysis is usually temporary.

Your baby is immunized when he is given his DPT inoculations.

Whooping Cough

Whooping cough refers to a characteristic sound, accompanying the deep intake of air following a series of coughs. The early symptoms are similar to those of a bad cold. Anywhere from a few days to two weeks later, the characteristic whoop begins. The child begins to cough eight to ten times on one breath, gets red in the face, may turn blue, and frequently throws up. The cough ends in a whoop, the crowing noise he makes trying to get his breath back.

Whooping cough lasts weeks and weeks. It can be especially serious in babies under two, where complications are exhaustion and pneumonia. Since an infant's larynx is not fully developed, the whoop is rarely heard. It is a bacterial infection spread by contact and is contagious during the cold period and first three weeks of the whoop.

Whooping cough can be avoided through vaccination. The *P* in your baby's DPT inoculation is pertussis, or whooping cough.

Poliomyelitis

Poliomyelitis, a viral disease causing inflammation of the nerve cells leading down the spinal cord, has been almost eradicated wherever polio vaccine is systematically used. Every child should be immunized in early infancy. Formerly it was the major cause of crippling and there are many adults limping because of its damage. In some persons the nerve cells were not severely damaged and paralysis was temporary. In others, nerve cells were completely destroyed and paralysis was permanent. Frequently, breathing muscles were severely damaged and polio victims died or spent years in an iron lung.

Infantile paralysis starts with fever, headache, and a general sick feeling, followed by a stiff neck and arm and leg pains. Muscle spasms occur later. It is communicable *prior* to the first symptoms and through the first week of acute illness. All ages are susceptible. It is contagious and can be transmitted through droplet infection, contaminated food, and by contamination from the feces. Prior to the use of polio vaccine, it would reach epidemic proportions during the summer and autumn months.

6

Sensory and Social Powers

INTRODUCTION BY ASHLEY MONTAGU, PH.D.*

The senses are our means of perceiving the world. The kind of world we perceive and the kind of world we make are largely dependent upon the manner in which our senses have been trained to see the world. The parents' clear understanding of how they can train their children to use their senses is obviously important. It is toward helping parents to help their children achieve these ends that the present chapter is dedicated.

The newborn infant arrives in the world with all his senses marked "Go." He is ready to take on everything the world has to offer him through the agency of his senses. Contrary to the conventional wisdom in these matters the newborn has a highly developed visual system of which he is able to make good use virtually from the moment he is born.

The baby scans her mother's face, her expression; in turn, the mother conveys the most significant messages to her infant. But perhaps even more important are the messages conveyed through the sense of touch—the sense that has from earliest times been described as "the mother of the senses." We can appreciate the difference that adequate or inadequate early tactile experience has made in tactile behavior in later life.

* Anthropologist, scientist, teacher, and writer, Ashley Montagu has integrated the diverse thinking that is appearing on the sensory and social powers of infants and preschoolers. Born in England, he secured his Ph.D. at Columbia University and has done research at New York and Harvard Universities. He was chairman of Anthropology at Rutgers University and has written, among many other books, *Life Before Birth, Touching, The Reproductive Development of the Female, Human Heredity,* and *Racial Awareness.*

Editor's Note: Dr. Montagu is very controversial in his attitude toward the role of working mothers and fathers during the first years of life of a child. PCI believes that in the future we are going to have to work out life-styles that take into account the needs of babies and their parents.

It has been said that adults are deteriorated children. That statement defines a very real and disturbing truth, namely, that in the Western world, as the individual grows he tends to become progressively desensitized. His senses and sensitivities tend to become blunted. Aware of this, prepared parents will provide their children with all those sources of stimulation (without overstimulation) for the growth and development of their senses. It is through this process that children will become personalities with minds and sensibilities of their own.

We have learned a great deal about the requirements and behavior of the human infant from the study of other animals, particularly the class of animals to which we belong, the mammals. Indeed, some of our most significant insights have come from this source. Hence the attention to animal research in these pages.

Throughout, the reader will be impressed with the fundamental role the mother has to play in the growth and development of her offspring—the importance of which was long ago recognized in the saying "Since God could not be everywhere he created mothers." With all due respect to some who think otherwise, the evidence reads quite clearly to me that a day-care center can never be a substitute for a good mother, any more than a bottle can be for the mother's breast.

The basic family unit is mother and child and the making of humanity through the child is in the power of the mother. The father is, of course, a parent, too. But his role can never be as fundamentally important as that of the mother in relation to the child during the first few years of its life. This does not mean that the father's role is unimportant. It is very important and should never be underestimated. Nor should the father's role ever be conceived to be merely ancillary or subordinate to that of the mother. It is different and important. During the birth of the child he should be present giving his wife all the support, love, and encouragement she needs. Following that role is not merely complimentary, but uniquely contributory to the growth and development of both his wife and his children.

Boys usually have a harder time with their gender roles than girls. In most societies girls grow and develop with their mothers as the model with whom to identify themselves. Boys also begin and maintain for the first few years of their lives this identification with their mothers, but sometime along the course of their development they have to give up this identification with the maternal loved one and switch to the role of the male. Sometimes, depending upon circumstances, some of them don't make it, especially where the image of one or the other parent is weak or inadequate. Overt anti-feminism, if not homosexuality, may be one result of such experience in the male.

In the Western world, and especially in the English-speaking part of it, we still suffer from Victorian hangups in all matters relating to sex and sex education. Happily, in recent years we have freed ourselves from many of these unfortunate and damaging taboos. Healthy sexual development is a function of healthy personality development. By healthy personality development, I mean the ability to love, to work, and to play.

Socialization directed toward the making of a healthy personality would include the development of personal qualities first and education in the understanding of sexual behavior and sexual relationships second. Personality development as a considerate, sensitive being is primary and, indeed, essential to sexual understanding. Otherwise "sex education" becomes mere instruction or information. Too much, alas, for too long has passed for education that has been nothing more than instruction. Instruction is training in techniques and skills principally of the three R's. Education is training in the techniques and skills of being a responsive, loving, humane being. There is a world of difference between instruction and education and yet instruction is what mainly goes on in our educational institutions at all levels.

Hence the importance of what goes on in the socialization of the child in the home and the great value of a volume such as this, which can be of such substantive help to parents, their children, and the world in which they and their descendants—we may hope—will live.

The quality of parenting is measured by the success with which the inner needs of the child are met. The worth of a civilization, Thoreau pointed out, over a hundred years ago, is measured by the same test —applied to the needs of men. Parents are the unacknowledged legislators of the world. I am, therefore, inclined to say to the reader, "Act well your part, for there lies the fate and the future of humanity."

VISION IN THE NEWBORN

Brandon Sparkman and Ann Carmichael, in *Blueprint for a Brighter Child,* write that "the senses are the doors to your baby's mind. All the information he receives will come through the doors of the five senses: seeing, hearing, tasting, touching, and smelling."

Every baby needs many things to see, hear, touch, taste, and smell, and early stimulation of his senses will make him actively aware of his world. His reaction to each new stimulus will help him discern more, permitting him to make sharper distinctions between the specific elements in his ever expanding world. Early stimulation of the senses will set a learning pattern that will be decisive to the baby's ongoing learning experience.

Remember that all the senses work together to reinforce each other and one learns to experience the world through this process.

What Can Newborns See?

Although much still remains unknown about the visual world of the newborn, we have come a long way in a very short time. It was not so very long ago that journals were advising us to ignore baby's vision since he could not "see" until about six months of age. The fact is that important visual powers are functioning in the newborn, powers that become tools for communication and stimulation.

1. *Visual patterning.* The research of Dr. Robert Fantz of Western Reserve University reveals that from birth human infants do see and have certain preferences and that visual patterning is more stimulating to them than is color and brightness. By the age of three months, complex and novel patterns are preferred. For example, in one test situation, the infant lies in a crib in a chamber and stimuli of varying complexity are hung from the ceiling. An observer watches the infant's eyes through a peephole in the ceiling and records how long the infant gazes at an object. The in-

200

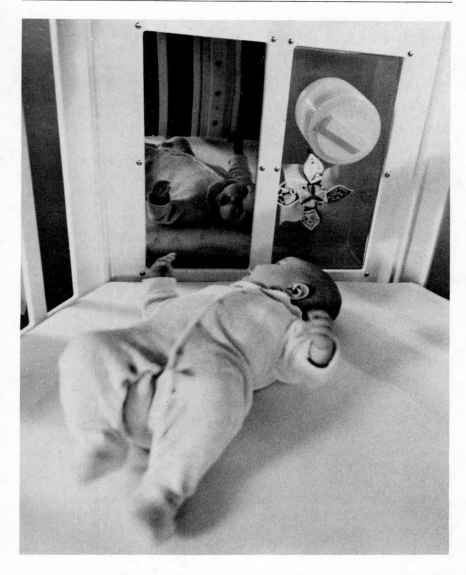

fant gazes significantly longer at a checkerboard or bull's-eye pattern than at a black square, circle, or triangle. Infants from four days to six months old look longest at a real face, somewhat less at a scrambled face, and typically ignore a black patch.

201

2. *Response to bright light.* The newborn responds to a bright light shining in her eyes by tightly shutting her lids. She reacts to moving objects, such as a red or soft yellow object dangling in front of her, by looking intently. She will follow an object with her eyes, and turn her head when the object is moved slowly from one side to another, and even follow it up and down.

3. *Visual accommodation.* In a research effort that spanned the period 1960–66, Dr. Burton L. White, Director of Harvard University's Preschool Project, and some colleagues systematically traced the evolution of visual acuity from birth on, looking for clues as to how the environment affects the process. Visual accommodation is an activity by which the image of a target is focused on the retina of the eye. According to their findings, as set forth in an article entitled "Visual Accommodation in Human Infants," written by Harold Haynes, Burton L. White, and Richard Held, that appeared in *Science* (the magazine of the American Association for the Advancement of Science), 148, 528–30, April 23, 1965, infants under one month of age cannot adjust to changing distances; their immature system is locked at about seven and a half inches. However, by the "ripe" age of four months, adult accommodation has developed.

4. *Visual attention.* During the first four months of life, the infant's *tendency to explore* her visual surroundings parallels an increasing expansion of her visible milieu. Simply stated, as the baby gets older and develops greater mobility and co-ordination skills, her visual environment also extends, offering her fresh and stimulating visual opportunities.

5. *Form perception and early reading.* A research digest, published in 1970, "Modes of Biological Adaptation and Their Role in Intellectual Development" by Dr. W. Ragan Callaway, Jr., discusses this subject in detail.

Infants do respond to patterned visual input, even like and are motivated by it. If this attribute is developed systematically from birth until four months, there is every reason to expect that the teaching of reading may begin much earlier. The traditional notion in public education is that at the mental age of 6.6, somewhere in the middle of first grade, children are ready to deal successfully with the form perception tasks required by beginning reading.

Recent research has babies of three months discriminating, remembering, and motivated to look at complex patterns. Perhaps the number 6.6 is not magical and reading might successfully be started earlier.

Another way of looking at this concept is to ask, "Why is it that some children are not successful readers at the mental age of 6.6?" Could it be that they have not received appropriate environmental stimuli in the way of patterned visual input during the period from birth to four months? Perhaps the seeds of success or failure in the complex task of reading are sown in the crib!

PCI Point of View

The days of putting baby aside in a neutral, bland room or cubicle are gone forever. Principles of growth and development dictate that emerging abilities should and want to be practiced. Since newborns are unable to tell us directly what they want, it is up to the parents to assess abilities and provide appropriate stimuli.

The world of the infant should include many moving objects, as well as objects of changing light intensity, graphic arts (bull's-eye strobes), and things that are patterned. (See Chapter 10, "Play and Playthings," for specific suggestions on stimulation.)

HEARING IN THE NEWBORN

Hearing Matures at Birth

Not only do newborns hear at birth, they are known to hear while they are in utero and to respond differently to varying kinds of sounds. Many mothers-to-be report that their unborn infants jerk suddenly at a loud noise. Some expectant mothers report the need to stop typing because every time the carriage returns, the fetus jumps, and this becomes very uncomfortable. Often mothers attending a concert feel the baby moving more than usual.

Research is proving these very early responses to sound. Thus it may never be too early to expose your baby to music and pleasant sounds in his environment. Avoid loud rock music or too many people in your infant's room. These will shut out his ability to discriminate one sound from another. Distinguishing sounds is an important learning. If the room is constantly full of sounds that cannot be differentiated, a baby gives up listening and differentiating.

The startled response of a newborn infant to a loud sound is called the *Moro reflex*. This can be demonstrated when a door slams shut, a radio is turned up, or if a book drops. Your baby will display this reflex by contracting the muscles of his arms, legs, and neck. Sometimes an eye blink occurs simultaneously with the muscular activity that characterizes the Moro reflex.

If your baby does not respond to a loud sound, it does not necessarily indicate a hearing impairment. Many babies are born with fluid in their ears that produces a temporary "deafness," but this condition usually clears up in a short time.

There has been a great deal of research on the hearing ability of newborns. One of these studies, by A. I. Bronshtein and E. P. Petrova, tried to correct the misconception that noise had no physiological effect on newborns. They found that newborn infants from twenty-seven to seventy-seven hours old definitely react to sound stimuli. These infants were also measured as to the effect musical tones had upon their sucking activity. It was found that these tones had a clear-cut effect upon them.

Try this with your infant while she is nursing or sucking a pacifier. Introduce a new sound, such as a radio or a rattle, while she is sucking. The sucking will probably be inhibited at first. After a while the sound will become familiar and cease being a stimulator or inhibitor of her sucking. From this information you can see that it is not necessary to keep a quiet house for your baby since she will become accustomed to the normal sounds around her.

At two months of age a baby can recognize her mother's voice. If she is fussing and upset, others may try comforting her, but nothing seems to be as effective as her mother's voice and handling. This is also the age when a baby is beginning to locate sound.

Frank Caplan, editor of *The First Twelve Months of Life,* describes a research experiment conducted on three eight-week-old infants at Radcliffe College. The purpose of the research was to see if these infants understood that a person's voice comes from where the person is located. The researchers used two stereo speakers that separated the sounds of a voice from its source. The babies were seated before a glass partition separating them from their mothers just two feet away. As long as the speakers were balanced so that the mother's voice seemed to come directly from her, the infants remained content. When the phase relationship between the speakers made the voice appear to come from a different spot, the babies cried, looked around, became agitated, and clearly indicated by their frustration that their expectations were being countered.

Perception happens only when there are things to see. You have to provide the stimuli for your baby. Since the sense of hearing is one of the most important senses in acquiring information and for future learning, it is important that you stimulate your baby very early in this area. (See Chapter 10, "Play and Playthings," for specific suggestions on stimulation.)

TOUCH AND SKIN STIMULATION

One of the most important sensory powers that an infant experiences and practices is the sense of touch. Through this sense, we feel, love, and hate; it gives us knowledge of depth, thickness, texture, and shape. Helen Keller, who became blind and deaf in infancy could still continue to learn and communicate through touch and skin stimulation. It is our first medium of communication. Dr. Montagu believes that the skin as an organ of communication is the most important of our organ systems, next to the brain.

Touch is the earliest of the senses to develop in the human fetus. When the embryo is only eight weeks old and has neither eyes nor ears, stroking of the lip wings of the nose results in a bending reaction of the neck and trunk. The skin is also called upon to make many adaptive responses to the environment—air movement, viruses, bacteria, changes in temperature, humidity, light, etc.

Tactile Research on Animals Is Considerable and Conclusive

Countless animal studies reveal that gentled animals (handled or stroked by humans) reveal behavior strikingly different from ungentled animals. When handled, the former are relaxed and yielding; they are not easily frightened. The opposite is true of animals that receive no gentling.

Dr. Frederick Hammett, in the early 1920s, proved conclusively that differences in mortality rates in rats were strikingly correlated with gentling. There were two colonies with which he experimented, one handled and the other subject only to routine feeding and cage cleaning. Taking 304 rats from both groups, he removed thyroid and parathyroid glands from both groups. Within forty-eight hours of the operation, 79 per cent of the non-handled animals died while only 13 per cent of the gentled rats died—a difference of 63 per cent in favor of the gentled animals. Studies with other types of rats revealed that the more gentling and handling the rats received, the more resistance they had to dying.

Ashley Montagu's Views on Tactile Stimulation

Impressed with these animal studies of the early 1920s and 1930s, Dr. Montagu began checking with animal breeders, veterinarians, staffs of zoos, etc., for confirmation of similar experiences. "It occurred to me,"

205

wrote Dr. Montagu, "that the washing the mammalian mother gives her young from the moment they are born in the form of licking serves . . . a very different purpose than cleaning." (His book *Touching* is a scholarly yet readable work that digests all the pertinent research in sensory experience. It belongs in every parent's library.)

Animal researchers have revealed that newborn animals must be licked if they are to survive. The areas receiving most of the licking are the genital region, the back, and sides, in that order. While having the effect of cleaning, actually it keeps the bodily systems (respiratory, circulatory, reproductive, nervous) adequately stimulated.

The animal research of the 1950s, 1960s and 1970s provided many verifications of such animal findings, i.e., the work of Dr. Harry Harlow with monkeys, Moore and Richmond's work with goats and sheep, and the work of G. Alexander and D. Williams with newborn lambs. The results are conclusive: animals without bodily contact, clinging, grooming, warmth, and sucking develop behavior problems and die more often in infancy.

If this licking type of bodily stimulation is important to animal infants' survival, what is its equivalent in the human maternal–child relationship? Dr. Montagu believes that one of the human equivalents is represented in part in the long period of labor that women undergo. During the average fourteen hours of labor with a firstborn and average eight-hour labor with subsequent births, the contractions of the uterus provide stimulation of the fetal skin. Infants who are born by means of Caesarean section and do not pass through the birth canal lack this stimulation and do not function well in the postnatal period. They tend to suffer more frequently than normally delivered children from upper respiratory infections. Children born prematurely who are confined to incubators more often exhibit the effects of such tactile deprivation than do term children and tend to be somewhat slower in manual and linguistic control. In later life, such touch-deprived children tend to be jumpy, anxious, shy, have a short attention span and are apt to have more emotional problems.

Based on many follow-up studies of premature and Caesarean-delivered babies, overwhelming implications for parents are clear.

1. Hospital procedures must be revamped in order to compensate for the sensory lacks incurred both perinatally and postnatally.

2. Upon birth every attempt must be made to increase mother–infant contact. Caressing the baby is pleasant in and of itself and a good way to stimulate his respiratory and gastrointestinal functions. Traditional hospital policy regarding birth procedures varies widely. Some hospitals do not permit the mother to have her baby for twenty-four hours. Others, more

innovative, leave it up to mom. Still others, enlightened regarding the newest research, encourage a reluctant mother to keep her baby with her.

Breast Feeding and Touch

Breast feeding, Dr. Montagu feels, is an important part of skin and touch stimulation necessary for properly working bodily systems. Even a newborn looks forward to a continuation after birth of the pleasant sensory experiences in the womb. Instead, what Western society gives the newborn is a very abrupt change. The moment he is born he is left lying on a flat stand, screaming. The umbilical cord is cut or clamped. The baby is exhibited to its mother and then taken to a "nursery." Here he is weighed, measured, and a number is put on his wrist. Then he is placed in a crib to howl away to his heart's discontent.

The mother's whole organism is prepared for and geared to minister to her newborn's needs—to make loving sounds to him, to nurse him at her breasts, and to caress him. At birth, mother and child need the reassurance of each other's presence. For the mother it is the sight of her baby, the first cry, and the closeness to her body. For the baby, it is the warmth of the mother's body, the suckling at her breast, the caressing, and the welcome into the bosom of the family.

Dr. Montagu makes a distinction between sucking and suckling, maintaining that a five-month-old fetus can do the former, but the newborn must *learn* to suckle. To Dr. Montagu, suckling is a more complex and socially important experience than sucking. A baby sucks on a bottle, but suckles at the breast.

The distinct advantages of breast feeding on the health and emotional behavior of a baby are treated elsewhere in this book. Suffice it to say that through the skin contact at the breast, the infant makes her first contact with the "other" in her life who offers comfort, warmth, and increasing aptitude for new experiences.

Thoughts and feelings are often communicated non-verbally through movements of the body. Dr. Ray L. Birdwhistell is convinced that this kinesthetic behavior is learned and it is at the breast where this learning and communicating take on importance. At this point the lips and mouth are stimulated. Many psychiatrists and psychologists (Freud, Hall, etc.) make the lips and feeding at the breast the base of their theories of sexuality and interpersonal relations. At the breast, through touch, the infant attests to objective reality in the sense of something outside herself.

By having been gentled, caressed, and cuddled, the infant learns to love others, which implies involvement, tenderness, and awareness of the

207

needs of others. All this is communicated to the infant through the skin in the earliest months of life.

Sexuality and Touch

Satisfying body contact is important in social development and also influences sexuality. In most non-literate cultures, the infant is held close to the mother or child caretaker a good part of the day. Clothing, if any, is loose and is used only to bind the infant's body to the mother's.

The child–mother relationship whether animal or human goes through four stages: (1) A reflex stage in which the infant reacts automatically to the mother's stimuli, heartbeat, and general motion of the mother's body. This stage lasts only a few months. (2) An affectionate stage that begins at three months and lasts to twelve months. By smiling and cuddling, the child shows voluntary affection for the mother or constant mother figure. Clinging, visual following, and responsiveness to the mother are at their highest. (3) A security and attachment period. (4) A stage of independence.

Dr. Anna Freud points out that "at the beginning of life being stroked, cuddled, soothed by touch frees various parts of a child's body, helps to build up a healthy body image and ego, and promotes the development of object and mother love."

PCI Point of View

The little research that has been done in the field of sensory stimulation and learning, primarily animal studies, shows a strong relationship between touch and learning, physical growth, weight gain, and social and emotional development. The nurturing of a secure personality dictates that tactile stimulation should begin with the newborn being placed in the mother's arms, nursed as soon as possible, and allowed to remain as long as the baby desires. PCI believes that those in charge of hospital obstetric rooms should consider implementing the theories of the French obstetrician Frederick Leboyer. (See Chapter 1, Birth Without Violence).

EARLY INTERVENTION

A neonate is already conditioned by previous in utero experiences. Listening to mother's heartbeat, being vertically jostled in her bag of waters, reacting to prenatal body stimuli with reflexive actions—all these contribute to the newborn's sensory powers.

Desirability of Early Sensory Stimulation of Infants

There is widespread agreement that the potential receptivity of young infants to sensory stimulation not only can but should be utilized to promote learning and development in later childhood. It would seem plausible that maximizing the number and variety of sights and sounds a baby is exposed to during the period of her most rapid sensory development (i.e., two to five months) would enable her to make finer visual and auditory discriminations that would later be reflected in superior reading and speaking abilities. Unfortunately, there is not much direct research on the effects of infant sense experiences on later learning.

Arnold Arnold aptly describes the presumed role of sensory stimulation in the learning process of preschool children as follows: "Sight, hearing, touch, smell and taste . . . are your child's instruments of learning. A healthy newborn can use each in an elementary way, but he uses them singly. He cannot, as yet, relate what he can see to what he hears and feels . . . Before a baby can make sensory associations, he needs the experiences that allow him to develop each of his sense instruments. He thus sensitizes the pathways from each brain center to all others. Eventually this allows him to test each impression against those received by all of his other senses."

There are a number of studies that suggest that early stimulation fosters greater learning *indirectly* in a number of ways. Laboratory animals reared in dark, stimulus-deprived cages show permanent impairment of the nervous system, endocrine system, and muscles. They also display behavior characteristic of childhood schizophrenia. By the age of six months, babies raised in institutions may appear to be autistic or mentally defective. Monkeys raised by Dr. Harry Harlow with terrycloth mother figures (soft and warm but inanimate) grew up to be aggressive and not adept socially or sexually. Dr. T. Berry Brazelton, Dr. Lee Salk, and Rita Kramer suggest that the missing link here is the lack of active, give-and-take interaction between mother and child. They and other psychologically oriented observers tend to view sensory stimulation as a basic need on a par with food, warmth, or relief from pain. A familiar example would be the need for oral gratification, e.g. sucking. A less familiar one would be a need for movement or inner-ear stimulation, e.g., to be picked up and carried around.

In their recent book *The Power of Play,* Frank and Theresa Caplan suggest that failure to respond to the infant's sensory needs, as with other needs, can weaken the fundamental coping capacity of the ego and lead to anxiety, insecurity, aggressiveness, and impatience in the preschool child.

Other studies suggest that the lack of sensitive and loving responses to a baby's sensory needs can set up a fear of failure and diminish her interest in exploring the environment or in practicing her skills.

Control of Sensory Stimulation

Several of the aforementioned writers warn that sensory stimulation of infants can be excessive and harmful if it is inappropriate to the child's stage of development or to his particular temperament and abilities. Mr. Arnold urges that we teach each sensory modality singly (e.g., see if the child can identify an object solely by listening) "instead of swamping all his senses at random."

Babies differ in terms of how much and what kinds of stimulation they can best respond to and it is important for a central, sensitive figure to discern and cater to these differences. Otherwise a child can become "turned off" to learning either through boredom or frustration and enter a negative spiral leading to the atrophy of his potential capabilities.

PCI Point of View

Parents must always keep in mind the needs of their own baby. If your baby is very active, always on the go, PCI cautions against too much sensory stimulation. For this type of temperament, physiological and other internal demands need external stabilizing. Offer structured, orderly types of activities with lots of rest periods. Above all, always take the cue from *your* baby.

THE IMPLICATIONS OF ANIMAL RESEARCH

Primate Laboratories

In the early 1960s, the United States Government established primate centers in four locations in the country where controlled medical, mental, and developmental/psychological experiments with many species of monkeys and apes could be conducted. In the Atlanta, Georgia, center extensive experiments on the life of infant apes have been carried out.

In one experiment, monkeys were treated as human infants. They were given the same care (diapering, powdering, hugging, etc.) and long periods of supervised play in and out of doors with carefully selected play equipment.

211

In other experiments, play materials were placed in the environment of the experimental group while the control group had no playthings. After considerable periods of play, the brain weight of the playing monkeys was taken and studied and compared with that of their non-playing peers.

In all these experiments, the data revealed overwhelmingly that the environment of play and loving interaction with adults resulted in a more alert, socially mature monkey (with a heavier brain) than was the case with the control group of "deprived" primates. The relevance of these studies for human growth in early infancy and childhood merits further serious consideration.

Despite this pointed evidence, there are many pediatricians and psychologists who complain that these studies may be appropriate for animals, but have no meaningful significance for humans.

In "Social Deprivation in Monkeys," the now classic article by Dr. Harry F. Harlow and Margaret K. Harlow published in *Scientific American* in 1962, the researchers described experiments in which baby rhesus monkeys caged with their mothers, but permitted no play or social contact with other monkeys, displayed gross abnormalities in their adult sexual and social roles. Young monkeys permitted daily play with their peers, even though isolated from their mothers, showed nearly as normal behavior as adults.

One of the areas that concerns educators and pediatricians is the effects of malnutrition on the development of the brain and of intelligence. Some investigators, such as Drs. George G. Graham and Blanca Adrianzen of Johns Hopkins University, School of Medicine, have proposed that certain effects of malnutrition may actually be secondary effects of environmental impoverishment. Since a prominent effect of malnutrition is to make the person or animal apathetic and unresponsive to the environment, the individual then suffers from the lack of stimulation, and this may be the direct cause of some of the symptoms usually associated with malnutrition. Current research suggests that some of the effects of malnutrition may be offset by programs of environmental enrichment.

Rodent research verifies the importance of social play and an enriched environment. One of the most conclusive pieces of animal research on the values of an enriched play environment was undertaken over a period of twelve years, from 1960 to 1972, by a team of biologists and psychologists led by Dr. Mark R. Rosenzweig. As described in the February 1972 issue of *Scientific American,* he used rodents from the same litter in his work. Rodents proved convenient because they bear large litters; the littermates have a common genetic background, and some

212

can be sacrificed (the brain could be removed to be weighed and studied chemically).

Very early in the experiment it was found that the rats that spent four to ten weeks in an enriched environment with frequent play changes differed markedly from the rodents in impoverished milieus. For example, rats with enriched play had greater weight of the cerebral cortex, stronger nerve endings and transmitters, and greater enzyme activity.

To check whether brain changes were brought about by the amount of handling, stress, or maturation differences, a series of experiments were undertaken to handle one group of rats several times a day while their other littermates were never handled. It was found that there were no differences in brain weight or enzyme activity between the handled and the non-handled rodents.

The research did indicate that two hours a day of enriched play experience over a thirty-day period were sufficient to produce changes in the brain weight of the experimental rodents.

Current findings suggest also that learning occurs more readily when animals (and young humans, we believe) are put in a responsive social setting with their peers. Peers can teach each other by their example and interactions. It is participation in family life and peer groups that provides the important one-to-one relationships that child psychologists tell us motivate early learning. Social development is an essential part of the growth process. Becoming a social animal is a complex learning task.

PCI Point of View

What does animal research teach us? We believe it points conclusively to the need for frequent changes in environmental challenges, especially for infants. Current research demonstrates that long-term containment (in a crib or playpen) can be a disaster for an infant unless his parents intervene and encourage their infant's interaction with the elements of play in his environment.

THE MOTHERING ROLE

In today's society, mothering is not simply a duty that all females are are expected to perform; it is a very definite profession that requires knowledge, patience, and skill. Not only must a mother of today raise her children to accept the changes in our society and its complexities, but she must also cope with her own role conflicts.

In this section we refer to the mother; however, other individuals such as a caretaker or a father who is at home may perform these functions.

(See Chapter 12, The Working Mother, for a discussion of mother substitutes.) Dr. Leon Yarrow, in "Measurement and Specification of the Early Infant Environment," assigns three major functions and activities to the mothering role:

1. Mother is a source of social and sensory stimulation via such activities as handling, cuddling, touching, and playing with her infant.

2. Mother is the primary need-gratifier via such activities as feeding, changing, and rocking her infant.

3. Mother interprets reality, recognizing both the changing needs of the infant and the changing environmental possibilities—and adapting both of these variables to correspond to each other.

The so-called "feminine" characteristic of soothing, which is a part of need gratification, has been studied in depth. Dr. Yarrow reports that at

least in very early infancy, many experiences with tension and disequilibrium do not increase the baby's capacity to handle stress. The baby who is gratified much of the time and who experiences tension infrequently is better able to handle stress than the infant who has experienced large doses of frustration.

Mothering Personality Traits

A sense of humor, intelligence (the commonsense kind), and flexibility are paramount mothering qualities. These will enable you to react to, help develop, and influence your child. Most important, however, is knowing yourself. If you are able to identify your own personality traits, both shortcomings and strengths, you can try to avoid passing your weaknesses on to your child.

THE FATHERING ROLE

Traditionally the father's role was that of distant disciplinarian. His love was conditional and demanding. Father was unemotional and not involved in the mechanics of child rearing (diapering, feeding, etc.) whereas mother was the all-accepting, totally involved, nurturing figure. These role stereotypes are crumbling. Fathers are recognizing their importance and joining their wives in parenting from pregnancy onward. An increasing number of pediatricians are emphasizing the importance of the father being involved in the process of labor and delivery as the beginning of the new father's role. Many fathers are becoming increasingly involved in the routine daily care and nurturing of their infants and children.

The father–child relationship should be satisfying to both child and father. There is no *one* procedure that every "good" father ought to follow. Each individual parent and each individual child relates to the other as a unique personality. Fathers play: one father plays in a physical roughhouse fashion; another playfully creates rhymes and riddles that delight his toddler. Fathers teach: they set examples as they go to work, or garden, or shop and clean. Fathers have feelings: they express their feelings of joy, sorrow, pride, and anger in a way that validates their children's own feelings and encourages their expression of them.

The *quality* of time spent with a child may be at least as important as the amount of time spent. The small child can absorb a great deal of the father in a very short time and can benefit more from the shared experi-

215

ence by enlarging upon it all day long. It is far better for father and child to play together enjoyably for fifteen minutes than to spend hours in the park miserably.

Father Power

"Father Power" is a phrase popularized by two young male parents, Henry Biller, a psychologist, and Dennis Meredith, a writer, in their book of the same name.

The special power every father may achieve via his relationship with his children is not mystical, elusive, or restrictive. Father power is based on a father's conviction that he is naturally, uniquely important to his children—"that he has the power to affect children, guide them, help them grow."

Research Supports Father's Importance

There is evidence to suggest that an affectionate relationship with father during the first several years of the child's life is critically important in helping to develop a healthy sexual identity and orientation toward sex.

216

Early father warmth and nurturing have also been linked to later levels of intelligence and to a child's ability to show affection for others.

Guidelines for Successful Child Rearing

Following are guidelines that have been developed by Harvard University's Laboratory of Human Development, based on findings of the Preschool Project directed by Dr. White. When a child wants the parents' attention, the latter should respond promptly and favorably as often as possible; make some effort to understand what the child is trying to do; set limits—not give in to unreasonable requests; provide encouragement, enthusiasm, and assistance whenever suitable; talk to the child as often as possible; use words to provide a related idea. If the child shows you a ball, ask him to "Throw the ball" back to you; take only as much time as is needed in a situation, even if it's only a few seconds; be available to your child at least half of his waking hours; encourage "pretend" activities.

On the basis of their observations, Dr. White's staff also drew up a list of practices for parents to avoid:

1. Do not cage the child or confine him regularly for long periods.

2. Do not allow him to concentrate his energies on you to the point where he spends most of his time following you around or staying near you, especially in the second year of life.

3. Do not ignore attention-getting devices to the point where your child throws a tantrum to gain your interest.

4. Do not worry that your baby will not love you if you say "no" from time to time.

5. Do not try to win all the arguments with a child, especially from the middle of the second year, when he may start becoming negative.

6. Do not try to prevent him from cluttering the house; this is an inevitable sign of a healthy, curious child.

7. Do not be overprotective.

8. Do not overpower your child; let him do what he wants to do as often as is *safe*.

Although the question of a baby's learning to be a social being is important, there is sheer pleasure in playing with a baby, learning what he wants, and enjoying each new sign that he is reaching out to his mother with his needs.

Father should not be left out of the picture. He, too, is an important caretaker and can be even more in tune with his baby at times than is mother. Mother can help the baby establish trust in the father and so give both the benefit of mutual give and take.

In a few cases, neither parent feels truly able to respond to their baby —perhaps their personalities at this time clash! Eager to be "perfect," they are too hard on themselves, overreact, and then feel useless. If parents can honestly assess their own personality characteristics and find themselves totally unable to meet their baby's need for trust, consistency, and warmth, then a short-term baby-sitter or alternative caretaker can be hired if that person *can* respond appropriately.

When a mother feels she cannot cope, even uneasily, with a baby whose temperament is markedly different from her own, she should remember that this stage is short-lived. With insight and the help of a loving, responsive partner, or an outside professional such as her doctor, she will be able to supply the baby's social demands, learn to interpret his different cries, and respond to his smiles and gestures.

ATTACHMENT BEHAVIOR

In 1958, Dr. John Bowlby challenged the secondary drive theory of attachment that assumed that the child became attached to his mother because she satisfied his needs (food and warmth) with his theory that attachment is instinctive behavior. Bowlby theorizes that attachment to mother develops as a result of the infant's repeated interactions (in the forms of sucking, clinging, following, crying, and smiling) with the environment (usually the mother).

He bases this theory in part on studies made of animals and their young. In mammals and ground-nesting birds, attachment between the mother and her young is exhibited soon after birth, whereupon both try to maintain close proximity with each other. Within a few hours after birth parents recognize their own young and the young recognize their own parents and behave differently toward each other than they do to other members of their species.

Dr. Mary Ainsworth, a professor of psychology at Johns Hopkins University, attempted a study of attachment behavior and individual differences in white, middle-class American families. She found that during the first three months of life there is little tendency for infants whose mothers are unresponsive to them to cry more (or less) than infants whose mothers are responsive. However, in each of the subsequent quarters of the year—especially the third and fourth quarters—there *are* significant tendencies for babies whose mothers have ignored their crying

218

in the previous quarter of the year to cry more frequently than do those whose mothers were more promptly responsive.

Dr. Ainsworth's findings are inconsistent with the views of those who assume that babies who cry more are spoiled. The babies who responded positively to being held, showing strong attachment behavior, tended to initiate being picked up by active reaching or approaching, but did not protest being put down. All babies showed clear signs they had become attached to their mothers by the end of the first year, but the study showed that the quality differed.

Critical Periods for Separation

In a study of the effects of change in mother figures in infancy (foster homes, adoption, etc.) "Some Conceptual Issues in the Study of Mother-Infant Interaction" by Dr. Leon Yarrow and Marion Goodwin, they provide the following statistics on the vulnerability of infants:

Under three months 55 per cent of the children show *no* reaction; 45 per cent indicate a very mild reaction.

Between three and four months, many more infants (40 per cent) show moderate or severe reaction to separation.

By four months there is a clear change; 72 per cent show moderate-severe to very severe reaction.

By six months 91 per cent of the infants show clear signs of *disturbance*.

By nine months all the infants are markedly disturbed.

Although this project is involved with change in foster mothers, and adoptions in the first year of life, the statistics have meaning for all parents and perhaps point to the strong attachment behaviors of babies to their constant caretakers.

PCI Point of View

During the first year an active relationship between mother and child results in more confident behavior patterns. Fatigue, illness, pain, and hunger can affect attachment behavior and cause it to vary. It is increased after the absence of the mother and can become more intense when the baby is alarmed.

With the security of a strong attachment, a baby has the confidence to explore more and learn new skills more quickly.

SEPARATION ANXIETY

Babies exhibit separation anxiety when they feel cut off from those to whom they are strongly attached. An individual baby's reaction to separation will vary with differences in maternal behavior.

In an article in the *Scientific American* March 1972, Dr. Jerome Kagan reports on infant studies conducted at Harvard that "the intensity of the attachment to his mother often is measured by how long the infant cries when he is separated from her." He found that crying can be the result, at least in part, of the infant's inability to interpret a discrepant event (seeing his mother leave him alone or with a stranger in an unfamiliar situation). Before eight months of age, an infant cannot discriminate such an event. However, by eight to twelve months he may develop the ability to hypothesize from a series of prior experiences.

Dr. Leon Yarrow, of the National Institute of Mental Health, says, in "Measurement and Specification of the Early Infant Environment," "A focused, individualized relationship with the mother does not appear suddenly but is a gradual process. We find that this process begins for many infants before the commonly assumed age of five or six months."

Short-term Separation Anxiety

Babies react in different ways. Some object to nap time and bedtime; others lose interest in food. However, in general, all babies protest when they are left alone even if for only a short time period.

A baby's strong attachment to the mother or mother figure arouses the fear that when she is not there, she is lost to him. His separation anxiety then becomes a problem for the parent, as well as the child. In order to avoid a crisis, the parent must begin early in the life of the child to teach him the ability to postpone immediate satisfactions for long-term goals.

A child can withstand small amounts of anxiety and discomfort if, when really upset, he knows that he will get proper reassurance. Dr. Spock reports that "children who from infancy have been around different people and who have been allowed to develop independence and outgoingness are less apt to develop such fears."

A child who wakes at night generally needs only to hear the voice of the parent or to be momentarily soothed in order to obtain the reassurance that the parent is nearby. It is not a good idea to offer your baby a drink of water or walk with her for long periods of time, because she is apt to

equate this with pleasure and want it on a routine basis; nor is it a good idea for the tired parent. In general, it is not psychologically healthy for parent or child.

Long-term Separation Anxiety

This is never a desirable situation, but sometimes a necessity due to illness, war, etc. The absence of the mother causes a threatening reaction in the child because of his orally based drive. Separation anxiety is far more severe in the breast-fed baby who has to undergo weaning simultaneously with the separation. Weaning is not a pleasurable sensation and the loss of satisfaction is a form of separation itself. When the mother reappears several days later the baby is not likely to recognize her. This detachment is an unconscious type of defense mechanism. In a short time, the child will try again to be as close to the mother as possible.

To avoid upsetting a child needing prolonged medical treatment, today many hospitals invite the mother to remain in the same room with her child.

Fear of Strangers

In the middle of the first year, the child is likely to develop a fear of strangers and strange places. On seeing a new face, he will bury his head in his mother's neck and/or scream. Unfortunately, many times the onlooker is a grandparent. Joseph Church comments that grandparents may then feel rejected by the baby and may suspect (however irrationally) that the baby's hostility has in some way been picked up from his parents. This is an easy problem to overcome. Left alone to adjust, the baby will eventually seek out the stranger, first with his eyes, and then with an outward overture of friendship.

Baby-sitter

Occasionally the baby awakens at night and cries out expecting to have his mother's face appear; instead, that of a stranger appears, disturbing the child. To prevent such disturbance it is better to introduce the baby to a baby-sitter in the mother's presence. In this way the child will not consider the person a stranger and will be able to form a substitute attachment. A certain amount of separation, sometimes accompanied by separation anxiety on the part of mother and child, is almost inevitable and causes no lasting harm. Actually, the ongoing process of letting go has to begin almost as soon as the attachments are firmly cemented.

EXTENDING RELATIONSHIPS WITH OTHERS

In *The Power of Play,* Frank and Theresa Caplan point out that the one-year-old has social status—he can influence others to watch him and may repeat a performance that brings a good response. In *Infant and*

Child in the Culture of Today, Drs. Gesell and Ilg amplify this thought when they describe the pattern of psychological development in children as innovation-integration-equilibrium. That is, at each stage, the child tries a new action, perhaps a new impulse to contact the outside person, then practices this, and finally the new phase becomes part of his own self. He no longer has to consider how to perform the action before he can perform it.

This achievement of equilibrium is part of his developing sense of self. With each new step mastered, he is becoming more like the people around him and one step nearer to realizing that he is an individual who, though separate from his family and friends, can function as they do.

It is important for parents to understand that the learning of social skills falls into three categories: playing near other children, learning to join the family at the table, and meeting strangers; also that a child's social development, like physical development, does not progress steadily. A one-year-old baby may spurt ahead in interest in other children, but regress to babylike play at other times. Actually such regression is still to be expected even beyond the third year. Reliving his earlier life a little before reaching a new equilibrium is an expected part of the integration of new skills; that is, readiness for the next stage toward independence from mother.

Many researchers have studied the problem of how the mother's behavior encourages social development in the one-year-old. Most agree that satisfying physical needs do not appear to affect the social skills of the year-old infant. It appears that "contact comfort" or at least frequency of physical contact in the first six months may be important in strengthening a child's social behavior. Some researchers have found that the more frequent the mutual visual regard between a mother and her infant, the more the baby will make approaches to strangers.

Dr. Mary Ainsworth suggests five important variables for building social strengths: frequent physical contact, sensitive responses from parents to baby's signals, giving the baby sufficient freedom to explore, an environment in which baby derives a sense of consequence for his own actions, and mutual delight of the baby and parents in their interactions with each other.

The new social movements of the year-old may consist of offering toys (but wanting them back immediately), saying a word or two, giving his empty bowl to his mother, and echoing a word here and there of his parents' remarks. His social world opens up rapidly with these advances and, at the same time, this may be a period when he needs more affection and reassurance as he discovers increasingly how complicated his world is.

223

The year-old needs to be exposed to other children, preferably babies his own age rather than a noisy group of older children. He may do nothing more than make noises, but he will derive stimulation from the presence of other playing children. He also may look upon the other babies simply as moving objects to push, feel, or bite. Nonetheless, he needs this early preparation for the more active interaction he will get when two years of age and older.

If his mother has been his only caretaker up to this point, she should try to get him used to staying occasionally with another adult.

The play group (in which a small number of agemates are brought to visit in different surroundings with interesting toys) is probably as good for the mother as the child at this age. In this way she gets the chance to compare notes with other mothers and observe a variety of behaviors in different very young children. This can increase her sense of security in handling her own child. (See the section on Play Groups in Chapter 12.)

PCI Point of View

This can be an exhausting stage for parents since baby is probably walking by now and full of curiosity about his surroundings. The toddler is avidly getting into the cupboards, tirelessly exploring the contents of drawers, and making all kinds of messes. However, it is also the time when he is really starting to feel his power as a person and he needs to have his curiosity satisfied, his needs met, as well as interesting contacts with other adults and children.

If the child is beginning to acquire a vocabulary, he needs feedback and chances to try his new words on others in order to learn that words bring a response. Then he will be encouraged to learn more words, more complicated ways of expressing himself, and to integrate himself a bit more into his enlarging social world.

PEER GROUP EXPERIENCES FOR TODDLERS

A Definition

Paul Mussen, Jerome Kagan, and John Conger, in *Child Development and Personality,* define socialization as the process of "acquiring those personality characteristics, behavior, values and motives that the culture considers appropriate." Parents, as the first agents of socialization, encourage the desirable characteristics and behaviors, while discouraging the undesirable elements. Socialization is a moving-out process.

A Growing Process

The different desirable and sophisticated aspects of social development (sharing, co-operating, developing friendships, and taking satisfaction in human relationships) constitute a slow growth process, one that cannot be rushed. Successful socialization depends not only on guidance and training, but also on the child's readiness for acquiring certain behaviors.

Heredity Versus Environment

Although the temperament a child is born with (whether he is quiet or active) will somewhat influence his social development, his *experiences* with others are most important. Parents can help a child learn to be sociable by exposing him to other children, preferably those his own age. Bullying behavior on the part of older children, for example, might damage the urge to interact with other children. All authorities agree that a child should never be pressured into relationships. Such an experience would be threatening and confusing, possibly damaging later social interactions even into adulthood.

Basic Ingredients

Authorities agree that the rudiments of social development go back to early infancy as parents instill the basic trust necessary for later social interaction by giving their child plenty of accepting emotional support. Children reared lovingly tend to be highly social and to make friends easily.

Peer Interaction and the Two-year-old

With mother or mother figure nearby and communicating approval, the two-year-old will begin to be aware of her peers. Although still too young to play with other children, she is stimulated by them. She will inspect another toddler with great interest, often ending with a hug, the offering of a hand or toy—all done in silence. Verbal interaction is usually negative—to shout "no" or "mine" in angry dispute over a toy. Of course, hitting and fighting might ensue at this point.

225

A Complicated Time of Life

The toddler is becoming more aware of himself as a person and developing a strong sense of ownership. At the same time, he is becoming more aware of his peers. This self-awareness and the awareness of others are opposing tendencies to some extent. Inevitable conflicts are usually resolved by what parents label as selfishness and unreasonable behavior. Eventually time, growth, guidance, and patience will bring these tendencies into balance and co-operation. Scolding is not recommended for property disputes occurring at this age.

Much of the aggravation between parent and child occurs because the parent heedlessly or ignorantly insists on treating the child as if he were in a "continuous state of equilibrium." Growth, however, consists of disharmony as well as harmony. Most of what adults label as unreasonable behavior is really an immature stage of social development.

Peer Interaction and the Older Two-year-old

The older two-year-old is in a state of better equilibrium. He has passed through his earlier "self-assertion" stage and can now play side by side (parallel) with another child, enjoying the company and not disrupting the play of others. Any interaction is still usually material, involving a toy, or physical. Adult supervision is still needed, especially after the first twenty minutes. Unpleasant experiences can probably be avoided if the parent anticipates roughhouse behavior and exercises the necessary control.

"How can successful socialized behavior with minimal parent–child conflict be achieved?"

Mussen, Conger, and Kagan pose the above question. The answer, unfortunately, is that there are few solid facts about "best" ways to attain this goal.

By the end of the first year, the child is highly motivated to please his parents and to avoid the unpleasant feelings generated by punishment or rejection. Parent–child conflict usually begins when the child is two years old since this is the time when parents begin trying to correct undesirable behavior in their children. Friction occurs because the child enjoys his behavior and dislikes being thwarted.

Successful socialization will occur if the child is encouraged to give up

226

his unacceptable behavior in return for the continued love and affection of his parents. However, if the parents have not elicited the necessary love and warmth during the child's first year, a medium of exchange will not exist.

PCI Point of View

Going beyond just offering guidelines for parental reaction in undesirable situations (e.g., two toddlers hitting and pulling one another's hair in dispute over a toy), PCI recommends the following books for more thought-provoking suggestions: *Between Parent and Child* by the late Haim Ginott, and *P.E.T.* by Thomas Gordon.

If a two-year-old does not have vocabulary enough to handle the sharing activity in a sandbox or on a playground, his parents may have to intervene when a conflict arises and give their child the words necessary to bring about sharing. Example: "This is Johnny's pail and maybe he will

227

share it with you when he is finished using it." "Let's ask Mary to come and play with you."

A parent does not teach sharing by taking a toy from one child to hand it over to another. Substitution or distraction might be recommended in such a case. Hitting a child to teach her that she "must never hit Tommy again" is not an effectivᵥ way of eliminating violence and force from the child's behavior. In fact, it is contradictory and confusing.

SELF-PLEASURING/MASTURBATION

Discovery of the Genitalia

At about five months of age, the baby finds his genitalia and explores this area with perfectly normal curiosity in much the same way that he plays with his feet, toes, earlobes, etc.

Discovery of Increased Sensitivity

Sexual stimulation in a little baby usually occurs inadvertently. A little boy gets an erection during a diaper change. A little girl demonstrates pelvic thrusting from clitoral sensations, perhaps from bounding on a parent's knee. Your child may obtain pleasure at bath time by rubbing against clothing.

In any case, according to Dr. Virginia Pomeranz and Dodi Schultz in *The First Five Years,* once children become aware of the increased sensitivity in the genital area, they masturbate deliberately. Pomeranz and Schultz claim this will not harm a child in any way and is a normal human activity.

Pediatricians caution against giving baby an idea that his activity is bad or to draw undue attention to the masturbation. The young child should develop wholesome feelings about his entire body and every part of it.

Toddlers will discover subtle ways of self-pleasuring that are acceptable in public. They may derive stimulation from tricycle seats, swings, slides, and seesaws. They usually save direct genital stimulation for private moments.

Sex Play

It is perfectly normal for little children to engage in sex play in a group. This may take the form of "playing doctor"—"You show, then I'll show you" satisfies children's natural curiosity in the opposite sex. (Doctor games also have respectable dramatic potentials. Illness, followed by medicine, followed by tragedy or good health, etc.) Some children may "mutually masturbate," which is not harmful in normal healthy children. This stage usually passes quickly once initial curiosity is resolved. If, however, a child is basically unhappy or has experienced a trauma recently, he may continue masturbation to an excessive degree since it provides him with the only satisfying or pleasurable experience he has had recently. This situation requires tackling the cause of the unhappiness rather than the masturbation itself.

In a lighter vein, there are those children who dance around with legs crossed, clutching their genital area. This is in no way related to masturbation. These children may merely have the urge to urinate!

Attitudes Toward Masturbation

In his book *Understanding Your Child from Birth to Three,* Dr. Joseph Church reports that according to folklore masturbation was said to debilitate people physically, mentally, and sexually. Some thought it would stunt growth and cause mental illness. In spite of the fact that these horrors have been disproved, some parents have been brought up with an attitude of shame and guilt regarding masturbation.

PCI Point of View

Serious consideration should be given the parents' own attitudes regarding masturbation at any age. Feelings of shame and guilt should be recognized and the fact that many specialists in early childhood behavior claim that masturbation is completely harmless should be thoroughly understood.

Masturbation in babies and children should be met in as nonchalant and understanding a manner as possible. If, however, masturbation *bothers you,* the child should be casually distracted so as not to perpetuate your feeling of shame. Pleasant and interesting play experiences will usually divert the child from playing with his body excessively.

It should be a relief to parents to know that some masturbation at any age is normal and only when it is inordinate—a child's major recurring mode of obtaining pleasure—does masturbation indicate an underlying problem.

PARENTS AS MODELS OF BEHAVIOR

Children develop a sense of identity through identification with their parents. Identification is largely an unconscious process, based on what parents do and don't do, rather than what they consciously would *like* to do or be.

The Research

It was once a commonly accepted theory that little girls automatically imitated their mothers' behavior and therefore became "proper ladies," while little boys modeled their fathers' behavior and grew up displaying "masculine" traits.

Many recent studies have disproved this theory. A major research study conducted by Dr. Albert Bandura, Dorothea Ross and Sheila Ross, found that both boys and girls selectively imitate a dominant parent *regardless of sex*. The dominant figure was defined as the one who controlled the resources of the family and had rewarding power. Children demonstrated cross-sex imitation, although this occurred more frequently with the girls. One explanation of this is our differential cultural tolerance for cross-sex behavior. Also, in our culture there is privileged status and greater positive reinforcement of masculine-role behavior.

If you were to examine your own attitudes on masculine- and feminine-role behavior, you might find that your own home was dominated by *one* person and that you and your children could easily determine which parent was the controller of the family resources and, therefore, had the power of reward.

In many cases, father plays this role and the girls in the family learn that their adult lives will also be male-regulated. Unfortunately, placing females in a subordinate position deprives our society of a valuable resource; namely, *woman power.*

Many of the traditional roles once assigned to a husband and a wife have been dissolving. Either partner is able to support the other financially, is capable of soothing a crying infant, can do the food or other marketing and can prepare the meals.

The dissolution of stereotyped attitudes toward the roles of women and men in our society is a heartening sign. If this permits women and men to arrive at more satisfying ways of reconciling their personal interests, their family's financial requirements, and their children's needs, society will be strengthened and parents and their children more fulfilled.

No longer is father the sole breadwinner or problem solver. As this occurs, parents are presenting new models to their children. Children will selectively imitate the behavior of both parents, depending upon who is dominant and rewarding in each situation.

Development of Imitation

From the age of six months babies will be discovering the joys of imitation. They will imitate the hand gestures parents make, such as wiping up food with a sponge, as well as the sounds they hear. By eleven months of age their imitating technique is more deliberate, sophisticated, and useful. They remember behavior from the past and can call upon this memory to produce present imitative behavior. They are also beginning to associate behaviors and qualities with people and things, for example, when they are shown a dog and they try to say "bow wow."

Through imitation, babies learn to speak and dress and undress themselves. Their gibberish includes adult inflections and their facial expressions also include adult manifestations.

During the second year of life, imitation flourishes. Many "good" habits that you want your child to acquire can begin at this age. As two-year-old boys and girls watch daddy shave, and wash his hands and face, and mommy clean house, mow grass, and fix the car, they are also incorporating these activities into their own work and play.

Through the identification process, children learn cultural conventions such as language and daily routines, and more subtle personality traits. It is not accidental that some families seem to produce independent self-starters while others do not. Similarly it is not accidental that some countries produce many creative leaders who exhibit high degrees of risk-taking behavior while others encourage the development of conformists, with little or no imagination or daring. Attributes such as flexibility and responsibility, traits such as a sense of humor and wit are handed down from parent to child by the conscious and unconscious examples they set.

Parents as Conscious Models of Behavior

Traditionally, child rearing consisted of raising your children as you were raised. Bombarded with articles that blame all societal ills on the parents' failure properly to love and discipline their children, it is natural for parents to question their adequacy. Parental permissiveness has been related to student riots, being authoritative has been associated with the drug abuse problem and other forms of rebellion. Teachers blame parents for the child's learning problems, while doctors blame parents for causing psychosomatic illnesses in the child.

What Are Parents to Do?

It is possible for you as parents to look at yourselves in your roles as parents, to discover how you may *consciously* influence the lives of your offspring, and to establish some goals for behavior. Keeping in mind the fact that much rearing is accomplished through unconscious identification, families should still think ahead to the goals they hope to achieve. Prior to setting behavior standards, one must first ask the question, "What kind of a person do I want my child to become?" Of course, you want him or her to grow up healthy and whole, so you must be concerned with personal safety. You would like your child to have self-confidence and a feeling of self-worth—to be independent. To become independent, a child must have adequate freedom to make choices that become more involved as the child grows older. Along with self-respect, you want your child to have respect for the rights of others, to develop some inner controls to govern his own behavior and to have a healthy attitude toward authority.

A knowledge of child development helps parents set realistic goals for their children.

SEX STEREOTYPING

What will your little boy be made of? "Independence, aggression, leadership, activity, courage, confidence, emotional control." What will your little girl be made of? "Dependence, passivity, fragility, sensitivity, shyness, non-competitiveness." These behavioral traits assigned on the basis of sex differences have begun to be challenged as a result of what has come to be known as the Women's Liberation Movement. Since these patterns of behavior are found in early childhood, as parents you will want to know something about their origins.

Origins

From the day you learn of your impending parenthood, does the twinkle in your eye register hope for a male child? After birth, will the sex of your baby determine the color of the room and clothing? Studies reveal that the ways in which parents pick up, hold, talk to, or play with and feed their baby convey to the infant a distinct sex orientation. It seems that infant girls are touched and talked to more than are infant boys.

The toys purchased for play reflect a pattern of sex separation—trucks and cars for boys; dolls and tea sets for girls. Even books read to children reinforce and illustrate sex-stereotyped roles that our culture has assigned to males and females. Men are often portrayed as doctors, pilots, scientists; women, as nurses, mothers at home, teachers. The message is loud and clear. Many sexual difficulties reported for American males and females are related to their not having had a chance as small children to practice a wide range of feelings.

Socialization Process

In her article "Psychology Constructs the Female," Naomi Weisstne writes that human behavior is often claimed to rest on an individual and inner dynamic, perhaps fixed in infancy. However, what people do and who they believe themselves to be will in general be a function of what others around them expect them to be. Thus the influence of the social context is overwhelming.

As parents, you affect the socialization of your child through communication of behavioral expectations. Through these social/cultural expectations, sex stereotyping is determined. What you feel about the "nature" of men and women will influence the subsequent behavior of your children.

In her study of three primitive societies, Margaret Mead describes a variety of personalities and sex roles very different from our own. Among the Arapesh, men and women are trained to be co-operative, unaggressive, and responsive to the needs and demands of others. Among the Mundugumor, both men and women develop as ruthless and aggressive, with the maternal-cherishing aspects of personality at a minimum. There appears to be no contrast between the sexes. The third tribe, the Tchambuli, exhibits a reversal of the sex-linked roles of own Western culture. The woman plays the dominant, impersonal, managing partner while the man is less responsible and more emotionally dependent.

Thus we can no longer state with certainty that these aspects of behavior are sex-oriented, but rather as Dr. Mead does, that "many, if not all . . . personality traits . . . called masculine or feminine . . . that a society . . . assigns to either sex are lightly linked." She stresses the social conditioning, especially the impact of the whole of the integrated culture upon the growing child as communicated by the parents at first.

What the Women's Lib Movement is challenging are the culturally instilled behavioral roles assigned on the basis of sex alone and not on what may be proper or right for a particular human being, your own child.

In early infancy, children begin to exhibit behavioral tendencies that then evoke parental responses. Via these responses (reward, punishment, ignoring, etc.), the child's behavior will begin to conform appropriately. While studies often claim so-called sex differences in behavior modality from the earliest months, it is now apparent that there are other factors at work. Many characteristic responses are acceptable in girls—from feminine to athletic "tomboy." Boys do not have such a wide range of behavior patterns allowed them. Neither the passive "sissy" nor the aggressive "bad boy" earns approval or acceptance. More boys than girls from the age of two experience prohibitions for a wider range of behavior.

Overcoming Sex Stereotypes

1. Treat and see your child as a human being, not as a member of a particular sex. Expect and demand the same achievement goals from both sexes.

2. Encourage varieties of behavior, i.e., crying, aggressiveness, courage, leadership, exploration, etc.

3. Use a variety of different colors in decorating her or his room and dress.

4. Feel free to handle and fondle your child. Be as rough or as gentle as you feel with either sex.

5. Verbal communication, tone of voice, etc., should not be differentiated for males or females. Cooing is soothing to both.

6. All children like active and passive toys. Provide both sexes with suitable trucks, dolls, games, etc.

7. Critically examine the books you select to read to your child.

8. Become aware of your own values and begin to examine them in light of the preceding information. There is much published material available to help you. One example is *Women in Sexist Society* by V. Gornick and B. K. Moran; another is *Our Bodies, Ourselves* by the Boston Women's Health Book Collective. Fathers will enjoy reading *Father Power* by Henry Biller and Dennis Meredith.

SEX EDUCATION

If sex education is taking place continuously—whether consciously or unconsciously—why is it such a topic of self-conscious concern to young parents?

Part of the answer is that despite Freud and the "sexual revolution," sex is a topic that is somehow taboo in many families. Sex is "for adults," "private," and may be infrequently discussed, particularly in family conversations. Some parents may have been brought up to believe that sex is somehow "dirty" or at least an "embarrassing" topic, causing them to feel self-conscious when talking about sex with their children.

Wardell Pomeroy, in his excellent reference book *Your Child and Sex,* deals directly with these problems. A good deal of his book is devoted to discussing with parents their own sexual lives in order that they might come to grips with their feelings about sex and sexuality and consequently be better equipped to deal with this topic and their children.

Sex Identity and Identification

Child-rearing experts are unanimous when discussing the importance of gender identity and identification with the parent of the same sex. As Selma Fraiberg writes, in *The Magic Years,* "This means that sex education in the broadest sense must educate the child for the fulfillment of his sexual role, to give optimum satisfaction in being a boy or in being a girl, and that the ties to parents must be strong enough and tender enough to ensure the possibility of a rich love life, yet not so strong or so all-consuming as to prevent the child from later forming new love attachments in mature love and marriage."

Difficulties are arising because feminine roles are undergoing change and this can cause some parental confusion. In other words, it is important that your child know that daddy can be warm, sensitive, and nurturing, and do dishes and change diapers—but that he is still a *man* doing these things. In the same way, it is important that your young child have the freedom to play with a whole range of toys: girls with trucks and trains, boys with dolls and housekeeping sets, etc.—but to understand clearly whether he is a boy or she is a girl.

Where Do Babies Come From?

It is not unusual for your two- or two-and-a-half-year-old to notice your pregnant body or a neighbor's becoming larger and ask, "Where do babies come from?" What do you answer? Child-rearing authorities agree that the truth, simplified to the child's level of understanding is best. In other words, at age two, the answer "Babies grow inside the mother's body in a special place" will probably be sufficient. This may not satisfy a two-and-a-half- or three-year-old, who may ask, "How does a baby get inside the mother?" Again, do not immediately launch into a detailed, start-to-finish lecture! The key is to gear your answer to your child's maturity and comprehension. Your child needs different answers at age two, three, four, and five. But at each age, answer your child's questions honestly, directly, and as "naturally" as possible. Try not to get uptight about the whole subject. This is harder than it sounds, especially if your child asks these questions in seemingly the most inappropriate places, such as in the supermarket or in a crowded bus.

Body Parts and Functions

Young children, upon discovery of the opposite sex, may experience anxiety about their own genitals. Little girls may feel deprived at not having penises until they learn about the special parts of their own bodies. Little boys may feel anxious about the possibility of losing their penises until they learn that girls and boys are born with different genitals. Little boys may feel left out of "pregnancy and birth" until they learn about the masculine contribution to conception. Authorities agree that the correct labeling of body parts and functions is best. Wardell Pomeroy advises that prior to entering school the preschoolers should:

1. Know the names of the body's sexual parts.
2. Know and be able to use the correct words for elimination.
3. Understand the basic fact of a baby's growth within the mother's body.
4. Know enough anatomy by direct observation to understand the differences between boys and girls.
5. If children ask about it, they should know that babies are made by mothers and fathers together.

Nudity

Authorities vary as to their opinion regarding nudity in the home. The majority feel that nudity on the part of parents arouses uncomfortable and confusing feelings in the child. In contrast, Wardell Pomeroy feels nudity in the home—without "sexualization"—is healthy. All are in agreement, however, about the importance of keeping your own sexual life private.

Public Versus Private

Along with healthy feelings about his or her body, it is important for your young growing child to realize the difference between public and private, i.e., some things are done in public—others only in private. Failure to establish this idea can lead your child into embarrassing situations. While certain activities are "cute" in a young child (appearing nude in the midst of your dinner party, for instance), nudity in an older child or teenager might be a sign of disturbed development.

Self-protection

As children grow older and begin to play farther away from home and their parents' direct supervision the parents will need to equip them with some knowledge for their own protection. The parents must prepare their children for the world *without* making them overly frightened or traumatized.

Dr. Lee Salk suggests that children who are old enough to understand should be cautioned that there are sexually "abnormal" people who may sometimes show their genitals to others and that there are some older people who like to undress younger children and play with their genitals. You should stress that such people are this way because of some bad experiences in their lives. If something unpleasant does happen to your child, do not overreact, but "give your child as much support, reassurance and acceptance as you can, while giving him every opportunity to talk about what happened," advises Dr. Salk.

Communication

In sex education as in other aspects of life, communication is of utmost importance. Ideally, you should feel that you and your child have an open, honest relationship, free from fear and guilt. Your child should be able freely to ask you questions to satisfy his curiosity. Apart from dealing with your child's natural curiosity, the ideal of sex education should be your child's development of positive feelings about his or her body and sexual identity.

As Dr. William E. Homan writing in *Child Sense* believes, "The one ultimate goal of sex education is that the individual will arrive at attitudes which over the years will bring him the greatest amount of happiness and will subject him to the least amount of hurt."

Highly Recommended Reading:

How Babies Are Made, Andrew Andry and Steven Schepp
What to Tell Your Child About Sex, Child Study Association of America

The Wonderful Story of How You Were Born, Sidonie Gruenberg
Your Child and Sex, Wardell Pomeroy
Let's Find Out About Babies, Charles and Martha Shapp and Sylvia Shepard
Where Do Babies Come From, Margaret Sheffield
Before You Were a Baby, Paul and Kay Showers

RACIAL AWARENESS AND PREJUDICES

The tolerant child is one who is self-confident, creative, considerate of others, and generally successful in her activities. Parents would like to nurture these traits and probably do to some degree. Author Suzanne Ramos notes in *Teaching Your Child to Cope with Crisis* that parents of tolerant children "tend to be warm, affectionate, sensitive to their child's needs, consistent about rules, and accepting of the child's weaknesses as well as his strengths."

Most parents are not actively prejudiced. They really believe that no race or religion is inherently better than any other. Their problems begin the day they buy that single-family home they can barely afford in order to provide their babies with "the very best," a fenced-in back yard that reveals a series of similar jungle gyms as far as the eye can see, a playroom filled with so-called educational playthings, a good socialization experience in the neighborhood nursery school followed up with equally good academic preparation in the neighborhood elementary school. "So far so good," you say: "What's the problem?" Passive prejudice is, unfortunately, the price we pay for this so-called "good life." It is human nature to be fearful of the strange and unfamiliar. Thus children develop with untried and untested concepts of "love thy brother" and equal opportunity, coupled with other feelings that black, and old, and poor are somehow different and inferior.

Most people probably do not realize that children become aware of racial differences at a very early age. Studies have shown that by the age of eight months a baby distinguishes between black and white skin colors. When a white baby sees a black person or vice versa for the first time, he will most likely become upset and not let this new phenomenon get near him. If the mother pulls the baby away and also shows mistrust of the other person, the baby's initial fear of something different will be reinforced and may one day become a dislike of all people of a different race. This is when prejudice has its beginninngs.

However, if the mother accepts the new person, the baby will most likely accept him (and his skin color), too. Of course, some children do not actually meet people of other races until they are older and parental attitudes may already have formed their ideas of other races. Thus an older child's first contact with a person of another race may be confused by his parents' attitudes and the initial reaction may not just be mistrust of something different.

It is important for a child to see people of other races and colors at a very early age and to have personal contact with different people and meet them in situations of trust. Many studies have revealed that prejudice and racial misunderstanding undeniably hurt children both black and white. They harm the prejudiced child (and later the adult) by making him oppressive in action and dogmatic and narrow-minded in thinking. At the same time, the child punished by prejudice learns self-hatred and misplaced identity and suffers from the obvious economic and social consequences.

How Prejudice Develops

A child becomes more racially aware as she grows older. By the age of two, a child senses (if she has not already internalized) her parents' racial attitudes. Incidents occur and the child watches her parents' reactions to them. A two-year-old black child stands with her mother at a Little League game. A two-year-old white child comes over to play with the black child. The white mother pulls her child away. The white and black children quickly learn the significance of this action.

At the age of three, a black child looks at the white mother of an interracial child and states, "You can't be her mother because she's black and you're white." She goes on to say that she doesn't like the white mother because her grandmother told her that white people are bad. This child has learned her lessons well. How can mothers raise their children not to be racially prejudiced?

Identifying with One's Own Racial Group

A child must first identify with his own race and skin color to get his bearings on himself and the world. For most white children this is not a problem since white people form the ruling society. A white child sees his white parents and the white society around him and identifies himself with them. However, the white child must learn that there are other people in the world who may look different and may have different values but should not be suspect because of this. He can learn this through books and

239

social contacts. If your child asks questions, don't shut him off with stereotyped answers.

A black child also sees his black parents and most often a black society around him, but as he grows older, he becomes increasingly aware of the many white people, too. He sees them on TV, in stores, as policemen, and firemen. (It is more likely for a white child never to have met a black person than vice versa.) By nursery school age, a black child may have sensed a double standard in the society around him and often equates good things with being white. He has undoubtedly sensed his parents' reactions to incidents of outright racial prejudice.

A black child should be taught that being black is something to be proud of, not ashamed of. Whether you are a black or white parent, be aware of the sinister connotations of the color "black" and the pure connotations of the color "white" in the English language. Be especially aware of this as you choose books to read to your child. Also when choosing books, try to find books that mirror the child's own image. Look for books about black children or black and white children together.

Interracial Marriage and Adoptions

If you are the natural parent of an interracial child, your child may have special problems of identity. She may be confused as to which group she actually belongs in. Have your child look at her skin and look at your skin and she will see, yes, she is one color and you are another. She should be taught that people will call her black (as they call her daddy) and they will call you white, or whatever the case may be. Most importantly, she must be taught that black is good and white is good—they just are different.

Choose black and interracial books that your child can identify with. If you do not live in a black neighborhood, make sure your child comes in contact with black people and playmates often. An adopted black child with white parents also needs special attention. In addition to the careful choice of books and the teaching of pride in himself and his color, the white parent of an adopted black child must make a special effort to see that her child has a chance to play with other black children and to associate with black adults. He should not be a black oddity in a white world.

At around the age of two or two and a half, a child (given the opportunity of contact) will probably start noticing differences in other children, such as hair texture, differently shaped eyes, and assorted skin colors. He may say something about his observations, for instance, "Sally needs a bath." The observations are normal and healthy. Try to answer his questions or explain observations by telling your child about different people. Do not be derogatory and your child will not be.

Above all, do not say one thing and act another. Your child learns by what you do, so try to adhere to what you teach. It is important for children to meet and play with children of other races not just for experience, but so that when they become adults they will be able to live and work together without fear and hatred in full friendship and mutual respect.

Note: Some recommended books are *Stevie* by John Steptoe, *Spin a Soft Black Song* by Nikki Giovanni.

PCI Point of View

If you consider tolerance a high priority, you will expose your children to all kinds of people.

Enroll your child in a play group or a preschool Y program that draws upon heterogeneous racial and financial backgrounds.

When selecting a day-care program do not immediately head for the most expensive one. High tuition rates may guarantee fancy equipment, but will definitely exclude many interesting children from the program. If parents do not demean cultural differences and imply people are inferior because they are different, in all likelihood, their children won't.

IMAGINARY PLAYMATES

A normal phase of a child's growth is the development of his imagination. Situations, games, and even playmates are created by the child's fantasy. Allan Fromme, author of *The Parent's Handbook,* explains that the young child's experience with reality has been limited and his world protected enough to allow his escape into fantasy. While an adult expresses much of his life in work, a child does so in play. His emotions and ideas are released in his play, often allowing him to create imaginary situations and companions.

Frank and Theresa Caplan, in *The Power of Play,* emphasize that children should be allowed to create their make-believe world. Since the child's control of the real world is still limited, his imagination allows him to create a world in which he can have control. Make-believe is an integral part of a young child's life.

Around three years of age, a child may suddenly have one or many new "playmates." Her vivid imagination has created these new personalities. Each child has a different capacity for fantasy. While one child may be satisfied with a lone imaginary playmate, another child may have a house full of them. These imaginary friends may take the form of children, animals, or adults.

The parent may question why a child would want to "create" friends if he has real friends with whom to play. The preschooler is learning to control his emotions and actions. Edith Neisser, in *Primer for Parents of Preschoolers,* writes, "Even as his actions come under control, the wish to hit out aggressively, the frightening anger, persist within him." The child soon learns that a real playmate may not accept these actions and feelings, and transfers them to an imaginary playmate, who becomes a healthy release for his emotions while he is learning to cope with them.

Invisible friends will most probably materialize with the child who must be confined to bed due to an illness. An imaginary friend or animal fills the void created by loneliness and the need for companionship and understanding. The child speaks and creates situations with her new friends and may even ask for extra food on the bed tray.

If you could trace the early childhood behavior of some of today's adult achievers, you would find that many were only children who conjured up imaginary playmates as a social activity. The child who plays many roles is often verbally competent, creative, and inventive, and these abilities are useful at every stage of life.

Parent Reactions

How should a parent react to a child's fantasy? Dr. David Hellyer, in *Your Child and You,* warns that overencouragement on the part of the parents can stimulate the relationship of the child with his "friend." A casual acceptance is preferred. Since a child does have a vivid imagination, he can confuse his fantasy with reality.

One parent had a three-year-old girl who had created an imaginary friend, "Cathy." Whenever the child wanted her friend introduced to real people, the parent would say, "This is Cathy, Jennifer's *pretend* friend." Thus, while the parent accepted the imaginary playmate, the child realized that the parent knew that Cathy was only make-believe. The child was also reminded that her friend was not real.

Unfriendly Intruders

Some imaginary creations are not friendly. A child is convinced—repetitively—that a bear or tiger is hiding under the bed or behind the curtains. These imaginary fears are very real to him. Dr. Fitzhugh Dodson, in *How to Parent,* warns against telling a child that he is lying. The parent should reassure him that his room is safe, and the room might even have to be "checked out" in order to appease the child.

Imaginary Playmates Who Fail to Disappear

Sometimes imaginary playmates fail to disappear. This is not unusual. However, there should be concern when the child cannot share his fantasies with others or allows his make-believe to isolate him from other children and normal play.

If a child is spending most of his time in his fantasy world, the parents need to make sure that he is receiving enough of their love, attention, and acceptance and that he also has enough playmates to occupy his time.

The child may not be satisfied with her real life. If her parents are always critical of her, she might create a wicked imaginary companion upon whom to blame the naughty things she has done or would like to do. Of course, if a child continues to spend too much time in her make-believe life, help should be sought.

Often parents question a child's use of fantasy as not being a good preparation for adulthood. When it is *not* the only form of play or release, make-believe play helps give a young child a rewarding sense of self-expression. The use of her imagination can enhance all the days of her life. (See the section on Fantasy in Chapter 10, page 381.)

7

Physical Development

INTRODUCTION BY MYRTLE B. MCGRAW, PH.D.*

The multiplicity of ideas, often controversial, to which the parents and educators of young children are exposed is bewildering. Their big challenge and the challenge of current professionals, mass media, the consumer of theories, and the institutions that implement them is to find a way of disseminating ideas so that they do not become grossly distorted and misinterpreted. It also has to be recognized that ideas that proved useful under other circumstances (agricultural, kinship, families, island tribes) will not necessarily be applicable in a highly mechanistic, mobile, changing society.

But knowledge gained about young children through academia and the media alone will not cultivate the kind of observational acuity and intuitive sensitivity so necessary to the restoration of parental confidence. The upbringing of young children requires knowledge plus intuitive sensitivity on the part of parents.

Today's parents are eager for information about any subject matter pertinent to their baby's growth and development. A revolution in research relating to the capabilities infants possess, coupled with increasing evidence of the long-range importance of the prenatal and earliest years, has created "the professional parent."

Record keeping—via the use of anecdotal diaries, tape recorders and photographs—is the "tool of the trade." Parents educated in the ages and stages approach to learning will be able sensitively to iden-

---

* Dr. Myrtle B. McGraw is one of the "first generation" of psychologists who in the 1930s turned to infancy for insights into human growth and development. One of her many books, *The Neuro-muscular Maturation of the Human Infant*, remains a classic in its field.

As a director of the Developmental Psychology Department at Briarcliff College in Briarcliff Manor, N.Y., she founded and directed a Baby Teaching Laboratory. Her research on the physical powers of infants led her to experiment with infants less than a year old in swimming, roller-skating, climbing almost vertical inclines, and climbing on push pedestals to attain a position on the top.

247

tify the particular skill their baby is working on, and on this basis anticipate future stages by providing appropriate stimulation and practice.
The ability to read baby's own "body language" will be cultivated
through sensitive observation based on information.

"Reading body language" means the ability to recognize the intricate development of an infant's motor powers. An infant will not acquire specific skills until certain hookups are established between
nerves and until associated muscles are strong enough. Babies hold up
their heads, then control their torsos before they can use their legs to
crawl at will. The maturation of the nervous system depends partly on
heredity. Within these limits, parent stimulation and a challenging environment can and do to a great degree enable children to use their
senses to talk and walk sooner.

We are not merely concerned with physical exploits. Equally important are the infant's own sense of accomplishment and interaction
with adults who understand him. If the child of one or two gains
confidence in handling his own body, then it is reasonable to assume
that this confidence will subsequently generalize to other areas.

Growth is not a straight onward and upward line of development. It is a jagged process of spurts and regressions. Older is not necessarily more advanced. Behaviors need not occur at a specific month.
Development in one area can interfere with development in another.

One of the most important features of observing human growth is
the ability to recognize critical periods. A critical period is that period
of time in which new behaviors appear most easily or optimally with
respect to the baby's personal learning readiness. These periods could
be considered "opportune" periods for learning a particular ability.
With the utmost energy expended by the child and the least amount by
the parents and least distraction from other learning processes, the
baby will more easily master a particular motor or learning skill.
Teaching and learning are more costly before or after the opportune
period and the probability of change is smaller with each successive
year.

This chapter hopefully will provide a description of the physical
growth and development of infants and toddlers so that parents can
better interpret their baby's behavior and also be prepared for what
comes next.

MATURATION

"Maturation is the development of innate patterns of behavior in ordered sequence" (from J. A. Hadfield's book *Childhood and Adolescence*). For example, walking and talking are inborn capacities and do not depend on training. The child needs opportunities for practice in these areas, but the seeds for these abilities are already there. Mastering an ability is dependent upon when his nervous system is biologically ready to perform a task. For this reason, it is important not to try to teach a child to do something if he is not ready, for this only frustrates him.

Each child progresses and matures at her own rate. She gives certain signals to her mother when her body is physically ready for a task. Therefore, in the early months, non-verbal communication between mother and child is especially important. This permits the mother to recognize her baby's periods of growth and to help her practice her burgeoning abilities.

Timing of Parent Intervention

There is some disagreement as to when parents should help and encourage their child's exercise of his abilities. Dr. McGraw thinks that a child can and should be encouraged at the first sign of an ability maturing. Professor Hadfield, on the other hand, maintains that parents should wait until the maturing process is fully developed.

Lack of practice will not stop *basic* maturation patterns. However, physical maturity, as evidenced by the ability to walk, for instance, will free a child to practice social relations and also broaden learning vistas.

Maturation and the Environment

When a child is physically ready to walk, it is much easier if there is a space in which to walk. When he has a capacity to talk, he will learn faster

249

if he is spoken to. Practice and training will determine whether a child will be good at something. Hadfield believes that the environment "determines which of the child's native potentialities are developed or exaggerated, which left in abeyance, and which are repressed."

Hence an aggressive capacity could be developed into an overaggressive personality. By the same token, a child who is innately aggressive may actually become a very timid person due to severe discipline imposed by parents, grandparents, military school, etc. The direction of the capacities is decided by the environment. Environmental influence is so strong that it can even modify hereditary factors.

A child's *temperament* results from the influence of her body on her mind. It is completely physiological. *Disposition* results from factors of the environment. Crawling, walking, and talking depend on physiological development. Thus, when the system for walking matures, the child will begin to walk; when the bladder matures, she will begin to learn to control it. Her body cannot perform these tasks before it is ready. This is why it is important not to force walking, talking, toilet training, etc., until the child is ready.

That one child starts to walk later than another child is an example of individual differences in maturation and is not a precursor of slowness in general. When a child is ready for a task, she needs encouragement and practice. An unresponsive environment can stunt a child's natural physical and intellectual growth patterns.

Repetition

When a child repeats a sound over and over again or crawls endlessly with no apparent goal, he is practicing his biological functions. Repetition of sounds prepares the vocal cords for actual talking. The crawling infant eventually discovers that he can get a toy by crawling to it. Beginning with a simple physiological urge and then through repetition, a child inevitably finds a purpose for his actions.

Repetition contributes to the development of *orderly patterns of behavior* that are beneficial for both the child and those surrounding him in that they reduce frustration and predictability. Repetition develops, too, such qualities as *persistence* and *perseverance*. A child will do something over and over until it is right, but he needs to be helped in difficult places so that he does not always fail and become discouraged. (This same stick-to-itiveness might at times provoke a conflict with parents' goals for their child.)

Characteristics of Developmental Stages

Dr. McGraw has compiled a list of facts that are true about all stages of the acquisition of different kinds of skills.

1. Behavior does not occur at a specific month, but will probably occur within a span of months.

2. Order of growth is not rigidly prescribed. Some aspects of growth are completely individualistic.

3. Infant behavior may vacillate between extremes before it settles down to an integrated system of action.

4. Growth is not a straight line occurrence; it is a jagged process of spurts and regressions.

5. Development in one area can interfere with development in another.

The key is knowing when the earliest sign of readiness occurs and then offering a concentration of appropriate learning opportunity. If someone tries to teach a child a skill before or after his stage of readiness, it will take longer and be harder to get the optimum results. It is comforting to note that Dr. McGraw does not go along with those who say it is impossible to get results—it is just much more time-consuming. Moreover, the method of instruction will necessarily be different. One would not use the same method of teaching an infant to swim as one would for a five-year-old.

REFLEXES, PART I

The human newborn behaves in a complex manner, reacting to the world around him via patterned, organized actions that are at once adaptive and automatic—technically referred to as *reflex responses.*

Parents should be reassured by the extensive repertoire of reflex responses the newborn possesses, for most of these behaviors contribute to the baby's physical well-being. Even though newborns are helpless and completely dependent upon their parents, given the appropriate stimulation they usually will act in a self-preserving, self-enhancing way.

Another element of reflex behavior of interest to parents is that it most often is a precursor of skills the older child will voluntarily learn. Writes Dr. Brazelton, in *Infants and Mothers,* "Much of the complex behavior we use later in our human development is anticipated in early infancy in the form of reflexes. The infant builds upon these reflexes. After they appear they may go underground and with a lapse of time return as controlled, voluntary behavior. Walking is an example of this."

As you become attuned to your baby's growing behavior repertoire, you will be able to distinguish between the reflex responses of newborns and the more developmentally bound traits that appear later on. As your baby displays reflex responses appropriate to her particular stage of development, you will be able to study her own *unique* patterns. Each baby varies in an infinite number of ways from another; some fall into the average middle-of-the-road category; others are more active and were that way prenatally; still others are more quiet.

Protective-Defensive Reflexes

The infant has amazing capacity to survive even under adverse conditions. When an object that could conceivably stop his breathing is placed over the baby's nose and mouth, he begins vigorously to mouth it, as if to displace it, and then twists his head violently from side to side. If these head maneuvers are unsuccessful, he begins to flail; each arm is brought across his face as he attempts to knock the object away.

Stroking one leg causes the other leg to flex, cross over, and push the stroking object away with the other foot. When an upper part of the baby's body is stroked or tickled, he will close the fingers as if to grip an object. When a painful stimulus is applied to any part of the baby's body, he will withdraw from it, even bat at it. Placed on his belly, head down, the infant has a set of reflexes that make it almost impossible for him to smother in that position. He picks his head off the bed, then turns it to one side or the other. He begins to crawl with his legs and lifts himself up on his arms. Newborns can even flip themselves completely over to one side or the other.

Startle/Moro Reflex

If a newborn is startled by a sudden sound or an abrupt change of position, particularly one with a sensation of falling, her arms and legs respond in a characteristic way. They move symmetrically, first outward, then upward, and then inward. The hands open first and then clench tightly into a fist as though the baby were trying to grasp the branch of a tree to prevent a fall. Her legs go through a similar sequence of movements although less consistently. In addition, the baby's head bends down and forward. It has been found that immediate repetition of a sudden noise usually elicits no reaction. The infant seems able to "shut out" the painful stimulus as a kind of self-protection.

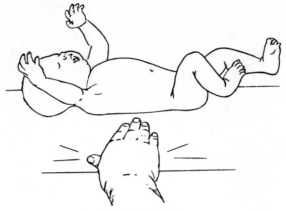

Startle/Moro reflex.

The Moro reflex is triggered by the baby. As she cries, she startles, cries because of the startle, and sets up a vicious cycle. If the parent applies steady pressure on a part of the body, as described below (tactile reflex), it seems to break into this cycle and results in calming the baby.

Tactile Reflex

A fussy baby will be quieted by being picked up and held. Sometimes just placing a hand on the baby's abdomen or restraining an extremity will do it. In some cultures, swaddling is used to produce the same effect. The quieting, soothing aspects of touch, plus the effects of firm, steady pressure combine to quiet the baby.

In a research study performed by William A. Hunt, Frances M. Clarke, and Edna B. Hunt (*Behavior in Infancy*), it was concluded that around the age of four months, the Moro reflex disappears and is followed by the regular startle pattern typical of adults. The latter includes closing the eyes, head movement, raising and bringing forward the shoulders, clenching fists, and other contracting movements, all of which persist throughout adult life.

Tonic Neck Reflex (TNR)

This is a position that babies from birth to sixteen weeks of age prefer. At sixteen weeks it seems to disappear. The baby's head prefers the

253

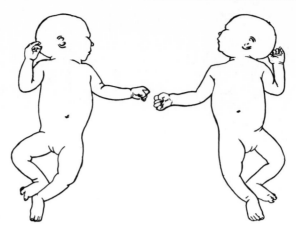

Tonic neck reflex.

horizon or side position and for good developmental reasons. This position enables a baby to catch glimpses of his hand, for he often holds his arm extended toward the same side to which his head is directed, the other arm being flexed at the shoulder.

Parents will recognize this asymmetrical positioning when their baby assumes this favored side and are reminded that this is a normal stage of growth, one that should not be tampered with. It is a natural form of asymmetry that serves to bring the hands and eyes into co-ordination. Such positions help the baby learn to use one side of his body separately from the other.

Many researchers agree that the earliest manifestations of handedness are connected with the TNR. Normative studies of full-term and premature infants indicate an unmistakable predilection toward rightward orientation.

Righting Reflex

When a newborn to one-month-old baby is pulled up into a sitting position, he attempts to maintain his head in an upright position in line with his backbone or spinal column. As he reaches the sitting angle, the head flops forward and he tries to bring it up again. It overshoots and flops backward. He tries to right his head again and it falls forward. During the first few months, parents are advised to support their infant's head inas-

254

much as it will be a while before the infant develops enough self-control to assume the upright head position independently.

Doll's Eye Reflex

This reflex is also produced upon pulling a newborn to one-month-old baby to a sitting position; the eyes tend to open much as the weighted eyes in the old china dolls.

Nystagmus

If you pick up a newborn baby and spin about with her, her head will turn reflexively in the direction of the spin and the eyes (in a rhythmical series of alternating fast and slow movements known as nystagmus) will try also to keep up with the spin. Upon stopping short, the baby's eyes will continue the quick rhythmical movement in the direction of the spin for several seconds. These reactions depend upon a complex system in the ear and brain for sensing position.

REFLEXES, PART II

Rooting

Rooting is the searching movement the baby makes while looking for something to suck on. It is elicited by stroking the infant in special parts of his body. If you touch a baby's cheek with your finger, he will swivel his head around and take your finger in his mouth. Rooting serves to zero the baby in on his source of nutrition before he "knows" where food comes from.

Sucking

Babies are born with the need to suck. Many babies have in fact gotten their thumbs into their mouths while still in the uterus and may be born with calluses on their thumbs. The sucking reflex facilitates contact between the baby and another object—usually a nipple. This kind of behavior usually leads the baby to a source of food, thereby serving a strong survival function.

The sucking and rooting reflexes are intimately associated. If one hour after a successful feeding, your baby is rooting around for something to eat or happens to find her thumb, she might not really be looking for food, but just to suck. Many parents, especially those who are breast feeding and are somewhat unsure about how much milk their baby is getting, are inclined to interpret any rooting or sucking activity as symptoms of hunger; this is not necessarily the case.

The need to suck is probably most urgent during the first four months of life and it is in this period that the pacifier can be put to good use. The sucking reflex occurs when the following parts of the mouth region are touched: most sensitive is the soft palate; next is the interior of the mouth and the lips; last is the cheek and chin area. Even a sleepy baby will suck when his soft palate is stimulated.

Hand-to-mouth Reflex

This behavior is elicited by stroking either the cheek or the palm of the hand. Simple stroking of one end or the other of this hand-to-mouth chain causes the infant's mouth to root and his arm to flex at the same time as he brings his hand up in the region of his mouth. His mouth opens in anticipation and he brings his fist up to it.

The hand-to-mouth reflex serves two functions for the infant: there is tactile gratification around the mouth and hands, coupled with the infant's ability to reproduce *for himself* his sucking need that is satisfied every time he feeds.

Grasp Reflex

If pressure is applied by a finger to the palms of baby's hands or to the balls of baby's feet, the fingers and toes will curl in to "grasp" the pressing object. The hand grasp is so strong that an infant can be lifted off

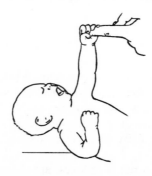

Grasp reflex.

256

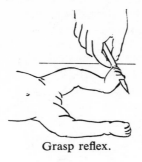

Grasp reflex.

the crib with it. This behavior is sometimes called the "Darwinian reflex": a residual vestige from our arboreal ancestors.

Babinski Reflex

So named for the neurologist who first described it. If the soles of baby's foot are stroked, his foot will pull up, toes fan out and large toe elevate. Thus stroking the soles of baby's foot can set up two opposing reflexes in the toes. One is the grasp reflex, described above, set off by pressing the end of the foot at the base of the toes. The other is the Babinski.

Precursors to Voluntary Skills

CRAWLING REFLEX

When placed on his belly, baby may make crawling movements with his legs and parents will find that upon placing their hands against his feet, he will push against their hands and propel himself forward, as if trying to crawl. The infant is *not aware* of propelling himself across a space. This will be learned at a later date. According to Dr. McGraw, some mothers have reported to her that their babies began to crawl at three weeks. Typically, the mother leaves baby at one end of the bed and after a short time finds him at the other end.

STEPPING REFLEX

Elicited when baby is held in a standing position. The soles of one foot and then the other are pressed gently on the bed. Each leg is drawn up in succession as baby seems to step. A brand-new infant can be helped

257

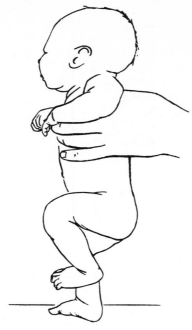

Stepping reflex.

to walk across a bed in this fashion. This stepping reflex will fade out before the baby develops real walking ability.

SWIMMING REFLEX

A series of reflexes that combine to propel an infant across a bed or even through the water. A baby can rhythmically extend and flex her arms and legs at the same time as she swings her trunk from side to side.

This activity is reminiscent of an amphibian and relates human beings to them in the hierarchy of evolution.

The newborn also has the ability to inhibit breathing when her head is placed under water for a short period. If by accident her head is allowed to dip under water, rarely does she choke and aspirate water. However, don't be stimulated by this reflex into experimenting on your baby. *Avoid* getting your baby's face underwater by supporting her under her chin.

Dr. McGraw has studied the swimming behavior of the human infant during the first two and a half years of life. She has observed and recorded the swimming reflex and notes that at about four months of age, the early behavior becomes disorganized and struggling. Toward the beginning of the second year, the child again shows the rhythmical movements of the newborn, with some difference. Activity is now deliberate, voluntary.

Dr. McGraw's detailed approach to the observation of infancy unfolding can be useful for parents. As parents sensitively watch their baby grow and develop, they can introduce new activities and experiences, such as swimming, on the basis of what their baby is now muscularly ready for. It may be that providing an opportunity for the young infant to experience the movements of arms and legs in water when very young will prepare him for learning to swim later unhindered by fears of water.

PCI Point of View

The reflexive (involuntary) behavior of an infant has a marked effect on his intelligence and learning. Jean Piaget, in his book *The Origins of Intelligence,* claims that it is from these early unco-ordinated acts (among them grasping, sucking, and glancing) that mature intelligence develops. British infant researchers are finding to their amazement that what appears to be reflexive action in infants sometimes is actually "intention" or purposeful behavior. When tracking interactions between baby and mother, father, grandparent, or strangers—using a slow-motion camera—the physicians and psychologists discovered that for each different interpersonal interaction there was a different type of reflex hand response.

We believe that as more research is undertaken, it may well be that these reflexes will be proved to be deliberately controlled!

"NORMAL" DEVIATIONS OF THE NEWBORN

A baby is often born with unusual characteristics or conditions that will be of concern to a new parent. In most instances, these "problems" are temporary and quite normal.

Skin Conditions

Many babies are born with whiteheads on the nose, blotchy rashes (often resulting from drooling or temporary allergies), and flat, red "birthmarks" on the forehead, nose, and neck. Dark-skinned and some light-skinned babies may have a blue patch, usually on the lower back, due to a high level of pigment in that area. Often there is fine, dark hair covering the body.

The newborn may also appear fat and swollen. All these conditions are usually temporary and soon disappear without treatment. Lip blisters and peeling are common in babies who are sucking intently. Pediatricians often suggest Vaseline as a protection.

Impetigo, a contagious skin infection, can occur during the first week after birth. Small water blisters appear and become a reddish-brown crust. Drs. Robertson and Wood, in *Today's Child,* suggest having the condition diagnosed by a physician. Treatment will involve a salve prescribed by the physician and bathing the infected area until the scabs are soft and removable.

Thrush, a severe form of diaper rash, is caused by a fungus. It can also occur in the mouth. It appears as white patches of milk. Your physician will probably recommend an anti-fungal medication.

Cradle Cap is a condition involving brown, greasy scales on the scalp that may result from the mother's hesitancy to wash with soap the "soft spot" on the baby's head.

Jaundice is a yellow appearance to the usually pink skin and to the eyes. A newborn has many extra red blood cells that were necessary before birth, and give the baby a lobster-red appearance at birth. The additional cells begin to break down after birth since they are no longer required. The result is the formation of bilirubin, which is yellow. The liver usually excretes this substance. In newborns the liver is still immature and cannot handle the higher levels of bilirubin, so it is absorbed into the skin and gives it a yellow appearance. At this point there is no cause for concern since jaundice is fairly common in the first week of life. Babies of all races experience jaundice symptoms. When the baby begins to absorb milk, the jaundice is flushed out of the system.

Protruding Navel

The navel of a newborn often protrudes, which usually is due to the skin growing along the umbilical cord. The skin becomes loose and folded when the cord falls off, but eventually it flattens. Another cause could be an umbilical hernia, which can vary from the size of a dime to a half-dollar. Whenever the infant strains himself, it may protrude even more. This protrusion will usually flatten without treatment.

Dr. Marvin Gersh, in *How to Raise Children at Home in Your Spare Time,* mentions that many physicians suggest strapping if the size of the hernia is larger than a dime. There are pediatricians, however, who believe that this treatment is not necessary.

Eye Problems

During the first month after birth, a baby may show signs of a blocked tear duct. The eye drains constantly and appears to have a film over it. A crust may also form on the eyelid. (See Chapter 4, section on Eyes and Eye Care, for more information.) Other common abnormalities that newborns display are colic (refer to Chapter 2 for further discussion); genital problems and bowed legs (refer to Chapter 4 for discussion); and vomiting (refer to Chapter 5 for discussion).

SITTING

Physical development depends on physical readiness or maturation. An infant's motor development, the ability to move, is orderly and sequential. There is nothing parents can do to teach their baby how to move. They can merely observe their baby's signs of readiness to move and provide an environment that is conducive to mobility. Sitting is one stage of development that combines physical growth and readiness with environmental opportunity.

To prepare for sitting, an infant's body must develop a complex network of nerves and muscles needed to maintain balance. Because the process of motor development proceeds from head to toe, a baby cannot sit until movement and control first occur in the head, neck, arms, and hands. As the baby develops and uses these parts of his body, his back muscles and nerves grow.

A newborn infant can move her head and raise it slightly. After head movements, she learns to control her neck movements. By three months of age, she can raise her head completely when lying prone. Proceeding downward, we come to the arms. An infant begins moving her arms in response to an object. In the next few months, the baby learns to use arms and hands in a skilled manner. Through the use of her arms and hands, the baby attains the balance mechanism that helps her maintain a sitting position.

"Even after an infant can sit alone," remarks Dr. Brazelton, in *Infants and Mothers,* "an observer can estimate how new the skill is by watching his hands. When he no longer keeps them ready to catch himself, but frees them to manipulate objects, he has become sure of his prowess in sitting." Therefore, it is not physical strength, but physical ability that determines readiness for sitting.

What Versus When

What a baby does is much more significant than *when* he does something. The sequence of events in the achievement of sitting, for example, unfolds over a period of about a year from birth. When specific abilities are manifested is not important because individuals vary in their development. What parents should know are the orderly stages of sitting progression so that they may recognize them and perhaps provide more comfortable positions for their developing infant.

The "comfortable positions" refer to our understanding that babies eventually tire of a passive position lying down. Awareness of this fact will alert parents to this cause of some infant fussiness. Solutions will depend on what stage of development your baby has reached.

Sequence of Events

Parents notice that following birth the head falls backward or forward when the baby is pulled to a sitting position. Gradually the baby may hold his head in line with his back. Weeks later he keeps his head erect while sitting, but there is still some bobbing. By the third month he can sit supported with a minimum of head bobbing. At four months the infant's back is firm and his head is erect and steady. Now he can sit supported for ten to fifteen minutes.

When your baby can sit supported for a period of about thirty minutes with his back firm, it will be appropriate to place him in a bounce chair or swing at a reclining angle to support his lower back. Care should be taken that the chair or swing is weighted to avoid toppling. A carriage and high chair also may be used now if the baby is propped on a slanted pillow. Propping does not hurt the back, but Dr. Spock recommends that "in general it's better not to prop a baby straight up until he can sit steadily himself for many minutes." Dr. Gersh indicates that only when rickets is present can early sitting or walking distort the soft bones of the spine or legs.

At about five months, the baby holds and balances her head erect continuously. She helps, too, in pulling up her body, flexes her head forward, flexes her trunk, and draws her legs toward her tummy. Seated, she can grasp an object.

Dr. McGraw suggests that the next stage, as reported to her by mothers, is "sitting alone." The baby now can support herself with her outstretched arms on the surface and her back at an angle, not upright.

Over the next three months the baby requires less and less support as he sits. His hands help him to balance and gradually they will be free. He can also balance on an adult's shoulders holding onto the person's head. He may also learn to sit from a crawling position. The techniques are many and vary with each infant. Often babies sit steadily by having one leg stretched out in front and the other flexed.

Another development is bouncing. Some babies may bounce across the floor on their buttocks, a mode of locomotion they use in place of creeping.

Until he is about one year old, the infant practices and polishes his sitting performance. He can sit well in a chair and steadily and indefinitely without one. He learns to sit down from standing and to get onto his stomach from sitting. He squats, stoops, and lowers himself to sitting grace-fully. Upright and mobile, he is indeed "sitting pretty."

CREEPING AND CRAWLING

After the infant is well on her way to sitting with less and less sup-port, her body prepares for the next step in motor development: creeping and crawling. This is a stage that takes place only after the downward de-velopment from head to toe has reached the lower back muscles and nerves.

Legs and feet need toning now. The baby gets them ready kicking them in the air when lying on her back. To direct this exercise, parents should try tying a bell-ringing object on the crib within reach of the infant's feet only. As she kicks, the infant is rewarded by the sound of the bell, which encourages her to repeat her success.

Readiness

Just as the ability to sit is independent of parental or environmental interference and relies directly on physical growth, so creeping and crawling are mastered according to an infant's readiness. The right mo-ment, however, will allow a baby to learn a physical skill with the utmost energy expended by him and the least amount by his parents.

When at about the sixth month the infant learns to roll from his back to his stomach, parents can be ready to meet their baby's needs. It is now that the gradual work toward creeping begins. The baby may get up on his hands and knees in a crouch position and hurtle forward by flinging his limbs out. The result is often a series of flops aimed at a desirable object. He may also try to conquer space by twisting and rolling across a room. To help the baby achieve his goals at this stage parents should provide room for movement. The firm, flat surface of a floor is suitable. The infant will arch his back, flex his muscles, and generally perform a sophisticated physical workout.

When he propels himself on his tummy with his legs and steers with his arms, he is creeping. Creeping is distinguished from crawling by the fact that the infant's abdomen is on the ground. A crawl results when a baby gets up on his elbows and bent knees.

Backward Versus Forward

In both flopping and creeping, a baby often goes backward first. The muscles that help her push backward are stronger at this point than those that permit forward direction. It will take time before she is able to favor going forward and achieving mastery of creeping that way.

When she does go forward, after about the seventh month, she may creep with an object in one or both hands. She may start from a crawling position and also experiment with other means of locomotion, such as raising and lowering the buttocks while on her back or sitting on the side of a flexed leg and propelling herself with a corresponding hand and opposite leg.

Achieving Style

While babies usually creep backward first, they often crawl in a forward direction when beginning this more advanced method of locomotion. Dr. McGraw recognizes that "nowhere is the struggle between higher and lower brain centers for the control of behavior more clear than in the de-

265

velopment of crawling." The higher brain (or cortex) does not take over the movement of all muscle groups in this activity at the same time. It reaches the legs later than it does the shoulders and arms.

For a while the infant must experiment. He tries over and over different methods until he learns how his legs and arms work together as a team. Many pediatricians think there may be an inborn correction mechanism that sends signals to the brain when motor acts seem "right," so that the baby can identify and use those movements in succeeding efforts.

Moving Out

Once the infant has chosen and mastered a style of crawling that will most likely be unique, he spends his time using this new freedom of movement to explore his world. By about a year old he has gathered speed and straightened his limbs. He can crawl with one hand full of booty. His curiosity is stimulated by crawling so that the physical act now leads to mental development. He becomes goal-oriented. He sees, touches, explores, and manipulates as a result of this new power of locomotion.

"The moment your child has the freedom of the house it is time for babyproofing, recommend Dr. Virginia Pomeranz and Dodi Schultz. The time to start the task, however, is not when the baby is already speeding out of sight, but before he achieves any movement on the floor. An environment that promotes and encourages movement is free of hazards. Parental shrieks of "no" every time the baby moves toward a forbidden object only confuse him and reduce his confidence.

Whatever the method of locomotion, every baby has her own very personal timetable of development. "The baby who learns to be a speedy crawler," suggests Dr. Spock, "may be late in walking, and the one who is a clumsy creeper, or who never learns to creep at all has a good reason for learning to walk early." Then, too, there are a fair number of perfectly normal children who never creep or crawl. They simply stand and walk when they are ready.

Parents can learn how to meet their baby's needs by carefully observing his individual style and progress and providing him ample opportunity to practice all his maturing physical skills.

STANDING

"A baby needs no teaching to 'complete the course' of gross or small motor skills. Bodily know-how just *comes!* But as each skill 'is born,' opportunity to use it, to improve it, to practice it is necessary." We see how this observation by Dr. George Engstrom, Director of Well-Baby Clinic, in Concord, North Carolina, is valid in the cases of sitting, creeping, and crawling. It is equally applicable to standing, the next sequential stage of physical development that urges the infant to achieve an independent upright posture.

A Gradual Process

Physical development in the first six to eight months reveals the gradual process that unfolds to enable a baby to reach a standing position. In the early months, when the infant is pulled to sit, he may bypass sitting and come up to stand. "The standing a baby is doing now," according to Dr. Brazelton, "is no more than a responsive or reflex stiffening of his body, but as he learns he can do it, he becomes delighted with the act, and repeats it over and over." However, only when the muscles of the neck, back, and hips are strong enough to bear the baby's weight will he be able to stand firmly with support.

When he starts to bounce, step in place, and watch his feet when standing supported under his arms, the baby is getting ready to experiment with pulling himself up to stand. Seated in the crib or playpen, he will spread his feet, draw up his knees slightly, and tug on the side until he is in a flexed, half-standing posture with his bottom out and wavering. The art of "scaling" follows. By letting go of one hand at a time, he uses a hand-over-hand movement until he is upright.

Practice and Determination

Endless hours of practice are needed to gain co-ordination and balance. They may be painful for both parents and child, because when the baby first learns to pull herself up to stand, she may not know how to get down. She cries until helped down and when seated immediately practices standing again. It is a frustrating experience for the parents, but one that does not alter the baby's determination to achieve this new skill. The urge upward is so powerful that no obstacle, no accident deters the infant.

It is through this repetition of experience that hazards are overcome and anxiety diminished. Soon thereafter the infant very carefully lowers herself as far as she can and eventually lets go. She finds that it really was not such a long drop and that her bottom is well padded.

Now, the practice sessions grow more vigorous as the baby's confidence increases. She stands briefly with her hand held and she begins to stand alone for a few seconds. Using furniture for support, she develops a side-stepping "cruise" along the sofa. As practice perfects this maneuver, a new one follows, the ability to stand alone with little support and to stand up independently. The baby pushes herself up from the tummy with both arms, places one foot, then the other on the floor, straightens legs and arms, and comes to stand by herself by lifting her trunk and using her waist as a pivot.

Through repetition and experimentation the baby learns to flex the knees and push off from a squatting position and when standing to pivot his body ninety degrees. When he wants to sit, he does so gracefully. These achievements are usually made by the end of the first year. Remember, please, that it is not age, but the sequence of events in the development of a motor skill that is significant. Each human being has a personal timetable of development.

Achievement and Change

The infant has put together remarkably a series of maneuvers in order to reach the end result, requiring both physical growth and a strong determination to achieve one's goal. During this growth the infant undergoes a personality change. No longer willing to lie passively flat on his back, he is impelled to upright himself. This urge is so strong that it sets him in motion practicing until the point of exhaustion.

During this time some babies may be observed sleeping while standing. They resist interference and persist in standing for dressing, for feeding, in the stroller, in the doctor's office. It may help parents to realize that the urge is an inner necessity having more to do with challenging gravity than defiance of mother.

Hazards, Risks, and New Skills

The baby's persistent attempts to stand will result in many falls. A harness may be used in the stroller, high chair, and perhaps the shopping cart at the supermarket, all sources of dangerous spills. Newly acquired agility in standing will lead to other skills, such as climbing. The baby's urge to get moving once he is upright will propel him onto chairs, into cabinets, into the bathroom sink and tub, out of the crib and stroller, and up the stairs.

Watchfulness is the key here to protection and guidance. Be aware of where the baby is at all times and what she is doing. When climbing stairs, most babies will insist on forward motion at first, so it is important to teach them both directions. The dangers involved make it worth your time, effort, and persistence in this task once your baby consistently heads for the stairs.

Through guidance and control, therefore, parents direct their infant's use of motor skills. When their offspring stands up before the world, they all share the delight. Now the baby is one step closer to becoming an independent human being.

WALKING

Walking is a very special human achievement. It marks the culmination of a growth process that urges the body to assume an upright position. Every completed motor skill drives the infant forward to the next developmental step in an orderly sequence from the time the baby raises his head when lying and begins to turn it from side to side. His personal timetable of readiness and growth leads him through sitting, creeping, crawling, and standing. When he takes his first steps, the infant achieves the capacity for physical independence that frees him to discover and become his solitary self.

Myths and Misconceptions

If parents want their child to realize his own self and experience the incomparable fulfillment of having walked himself, then they should refrain from the harmful attitude that often exists in our society that the earlier a child walks, the more intelligent he is. According to Drs. Mussen, Conger, and Kagan, "There is no strong relation between age of walking or rate of physical development during the first 2 years and intelligence during the preschool or early school years."

It is not up to parents to determine when their baby shall walk. This crowning ability depends upon the child's physical growth and his successful achievement of prior required skills, such as standing unsupported. Parents who overwhelm their infant with urges to walk before he is ready only destroy his great chance of self-realization when he knows he has taken these wonderful steps *himself*. Walking is a complicated and gradual achievement.

Conditions for Stepping Out

The stepping reflex is present in the first weeks of life. Parents may notice how their newborn infant when held moves her legs and feet one after the other as if stepping. This reflex disappears while the baby is busy

269

developing more immediate skills while lying down, such as raising the head and rolling over. However, it reappears around the fourth or fifth month as the baby lies on her back kicking in step. When pulled to stand, she again moves her legs and feet in a "walking step," but she cannot walk until her body is ready and antecedent skills have been acquired. The skills involve control and use of head, neck, shoulders, arms, hands, back, legs, and feet—in that order.

A baby cannot roll over until her head muscles and nerves are strong enough. She cannot sit until her lower back reaches appropriate neuromuscular maturity. She cannot stand until her changed body proportions allow legs and feet to bear the weight of her trunk. She cannot walk until her whole body works together to stand steadily unsupported.

Intricate Maneuvers

First steps occur with support, as when the baby "cruises" along the sofa or crib. Parents may participate in this new exercise by placing toys a little out of reach along the sofa to encourage their baby and help build his confidence. Gradually he shows signs of enjoying walking with his two hands held. Then he walks with one hand held.

When he finally gathers courage to walk unsupported, he uses his arms for balance. They are outstretched and held high like wings. He glues his eyes on a target and totters forward on his toes. It is quite a sight. With stiffened knees and a wide-legged gait, the baby clumps along swinging sideways as each leg is thrust forward. His next accomplishment is slowing down, catching himself, and turning around. The final maneuver is stopping in the middle of the floor.

As practice smooths all these gradually attained skills into the total ability to walk, more subtle maneuvers are acquired. Waving, backing up, and carrying toys are some of them. Walking backward is especially popular when infants pull toys along the floor. With eyes riveted on the toy, the baby concentrates on what he is doing and walks with a purpose. As he becomes more competent, he lowers his arms when walking, indicating he has mastered balance and the control of his trunk muscles.

Factors That Influence Time of Walking

When a baby walks depends on dozens of factors, the most significant being the age at which she achieves the basic skills needed for walking. The average age is between twelve and fifteen months. Usually babies take their first steps around twelve months, but do not achieve independent walking until fifteen months.

Dr. Spock suggests that ambition, temperament, creeping, illness, bad experiences, and the like may influence the timing. For example, a baby who gets where she wants to go effectively by creeping may be too busy at first to stand and then walk. Environment is also a factor. A large room that has little furniture in it for "cruising" does not provide the support needed for the first practice steps.

Most pediatricians do not recommend walkers. They take away initiative and deny the baby the discovery and use of her own body. If a "crutch" is needed, the baby will find one in the way of a chair or a carriage to push. Observant parents, therefore, should not create needs, but respond to those indicated by their baby's behavior.

From Infancy to Toddlerhood

Through walking the infant enters toddlerhood, with new tasks, new explorations, and new opportunities. It also exposes him to a new area of vulnerability, including, according to Dr. Dodson, in *How to Parent,* "feelings of self-doubt, if he is excessively punished or made to feel he is 'bad' for exploring his environment." Walking, then, is more than a physical feat. It also is a manifestation of self-confidence and trust that grow with parental and environmental reinforcement.

SWIMMING INSTRUCTION

There is much current interest in teaching the acquisition of skills to children. The implied message for parents seems to be "the more the better" and its corollary, "the earlier the better." Example: three-year-olds learn to swim. In many instances, increasing the abilities of young children is desirable, as in the case of teaching the three-year-old who can dress himself how to zip and unzip. This skill is useful, encountered daily, and certainly within the range of the toddler's muscular co-ordination.

Controversy has surfaced around the issue of infants learning how to swim. Areas of dissension revolve about the long-range effects of instruction (will nine-month-old Tommy retain his swimming abilities when he is nine years old?), the physical dangers water presents (does a one-year-old know what drowning is?), and the special health requirements pools should conform to when their users are under three (and not toilet trained). These are some of the questions parents need to ask themselves before running down to the local Y to sign up for swim instruction.

Babies Can Swim

The swimminglike behavior of infants was observed and recorded forty years ago by Dr. Myrtle McGraw. While affiliated with Columbia University, Dr. McGraw conducted an intensive analysis of forty-two infants ranging in age from eleven days to two and a half years. Through detailed observations and films, three stages of swimming behavior emerged. During Stage One the infant exhibits reflexive movements when placed in the water, forceful enough to propel her a short distance. Another interesting feature of the newborn apparatus is breath control. She reflexively does not breathe while submerged. Stage Two occurs after four months of age: the infant displays disorganization in swim behavior. She struggles with the experimenter or may passively sink. During this stage baby swallows a great deal of water, coughs, etc. Stage Three occurs toward the beginning of the second year. The child is again ready to propel herself through the water in a fashion more deliberate, more voluntary than was Stage One behavior.

How to Teach Infants to Swim

In her book written for parents, *Teaching an Infant to Swim,* Virginia Hunt Newman details the process by which she teaches infants to propel themselves through the water and come to the surface to breathe. The stroke she teaches is commonly referred to as the "doggy paddle," which, according to the American Red Cross, is the crawl with a two-beat kick and underwater recovery of the arms, or the *human* stroke. Some people may not call this swimming, but it is propulsion through the water and this fits the dictionary's definition. More accomplished strokes can be learned later on.

Mrs. Newman believes the best time to learn to swim is *yesterday,* but she cautions that parents should check with their pediatricians before beginning a swimming program. She maintains that every child exposed to water should learn to swim for safety's sake.

Lessons can be given every day or three times a week, depending upon pool availability. Cheerfulness and confidence are very important, because your child will reflect your attitude. He will learn by watching you, by repetition, and by praise.

PCI Point of View

There is no one right directive in this issue. Whether you decide to teach your little one to swim will depend largely on the kind of questions you ask yourself beforehand and the kind of outcomes you desire for your child. There is no longitudinal research to date to support the thesis that an infant swimmer will sustain this ability in later years, nor is there any research to suggest that infant swimmers get sicker oftener or drown more frequently than non-swimmers.

The evidence seems to suggest that if parents want to spend worthwhile time with their little ones doing something that is fun in and of itself and also has ego-building potential, then try swimming. Water play helps build strong bodies, develops co-ordination, increases the appetite, and, most important of all, may enable your child to save his own life one day.

ACTIVITIES FOR MOTOR DEVELOPMENT

By the time she is eighteen months old a child is ready to spend a short period of time each day (perhaps fifteen minutes) "working" with a parent in a specific endeavor to widen her interests and extend her knowledge. Just how that time is spent, however, is critically important to the amount and type of learning that will take place. As Ira Gordon, the author of *Child Learning Through Child Play,* put it, "What we ask children to do, how we ask them to do it, what experiences we provide for them, how we react to their successes and failures, what behavior models we expect them to copy—all influence whether or not they will become competent, will see themselves as competent, and will develop a sense of security about themselves."

Motor skills (the development of co-ordination and manual dexterity) play a vital role in a child's self-image, and her feelings of security and self-confidence. Learning to master control of body parts and using her crudely developed gross-motor skills in testing the influence of her environment—all these are tied up with the toddler's self-contentedness and self-image.

Working with the child, a parent can do a great deal to encourage personality and physical growth. However, the *learning should at all times be kept pleasurable* and should be stopped before the child becomes overtired, bored, or disinterested.

In planning for formal physical activity, several materials are invaluable: a *2"×4" walking beam* set on the floor is excellent for developing eye-body co-ordination and balance. The toddler can crawl across it and then walk across it, first with the steadying help of parent's hand, later alone. Both parent and child can suggest other ways to use the board and many action words can be introduced to accompany this play as a bonus in language development (jump, crawl, over, under, off, backward, etc.).

A *large ball* is also useful. This can be rolled back and forth between parent and child with the distance between the two gradually increasing as skills improve. The ball can be bounced back and forth. Finer co-ordination is called into play in catching a ball. A game can be made of rolling the ball into a large wastebasket turned on its side, the distance of the basket to be extended as dexterity increases. Later the ball can be bounced into an upright basket.

Balloons can be used in much the same way as a ball, but will respond differently to being thrown, kicked or hit.

A *large three-foot clown punching bag,* weighted at the bottom so it cannot tip over, is marvelous for wrestling, kicking, hitting, and chasing.

There are other materials that are useful in motor development: *water* and *containers* in *many sizes* help develop co-ordination through the act of pouring water from one container into another (as well as providing scientific observation as to the nature of liquids). The bathtub is great for this kind of experimentation. *Hammering pegs* requires precise eye-hand co-ordination and produces special sounds that are interesting to listen to.

Beads for stringing develop muscular dexterity and provide an opportunity for the child to sort and match colors, sizes, and shapes and to see and use numbers.

Running, walking, jumping, galloping, marching, spinning, rolling, and swinging, with or without music, are all excellent means of developing physical co-ordination. *Music,* when used as a background for the running, walking, galloping, dancing, etc. provides an additional source of pleasure and an objective boundary within which to play. Rhythmic activities have many values, especially in the development of balance, co-ordination, and good posture.

PCI Point of View

In working with your child in motor development—as in every other area of his growth—it is important to remember to keep all activities enjoyable and free from pressure.

8

Language Acquisition

INTRODUCTION BY ERIC H. LENNEBERG, PH.D.* †

I would like to address myself to two popular beliefs about language acquisition which on careful study appear to be little more than superstitions and briefly to three of the questions most frequently asked of me by parents of small children acquiring language.

I. The first popular but erroneous belief: Parents *must teach* their children to talk.

We have every reason to believe that actually the child is *not* taught language. Rather, the parents' role is simply to provide him with the opportunity to "teach himself," so to speak, to pull himself up by his own bootstraps. If the child is talked to, if he is surrounded with language, if he hears people talking to one another, he will naturally go without any teaching from stage to stage in his own language development.

Nor can this development be pushed by anxious parents. The child has his own strategy of language learning and will develop at his own pace, regardless of how much one tries to teach him. An excellent demonstration of the natural language-learning strategy of children is provided by kindergarten or first-grade classes in many schools for the

* The late Dr. Eric H. Lenneberg was an eminently qualified expert in language acquisition. At his untimely death in 1975, Dr. Lenneberg was Professor of Psychology at Cornell University in Ithaca, New York. He received his Ph.D. in Psychology and Linguistics at Harvard University in 1956.

Dr. Lenneberg had published widely on such topics as the relationship of speech to thought and behavior, communication systems of higher animals, and how infants learn their own language. Based on the training he received in neurology and physiology at the Harvard Medical School, he researched and wrote about deafness and brain damage. He also served as a consultant to parents of handicapped youngsters.

† PCI does not always agree with Dr. Lenneberg on how a child masters language, but we believe that airing a variety of concepts helps parents to understand and arrive at their own language acquisition ideas.

deaf. These children are frequently "taught" language in the same way that a foreign language is taught to normal high school students, with the teacher paying careful attention to sentence structure, parts of speech, the grammar of the language, etc. Careful observation of the young deaf child, however, reveals that he is not learning language in the way it is being taught to him at all! Rather, he is following a strategy very similar to the strategy of normal children, picking and choosing out of all he is offered just those things he is ready for, ignoring the niceties of grammar and syntax, however systematically these are taught.

A simple and harmless "experiment" on normal nursery-school-age children will provide another demonstration. If your child is at the stage where he is beginning to string words together to make little sentences, try having him repeat after you sentences like these:

> Johnny doesn't like dogs.
> The cat is chased by the dog.
> You like cookies and so do I.

You will find that your child will not repeat such sentences verbatim; instead, he will restructure them into his own language ("Johnny no like dogs," perhaps). This is not a question of the length of the sentence; he might do very well if you asked him to say, "Mommy, Daddy, and Johnny want to go" ("wanna go"). The reason the child cannot repeat sentences like those above is that their structure is more advanced than he is ready for. He constantly reformulates what he hears according to his particular stage of development.

All this is not to say that language grows as does a hair or a nose —or that the language environment surrounding the child is of no importance. As a general rule, the more verbal, vocal home will produce the more verbal child, at least initially; the quiet home, the taciturn child. However, extended studies I have made of children growing up in markedly impoverished language environments (hearing children of deaf parents, for example, or children living in institutions for the retarded) have shown that if a child has the capacity for language acquisition, a remarkably limited exposure to language will be sufficient for him to develop normal language himself.

At this point, mention should be made of some of the various experiments on language reinforcement that have been discussed in this chapter. It has been shown that if small infants are "reinforced" for making babbling or cooing sounds (if the mother immediately responds vocally and with a smile), the baby will make such sounds more frequently. When reinforcement is no longer contingent on the baby's vocalization, he quickly returns to his base line level of vocal output. The point being made here is that human beings rarely go to the limits of their capacity without encouragement, in language or anything else; we generally walk, we don't run all the time. Reinforcement can encourage the child to do *more* of what he already knows how to do. However, I stress again that this must not be interpreted to show that the rate of *development* is contingent on or advanced by reinforcement.

To summarize: we do not teach our children to talk. We simply provide them with an environment in which they acquire language at their own pace and by means of their own strategies.

II. The second superstition: The child acquires language in order to communicate.

Every careful student of child language has discovered that the first steps in language acquisition are taken without any evident purpose of communicating whatsoever. In fact, the child's first sounds are frequently described as "egocentric speech." The baby lying in his crib, babbling and cooing, the older child saying his first words over and over again, are evidently enjoying making these sounds just for their own sake. Even after they have begun to acquire a vocabulary with which to communicate, many children express their demands by extra-linguistic means, such as crying or taking mother by the hand.

III. The three questions I am perhaps most frequently asked by concerned parents are these: (1) My child is not acquiring language at the normal rate. What should I do? (2) Will growing up to be bilingual hurt my child or help him? (3) Should I use baby talk with my child, or is that wrong?

1. Perhaps the most important thing for parents to remember about language development, and about *all* development, is that there is a wide range of individual variation. In a study done in Boston, I found that roughly 10 per cent of all three-year-olds may be said to be slow language developers. If by his third birthday a child has not yet begun to string sentences together, if he is not understanding most of what is said to him, parents are right to be concerned. The pediatrician should be consulted. However, most of these three-year-old slow speakers are slow for entirely benign reasons and will outgrow

their problems within a year. Some, of course, have language delays owing to more serious causes, such as a hearing defect or a retarding disease. In about 1 per cent of our sample there were severe language delays or marked unintelligibility for no apparent reason. Even these children, however, will sooner or later acquire language, although they may often need the help of a speech therapist.

2. Most children can learn two different languages simultaneously without difficulty and no one will deny that being proficient in more than one language is an advantage. However, if a child is exposed to more than two languages during the early years of development, and is also required to speak more than two, problems may occasionally ensue—delayed language acquisition, extreme shyness, or other psychological symptoms of disturbance.

If the child is to grow up with two languages, it is usually beneficial and helps to avoid confusion if one parent speaks one of the languages with the child and the other parent the other. If the parents are bilingual themselves, and both use both languages, the child will most probably confuse the two at first. However, as long as the parents recognize this as a natural confusion and not a serious problem, no harm will be done.

If tension about the situation is avoided, the child will straighten out the two languages naturally and quite rapidly. (One last point: it must be remembered and considered that if a child is required to speak a language that identifies him with an ethnic and linguistic community that he and his peers consider less than prestigious, he may refuse to use that language when he reaches school age and thus conflict may be added to the household. Before embarking on a bilingual environment for their child, parents might give serious thought to such problems.)

3. My answer to the problem of baby talk is brief indeed. I certainly do not recommend it as being "good" for the baby. On the other hand, the important thing for the baby is that his parents love him and talk with him naturally. If your way of doing this is with baby talk, certainly a moderate dose of it is not going to harm his language development!

STAGES OF LANGUAGE ACQUISITION
IN THE FIRST YEAR

Vocalization from Birth Cry to One Year

The acquisition of language in the growing baby should be approached from a point of view that always focuses on its dual nature: language is both an active (vocalization) and a passive, responsive (comprehension) process. At birth, it is entirely a vocalization experience; the newborn cries. However, by the age of one month, he is crying, making small throaty sounds, and responding to a voice. The baby *is* aware of and is paying attention to the sounds around him even though he may not indicate this overtly. Indeed, in the area of language, the research shows a time lag with comprehension consistently preceding verbalization.

Universal Stages of Language Acquisition

1. All babies learn language similarly and within a few years. The most important aspects of grammar are achieved by the age of three and a half.

2. A baby learns language in spurts—a spurt of syllables around six months; a dramatic increase in number and clarity around eighteen to twenty-four months. A one-year-old has a vocabulary of several words; a three-year-old has a speaking vocabulary of more than a thousand words and an understanding of more than twice that many.

3. A baby moves from a blurred understanding of what's said to a grasp of clearly defined relationships between sounds and words. By the age of two, 70 per cent of his sounds are fairly clear and 50 per cent of what he says is understandable.

4. Language development is a maturation-bound process. It is similar to other motor skills, such as walking or reaching.

For a parent, the cry of a newborn baby is an exciting sound. For a doctor, the vigor and quality of the birth cry suggest the condition of the infant's lungs, airway, vocal cords, and general strength.

By one month, in addition to crying, the baby also coos, making vowel-like sounds, usually uninterrupted by consonants. These sounds are not like adult vocalizations in that they cannot be reproduced easily. The reason for this is that a baby's sound-making organs are in the process of development and are still unco-ordinated. Only by the twelfth month does the baby begin to produce some sounds acoustically close to those in more mature speech.

About the end of the fourth or fifth month, babbling, a chain of rhythmic, syllable-like sounds, appears. Reduplication is common in babbling—mama, bebe, dada. Thereafter, babbling increases in complexity and in frequency. Parents and grandparents at this time may be convinced that their little darling is calling them because the baby does attempt to imitate adult inflections. However, in reality, these repetitive syllables are produced spontaneously, for baby herself and perhaps for her toys.

Somewhere in the babbling period the baby starts noticeably to superimpose adult intonations and patterns upon her vocalizations, similar to those heard in questions and exclamations. By the eighth month of life, the baby's language environment assumes primary importance in influencing the mode and rate of her developing speech. Identifiable words emerge around the end of the first year.

Generally the first words consist of single or duplicated syllables, such as bye-bye, mama, or dada. Keeping in mind the growth principle that language comprehension precedes language production by several months, the year-old baby has in fact been in possession of some language knowledge for several months.

Social Influences on Language

Researchers agree that infants from a very early age do react vocally to adult (usually parental) speech. However, at what age, what type of language contact, and for what purpose still remain to be ascertained.

In a study made by Dr. Lenneberg and his colleagues in 1965, comparing the frequency of cooing among infants of hearing parents, hearing infants of deaf parents (who provide much less vocalization), and deaf infants born to deaf parents, there was no difference in the frequency of cooing during the first three months of life. This study implies that the amount of stimulation and reinforcement is not a factor in the initiation of these early sounds.

On the other hand, Rheingold, Gewirtz, and Ross, in 1959, performed an oft-quoted study with three-month-old babies that seems to contradict Dr. Lenneberg's findings. Rheingold, et al., reinforced any sound the baby made (that was not crying or fussing) with a smile, a touch on the baby's abdomen, and a vocal click ("tsk"). Infant vocalization frequency increased through this treatment. Perhaps the age factor can reconcile apparent contradictions. Dr. Lenneberg's babies were up to three months old while Dr. Rheingold's babies were all three months old. Furthermore, Dr. Lenneberg studied the children's total vocal output around the clock, whereas Dr. Rheingold and her collaborators reported on the babies' responses during the period immediately following the reinforcement.

Michael Lewis, Ph.D., at the Educational Testing Service in Princeton, New Jersey, conducted an experiment that draws attention to the infant's need to hear the speech of others in order to practice vocalization. In an atmosphere of "contentment, attention, and encouragement," a ten-week-old baby boy made a total of only four sounds in three minutes of observation during which his father was silent. The same boy, however, during alternate minutes when father said "hullo" every ten seconds, made a total of eighteen sounds. On the other hand, it is well to remember that babies need an occasional silence. Babies do best in homes where language is used in normal ways for communication.

Emotional Atmosphere

Sara D. Gilbert, in *Three Years to Grow,* reminds us that "words are the primary symbols, standing for things, ideas, and feelings. The better our baby's use of words—his verbal ability, as the aptitude tests call it—the better may be his thinking power." It is important to talk to, at, and around your baby. Diaper changing and feeding are two ideal conversational situations.

When you run out of your one-sided conversations you can switch to reminiscing, singing, reciting poetry, and debating current events. While the words in themselves will not be understood, the sounds you make, the love in your voice, and the comfortable atmosphere your attempts to communicate establish will be sufficient. Dr. Church advises parents to "bathe the baby in speech" right from birth.

Many parents naturally talk to their baby. Others feel awkward and foolish in this early one-way conversation. However, every child expert agrees that this accustoms parents to communicating with their child in words. For parents who are uneasy with infants, talking establishes rapport.

Once your baby begins to smile, your voice is a good way to induce her to smile, which will encourage you to continue talking. After two or three months, you may find her listening attentively and working her mouth in an attempt to reply.

PCI Point of View

PCI suggests that parents consider the following as they and their baby jointly go through the process of language learning:

1. *Emotional climate:* the adult who presents security by feeding, changing diapers, and fondling the infant; the adult who comforts the crying baby by rocking or singing to him, thereby teaching him to hope, wait, and expect; the adult who does all this and then verbalizes what is being done is creating the atmosphere in which language is learned.

2. *Secondary reinforcement:* according to learning theory, the following occurs:

   a. Parent talks to baby while attending to his needs; baby tries to imitate these pleasant, emotionally toned words.

   b. In parent's absence, baby reinforces himself by self-initiating pleasant sounds.

3. *Non-verbal communication:* the infant in the process of developing a language repertoire to express his thoughts, wishes, and needs, relies heavily on non-verbal referents, gestures, and facial expressions.

Some language specialists believe that the capacity for speech is biologically determined, i.e., it is a by-product of growing up. Peter Farb, in his excellent book *Word Play,* puts it this way: "The child hears a small number of utterances, most of which are grammatically incorrect or misunderstood and yet on the basis of scarcity and flawed information and without instruction, he discovers for himself the complex grammatical rules of his speech community."

This is the direct opposite of the behaviorists (B. F. Skinner and Ivan Pavlov), who visualize the child's mind as a blank with no inborn capacity for language; that solely as a result of training, parental rewards, and reinforcement (feedback), the child builds up language.

Dr. Jerome Bruner, formerly professor at Harvard and presently at Oxford, England, believes that language comes from voice play (babbling) and games between mother and child (peekaboo, cough games, etc.).

Whichever theory you adopt, the unfolding of language in infants and toddlers is an exciting experience to watch.

PREVERBAL LANGUAGE

It is said that language sets man above other animals. Dr. Joseph Church, in *Understanding Your Child from Birth to Three,* refers to language as the "ultimate humanizer, the raiser of the human being to full consciousness." The importance of cultivating the child's linguistic abilities to the fullest cannot be overstressed.

287

Preverbal Communication

Your baby will find ways to let you know what he wants before he can talk. Two emotional states, "pleasant" and "unpleasant," have been isolated for the newborn. When she is full, dry, and warm she is feeling pleasant. When hungry, gassy, wet, or cold she is feeling unpleasant. When she awakes, her screams are not of rage, but of unpleasant feelings due to an empty stomach or boredom.

Likewise, her smiles are not indications of friendliness, but of pleasant and comfortable feelings. The responses she gets from these early emotional signals will teach her how to use screaming and smiling as social tools. She learns to feel and show affection for those who make her feel pleasant and anger in those situations that are frustrating and unpleasant.

The process of communicating begins long before your baby can talk. As sensitive parents you will come to understand your baby's "language of behavior," to distinguish his various cries, and tune in to his gestures and other non-verbal signals, and understand what your baby is communicating. By understanding your baby's needs, not only the physical, but his emotional needs for affection, attention, and play, his behavior will become meaningful.

Language Development

Talking is a social, intellectual, and physical accomplishment that requires development of the mouth and throat, as well as good hearing. It is also greatly influenced by a child's emotional environment and experiences. If your baby's emotional environment is unpleasant, he may not be communicative. Responding to your baby's early cries of hunger or discomfort is important to his language development. Babies realize quite early in life that they can use their voices to communicate and so they babble and cry to evoke desired reactions. Your response will teach your baby to use his sounds as expressions and signals.

During her second or third month, your baby will probably begin non-crying noises that increase and develop until by the end of the first year she is using real words, in addition to babbling—conversation-like sounds meaningless to all but you. Responding to these sounds reinforces the idea of language and communication.

288

PCI Point of View

Body movement can be as meaningful as speech in communication. While your newborn's movements are spontaneous, she will soon learn to use her body in a controlled way. By closing her eyes and turning her head, your baby is communicating to you that she is turning off her environment. This is a voluntary, meaningful act. By tuning in to your baby's body movements and facial expressions, in addition to her cry and babbles, you will be aware of her willingness and need to communicate.

LABELING

Labeling represents the one-year-old's realization that through countless repetitions in various circumstances a word brings about a desired response. The word and the object are one to him. "Mama" brings mother. From twelve to sixteen months the association becomes more stable for two reasons: his repeated experience of hearing the word spoken by others and his own repeated use of the word, as well as the possible reinforcement he receives for using it. The feedback of his own sounds may be one of the most important reinforcements to the early learning of speech.

At this age, the toddler attempts to represent everything with single words. The first words spoken by the one-year-old usually are simple labels for persons, objects, or acts. Single words may represent entire sentences. "Shoe" may mean "Take off my shoe." "Eat" may mean "Is baby going to eat now?" "Truck" may label an entire play sequence with toys.

Mothers know that depending on the intonation, "Mama" can be a statement, "Here's Mama"; a demand, "I want Mama!" or a question, "Is that Mama?" In fact, intonation patterns at this age are the first bits of language mastery. At sixteen months, the toddler is using predominantly single words. Most of these words are nouns, but he may occasionally use adjectives, such as "hot," or verbs.

Frequently a toddler's words are enmeshed in streams of what adults think to be meaningless gibberish. This jargon peaks at eighteen months and generally disappears by twenty-four months of age, probably because it does not receive feedback. It has the rhythm and fluency of adult conversation, uses various sounds, and often accompanies an activity. The occasional real word may suggest what the child is trying to convey. These nonsense sentences are backdrops for words.

Words then begin to help in further classification. Words may stand for groups of objects. "Mama" means women. Eventually "Mama" labels only the most important woman in the toddler's life.

Progress in speech for the eighteen-month-old includes the use of "words" in preference to gestures in order to express wants and needs. His speaking vocabulary contains about ten words: a typical sample might be Mama, Daddy, cookie, drink, ball, bed, dog, milk, baby, water, doll, car. These words are associated with the toddler's past experience, physical objects, and the people important to him. Repetition of words he has overheard is not uncommon. The effective vocabulary (which includes the words the child both *speaks and understands*) of the average one-year-old is three words; by 15 months, 19 words; by 18 months, 22 words; by 21 months, 118; and by 24 months, 272 words.

When the child learns to name things, her labeling ability gives her a new power over them. She can refer to things and "manage" them mentally even when they are not present before her. With the beginnings of language learning and the realization that things continue to exist even when she cannot see, hear, or touch them, she begins to be capable of abstract thought.

Language learning helps define the boundaries of self and makes the toddler aware of the individuality of others. He names himself (me) and other people (Mommy) and also things around him (car). Perceiving differences in things allows him to act on them more efficiently, to plan, and to make better use of them. The labeling process is really fun for toddlers. They take great pleasure in learning how to use words. If it is interfered with and not encouraged at this stage, the child may have trouble learning later on.

The following is a list of things you can do to encourage your child to speak:

1. Name words in all activities, because your baby will understand more language than he can express.

2. Hire a baby-sitter with good speech. Your baby will imitate the speech of anyone around him a great deal.

3. Praise baby for his efforts.

4. Provide toys that allow your child to practice conversation with his peers, such as wooden miniatures of the family or puppets.

5. Sing nursery songs, recite rhymes, read stories.

6. Provide materials and playthings that your child can name and talk about—colors, shapes, textures, sounds, etc.—to encourage his interest.

Stimulation of Speech and Language

Here are some games you can play with your child. They are designed to stimulate and encourage speech and language development in all young children.

1. Try playing "A-Boom." Hold your baby so he is facing you and gently touch foreheads as you lean forward. As you touch, say "A-Boom." Smile and laugh for your baby so he knows this is pleasing to you. Keep trying this game and after several attempts ask your baby if he wants to play "A-Boom." Then lean forward and start to play. Soon your baby may lean forward to meet you as you say "A-Boom."

2. When you see your baby doing something, such as banging or shaking an object, pick up this cue and make up a game. For example, your baby is shaking a rattle. As he does this, you say, "Shake, shake, shake." Smile and imitate what he is doing. If you do this often, he will associate his action with the word and then you will be able to give him other objects to "shake." This will teach him that the word *shake* is not just for rattles.

3. Whenever you lift your baby into your arms, say, "Up we go."

4. Whenever you put your baby down on the floor, say, "Down we go."

5. When you hug your baby, say, "Mmmm, a big hug."

6. When you hand something to your child, always say the name of the object.

Most importantly, speech games should be fun for everyone. If your child sees that you are pleased with him, he will be pleased with himself and his accomplishments.

Things Not to Do

1. Do not use baby talk. Inasmuch as babyish first words are so appealing, you will be tempted to repeat them to your child. Don't! It definitely will not help your baby learn to talk. She thinks she is imitating the way you talk.

2. Do not try to change the way your toddler pronounces words. Just be sure you say the words she uses clearly and correctly each time you use them.

PCI Point of View

Realizing that human interaction is essential to a child's ability to produce language, start early by just talking to your infant and using non-verbal communication, too: smiles, eye-to-eye contact, and gestures. Your child is absorbing all the sounds of her environment. The day she labels "Mama" or "Dada" with meaning, you will stand in awe of her very real linguistic achievement.

SENTENCE FORMATION

It takes a while for a child to talk in real sentences. At first, each word represents a complete thought—"ma" may mean "Mommy, come here." (Does that ever change?) As he adds more words, the child can communicate more needs and feelings. When the toddler begins to put together two words to make a sentence—"Get ball," "Give cookie"—he is well on his way to piecing together a grammar that will grow more complicated, paralleling his increasingly complex thought processes.

The acquisition of the rules of grammar is a remarkable accomplishment. Some psychologists believe that it is the result of physical maturation. With each physical stage, there comes an advance in language. When he pulls up objects with his thumb and forefinger (eight months), his ability to pick out and repeat important words, such as Mama and Dada, improves. When he creeps on all fours, his ability to relate words to action is evident in his understanding of commands.

Linguist Noam Chomsky believes that children are born with a blueprint for language that they use to analyze utterances heard in the speech community and to develop a grammar system. Peter Farb shows a fine example of this when he refers to the constant use of "hisself" instead of "himself" until the child is four years old. Why is it constructed by children who hear "himself" and never hear "hisself"? "Hisself" is a reflexive pronoun, like myself, herself, yourself, formed by putting together my, her, and your with self. His and self should rightly produce "hisself." Children insisting on "hisself" rather than "himself" show that they have mastered a grammar system long before speaking; the inconsistency of the English language has not yet been accepted by them.

Grammar Reflects Internal Development

Grammar seems to appear with the ultimate step in mental growth: logical thinking. According to Jean Piaget, in *Play, Dreams and Imitation in Childhood,* toddlers at about eighteen months begin to combine and manipulate mental images of real objects so that they can figure out sequences of behavior without seeing or acting them out. They can imitate things they have not seen, can pretend, reconstruct memories, and correctly imagine the location of a ball by inferring its path instead of seeing it. At the same time, toddlers begin to combine words and symbols into sequences.

At about eighteen months of age, children begin putting two words together to make simple sentences. These beginning sentences appear to be abbreviated versions of adult sentences: "That ball" for "That is the ball," and "Where ball?" for "Where is the ball?" Function words (i.e., and, at, the, his) are almost completely lacking at this stage. It is a "telegraphic" language concept.

The two-year-old child is at an "early sentence stage" characterized by a predominance of nouns and a pronounced absence of articles, auxiliary verbs, prepositions, and conjunctions. This stage gradually gives way to the short sentence "telegraphic" stage, with sentences of an average length of 3.5 to 4.5 words having a somewhat more intricate structure than those of the preceding stage. Inflections have not yet been mastered and only one or two sentences out of fifty are likely to be compound or complex. Different areas of language develop at different rates. For example, only 32 per cent of the average two-year-old's sounds are clearly articulated.

Mentally an incredible achievement, these first attempts at piecing words together into sentences are terribly ungrammatical, frequently including noun and verb phrases: "Bad boy" or "Go home." Most often the

293

child produces them independently, though occasionally he combines them into a skeleton of a well-formed sentence. A toddler's first "sentence" is a comment on a topic: "Dog" in "Doggie go" is a topic; "go" is the comment.

Sentences include mostly nouns, names of things she has been attaching labels to in her explorations. She omits connecting parts of speech —articles, prepositions, "helping" verbs, and verb inflections are all candidates for omission—possibly because they are grammatically unstressed in adult speech and, therefore, harder to discriminate. A toddler will say "Adam go" regardless of when the event occurs.

Early two-word combinations (i.e., "My Mommy," "My milk," "Move it," "Close it," "Do it," "Push it") contain some systematic regularities of word order. Even at this age, the child seems to have her own grammar, her own set of rules for forming sentences.

The baby's two-word sentences are likely to consist of a noun with some indicator of an action attached, as in "Baby, crying," or "Car, backing up." (The commas represent pauses indicating the laborious hooking together of words).

There are at first no grammatical indicators of time and number; no words referring to the baby and his own states of being. He says "eat," but not "hungry"; he says "sleep," but not "tired." Some fairly abstract words do crop up rather early: "more" in the sense of "I want more," not in the sense of "There are more people than chairs"; "back" in the sense of "Back the way we came"; and "again."

PCI Point of View

At the same time that the toddler is mastering the grammatical rules, he is also learning the correct use of language in speech situations of his home and community. By two, children can use speech to get what they want and to influence the social behavior of others. Although most children acquire the grammar systems, appropriate use of speech and the growth of vocabulary depend on parents, siblings, and peer groups. If this "speech community" provides opportunities to use language, as in structured play experiences or interactions with a verbal mother, the child gains the vocabulary he needs.

LISTENING, SPEAKING, READING, AND WRITING

According to Dr. Gertrude Corcoran, in *Language Arts in the Elementary School,* available research evidence suggests a high degree of interrelatedness among the communication skills of oral language, reading, and writing. The child's ability to comprehend written material through reading and to express herself through writing appear to be directly related to her ability in speaking and listening. Let us look now at each of the language arts and their relationship to one another.

Listening

Until children have acquired considerable skill in reading, listening will be their chief tool of learning. Almost from birth, a child reacts to loud or sudden noises around him. Within the first few months of life, he associates familiar sounds with particular situations. Although normal hearing is essential, it does not necessarily enable children to interpret the world of sound. Children must *learn* to distinguish sounds. To do this they need the guidance of an adult to fill sounds with meaning. Non-verbal sounds are important to the child eager for sensory experience. The clanging bell, ticking clock, and bouncing ball all help to develop an interest in sounds and an alertness to differences that will stand him in good stead in his growing control over language.

Through listening to your speech and conversing with you, your child acquires language almost unconsciously. One of the reasons why the preschool child grows so naturally in the ability to listen is that much of the time he is an audience of one—remarks are addressed directly to him, the speaker adjusts the content of speech and the manner of speaking to the child's interests and needs.

Speaking

As the child hears, differentiates, recognizes, and finally attaches meaning to sounds, she becomes ready to imitate and respond, in short, to speak. The speech sounds of our culture constitute our language and speech sounds are learned in the context of meaningful words and phrases. A child is molded into speech patterns from babyhood. Words grow out of the recognition of objects and actions. As children are guided into careful listening and observation, a foundation is laid for verbal expression. Growth in conversation and vocabulary stimulates further language ability.

Dr. Fredelle Maynard notes that "speech and understanding come earlier if a child is constantly spoken to." Brandon Sparkman and Ann Carmichael go further and suggest that "a child who is seldom engaged in stimulating conversation is deprived." The reason for this strong position is that speech is not a skill a child is born with; it must be acquired through listening, a desire to communicate, social stimulation, and parental guidance. It may be learned well or poorly, but it is learned. (*This differs from Dr. Lenneberg's theories.*)

Reading

In reading, as in the other language arts, the parent is the pacesetter. If you read a lot, you are saying to your child that reading is important and enjoyable to you. However, it is your reading to your child that is vital to his future development.

Even at age one, a child loves to have a parent read to him. Although he does not understand much that is being said, he will respond to the rhythm of the words, variation in vocal expression, parental attention, and the sense that you are doing something interesting. At first content is of little import, but as the child begins to master some words, content becomes more significant. Discussion of the story is important, too, because it provides an excellent opportunity to develop your child's comprehension and verbal facility.

There is an important distinction between speaking and reading. To speak, the child learns a vocal symbol for a concept. When the child is ready to read, she must associate a visual symbol with her previously learned vocal symbol. Reading instruction should be given *only* when the child is able to hear and speak the language with success. Then the child may be asked to move on to the visual symbols of language, but only if she is herself so motivated.

Sparkman and Carmichael state that there are three basic ingredients to reading readiness. The first, *interest,* is developed by regular reading to the child. The second is *visual discrimination,* the ability to differentiate between shapes, colors, sizes, etc. The third essential is *auditory discrimination,* the ability to distinguish between different sounds. Oral communication, then, lays the groundwork for two of the three basic essentials of reading readiness.

Writing

Impression precedes expression; intake precedes outflow in all aspects of language learning. A baby listens and responds to words long before he says those words himself. Similarly, a child watches the process of writing language before he does any real writing. It is only after the child is able to recognize the symbols for sounds that he is ready to learn to make them.

Language takes two directions—receiving and transmitting. We receive when we listen and read. We transmit when we speak and write. A

296

child needs to grasp the concept that writing is talk put on paper. To forward this idea, let your child tell you a story, write it down in large letters, and read it back to her. Let her dictate to you a letter for grandma. Have grandma send back a letter addressed to your child. Such activities will help her see the interrelatedness of speech and writing. Each time you read aloud to your youngster, point this out to her.

Although listening, speaking, reading, and writing occur in this order, they also overlap. Children continue to develop new skills in listening after they are speaking. Effective oral communication continues after the child is reading and writing and, of course, children learn to write while their reading skill is still in its early stages. This interrelationship of the language arts continues throughout one's communicative life.

LANGUAGE AND THOUGHT

Various theories concerning the development of speech present different points of view about the relationship between language and thought.

1. The learning theory approach to the development of speech claims that language is fundamentally acquired by learning and responding to examples in the environment. The child listens to his parents, siblings, neighbors, and imitates them. We can train the child by saying a word and giving him some reward—attention, smiles, or the object he names—when he repeats it. The process is simply that of *stimulus and response*. In this way, we can teach the child any word.

Reinforcement theorists suggest that the world's three thousand languages give testimony to this approach; that is, every child learns to speak the language she hears in her surroundings. Children who do not hear much language or do not get sufficient rewards for saying words learn very little language. This approach to language acquisition does not assume any explicit connection between language and thought and sees the acquisition of language as a process by itself.

2. Many psychologists reject the "parrot" view of language acquisition. They claim that such a view cannot explain the child's ability to understand and produce complicated grammatical patterns and sophisticated sentences. They point to the role of internal processes and maturation. These theorists emphasize the unfolding, developmental nature of language acquisition. Certainly during the first year of life this model is most appropriate.

3. Other theorists claim that the development of language and speech aids and abets the development of thought. This view is based on the fact

that humans have language and the most developed thought patterns of animals. Dr. Jerome Bruner believes that through language we are able to play with ideas and share experiences with others.

We can speak or write about an object without the necessity of having the object present. Language frees a child from the need to manipulate the environment. By using symbols or words, she can select, store, and code a complex concept and communicate it. A verbal child may well attain a higher intellectual level than a child from a deprived area whose language is not well developed.

4. Dr. Jean Piaget has a somewhat different opinion. He thinks that the roots of logic are in actions, not in words. He found that infants begin to act in intelligent ways from the day of their birth as they practice their actions. We might even say that they are thinking with their actions. They learn that some things can be grasped, some cannot; some move when

they are pushed, some do not. All these insights are independent of language.

Dr. Piaget, in *Play, Dreams and Imitation in Childhood,* points out that thought precedes language and that it derives from the child's interaction with the environment. Even without language, the child is capable of developing a logical symbolic system by ordering objects in the environment, i.e., grouping objects, solving problems, imitating adult patterns.

In every stage of their development, young children are able to carry out activities that demand a good deal of intelligence without using language. Hence language often is a misleading indicator of the level of a child's understanding. If he really understands what he has been told, the child should be able to "act accordingly" and rephrase it in his own words. Comprehending words themselves and repeating them does not imply true understanding.

A child can learn by heart to count from one to ten forward and backward, but if she gets six cookies and is asked how many she has, she will not necessarily know. With language, the child can connect both words and thoughts; that is, to think in words. Piaget distinguishes two functions of language: the social and the egocentric. The first is directed to the listener and enables us to communicate with others; the latter is self-directed, an important tool of self-expression.

At early ages, especially between three to five years, the egocentric function is more important than the social one. The child talks and does not bother to know to whom he is speaking or whether he is being listened to. We see this sort of speech mostly in children's play and in the dark of the night before they go to sleep; they simply talk to themselves. This inner speech or imaginary dialogue with toys is addressed to no real person in particular.

In his book *Thought and Language,* Dr. L. Vygotsky defines inner speech as a "dynamic, shifting, unstable thing, fluttering between word and thought—thinking in pure meaning." Dr. Vygotsky believes that inner speech later becomes the basis for overt speech or talking. At seven to eight years, the child's desire to work with others increases and social talk begins to take on greater importance. The child uses his speech to put order in his world and plan his actions. The reason that at school age the egocentric speech disappears is that it becomes inner speech. Now the child can talk to himself soundlessly; he has learned to think.

Conclusions

We see that speech, besides being a means of communication, is a tool for our thoughts. It does not imply, however, that all our thinking is done with the help of words. Many studies have shown that the child can understand many things before he has acquired and used speech. Many aspects of thought are non-verbal—imagination, creativity, and art—and we should not devaluate them.

Such evidence indicates that thought and language are not identical. Nevertheless, from the fact that the deaf show much more intellectual deficiency than the blind, we can conclude that language is important for cognitive development.

Practical implications for parents should take into account the different points of view about the connection between language and thought.

PCI Point of View

Do not neglect your child's physical, concrete activities. He has to have many real experiences with different objects and situations. For example, in order to understand fully the word "dog," a child needs to see many kinds of dogs, to touch a dog, to hear its barking, to know what dogs eat, and even what smells they have. The child himself knows that a real understanding (or concept) of a thing comes only after he sees and experiences it from many angles.

SPEECH PATHOLOGY: DELAYED SPEECH

The chart at right, adapted from *Speech and Hearing Hurdles* by J. K. Duffy and J. J. Irwin, displays the normal language development of children.

Delayed Speech

M. Berry and J. Eisenson, the authors of *Speech Disorders,* have this to say about speech delay: ". . . we may consider that the speech of the child is delayed when (a) it fails to appear or is late in appearance; (b) there are deviations in the sound, syllable, and word patterns so marked as to disturb intelligibility; or (c) the vocabulary and language patterns are below the norm for one of his chronological age and sex."

Causes of Delayed Speech

What are some of the possible factors involved in delayed speech?

1. *Motoric characteristics:* The child must have proper breath control, be able to close and open her vocal cords, and move her jaw, lips,

300

AGE IN MONTHS	12–18	18–24	24–36	36–48	48–60	60
Numerical size of vocabulary	First word	20–100 words	200–300 words	900 words	1500 words	
Word type (each type appears with the most common at the top)	nouns	nouns, some verbs and other parts	nouns, verbs, and other parts	verbs, nouns, pronouns, and adjectives	verbs, pronouns, nouns	
Sentence length in words		single-word sentences	two-word sentences	three-word sentences		
Percentage of intelligibility in child's speech		25%	66%	90%		100%

tongue, and palate. Disabilities (such as cerebral palsy, cleft palate, or paralysis) may certainly play a deleterious role in these motoric skills.

2. *Symbolic language disturbance:* Language is related to thought. Charles Van Riper, in *Speech Corrections,* writes, "There is a progression beginning in meaningful gestures and tones, proceeding through a period in which the child acquires his first words, then increases vocabulary, and finally learns how to use it in the complex formulation of sentences involving commentary, prediction, and recall . . . comprehension always seems to precede expression."

Brain injury in children can cause an interruption in speech development or may retard it. *Aphasia* is a term used to indicate a disorder due to brain injury, causing difficulty in the meaningful use of symbols. Affected children find it difficult to formulate their thoughts in words, to express them verbally, or to comprehend what others are saying. They have problems sending messages and, less often, in receiving them. Children who are aphasic may have gaps in their comprehension and sometimes appear deaf. They may at times be unable to find or say words that they have often used before. They confuse opposite and associated words. It should be remembered that aphasia has no relation to intelligence. A child may be very bright and still be aphasic.

3. *Communication needs:* During the last half of the first year of life the baby learns that he can send messages by crying, by gesture, and by

301

speech. By using sounds, he later learns to influence people and obtain things. With proper rewards and models, he begins using his power of communication. Some children appear never to discover this power. It may be that their parents and/or sibling anticipate the child's every need before he can express it and, therefore, he does not have the need to speak.

4. *Emotional aspects:* Speech is the expression of the self. It is the need to identify and exhibit one's self that motivates much of our speech. Many speech disorders are produced or affected by emotional conflicts.

5. *Hearing loss:* Speech development may be delayed due to hearing difficulties. Different types of hearing loss result in different speech impairments. One type causes mainly articulation errors, while the other usually results in delayed speech.

6. *Retardation:* Mental retardation is often accompanied by physical retardation. Therefore, difficulty with the mechanics of speech may be present, as well as a general delay in language due to limited intelligence.

ARTICULATION PROBLEMS

Some children have speech problems. Based on norms for children of the same age, a two-year-old may have fairly unintelligible speech and yet not be unusual. A three-year-old who says "wabbit" for "rabbit" does not have a speech defect. However, if present in older children, it would be considered a speech defect. Remember that *young* children should be allowed to err in speech without direct criticism.

Timetables for Speech

Many children have quite intelligible speech without having mastered all of the twenty-three consonant sounds. The average ages by which these consonants are mastered are displayed on the following chart:

Age in Years	Sounds Mastered
3½	b,p,m,w,h
4½	d,t,n,g,k,ng,y
5½	f
6½	v, th (as in that), z (as in azure), sh, l
7½	s,z,r,th (as in thin), wh

Ruth W. Metraux, in "Speech Profiles of the Preschool Child," studied the speech of 207 preschool children of average or above average intelligence. The condensations below of their speech profiles are definitely *not* norms, but may serve as a guide:

Eighteen months: The child typically leaves off the beginning and the end of phrases. She is uncertain and inconsistent in the production of almost any word. She experiments a great deal with her voice and pitch and repeats syllables or words frequently in an easy manner.

Twenty-four months: The child usually telescopes her pronunciation. You will hear a beginning consonant, often a final consonant is present, and medial consonants tend to be omitted. A "squeaky"-sounding voice is common. The child repeats words or phrases constantly.

Thirty months: Telescoping of words continues. Word pronunciations are unstable and the same word may be said in different ways within a few minutes. For example, *cross* may be "kwoss," or "kwow," or "koss." The pitch is still variable, but is more stable than at earlier ages. Repetition, especially of phrases, is even more marked than at twenty-four months.

Thirty-six months: Shortening of words continues and final consonants appear more regularly. The voice is generally well controlled and usually is loud. Your child may begin to use a whispered voice to gain attention. Repetition is still present. Speech is easy and not self-conscious. The two-year-old uses short phrases to express himself while the three-year-old uses simple sentences. By three and a half years, practically all the vocal responses should be comprehensible.

Causes of Articulation Disorders

1. *Developmental factors:* Although articulation matures with age, the scale above is based on the child who begins speaking at an average age. If your child began to speak at a later age, his entire profile may differ in age of achievement. Such a child may naturally be expected to obtain mature sounds at a somewhat later age.

Children who are ill a great deal often have speech setbacks or display immature speech. The parents are often overconcerned and overprotective and the child continues playing the role of the "baby." Also, illness may occur during key speech learning stages in a child's early years and so cause transient delays.

2. *Foreign language influence:* A child's errors may be due to imitation of a parental accent. If a child comes from a bilingual home there may be confusion between similar consonants. (See Dr. Lenneberg's introduction to this chapter, page 279.)

3. *Emotional factors:* Children who come from troubled homes often have speech problems. Some children use defective articulation to get attention. Other children, if unloved, seem to refuse to speak at all!

4. *Organic abnormalities:* Any abnormality of the lips, tongue, teeth, jaw, or palate may cause articulation errors.

5. Children left often and for long periods with inarticulate baby-sitters or maids will not master verbal communication powers.

Children with delayed speech and moderate or severe articulation disorders need special professional help. A pediatrician or family doctor may be able to recommend a facility offering speech services in your community or you can obtain information by writing to the American Speech and Hearing Association, 9030 Old Georgetown Road, Washington, D.C. 20014.

Improvement of Articulation

There are many games you can play with your young child to help her become aware of sounds. Most of these involve improvement of listening skills.

1. Have your child listen to the everyday sounds in your home. Give words to describe the sounds; "pop" goes the toaster, "whosh" goes the vacuum, "tick-tock" goes the clock.

2. Listen to sounds outside your home; "wee-eee-eee" goes the siren, "beep-beep" goes the horn, "tweet-tweet" goes the bird.

3. Introduce animals and the sounds they make to your child. Show her pictures of the animals or take her to a farm or zoo and listen to the sounds.

4. Following instructions. Start by giving your child one simple instruction to follow, such as "Close the door."

5. Make sound books with construction paper stapled together to form each book. You and your child can look for magazine pictures of all objects that start with a specific sound (any sound you choose), cut them out, and glue them into the "book." Make a separate book for each sound.

6. Read nursery rhymes and other poetry to your child. All children enjoy lilting rhymes and rhythms.

STUTTERING: LACK OF FLUENCY

Stuttering or stammering is a disorder of speech that makes its appearance in a small proportion of children (estimates range from 1 to 5 per cent), usually at about the age of two to four years. It has been defined as a disturbance of rhythm and fluency of speech typified by occasional blocking, a convulsive repetition or prolonging of sounds, syllables, words, and phrases, or the posture of the speech organ.

A child may say, "I want to, I want to have that," or, "I go, go downstairs," or, "I g-g-go in here." Often parents become uneasy when they hear their child stutter or stammer, choke on a rush of words, produce garbled sounds or sentences, or in other ways depart from adult fluency. Dr. Joseph Church writes, "This is simply the way young children talk and there is nothing to be done about it, except to be patient."

At three or four, stuttering is quite common. Usually it means nothing more than that the child is in a hurry and cannot keep up with his own thoughts or he has not yet acquired the vocabulary to do so. It does not indicate any kind of psychological disturbance or maladjustment; rather, these children can talk faster than they can think or possibly they are not yet able to control their speech organs completely.

Dr. Spock thinks that children who are *urged* to talk and recite and "show off" are especially liable.

How Long Does It Last?

In most cases, stuttering lasts a number of months with ups and downs. Do not expect it to go right away; be content with gradual progress.

Causes

Dr. Neil C. Henderson says that persistent stuttering may be due to tension or a new environment. Speech specialists believe a child's emotional state has a lot to do with stuttering. Most cases occur in somewhat tense children. Mothers report that their children's stuttering is definitely worse when they (the mothers) are tense. Also, stuttering may start when a father decides to be a stricter disciplinarian.

Trying to change a left-handed child into a right-handed one sometimes triggers stuttering. The part of the brain that controls speech is closely connected to the part that controls the hand that a person naturally prefers. If you *force* a child to use his "wrong" hand, it seems to confuse his talking machinery.

Your toddler may be having difficulty in learning how to do all the things you want him to learn. Perhaps you have been demanding too much of him in learning toilet control or acceptable eating habits. Too much attention to a child's methods of speaking may also promote the onset of stuttering.

Who Is Affected

Stuttering can occur from preschool age onward. It affects rich and poor alike and is a little more than twice as common among males than females. Probably half or more children between three and six years of age show repetitive speech at some stage. Encouragingly, most two-year-olds who start to stutter will outgrow it by themselves in a few months.

What You Can Do

Let your child talk! Between three and five, your budding talker will probably become a chatterbox, discovering the fun of communication through words, wanting to attract attention, and to tell you things. If the chatter starts to wear you out, direct her interest to something else. Make sure she has other children and adults outside your family to talk to.

Do your child and yourself a real service and leave his speech alone. It makes perfectly good sense to suggest phrasings to him when he is having trouble making himself understood, but it is potentially harmful to worry about his lack of fluency. Help him articulate his ideas by all means, but leave his temporary stammering alone. If he is tense, discover what is bothering him and see whether you can do more to remove the causes.

When your child speaks to you, listen attentively, encouraging her by indicating interest and understanding. Show your delight in subtle ways at any obvious verbal achievement. Above all, do not make the mistake of calling attention to the stuttering in front of others or permitting others to mention it in front of your child. Do not compare your child unfavorably with her more articulate older sibling. Avoid interrupting her when she is talking or otherwise showing impatience (which will only create more tension). Never punish a child for stuttering or promise a reward for stopping it. Refrain from offering suggestions, such as "Now, take a deep breath," or "You must speak more slowly." Do not permit brothers and sisters to tease the stutterer.

If you do make "a case" out of this perfectly normal, transitory difficulty, you can create a problem. *Real stutterers are made, not born!*

9

How Do Babies Learn?

INTRODUCTION BY LEWIS P. LIPSITT, PH.D.*

It is a wise parent who knows that newborn children are affected by their environment from the moment they are born. Many nurses in maternity hospitals, even after they have been associating with infants for a long time, are often not fully aware of the full capacity of the infant even within the first few days of life. The fact is that recent studies of the neonate have demonstrated conclusively that in the first few days of life the child is capable of hearing many sounds, of detecting odors, of discriminating among different tastes, of feeling when he is touched lightly and reacting differently when touched with a heavy hand, and even of seeing some things!

While we cannot be fully sure yet of *all* of the sensory capacities and learning potential of the very young infant, because not enough research has yet been done about these interesting matters, there is a picture emerging of the child being born with all sensory modalities functioning and with the capacity for learning from his personal interactions with other people in his life. Needless to say, the most important, from the standpoint of amount of interaction time, is the relationship with the mother.

All of this is not to say that there are no hereditary or constitutional differences among infants. Indeed there are and they are apparent from the earliest moments of life. Just as new babies may be observed to be different in skin color, hair length, weight, and length, so also are there behavioral differences right from the start. It is not our purpose here to debate the old nature versus nurture argument, but only to point out that both sets of factors are operating from the start.

* Dr. Lewis P. Lipsitt, presently Professor of Psychology and Medical Science and the Director of the Child Study Center at Brown University since 1967, has researched and written extensively on the sensory powers of the newborn. His research has been published by literally hundreds of scholarly journals. He served as consultant to the National Institute of Neurological Diseases and Blindness, National Institute of Child Health and Human Development, and their counterparts in England. In 1972, Dr. Lipsitt was awarded a Guggenheim Fellowship.

Some babies at birth are jumpy and some seemingly are more at ease. This is so whether we are looking just at the spontaneous behavior of the newborn or "testing" responses to specific stimuli. Needless to say, all caretakers should want to take into consideration these individual differences in infants when interacting with them in any way— whether just holding them, loving them, moving them about, and so on. An interesting feature of the early mother–infant relationship is the extent to which each is capable of tuning in on and responding appropriately, or at least reasonably so, to the other's tempo.

So much happens to the young child, even within just the first year of life, that the adult observer cannot help but be amazed at the rapidity of the changes and thus the wonder of human development. The character of the newborn human is one of thorough dependency. Indeed, the human is much more dependent for a longer period of time than any other primates with which humans are biologically related. One supposition about this long period of childhood through which the human goes is that it is a necessary preparation for true humanoid existence.

Human beings have the most intricate and sophisticated communication systems. They are capable of engaging in very elaborate symbolic thinking, such as in very abstract mathematics. Man is capable of anticipating the future and contemplating the past, probably because of his mental dexterity with respect to the manipulation of symbols and ideas, in a way that would stagger a chimpanzee's imagination. Moreover, the human is capable of a wider variety and greater intensity of emotional reactions than any other animal, and this is the source for him both of enormous pleasure and of great pain. No animal knows better than humankind that life is bittersweet, because the human being is the only animal who laughs or cries, the only one who recognizes the difference between the way things are and the way they ought to be.

The wonder of infant development is that from the newborn state of dependency and passivity, coupled with interspersed occasions in which moments of distress are signaled through expression of seemingly inconsolable cries, the infant exits at the end of the first year with a ready smile for those to whose faces she has become accustomed, the ability to use a tool a bit crudely, the capacity for calling mother and making a request stick. The baby also has the capacity to walk around a bit or at least to create an uproar in the living room by her hobbles from one piece of furniture to another. It is a remarkable transition period, that first year. But then, so are all of the periods.

Any keen observer of the development of infants and young children cannot help but be aware of the fact that later development depends upon earlier accomplishments. The child cannot speak in sentences until he has mastered words. Most often he cannot walk until he has pulled himself to standing and has crawled or crept. He cannot express surprise until he has become accustomed to something. He cannot become annoyed over his mother's departure until he has become attached to her.

The extent to which later behavior and development depend upon earlier experience and exercise is a matter that we are only beginning to understand. After all, it is only since the turn of this century that we have really appreciated, from Sigmund Freud, that adult behavior and personality depend importantly on our early life circumstances. Based upon the discoveries and articulations of such famous psychologists as Pavlov, Thorndike, and Watson, we have learned that the effects of early experiences on our later behavior are mediated in large part through learning processes based upon our capacity for remembering. It is perhaps no accident that the most influential theories of psychological development that have evolved during the century have given *memory* a central spot.

We know today that it is quite possible for traumatic stresses or grossly deficient environmental circumstances to have a pernicious effect upon the development of young children, both cognitive or intellectual and emotional. While the kinds of parents and other children's caretakers who have contact with these instructional materials are very, very unlikely to have such effects upon any children, simply because they are already "set" to facilitate the behavioral development of children in their care, even the most well-meaning "infant handler" and competent parent can often learn new and interesting ways in which to facilitate the psychological growth and joy of a child.

When one is looking for new techniques of helping children with their learning or of facilitating their mental growth generally, it is sometimes easy to forget that an important aspect of life for the child is his or her capacity for joy. It is not terrible for anybody to enjoy living and the instrumentation and implementation of learning for the young child should never become so intense or overbearing as to preclude pleasure. It only remains to add, in connection with this point, that the more pleasure the adult has in his or her interactions with the child, the more likely is the child to appreciate the relationship and assimilate the objectives of the educational activity!

311

JEAN PIAGET: PIONEER IN LEARNING

Dr. Jean Piaget, the Swiss psychologist, has devoted his life to studying the development of intellectual growth in children. Close observation and questioning of his own three children led him to a general theory of how a child's mind progresses in a definite order from one stage to the next.

Dr. Piaget sees intellectual development as taking place in four major age-related stages. The first, from birth to two years, is the sensorimotor period. During this stage, the infant is learning how to direct the movements of his body continuously and practices his newly found sensory powers (seeing, hearing, touching, etc.). He takes in information through all his senses and learns how to use this information. For example, if a spoon is dangled over his head, he learns by trial and error how far to reach for it. He learns where to look to find out where a sound is coming from.

Psychologists have theorized that in the first few weeks of life an infant's world must be made up of successions of visual images, sounds, and feelings. The infant makes no distinction between herself and what is outside of herself. Gradually she will acquire a view of her surroundings as including objects and people that are different from herself and that exist even when they are out of her sight. She will be able to tell when a ball is really rolling or when it only appears to be because she herself is moving. She will learn some notion of cause and effect.

To a baby, out of sight is actually out of mind. An object simply does not exist as long as he does not see it. Parents can further their baby's understanding of his world by giving him play experiences with things that disappear and reappear again at short intervals. Simple peekaboo and hiding games can at a later stage be replaced by toys like Jack-in-the-boxes or a homemade variation. When the infant perseveres in looking for a hidden object, he has reached an important level in his intellectual development where objects are permanent to him.

Child watches and listens to moving beads activated by her fingers. These activities build drive and attentiveness, both assets for later reading mastery.

Somewhere toward the end of her second year, the child enters what Dr. Piaget calls the "pre-operational period," usually from two to seven years. The first part of this period, that ends at about age four, is called the "pre-conceptual period." It is during this time span—more so than in any other—that the child develops the ability to deal with symbols. She can understand the relationship between an object and the symbol or word for that object. The beginnings of symbolic play and drawing also appear.

Despite these giant forward steps in his development, the child still does not see the world as the adult does. For instance, if upon taking a walk he sees six fire hydrants, he does not know if he is seeing a series of different hydrants or whether the same one keeps turning up again and again. In any case, it makes little difference to his thinking as they all are simply "fire hydrants." Dr. Piaget calls this a "pre-concept"—meaning that it is somewhere between the idea of an object and the concept of a class of objects.

At about age four, the child enters the second period of the pre-operational or "intuitive" stage. Intuitive thought can be illustrated by one of Piaget's best-known experiments, in which the child is shown two identical drinking glasses filled with equal amounts of juice. The child is asked whether each glass holds the same amount. When she agrees that this is so, the juice from one glass is poured into a taller, thinner glass so that the juice reaches a greater height. When the child is now asked whether each glass holds the same amount of juice, she says that the tall thin glass has more. She is also unable to realize that if the juice is poured back into the original short glass it will once again appear equal to its twin. In another experiment devised by Piaget, it was shown that a child at this stage of development will believe that a belt arranged in a circle is shorter than an identical one laid out in a straight line.

Piaget's third stage, which he calls the "concrete operational," spans from about age seven to eleven. During this time the child develops the ability to do in his head what he would have had to do before through physical action. He can make estimates and is able to understand the concepts of relative length, amount, and so on. His ways of thinking are becoming increasingly like those of an adult.

Piaget's fourth stage, which he calls the "stage of formal operations" (from about twelve years of age and thereafter), signifies the child's ability to think abstractly, and thus hypothetical reasoning becomes possible for the first time.

The order in which these four stages appear are the same for every child, but the ages at which the stages develop and unfold depend partly on the child's inborn abilities and partly on the quality of the environment. Dr. Piaget believes in a variety of early sensory experiences in which the young child can practice new powers as they appear. He favors building on physical experience, not symbols, maintaining that a physical concept precedes a verbal one (counting beads and a variety of quantitative encounters should predate the role of verbal enumeration—"one, two, three . . . ten"). Many youngsters can parrot numbers and words with very limited real understanding of them.

Piaget's work has aroused some controversy, of course. Some critics think his research and testing techniques are unsystematic due to his reliance on a few subjects and a subjective procedure. Others doubt that each of his four stages of intellectual development is so rigidly fixed.

However, his main theoretical principals stand and the importance of his work cannot be denied. It is due largely to his theoretical framework— cognitive development viewed as unfolding systematically from infancy— that there is today such widespread attention given to the minds of babies. To many professionals, Dr. Piaget has provided the link between the sensory-bound intellect of infancy and the abstract reasoning of maturity.

PCI Point of View

There are several recurrent themes that parents may profit from:

1. You cannot really *teach* your baby anything. Address your energies to providing stimuli that enable your child to *learn* and discover by himself.

2. You must identify at what stage your baby is so that the external world can be incorporated into what Piaget refers to as existing "schemas."

3. Do not be fooled by your "seeming genius." There are many levels of "knowing." Sometimes "TV-jet-aged small-fry sophisticates" can fool their parents with their glib tongues and mature vocabularies. Build from the inside out. If a verbal concept precedes a real internal representation, you need to help your child refine, deepen, and anchor it through many sensory activities. Actual physical and sensory experiences give in-depth quality and meaning to words.

4. Practice "horizontal expansion" in addition to "vertical expansion"; that is the Piagetian way of saying *enrich;* do not just accelerate!

CAUSE-AND-EFFECT LEARNING

Babies Are Intelligent

Babies have highly organized systems of behavior, such as sucking, looking, listening, vocalizing, grasping, and motor activities of the trunk and limbs. Whether we decide to define intelligence as sudden insight, purposeful groping, problem solving, the ability to deal with means-end or cause-and-effect relationships, everyone will agree that infants do in fact display intelligent behavior through action and movement. (For example, the infant reaching for a distant or hidden object.) This very limited definition of intelligence is both practical and future-oriented. In an unconscious and self-centered way, the baby interacts with the outside world repeatedly until she gradually creates an internal representation of reality for herself. Part and parcel of this process is the infant's developing ability to construct notions of object permanency, space, time, and causality.

315

The Permanent Object

At first there is no object permanence. The universe appears as a shifting stage in which things appear, disappear, and reappear. Gradually the child learns that a thing does not cease to exist when it disappears.

Space and Time

At first there are many experiences with space and time without any co-ordination. Eventually various kinds of space—tactile, auditory, etc.—

Baby fingers and turns a sound chamber and then discovers self in mirror. These activities enhance self-image and confidence.

become organized so that an object can be located in space and logical operations can occur—reversibility, associativity, etc.

Causality

Physical causality relates to the cause and effect of mechanical and natural events. Causality develops in a similar manner as spatial and temporal schemas—through a long process of action. At first the baby is not aware of the necessity of spatial contact. He wants to hear the music box and pulls a cord, even though the cord is not connected to the music box or even if the music box is in the next room. In *The Psychology of the Child,* Jean Piaget and Barbel Inhelder offer another example of this "magical" causality: an infant squinting in front of an electric light switch in order to turn on the light.

This early stage in the development of causality is related to philosopher David Hume's formulation of the development of causal perceptions. He believed that adults who watched the same process repeatedly—such as the collision of billiard balls—were led to the expectation that one event usually followed another. In other words, "pulling the cord" and the musical sounds occurring simultaneously are sufficient for the infant to conclude that they are causally related. The other aspect of causality in infants is its "magical" nature. Babies do not consider at all the placement of objects in space; there is no awareness of where the self ends and the real world begins. Wanting to do something is all that counts. This characteristic of centering on himself—egocentrism—fades slowly in infants.

All the experts agree that the processes are learned more rapidly if the environment is varied and complex. It has been found that the attention span of babies lengthens when a novel element is added to the environment. By having your baby exposed to moving objects and playing with her, using varied colored objects, you can help her learn cause and effect, as well as other operations.

PCI Point of View

Young children learn how things happen by watching and participating. While the experts may disagree on how it happens, children do learn complex processes very early.

MEMORY

During the four-to-eight-month period, the baby tests his environment and gets a "picture of things." Parents have to make sure their child has a

317

broad variety of playthings so that he can experience their size, shape, texture, weight, volume, density, distance, and speed. A baby who spends most of his time in a crib can become bored. Well-chosen toys can relieve boredom and introduce a pattern of learning that will be developed throughout the baby's life.

A baby learns early to discriminate between things. He knows his mother's voice before he sees her in sharp focus; he recognizes foods that he likes; he waits for the crash that will come when he drops his plate on the floor. He has time from four to eight months to check and recheck, "What happens after I do this or that?"

One important way a baby learns is to try one thing over and over again until she is sure of it and when that happens it becomes part of her memory apparatus. As each item is learned, the baby uses that memory to learn something new.

Much is learned spontaneously by the baby by herself, but parents cannot trust this approach and should supplement their child's environment with fun-filled playtimes when new objects and sensory experiences are introduced and explored with her. These can help shape her patterns of learning.

As the late Lawrence K. Frank put it in his book, *On the Importance of Infancy,* "Children have different cognitive styles, their own individual ways of perceiving and understanding in the world, some visual, others auditory, while others prefer to deal with the world as it can be directly manipulated and felt. Various studies today, including accumulating clinical evidence, are showing that once a perceptual style has been developed it resists modification or replacement."

Babies vary as to how they put together learning tools to acquire mental skills. In experiments with one-to-ten-month-old babies at Harvard's Center for Cognitive Studies, patterns of faces and balls appeared briefly in each of two windows. Some babies found faces more interesting; some, the balls. Others were equally attracted by both. It may be that those who prefer balls are happier when playing with objects and toys; those who prefer the faces are happier in social interaction.

The use of memory, or the child's remembering things, is very important to learning at any level. It makes the acquisition of new skills possible. Often parents feel that their child has learned something only to discover that he cannot remember it. This is a very normal state of affairs. Babies need constant practice to learn or commit to memory certain skills. One caution is that in learning a new skill a child must learn what *not* to do, as well as what to do.

A child builds on simple skills to form complex ones. An example is reaching for an object, grasping it, hitting it on a table, and waving it about. If a new object is placed in a baby's hand, he will repeat all of these motions. If the object is a crayon and when it hits the table it makes a mark on the paper, the baby will see that. He will probably check the next object placed in his hand to see if it, too, will make a mark. After many trials and errors, a baby will learn or remember what a crayon does.

Only certain experiences have meaning for the infant; colors, numbers, and letters must all be specifically learned later. However, size, taste, and feel have real meaning to her and are more easily remembered.

One game you can play with your baby to help develop her memory is an eye-tracking game. The aim of this game is to help a baby follow moving objects with the eyes. Another aim is to help her learn to look at what she hears. Place your baby on her back. Twirl a shiny spoon, a bracelet of little bells, or a rattle until she focuses on the object. Then move the object slowly in one of the following paths—from left to right or right to left; from her chin down toward her tummy or up toward the crown of her head; in a 360° circle around the back of her head in either direction ending up in front of her, where she can see the toy well.

If the baby loses the toy with his eyes, help him "catch" the toy again by jiggling or tapping it. If he still finds following a bright-colored or jingling toy difficult, switch to the human object. Waggle your smiling face above his head and then move it in one of the paths. You may talk to him while you do it. Little games like this played for a few minutes every day will help your child develop skills of learning.

THE COMPETENT CHILD

What is competence in a three-year-old child? Until recently, we relied largely on intangible definitions and perhaps knew more about what *it is not* than what it is. In the older child (age six), we rely on IQ scores to test verbal abilities and intellectual skills, but just when does the development of educability and overall ability emerge? Research indicates that the concept of competence surfaces during the second year of life, specifically from the tenth to eighteenth month, and becomes quite substantial by age three.

In 1972, the Preschool Project of Harvard's School of Education, relying on thousands of simple, detailed observations, suggested that several major factors underlie the emergence of competence: the development of language, walking, a growing awareness of self and social orientation—all of these infused with natural curiosity and exploration.

Obviously, the first ten months of life are important to child rearing. However, the next eight months appear to "make the difference" in terms of the enhancement of competency or the retardation of overall growth in our children.

Parents should be aware of this period so that they may be prepared for it. What is it about the ten-to-eighteen-month-old infant that evokes special requirements on the parents' part?

1. *Locomobility* occurs and with it comes very serious parental choices regarding the creation of clutter, potentials for self-destruction, and intrusion on the domain of the older sibling.

2. *Language acquisition begins.* Some parents nurture it by talking to their infant a great deal, by carefully selecting suitable words, books, pictures, and records, by sensitively capitalizing on the baby's interests, however fleeting. Other parents try, but "miss the boat." Still others provide negligible language input.

3. *Onset of negativism.* This negativism, appearing sometime around the fourteenth or fifteenth month, is very stressful to some parents and they react variously to it, from the punitive to the overly permissive. (Refer to Chapter 11, "Personality Formation," for a fuller discussion of Negativism.)

Child-rearing styles are established on the basis of these three emerging phenomena. The research also suggests that these child-rearing styles are stable predictors of future behavior.

Since competency is not only achieved by certain developmental skills, but also by the caretaker's or mother's behavior, the Harvard study labeled five types of mothers: The *super mother* wants to provide educational opportunities for her child; she slips in from time to time to teach him something, but she is not frantic about it. The *smothering mother's* child spends the day responding to her commands. The *almost-mother* enjoys and accepts her child, but is confused and frequently unable to meet his needs. If she reads to her child, her spontaneous comments may be, "See the hill!" while the super mother may ask, "What's he going to meet at the bottom of the hill?" The *overwhelmed mother* finds just living from day to day so demanding that she has almost no time for her child. Finally, the *zoo-keeper mother,* who has a highly organized household routine, does not have time for her child and while materially well cared for, there is a striking lack of contact between mother and child.

Thus the five mothers represent extreme types not observed often in real life. The super mother raises an all-around "A" child. The smothering mother's offspring rates "A" in learning capacity, but not in emotional maturity (he tends to be shy or incredibly infantile). The overwhelmed mother produces a "C" child. The almost-mother does a very good job until her child is fourteen to sixteen months old, when the mind-stretching aspects of care become more important; and then she fails. While the super mother's child continues to grow rapidly, the child of the almost-mother reaches a plateau that eventually turns him into a "B" child.

Traits of a Competent Child

The Harvard Project also concerned itself with the coping behavior of the young child. Children judged to be high in this area were able to cope in superior fashion with anything they met, day in and day out. The other half were judged to be free from serious problems, but generally of low competence.

Based on observations of 400 children of varying socioeconomic status, residence (rural or urban), and ethnic background in moment-to-moment activities in kindergartens, nurseries, and homes, thirteen most talented and thirteen least talented children were selected. The average, or "B," child was not covered in the study.

The researchers noted that when something gets in the way of the inept ("C") child, he may be reduced to tears or throw a tantrum, while the competent ("A") child will be quietly persistent; he might even "con" someone into giving him what he wants in a socially acceptable way. Also, the "C" child may be locked into either sheeplike docility or rebellion, while the "A" child knows both how to lead and how to follow.

The Harvard group concludes that some fundamental learning patterns are set very early in life, well before the age of three, and that during this period the child is particularly open to environmental and interpersonal influences for good or for bad.

PCI Point of View

Although parenting styles have a tremendous impact on young, maturing personalities, parents themselves cannot take all the credit or all the blame for their offspring's traits. Every newborn brings with her a unique history both genetically and prenatally. Consider these factors before you assume that you are or will be an A, B, or C parent and automatically will nurture an A, B, or C competent child.

CONCEPT FORMATION

What Is a Concept?

From the first moment a baby is born he is bombarded by many different kinds of stimuli. These impressions are of an unconnected nature to the infant; they have no sequence and no meaning. To make a predictable world out of all these impressions, he must learn to assign meanings to the events that involve him. In this way, he begins to form concepts.

To understand fully what a concept is and how it develops, one must try to see the world as an infant does. For example, at first the baby experiences the mother as the feeder and cuddler. After many months, she has finally developed a concept of "mother." The infant will probably identify all women, if they are reasonably similar to her own mother, as a mother. A concept, therefore, is a classification of stimuli that have common characteristics. The concept is formed when the classification is carried beyond one event, as when the child identifies other women as a mother.

Concept Formation and Total Development

There is evidence that the development of concepts is closely tied to the child's total development. As the infant gains control over more of his own body, he is able to come into contact with more things. Accompanying this increased contact is the process of assigning meanings to events and things. Meanings are related to certain feelings, such as comfort or tension; for example, the baby smiles when he sees his mother coming with a bottle or cries when the nurse approaches with a needle. While this does not indicate a high level of thought, it does demonstrate the beginnings of concept formation.

Perhaps one of the most important ways baby learns about herself and her environment is by her sense of touch. When the baby sucks her thumb, the mouth feels the thumb and the thumb feels the mouth. This feeling and being felt is called *self-sentience*. It is from this beginning that the baby will learn about herself and form the concept of "me." Once the baby knows that she is separate from her surroundings, she has opened the door to forming concepts about those things that are part of her environment.

Since the baby is constantly forming and expanding his concept of himself, the way he experiences his world will affect the way he thinks about himself. He needs a safe world in order to develop a sense of adequacy. One way in which he does this is by relating to certain people, referred to as "significant others." These usually include the parents and other people the baby sees very often. Through these people he will develop a basic trust toward people that he will carry beyond the small circle of this significant group.

The process is a slow one, however, and many a parent will be dismayed when grandma comes to visit and the baby cries when she tries to pick him up. The problem is that the baby has not yet had time to develop

322

meanings about that person and, therefore, has not formed a concept of what grandma means to him.

The development of concepts is not a rapid process. Concepts are formed and then changed to fit a new set of experiences. A child develops new concepts by building on ones previously acquired. After the child has mastered some concept of himself, his parents, and other people, and some basic idea of his world, he will be able to begin to develop concepts of a more sophisticated nature.

Helping a Child Form Concepts

Since the development of concepts is closely bound to the child's total growth and because concept formation is closely tied to feelings, it is the opinion of most researchers and the PCI that parents can aid in conceptual formation. You can encourage your child to explore the physical world in a safe manner. Allow your child to roam through the house after you are sure he will not hurt himself on wobbly furniture or steep stairs. Gently but firmly teach him about those things that must not be touched, such as the hot stove.

To develop a satisfying concept of self, your baby will benefit from games, such as peekaboo. Games will help her strengthen her emotional ties to you and permit her to see herself as lovable and adequate.

As your child grows older, answer all his questions and ask some that will stimulate his interest. Most important is that you realize that the formation of concepts is a slow process and that your child will reach each desired goal when he is ready and able to do so.

PLANNING A HOME CURRICULUM

Objective of a Home Curriculum

Dr. John Meier, former director of the JFK Child Development Center and Associate Professor of Pediatrics at the University of Colorado Medical Center, presently Director of the U. S. Office of Child Development, HEW, in *Systems for Open Learning* presents four objectives of a responsive, autotelic (self-pacing) environment. These can be useful to parents as a basis for a home curriculum and setting up a learning environment. They are:

1. To develop positive self-image.
2. To increase sensory and perceptual activity.
3. To improve language functioning.
4. To improve problem-solving and concept-forming abilities.

In defining the autotelic environment, Dr. Meier points out that "an activity is autotelic if it is done for its own sake rather than for obtaining rewards or avoiding punishment." An autotelic home environment is one that satisfies the following conditions:

1. It permits the learner to explore freely.

2. It informs the learner immediately about the consequence of his action.

3. It is self-pacing and non-competitive, i.e., events happen within the environment at a rate determined by the learner.

4. Its structure is such that the learner is likely to make a series of interconnected discoveries about the physical, cultural, and social elements of his world.

Positive Self-image

The way a person views herself tends to affect the way she behaves and learns. A responsive home environment and parents contribute to the development of positive self-concept. The learner is free to explore anything in sight. Since the home environment is self-pacing and non-competitive, the child is not compared unfavorably with another child who speaks better or builds better.

In such an environment, a child can experience as much success as is possible. The concept of "me, my, and mine" is encouraged by putting up on the wall the child's drawings and paintings so that she can think "that's me," "my place," "my pictures." Mirrors also reflect the feeling of self.

Sensory and Perceptual Skills

Recent research with disadvantaged children focuses on the input of all the senses in learning by toddlers and preschoolers. These studies emphasize the importance of selecting and using equipment the learner can look at, feel, listen to, and move around. Included are pegboards, color cones, nesting cups, depth cylinders, puzzles, colored rods, etc. *Timing is also important.* Providing these sensory experiences at three to four years may not succeed as much as if they were offered at one to one and a half years of age. It is during their earliest years that children practice intently their newly found sensory powers.

Language Development

Language learning is a very important skill. It is accomplished in great measure by labeling objects, developing listening skills, and discover-

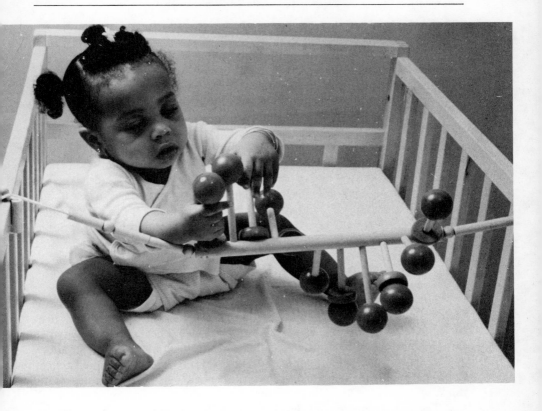

ing relationships ("over, under, and between," etc.). Mastering a language is a long, arduous trial-and-error process. Some of the slowness can be eliminated by understanding what is involved in the process. Learning to listen, using words to describe an activity a child is doing, etc., will aid the development of language. One must remember that children may have mastered certain concepts even though they cannot define them.

Problem Solving

Problem solving refers to the variety of learning concepts that toddlers and preschoolers have to master. These include such motor mastery as climbing, balancing, carrying, etc., as well as puzzle solving, discovering the rules of a game, and so on. Interactional problems include getting along with others. Affective or emotional problems include learning to take turns, finding a place in the group, etc.

325

Organization of the Learning Environment
Order and Orderliness

Perhaps the most important requirement for learning is order: the order of things, of space, and of time. Only from a sense of the orderliness of the universe can observations be made that can be of use.

To promote learning in the home, an infant's surroundings must be orderly since his home is his universe. Thus the materials that promote learning need to be kept in order. The child must know with certainty that they will always be in the same area. There must be a place, an open shelf, perhaps a box or two, for construction materials (blocks, beads, puzzles, etc.); another space for dolls and house play materials; a shelf for cars, trucks, trains, etc.; and other convenient containers for art supplies. Each container should be identified with a picture and perhaps a printed word description.

SIZE PERCEPTION FOR TODDLERS

The five senses interact dynamically, with visual perception playing the dominant role in the baby's learning process. Long before a baby has the muscle co-ordination to reach out and touch, she can see, and what she sees marks her memory with significant impressions. She will file these experiences away, using them at the same time to expand her intelligence. At first dependent on perception and movement, gradually she learns to think.

The baby's intellectual development is being formed by her "sensing abilities." Therefore, the baby who is active and full of movement is more likely to be more mature mentally and physically than the one who is confined to a limited arena of investigation, such as a playpen.

Size Discrimination

The baby's first mental images revolve about his ability to discriminate an object or figure from its surroundings. He sees the object with his eyes, but it is given more meaning *after* he touches it with his hands, feeling whether it is round or square, smooth or rough, etc. His initial reaction is that the object is an extension of himself, but later he learns that it is a thing apart from himself and other objects. This is the beginning of spatial concepts. The baby's ideas of space and the objects in it are determined by himself and where he is at that moment.

Learning spatial relationships is necessary before a child can differen-

tiate size. He must first experiment in reaching out to grasp an object in order to estimate distance. His concept of space gives him a sense of relationship to the objects around him. He needs to understand space in order to compare these things.

The very young child learns to measure space by muscular movements (squeezing into a small box, for example), but soon finds that vision gives her a more comprehensive picture of her world. She learns to depend on her eyes as a useful means of identification.

Size discrimination requires more sophisticated thinking than do color or form. The earliest a child is able to differentiate "biggest," "middle size," and "littlest" is not until she is three years old or more. Her most difficult concept is that of middle size, but biggest is also hard for her to grasp.

One of the reasons that size discrimination is such a difficult concept for the child to understand is that she must take into account perspective. We all know that objects look smaller when we are far away from them, but even adults tend to think the moon is larger when it is nearer the horizon than when it is high in the sky. Children are no exception. Studies reveal that children often have difficulty making accurate judgments when the distance of the object from the child increases.

Learning by Play

A full-length mirror is a good tool for teaching a child to distinguish different sizes. First you and your child stand together and you ask the questions, "Who is the biggest?" "Who is the smallest?" The answers will be fairly obvious to your child. Next introduce a third object, such as a doll, and ask, "Who is the biggest?" "Who is the smallest?" "Who is in the middle?" When you think that your child understands the concept of size difference sufficiently, you should sink down on your knees so that you are lower than your child's head and then repeat the questions. This will also help reinforce his awareness of size.

You have a captive audience and it is easy to take advantage of this while you go about your daily routine. The next time you are going to break an egg, show your child the whole egg; after it is broken, show him the two halves. By holding the two halves together and then pulling them apart, your youngster will be getting his first lesson in fractions in terms that he can understand and enjoy. As was noted above, middle size is the hardest concept of the three for a young child to grasp. The next time you are making a sandwich, ask him, "Where is the filling?" "Where is the middle?" etc.

Many learning experiences may be gleaned from the family's box of discarded buttons. Children love to match them by color, size, or even the number of thread holes used to sew them to fabric. (Be alert lest little children put buttons in their mouths and accidently swallow them.)

Research indicates that not only can intelligence be extended with early visual training (three to four months), but that the development of a mature visual-motor function is essential to reading readiness. Early difficulty in recognizing geometric shapes means later difficulty in recognizing letters and words.

PCI Point of View

The more a child has learned, the more he is ready to learn. In the beginning, he learns much by repetition, but as he grows older his thinking becomes more abstract. The things that interest you are the things you do best and they are what you can best teach your child. This will lead to strengthening his interest and cementing a warm bond between you.

COLOR PERCEPTION FOR TODDLERS

Visual perception is governed by two factors that interact: heredity and intellectual capacity. Heredity sets the outside limits of intelligence levels, but intellectual capacity allows these boundaries to be stretched. The earlier we begin to stimulate a child's sensory abilities, the more the child learns and the more he is capable of learning.

A child has to learn shape and color discrimination because this ability is not present at birth. This is followed by visual differentiation of form. Experimental work shows that an infant can discriminate a contour with different gradations of color. We know that she will respond to a mask of a face with eyes, nose, and mouth rather than an equal area with randomly distributed colors.

Color Perception

Response to color develops early in the child's life, but assumes less importance as she matures. The first color the child recognizes is yellow and the last usually is blue. By the time an infant is a year old, she will react to all the colors presented to her.

From the first day of life, the infant's perception of contrast and movement is well developed. By the time he is two weeks old, he can begin to discriminate colors.

Experts feel that few geniuses are born, but that many are literally made at home. A well-thought-out program beginning when the child is a few months old will pay off in increased learning dividends and need not cost much money. There are an infinite variety of household items suitable for instructing a child and increasing his potential.

Learning to Classify

Learning to classify is a prerequisite to developing good mathematical skills. Therefore, teaching your child to organize by matching colors will help him later on in life.

Colored cubes are available as a traditional toy to teach color matching. Stationery stores have colored tags of different shapes in stock. Colored tags offer the advantage of teaching color and shape and of being small enough to be stored in your pocketbook for those moments when you are waiting in the doctor's office or traveling on the bus. Your child will find it easier to pick out the different objects when you first begin to work with him. Asking him to pick out two things that are similar will prove much harder for him. The development of his visual discrimination will be stimulated by exercises requiring fine distinctions.

Tasks you give your child should be simple and brief, because her attention span is limited and her interest will wane quickly. The goal should be to teach her specific skills that allow her to utilize her experiences to the maximum degree and at the same time teach her classification. The progression of her learning process is dependent on her ability to organize.

Learning by doing is a primary approach to the development of the thinking process. For instance, letting a child have access to paints and the mixing of colors not only encourages a manipulative skill, it lets him experiment with color changes and variations of intensity. All this while he is having fun, too.

Putting the toys away after playtime always seems to be a chore to both parent and child, but this can be made into a learning game also. Ask your offspring to pick up all the red toys first, then the green, etc. In no time the job is done to your mutual benefit.

A game can be made out of identifying the canned goods in your kitchen pantry. For instance, carefully phrasing your questions, ask your child, "Can you find a can with a picture of a yellow vegetable?" "A Green Giant?" "A half-red and half-white label?" "Could a Green Giant be on any can we have?" "Is there a can that is half one color and half another?"

This type of technique reinforces color precepts and strengthens communication, increasing finger dexterity and eye–hand co-ordination at the same time.

Sensory Games for Visual Discrimination and Color Learning

1. Color memory game—Cut out and paint 2½"×4" cards (plywood, Masonite, or mat board can be used). Keep one side neutral and paint the other side with white, black, red, blue, yellow, etc., as well as tint shades of these. Make six of each color. The parent keeps one card of each color at the table and puts the others on shelves across the room. The child selects and looks at the color. It is then turned color side down, neutral side up, after which the child goes to the shelf across the room and selects the color that she thinks matches the turned-down color card.

Later on in the game the parent can ask the child to bring two cards that are the same color, etc.

2. Saying color names.

3. Color lotto. There are numerous companies and school supply houses that make or sell color-matching lotto or other games.

4. Montessori produces a color sequence wood game that has six gradations of the original color to be put in sequence. Check catalogues of school supply houses in your community.

PCI Point of View

Children presented with a routine of many varied learning experiences will profit the rest of their lives. However, the amount or quality of a child's education will not necessarily bring happiness to that child's life; the approach of the parents is critical. Calm, patient, and understanding parents will not only nurture a love of learning in their child, but help rear one who will be socially aware and probably more at peace with himself and the world in which he lives.

Dr. John Meier's handbook *Systems for Open Learning* offers 500 pages of lesson plans for sensorimotor, linguistic, attitudinal, and perceptual learning. A "must" for all parents, paraprofessionals, and preschool directors.

TIME PERCEPTION

Time is a complex concept that is especially difficult to get over to toddlers. Time is complicated because we cannot see, hear, touch, or taste it.

There are two distinct kinds of time: conventional, abstract time with a measurement system to be learned (hours, minutes, seconds), and our own personal temporal time (the time at which we eat, go to school, etc.). Most parents teach temporal time informally. The child is told, "Not now, wait a minute, Daddy will be home soon." Some time learning develops as a result of interaction with the environment—night, day, seasons of the year, etc.

Development of Time Conception

When the infant brings her hands to her mouth before sucking, we realize that her actions are arranged in a temporal series. However, an infant has no sense of past, present, or future time. Instead, she has vague feelings of her own actions mixed with other vague feelings of her needs.

As the baby develops, she becomes better able to see her own actions and to arrange them in regard to the effects they have on the environment. She gains a slight idea of time "before" and "after" as a result of a sequence in which her actions produce a result. However, the baby cannot yet conceptualize temporal events in which her own actions have not played a part. She is, as Piaget says, "egocentric." She understands only subjective time.

At about one year of age, the child sees one event happening first, another event happening second, etc. So he begins to view objectively the various happenings going on before him. He is now able to retain a series of events in which he did not participate and his view of events is no longer solely subjective. At about fifteen months, his objective view of events becomes well developed. By sixteen to nineteen months, the child can recall past events because his ability to view events objectively allows him to represent mentally events outside of his immediate perception.

Dr. L. B. Ames conducted a study of time concepts in children from the ages of eighteen months to eight years. A short compilation was made of verbal expressions of time over a two-year period during direct conversations. It was found that a child first responds to a time word, then uses it in spontaneous conversation, and finally he can answer questions dealing with the concept. For example, at eighteen months the child responds to "soon"—at twenty-four months he uses "soon"—and at forty-two months he can answer a question about the concept "soon." Words referring to the present were used first (twenty-four months); words referring to the future were used second (thirty months); and words referring to the past were used third (thirty-six months).

332

Parental Involvement in the Learning Process

What can parents do to aid their child in developing a concept of time? It is helpful to emphasize what is going on now, what has already happened, and then what will happen next. Through your own daily conversations with your child you can use such expressions as "That's something for after nap time" or "In a little while it will be time to go outside to play." Since children understand time concepts based on a sequence of events before they understand those based on intervals, the use of such words as "before," "after," "first," "next," "last," "soon," and "later" aid them in furthering their ideas of temporal order.

You can help your child achieve understanding of time concepts dealing with cause and effect by verbalizing the consequences of her actions, for example, by asking, "What happens when you press down too hard with your crayon?" when she breaks her crayon. Also, when she builds with blocks, pulls toys, makes sand castles, etc., ideas of cause and effect begin to take place in her mind.

Since auditory perception of time develops before visual perception, musical toys, records, and the human voice play a major role in a child's acquisition of time concepts.

Here are some activities that are part and parcel of a time-learning schema:

1. Authorities point out that time learning begins with simple associations. A hungry child will stop crying when he sees mother's breast, which is associated with the milk that follows.

Parents can call attention to the one-thing-follows-another scheme of time learning. Let the child look at a bottle before feeding him. Show him a diaper before starting to change him.

2. Parents can provide a solid foundation by calling the child's attention to specific times of the day. "It is noon now and time to eat lunch." "Today is Monday and that is the day we wash our clothes."

3. We must learn to be consistent in the use of indefinite time expressions. "Wait awhile" can mean anything from a few minutes to an hour. What parents must do is to relate these expressions to concrete activities— when we say a "long time ago" we should add "when grandma was a little girl." Even though the child does not have the concept of twenty to thirty years, he still will be getting a schema that will have use when he is using "time words."

4. Give your toddler practice in remembering several things in order

—a toy, a doll, a fork, a hat—then take them away and ask him which came "first," then which is next . . . and last.

5. Talk with your child about past events—"a visit to grandma last week," "yesterday his cousins took him to a zoo," etc. Show him pictures of how he looked when he was one year old, or two years, and see how much bigger he is.

6. Since counting is the basis of our system of measuring time, you might teach your child how to count. Later the counting can be related to groups of objects.

7. Teach him the meaning of time-related words, such as new and old, fast and slow.

8. Let your child play with an egg timer. A cuckoo clock which has different sounds for quarter, half, and hour intervals is a good learning tool.

9. Include in your playroom attractive calendars with spelled-out days of the week. Give each day its own personality. "Sunday is our family day," "Tuesday we go shopping," etc. "When does the garbage man come? No, it isn't Thursday, it is Monday."

10. Give your child a system for figuring out time words, such as "yesterday, today, tomorrow, before, after."

The quality of understanding of time is furthered only by activity-oriented home and school teaching.

SPATIAL RELATIONSHIPS: ONE TO THREE YEARS

When we talk about the development of spatial relationships in visual perception, we mean the relationship of objects to each other, as well as the relationship of objects to the individual. Form perception tends to cast the shapes we see into meaningful figures; space perception makes meaningful the relationship between forms. The child who has difficulty with space perception may also encounter difficulty with reading and arithmetic and generally find all abstract thinking difficult.

When a baby first begins to reach for an object he sometimes appears to be pushing it away. This is because he has not yet judged the distance correctly. When he begins to walk and crawl, he bumps into things and often falls down. When he first tries to sit down on a chair, he will walk up to it, put his hands on it, then hold onto it as he turns around and sits down. Accurate judgment of distance comes through experience.

All children become better oriented in space as they grow older, but some seem to use their visual cues better. The more varied and numerous sensory experiences a baby has, the greater will be the realization of her optimal intellectual maturation and functioning. Since the greatest amount of learning occurs visually and especially through visual-motor activities, parents need to see that this sense is fully and properly developed.

Up to the age of one year, the baby has been learning much about spatial relationships without any apparent effort on the part of the parent. He built up an awareness of himself in space as he discovered different parts of his body. Then he built up an awareness of different objects in space as he learned to locate them with both his eyes and hands.

Parents usually find their year-old baby dropping things from his high chair and then screaming until they are retrieved. Although the parents soon tire of this game, they can take real comfort from the fact that their baby is learning something about space. Now the parents can begin to bring some concepts of space into the baby's world as they speak of things being "near, far, up, down, big, and small." Even though the baby cannot talk, she will gain some knowledge of these concepts. When the parent says "Bye-bye" and leaves, the baby grasps the notion that someone is leaving her immediate spatial world.

PCI Point of View

Let your toddler work along with you in your housework. Even a simple chore such as dusting is a learning situation. When your child empties the wastepaper basket into the garbage can, he is learning the wastepaper basket must be right over the garbage can in order for the trash to go in properly. Be patient. Do not push him into learning things he may not be ready for, but always offer ample opportunities for learning to take place.

FORM AND SHAPE DISCRIMINATION

Reinforcing Early Learning

A positive attitude toward learning comes from parents. Dr. Glenn Doman had a fascinating experience involving learning at the Institute for the Development of Human Potential in Philadelphia. When the participating parents first became aware that they could teach babies to read, they found that those mothers who had the most success were not the most intelligent, but those who were the most enthusiastic. The mothers who approached their children less intellectually were more apt to shout, "Wow! That's great!" when their child succeeded. They showed by voice, motion, and commotion their elation with their child's success.

Children understand and appreciate "Wow" better than carefully chosen words of praise. They respond well to a general feeling of joyousness on the part of their parents. Probably the greatest benefit to the parent and child working together in a specific learning situation is the close relationship it affords them. The baby gains by having responsive individual attention and the parent gains through developing greater understanding of her baby.

A clear understanding of forms is necessary both for reading and math readiness. At first the infant sees forms as a mass; then he sees the parts that make up a form; then he can begin to differentiate between forms. You can begin to teach your baby about forms at the age of twelve months. The circle is the easiest form to recognize, then the square, and last the triangle.

The baby must learn to identify, classify, and then put into order what she perceives. These lead to her learning, reasoning, and, finally, her action. A simple form board can be made from a corrugated box by cutting out a circle, square, and triangle. Show the baby how the circle fits into the hole first, then repeat with the other shapes. After that all three shapes can be taken out at once and the baby helped to get them back properly until she is able to do it on her own.

From this beginning, the baby can move on to more complicated forms and form boxes. There are three-dimensional form boxes on the market (into which the child puts a triangular shape through the triangular hole, etc.) that are very helpful and sometimes make it easier for the baby's identification of forms. (Creative Playthings, Inc., has a wood form board with five different shapes and numbers from 1 to 5. There is one form for number 1, two of the same forms for number 2, and so on.)

The Classification of Forms

Classification is easiest by color, next by shape, and then by size. First, cut the same shape of different colors for your baby to match together. Then cut out several different shapes (circles, squares, diamonds, triangles, etc.) with all the circles, for example, colored green and all squares colored red. Finally, cut out different shapes with all having the same color. Help your baby arrange them at first by color. Later he can progress to classifying circles of different sizes, squares of different sizes, and triangles of different sizes.

336

PCI Point of View

Young children do not learn just through seeing with their eyes; they learn constantly with *all* their senses. Touching is essential in learning about form, and interesting textures and novel shapes increase the desire to touch.

NUMBER CONCEPTS

One aspect of intelligence on which our society has placed great emphasis is mathematical proficiency. Approximately one half of the time our children spend in elementary school is devoted to the study of numbers and all our children are expected to acquire a competence in mathematics far greater than that of the most intelligent Greeks of the sixth century B.C.

Because adults use many sophisticated mathematical processes in their daily lives and take them for granted, there has been very little study about how and when these mathematical processes become possible for the child.

Research on Quantitative Concepts

Jean Piaget did perform extensive studies on how children develop an appreciation of quantitative relationships. The results of his experiments show a picture of a slowly unfolding system of awareness of relationships between things, their number or quantity, weight, shape, and size. Dr. Piaget believes that before the age of twenty-four months the child's concepts of number relationship are undifferentiated. For example, a two-year-old would decide a piece of popcorn weighed more after it was popped because it was bigger.

The Two-year-old

During the period from twenty-five to twenty-eight months, developing number concepts are those of ordination (counting objects in sequence —one apple, two apples, etc.) and the process of classification (a dog is an animal, etc.). Maria Montessori's colored rods (developed long before the Cuisinaire rods that are used in today's schools) are one example of material that can help teach a child number relationships. Ten different colored and sized rods are used to symbolize numbers 1 to 10. Since the ordination process can be improved with practice, the mother who works with her toddler is providing necessary training and feedback.

By two and a half, the child begins counting and classifying objects (ordination). He can tell you, "Daddy is bigger than I am," "A dog is an animal," and "I have three cookies." Every few months, parents can see the development of increasing sophistication in dealing with quantity.

When you are measuring ingredients for a recipe is an excellent time to help teach your child more and less, full and empty, etc. Only after frequent exposure will your child learn these things, but once learned they will become permanent concepts. Counting objects in sequence is something that can be done any time. Count your steps out loud and soon your child will be joining you. Count the people in your family, the fingers on your child's hands, and the things you buy at the supermarket.

By the time your child is ten or eleven, the why of these concepts will be explained in school, but for now your child is struggling to understand complex mathematical relationships and perceptions. Anything done in the spirit of play for ten or fifteen minutes a day that employs the principles of ordination and natural numbers will help your child make additional sense out of his environment.

Parent-Child Activities for Learning Natural Numbers and Ordination

1. Take advantage of the counting potential in a child's play. If she is playing with pegboards, nesting cups, counting cubes, bead counters, or large beads or if she is working with clay making cookies or balls or snakes, count each item as it is finished. "Mary has made one cookie, now she is finishing the second one. One, two, three." "How many beads can fit into this box? Let's count them together."

2. When the child has learned to build a nesting cup tower, ask, "How many nesting cups are in the tower you made?" Using a bead counter, show the child how to move one bead at a time across the bar; then let him push the beads while you count. Learning the order of number series helps a child to count.

3. Some commercial houses sell "Number Pegs"—numerals cut out of wood or Masonite with holes punched through so that a child can put pegs in on either side. After several days of play with these, count with an interested learner the pegs in each of the numerals: "One, two, three pegs . . . and this is the numeral three."

338

THE EXPLORER

The Scientific Method

The preschool child is an avid explorer. He comes equipped with an insatiable interest that can be fostered and encouraged by the parent. As a child touches, smells, and looks at the world around him, he questions, looks for cause and effect, and tests his conclusions—*playing all the while.*

The name given to this questioning pattern is "the scientific method." There are five steps to this approach: state the problem, form the hypothesis, observe and experiment, interpret data, and state conclusions. A child will naturally follow this pattern even though there may be large time lapses between each step and he will not always verbalize his questions and conclusions.

In his book *The Development of Scientific Concepts in a Young Child,* John G. Navarra closely observes a preschool child and records his observations and statements that depict the growth of scientific concepts. The author reveals the step-by-step process over the space of many months by interpreting what the child sees and says.

State the Problem

The parent must observe this step in the very young child. The latter may, for example, merely repeat the action of pouring water from a sieve; an older child will ask why the water does not stay in the container. Of course, the more stimuli a child is exposed to, the more questions she will raise. Each problem should be allowed to arise naturally from a situation rather than be taught as a lesson.

Walks in a park, a city setting, or the country can be inspiring if the parent will point out leaves, birds, the height of trees, shadows, the feel of the air, the way the rain dries on the skin, the differences and similarities of things in the environment, to name just a very few. The child may wish to touch an object or see how it feels in his hands. This should be encouraged when possible. An excellent toy to stimulate curiosity at this stage is a large magnifying glass.

An important way parents can encourage their child in this first step of the scientific method is by helping her with her vocabulary. The two-year-old will profit from learning that "water" or "wet" applies to the hot and cold from the faucet, what's left when the ice melts, and the rain.

339

Form the Hypothesis

When a child forms a basic concept of water, for instance, he will begin to form certain expectations about the water. For instance, he may expect it to pour from a hole. This expectation is his hypothesis. Other expectations may be that the candle will go out when he blows it or that the blocks will fall if he piles them too high or crookedly. The expectation may or may not be clearly stated. After it is formed, however, the child will proceed to test his hypothesis.

Observe and Experiment

This step will probably take the most time and is the most easily observed by the parents. Parents who witness their child's curiosity can help focus it on one aspect. For instance, the child who is playing with ice cubes (letting them melt, feeling their wetness, etc.) might enjoy having the water refrozen in the ice cube tray and then letting them melt again.

Sometimes the parent will observe the child experimenting on her own. A child pouring water through a sieve may put her hands around it to prevent the water from coming through. A baby will demonstrate the same experimentation, although on a much lower intellectual level, i.e., at repeated games of peekaboo or "Which hand has the penny?" The parent can easily enlist the child's help in certain experiments, such as seeing whether a mitten in a warm spot dries faster than one in a cold spot or seeing what makes a pinwheel turn faster. Planting seeds in a paper cup on the windowsill is an ideal way for a toddler to see how plants grow.

Interpret the Data and State Conclusions

Parents need to listen to what their child says and try to understand the information or misinformation behind his remarks. This should guide the parent into providing activities that will help him attain more precise information.

A young child is not able to tell his parents that he has learned that water comes through a hole. Even an older child will not be able to tell by what steps he has reached his conclusions. However, he has learned something. The conclusion that the child comes to will be gradually refined and integrated into a more comprehensive concept relating to the passage of water. For instance, he may learn that water will pass through a cloth.

The development of scientific concepts is a dynamic process in which ideas are related to each other; for example, the child who learns that water falls down will also have learned something about gravity.

What Parents Can Do

Parents need to let their child have a large measure of freedom with limits that are reasonable and consistent. Parents need to be their child's helper, not the master or director. This will allow the child to be spontaneous and take the initiative.

During the preschool years, parents are the first teachers of science. It is during these years also that the child develops a basic orientation of himself and the environment. Combined with the child's curiosity, this makes the preschool years a most important time for parental interest in their child as an explorer of nature and science.

INTELLIGENCE TESTING

American interest in intelligence is to a great extent centered on achievement and specifically on comparing the relative intellectual standing of children of the same age. For that reason, numerous standardized intelligence tests have been developed for all ages. First, let us look at tests that are specifically designed for infants.

Infant Intelligence Tests

A popular standardized infancy test is the Bayley Scale of Mental Development. The following list of items, taken from the scale, illustrates the kinds of behavior that are sampled and measured in infant tests. (Numbers in parentheses indicate the age in months at which 50 per cent of the children tested passed the item.)

imitates words (12.5)
builds tower of two cubes (13.8)
says two words (14.2)
uses gestures to make wants known (14.6)
attains toy with stick (17.0)
imitates a stroke (17.8)
places two round and two square blocks in a board (19.3)
follows directions in pointing to parts of a doll (19.5)
points to tree pictures (21.9)
builds tower of six cubes (22.6)

> names two objects (23.0)
> mends broken doll (23.6)
> names three pictures (24.0)
> names three objects (24.9)
> names five pictures (25.5)

Most of the items on this test, like those on other scales, tap sensorimotor skills, although many of them involve simple understanding and use of language. Research by Dr. Nancy Bayley and others, indicates that scores obtained on infancy scales are *not* predictive of later intelligence. Some authorities believe that such tests indicate whether a baby has had a disease or injury to his brain and whether he has suffered emotionally from neglect.

In the first year, however, they do not tell anything about what the normal child's future intelligence will be. This may be due to the fact that while infant tests consist largely of motor tasks, tests for preschool and older children deal with language, abstract thinking, reasoning, and memory.

It appears that black and white infants of fifteen months of age or younger do not differ in their performance on this test, nor do these scores correlate with the socioeconomic level of the child's family. This is due in part, no doubt, to there being little cultural bias to a test that consists largely of sensorimotor tasks.

Intelligence Testing of the Preschool and School-aged Child

Standardized intelligence tests for preschool and school-aged children yield a score, the IQ, that is commonly considered an index of intellectual capability and potential intellectual achievement. The extent to which the IQ test has been used in this country in the last half-century is staggering.

It is estimated that within North American schools alone, over 250 million standardized IQ tests are administered yearly. It would be a rare individual indeed who has not been evaluated by an IQ test.

A child's intellectual growth is neither static, nor necessarily predetermined. It varies throughout her life, depending on the interaction between her inherited characteristics and her environment. Many factors may affect intellectual or cognitive growth: the emotional climate at home, whether she is encouraged or discouraged, whether or not her drive is strong, and whether there are sufficient opportunities for experience and learning geared to her capacities.

Therefore, the concept of the stable IQ score seems outmoded. Numerous factors influence scores on intelligence tests, most of which are capable of manipulation. Brandon Sparkman and Ann Carmichael report in their book *Blueprint for a Brighter Child* that the scores culturally deprived youngsters make on IQ tests can be substantially improved through concentrated efforts on language development, especially from the ages of eighteen to twenty-eight months. They reveal that an increase of fifteen to twenty points in one year is not uncommon. They further emphasize that "IQ does not measure the innate capacity of a child to learn; it merely indicates the degree to which he is able to learn at that moment."

Other studies indicate a child's ability to alter markedly her IQ score. Drs. Mussen, Conger, and Kagan report that "many children undergo significant changes in IQ between early childhood and later ages. In fact, there are marked changes—sometimes as much as twenty points—between the nursery school period and later childhood." They suggest that extremely favorable or unfavorable changes in environment may produce such shifts in intellectual performance.

Other research on personality and IQ change showed that qualities such as high achievement, competitive striving, and curiosity about nature were correlated with gains in IQ score because these qualities may facilitate the acquisition of skills that are measured by intelligence tests.

Criticism and Limitations of the IQ Test

In the post-Sputnik period, a growing number of critics have claimed that mental tests are unfair to the bright but unorthodox person, to the culturally disadvantaged, and to those persons who simply do not do well under the pressure of the standardized test situation.

For too long, society in general and our schools in particular have viewed the IQ test as the only measure of an individual's capability and potential. The IQ test measures convergent thinking—memory, recognition, ability to analyze, and to reason—but does not measure divergent thinking—the ability to be creative, exploratory, venturesome, flexible and inventive. Clearly, then, the IQ test provides us with only one index of personal capacity.

At the University of Minnesota elementary school children were tested for both intelligence and creativity. Seventy per cent of the most creative did not distinguish themselves on the IQ test, a situation very reminiscent of the young Thomas Edison and numerous other highly inventive persons. In another study, Donald F. MacKinnon, a psychologist, tested a group of successful young architects chosen as most creative by experts in the field. Their IQ scores ranged from very high to very low, with a mean of 113.5 (a very average score).

The traditional academic curricula of our schools and colleges are becoming increasingly dependent on verbal communication, verbal memory, and the same kind of abstract reasoning that is measured by mental tests. Our schools are trapped by the tyranny of the test. As society becomes more and more dependent on the test score to categorize people, schools provide a curriculum that tends to promote success on the tests, but not necessarily in life.

PCI Point of View

Parents, beware! Intelligence is not a fixed, objective trait to be identified and somehow converted into a score, once and for all. Ask questions about the tests administered to your child and do not stop asking questions until the interpretations presented satisfy you.

On the other hand, tests can be useful guidelines. Some of them are even quite good. They are remarkably acccurate scoring devices for *describing* behavior at different ages. At best they may provide insights and clues to your child's mind that would otherwise be lost to you.

10

Play and Playthings

INTRODUCTION BY FRANK AND THERESA CAPLAN*

Most parents believe that the powers implicit in play far transcend our present knowledge. In more recent years, their intuition has been proved correct and is being tested and researched.

Previously, most scientists and educational researchers steered clear of studying play because it was an unmanageable laboratory subject. Today, however, biologists and ethnologists are seriously studying the behavior and play of primates in natural settings and discovering that play serves a crucial learning function and forecasts adult competence.

A great body of animal and human infant research and observations by the most perceptive thinkers in the field of psychology and education leave little doubt that play is of significant value to the physical, emotional, and social development of the young child.

In spite of the fact that there are very few tests available that assess the elements of play, we believe that play precipitates such qualities as creativity, imagination, ingenuity, motivation, and daring. We are of the unequivocal opinion that a great deal of play and fantasy in early childhood builds self-image, self-confidence, and drive; helps satisfy in each child the urge to master a world of his own; and

* Frank and Theresa Caplan have been associated with educational toy pioneering for over twenty-five years. As co-founders of Creative Playthings, they initiated in 1945 a business that has served the play needs of millions of children. They introduced play sculptures to the American playground movement, initiated laboratory learning in mathematics and science, and simulation game play in social studies.

Frank Caplan served as president of Creative Playthings, Inc., until 1968, and was president of the CBS Learning Center and Edcom Systems, Inc., of Princeton, New Jersey. He is also founder-director of the Princeton Center for Infancy. He received his M.A. from Teachers College, Columbia University, and served a preschool teaching apprenticeship under Caroline Pratt at the City and Country School in New York City. As general editor of the Princeton Center for Infancy, Mr. Caplan has overseen the preparation of *The First Twelve Months of Life* and the extensive data collecting and writing that went into this *Parenting Advisor*.

encourages the exploration and make-believe that contribute to creative thinking in adult life.

Dr. Jerome Bruner believes that play has great cognitive values as well; that it provides practice of instinctive behavior and emerging physical abilities that come together later in problem solving. He wonders whether play is not also responsible for the origins of language in man. When mothers, infants, and toddlers play all kinds of exchange games, such as "peekaboo," "This little piggy went to market," etc., the children learn to signal and recognize certain expectations. From these playful games with primitive rules of behavior, children learn to put together and manipulate certain features of language that eventually take the form of sentences, grammar, and so on.

"Ages and Stages"

Play and playthings offer change and challenge at each age and stage of physical and sensory maturation. In the earliest years—newborn to two years—as each sensory and physical power matures, there is a great need to practice and test out these powers via play. Up to two years of age and beyond, the maturing powers and skills of sound, smell, taste, sight, touch, mouthing, babbling, creeping, standing, walking, and talking need parental intervention by means of an enriched environment of play and challenge.

Even more important, children require ongoing parental "feedback" and encouragement. These powers come so quickly that parents need to be educated and alert in order to provide the necessary stimulation and changes of environment. Without the foregoing, important "imprinting" periods can be lost forever. Play and stimulation at these critical periods help infants and toddlers to develop great sensitivities, self-ego, self-discipline, attending behavior, and talents that continue on into adulthood. For each emerging power, an infant has "full time" to devote to its mastery without worrying about peer group acceptance and other distractions that beset later age levels.

Change and Challenge

Each age level needs a different environment; for example, the newborn to three-month-old benefits immeasurably in a sensory environment of art and graphics, sounds, things to touch, smells, and tastes. In these earliest months, stimulating the sensory modalities can pro-

348

foundly influence the qualities that we later call "awareness," "talent," and "ambition."

What is it that often puts the "B" student ahead of the "A" student in adult life, especially in the creative professions and the business world? Certainly it is more than verbal skills. Research shows that in order to create, one must have a sense of playfulness and adventure. One needs toughness and daring to hazard the risks of possible failure. One needs a strong ego to be propelled forward in one's drive toward an untried goal.

Above all, one has to possess the ability to play, to see relationships easily, to pick out the relevant, and to put parts together until the insightful moment of truth comes through. Creativity and innovation do not come as a flash of genius; rather, they come from long years of early childhood playing, of looking at a problem from unusual perspectives, of "upside-downing" a situation, of staying with a challenge until several usable alternatives present themselves. The abilities to fantasize and to take risks are fundamental potentials of all children.

THE EXTRAORDINARY POWER OF PLAY

Spontaneous play during infancy and early childhood has such far-reaching implications for adulthood that we have summarized some of the thinking of many scholars and educators on the subject. Most parents have instinctively known that play has a vital effect on learning, curiosity, ego, drive, and sociability. However, few parents or researchers have been able to identify specific elements of play, types of play, and the play process as a total system of behavior.

Here are some theories on the nature and power of play:

Surplus Energy Theory of Play

In the mid-nineteenth century, the English philosopher Herbert Spencer drew upon the earlier writings of Friedrich von Schiller and proposed the theory that play is surplus energy in action. According to this theory most children (excluding those of underdeveloped countries or those of acute poverty) do not encounter problems of physical survival on a daily basis. Therefore, their energies are directed toward play rather than toward work. Few early childhood specialists today seriously support the notion of play as a buildup of energy that must be spilled out in some direction.

Psychoanalytic Theory of Freud

Dr. Sigmund Freud (1856–1939) felt that much of a child's play represents an attempt to satisfy drives or to resolve conflicts. There is built up in the child a great range of unsatisfied wishes that forms an increasing basis for elaborate fantasy and play life. Freud also believed that play was *mastery*—an attempt by repetition to cope with overwhelming anxiety-provoking situations.

Piaget's Cognitive Theory of Learning

For Dr. Jean Piaget (1898–), play derives from the child's encounters with reality through related techniques of assimilation and accommodation. Accommodation is the child's attempt to imitate and interact with the external environment, while assimilation is the child's endeavor to integrate externally derived percepts or motor actions into a relatively limited number of internal schemes. For Piaget, symbolic play goes on from about eighteen months to seven years, when it gradually disappears or is transferred.

Playtime, a Critical Learning Period

Dr. Benjamin Bloom, in his book *Stability and Change in Human Characteristics,* has indicated that the period of greatest learning spans the years from birth to about age eight. He discovered that for a seventeen-year-old, 80 per cent of all his learning is attained by age eight and 50 per cent by age four. This period is precisely when play is a child's primary way of life. In recent years, the concept of play has been treated as a vital means of learning and growing for children.

The PCI Point of View

The Princeton Center for Infancy believes that the power of play is extraordinary and supremely serious. Play is a child's way of life. Our culture gives him *time*—more than eight years—to imitate, explore, fantasize, and experiment with new ideas through play. Finding one's place in a culture takes time and our society is tender with children in their first eight years. Play gives a child relief from a sense of hopelessness that many children experience in the complex adult society.

Play Is a Voluntary Activity

Because of the self-choice nature of play, each child builds up play settings that are his own ideas and over which he has full control. In the play world, each child is the play master and decision maker. There are no superimposed directions, no rigid rules to which to adhere. Each child can carry on trial-and-error activities without fear of ridicule or failing. Free from adult interference, a child can pretend any real or imaginary situation and role-play any adult or animal character.

351

Play Develops Ego

Play is an autonomous pursuit in which each child assimilates the outside world to the support of his ego. The self-choice in play permits the child to build confidence in her own power. In her make-believe world, a child can be a giant, a lion, a train, a mother or father—and these play roles give her a sense of control.

Play Provides an Imaginary World That Children Can Master

The real world is brought down to manageable dimensions that allow a child to get a feeling of being "ten feet tall!" In a play setting, the child can imitate an action or oppose it. He can be the subject or the object. There is freedom and an absence of boundaries and restrictions we cannot give him in the adult world.

Play has unique power for building social relations between parents and child and a child and his peers. It fosters group life and offers a chance to work out interpersonal relations and learn adult roles. It takes countless play experiences to make a child a mature social being.

PLAYTHINGS FOR INFANCY

Toys for the First Three Months of Life

There are very few existing toys that have any effect on the first three months of life. (This might be a good field for designers or parents to explore.) An infant's head and feet are constantly in motion. If fitted with a headpiece attached to a mobile, a baby will soon discover that his head movements will activate the mobile. Researchers who attached the corner of a crib sheet at one end of a crib to a mobile and a sound system found that the mobile and sounds kept going all the time, set into action by the infant's feet during his awake period. Earliest toys have to be rigged up by parents. Toy makers find it is financially unsound to make toys for just a three-month period of a baby's life—which nonetheless could be the most important period of a child's life.

Planning an enriched environment for these earliest months should be part of the prenatal preparation for birth. In the early 1930s and 1940s, parents were so preoccupied with health and cleanliness that they set up a white, quiet, hospital-like atmosphere in the nursery—devoid of sounds, sights, smells, tastes, and touch. Such a milieu restricted interaction with adults and siblings.

However, new parenting styles encourage more sights and graphics to distinguish; provide more social interaction with family members, more experience with environmental sounds (tick-tock of clocks, music, etc.), and more contact with nature. Touch, bodily interaction, and wholesome sexual attitudes of today's parents are an important part of the world of

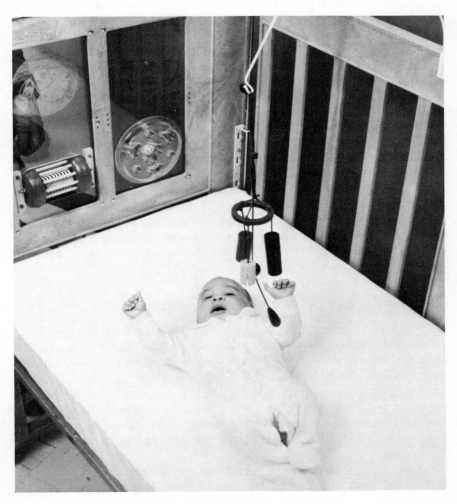

the newborn. The return of the rocking chair, the use of back and front carriers, for instance, are growing evidence of the acceptance of the need to increase all sensorial experiences.

1. *Visual and Auditory "Following."* Visual attendance of specific objects can be stimulated by passing selected objects across the baby's visual field so that he can track them with his eyes; also by having a mobile or fish aquarium at cribside. Infants can be exposed to the projection of large pictures in their cribs; that is, if one side has a screen. The baby can also be taken out of the crib for a visual tour of house or apartment.

Auditory following can be encouraged by toys that make a noise or make music. These toys also help build a baby's "vocabulary" of familiar sounds. Bells, chimes, music boxes, rattles, records, and sound tapes are useful in this regard. Additionally, there are cassettes of music and sounds that appeal especially to infants and often quiet them (heartbeats, among others).

2. *Oral Gratification of Sucking and Tasting.* The infant uses her oral sense by means of sucking, feeling with her tongue, biting to explore the softness, hardness, taste, and shape of things. Therefore, the baby should be given all kinds of safe, attractive teethers in different shapes, colors, materials, and textures, i.e., smoothly sanded hardwood, rubber, vinyl, etc.

3. *Fingering, Reaching, and Manipulating.* Infants discover touch early by their uncontrolled sideswiping movements at the edge of their cribs. If toys are provided that react to these uncontrolled actions, if pleasant sounds result from grasping, if reaching and pulling are rewarded by movement or sounds, then a baby will be impelled to keep on trying. It is desirable to change continually such "touch toys," exchanging teething beads for a rattle or a new mobile, etc.

Nothing Replaces Parents as an Important First Toy!

Mothers or fathers can modulate their voices, offer a familiar face, cuddle and comfort, provide food, etc. From these mutual primary experiences, infants develop social trust. They learn about the wide range of tones, different textures of skin, rubber, and cloth, and they discover movement when they are lifted and carried. It is the activities that babies engage in with their parents that count the most in sensory development. Take your baby on "learning walks" through your house or apartment. Together look in a mirror, feel different textures, and listen to music and folk singing.

Encourage vocalization! Although infants understand very little, it is good for them to hear and eventually imitate sounds. In due course, these sounds will become words and sentences. For parents who are beset with added family responsibilities, there are some aids: toys for hearing, seeing, fingering, sucking, etc. Here are a few:

For Listening

Tick-tock or pendulum clocks
Music boxes with changeable records
Record player
Slumber wind chimes
Bell on handle
Wrist bells on foot

For Seeing

Fish tank
Kick-a-tune (plush ball on string with music works)
Ceiling posters
Faces on the window
Framed metal mirror or crib mirror
Wind-up moving mobiles
Gloves with bull's-eyes (make it yourself)
Mobiles with or without music
See-through crib bumpers

For Kicking

Kick-a-tune
Tie a helium-filled balloon on his feet (while he is on his back)
Sew bells securely on his booties

For Fingering

Plakies (plastic discs on metal chain)
Dumbbells
Smooth clothespins
Plastic keys, balls, rings

355

For Sucking

Nipple ball
Nipple jack
(Write for catalogues to Childcraft Education Corp., 20 Kilmer Rd., Edison, N.J. 08817. Also Fisher-Price Company, Questor, Childhood Interests, Playskool—all at 200 Fifth Avenue, New York, N. Y. 10010.

PLAY FOR THREE TO SIX MONTHS

When infants are ready for grasping (at about thirty-six weeks), a new world of intention and imagery unfolds. During the first stage, from birth to three months, touching and handling are accidental and reflexive. Then infants practice their random movements. Soon they begin to discover the world of objects and their ability to act upon them. Intention begins to appear overtly.

During the second stage of development, infants establish relationships between looking, grasping, and sucking as they continue to apply a great variety of actions to the same objects, show increased purpose in play, build an inner imagery of familiar objects, and start to organize a sense of physical space, form, and texture.

Learning in the real sense has begun. Babies enjoy feeling a variety of things, exploring their contour, balancing them, and striking them against other things. As they turn objects around to view them from every angle, they are developing spatial understanding about objects, about nearness and distance, inside and outside, position and placement, and object permanence.

Programming a Tactile Environment

Learning is always an active process, replete with touch, taste, visual, and aural complexities. The infant organizes all his experiences into usable "schemas" in the course of maturing. Parents cannot afford to sit by passively during this stage. The urge of the infant to explore and manipulate is so strong that to neglect it will deprive him of stimuli that can foster drive and excitement for learning.

Parents must literally "program" a full tactile environment by supplying their baby with multiple playthings or safe household objects to touch, finger, squeeze, and stroke. Variegated textures need to be introduced:

smooth, rough, furry, soft, hard, etc. Many assorted shapes and quantities need to be experienced.

All the attributes of objects need to be compared and contrasted before a child can communicate his or her feelings about them. Parents can help by labeling each object and process for their child. When the child is able to associate words with objects and actions, verbal comprehension has begun.

Teething Toys

Some of the successful first teething toys are rubber beads or plastic discs or keys on a rustproof metal chain with which babies can rub their gums and later their teeth. There are small rubber rings and plastic tube rings with enclosed water and tiny, colorful floating objects that are perfect for grasping, sucking, and chewing. Jack-the-Giant Teether is a soft, pliable plastic teether toy that has differently shaped protrusions for a baby to explore. Many rubber toys with safely embedded squeakers are on the market. Some, however, may frighten an infant if he is not properly introduced to the sound effects. Sorely needed are sucking and chewing baby toys that have a cause-and-effect relationship built into them.

Correlating Seeing and Handling

As infants gain control of their fingers, they correlate seeing and handling and begin to show purpose in reaching for things (usually at three months). While on their backs in the crib, they need touching, pulling, and exercising challenges. Parents will enjoy gently exercising their babies by offering them fingers to grasp and then pulling them up carefully into almost sitting position. The "Cradle Gym" has become a byword in almost every home where there is an infant. This exerciser is used when mother is not at hand.

Another interesting cause-and-effect infant plaything is the Crib Activator. When the baby reaches for a bright wood knob and succeeds in grasping and then pulling it, a bell rings and a beater strikes a wood tone block or a mirror is set in motion. Such playthings help the baby begin to develop a primitive sort of motor intelligence. The baby learns that when she pulls, something interesting will happen; she sets something into motion that can be visually followed.

For four- and five-month-olds who peer longingly through the bars of their crib or playpen at their siblings playing or at a ball or other play object, placing them on an infant crawler offers the mobility their "stomach drag" and weak arm and back muscles preclude. This safe, comfortable crawler will enable infants to be a more active part of their environment and make exciting sensorimotor discoveries.

Crib Toys and Sleeping

In all the research and child-rearing literature, the importance of parent interaction with the child is repeatedly stressed. Yet research shows that in most cases babies spend 27 per cent of their day awake and alone in their cribs and only 15 per cent tended by their mothers. In some day-care and institutional settings, infants are in their cribs alone some three to four hours. This situation encouraged a team of researchers (Twardoz, Cataldo, and Risoly of the University of Kansas) to see if babies actually play with toys placed in their cribs and to find out if crib toys have any effect on the babies' sleep. The results of the study *conclusively* reveal that the babies did play with the crib toys for a considerable time while they were awake in the cribs; this was 37 per cent of the time. The study revealed further that the crib toys *did not* make it more difficult for babies to fall asleep. When parents and day-care professionals were asked whether toys would interfere with sleep, invariably they felt that toys would keep the infants from sleeping. This is not so!

Below are some toys for three to six months from many sources:

TEETHERS

Teething Jack	(Creative)
Textured Balls	(Creative)
Nipple Teether	(Childcraft)
Mirror Teether	(Playskool)

SECURITY AND CAUSE-AND-EFFECT TOYS

Terry Teddy	(Childcraft)
Snuggler	(Creative)
Activator	(Creative)
Cradle Symphony	(Childhood Interests)
Twirl Around	(Questor)
See Me Whirly	(Questor)
Feely Quilt	(Questor—or make your own)

SELF-IMAGE TOYS

Baby Mirror	(Childcraft, Creative, Childhood Interests)
Musical Mirror	(Questor)
Peek-a-boo Mirror	(Hasbro)

ACTIVITY TOYS

Texture Pad	(make it yourself)
Crawligater	(Creative)
Dolphin Crawler	(Childcraft)
Jolly Jump-up	(Childcraft)
Baby Bouncer	(Creative)
Birds and Fishes	(Creative)

MANIPULATIVE TOYS

Rubber-Wood Bell Cubes	(Childcraft)
Hour Glass Ball	(Childcraft)
Baby's Playthings	(Playskool)
Peek and Seek Sack	(Childcraft)
Baby's Flip Book	(Questor)
Water Ball or Transparent Ball with twirling toys	(Questor)
Helium-filled balloon tied to baby's foot	(Childcraft) (make it yourself)

Check local department or toy stores for other infant toys by Fisher-Price, Playskool, Questor, Hasbro, Creative, Childcraft, and Childhood Interests.

INTERACTION GAMES

When a baby passes his third month of life, remarkable changes in his brain allow dramatic increases in muscular control and attentiveness. By four months of age, an infant can double his playtime up to an hour or more when a parent or sibling gets down and plays with him.

Tickling Games

At this tender age, a baby appreciates the sensations of body contacts. Parents everywhere have invented tickling games remarkably similar in vastly different lands and cultures. In all of these games, the parent uses two fingers to simulate the walking of a mouse or rabbit up the baby's body from her toes or up baby's arm from her hand. Mother or father surprises the baby by tickling her at tickle spots under the arm, or chin, or behind the ears. Also some tactile games emphasize toes and fingers. They often are accompanied by a sensational tickling finish, as in "This Little Piggy Went to Market."

Months later, when a baby grows more aware of his body parts and his distinctness from other people, he can appreciate the separateness of his toes and fingers. Then, in a few more months, he will grow aware of yet another facet of these games: the counting and stringing together of similar items in a series, a basic of numerical reasoning.

Rocking Games

Play changes around the fifth month of life because the baby's increasing control of the muscles in trunk and lower back allows her to sit propped in a chair for long periods. From then on, her favorite people circle above her only a part of the day; for the rest of the time she is sitting up, surrounded. This is the time for vigorous rocking games. Chances are the baby is dissatisfied with just the gentle rocking of lullabies or cars, that used to mesmerize her before. By now, father's bouncing her on his foot may be far more entrancing.

Naming Games

Naming games involving a baby's nose, toes, feet, hands, and mouth also emphasize body parts and a concept of self. Your cue for such games comes from your baby. As part of exploring and comparing themselves to their world and the people in it, babies will poke at their ears, nose, mouth, and eyes (yours, too) and may even compare the feel of your features with theirs.

A favorite nursery rhyme directly contrasts the size of the parent's and baby's hands, at the same time showing their similarity in shape. The parent takes the baby's hands and claps them together. Later the baby may clap her hands against those of the parent.

> Pat-a-cake, pat-a-cake, baker's man,
> Bake me a cake as fast as you can,
> Roll it and pat it and mark it with a *B*
> And put it in the oven for baby and for me.

361

In fact, parent–baby clapping games the world over show that people recognize a basic of human education—the awareness of a physical self!

A Game for Every Skill

As you probably have guessed by now, games that parents and babies play foster different kinds of skills in the baby. They can strengthen muscles, expand attention, prompt vocalizing, and promote self-awareness. Parents can use physical games to motivate a quiet baby or satisfy an active one.

Critical Periods

In a scholarly collection of infant research studies, Dr. W. Ragan Callaway, Jr., of UCLA, determined that there are "critical learning periods" for reading that if missed could create reading problems later on. These periods include the *first three to six months* of life, when an infant practices seeing and distinguishing the varied outlines of the mother's and father's faces, bottles, etc. It is a period of intense listening to mother's voice and relating sounds to sights.

Another critical period seems to be *eighteen to twenty-eight* months, when walking stimulates contact and talking to people other than mother. At this time, parents (especially middle-class ones) concentrate on "labeling" with words much of their child's interactions with the environment ("This is a book"; "Be gentle with the dog"; "Ball, this is a ball"; etc.).

PCI Point of View

It is the belief of the Princeton Center for Infancy that out of early experiences with external stimuli a great deal of learning actively takes place —relationship thinking in associating faces and voices, ego building in baby's turning on a musical recording or activating a mobile by foot, hand, or voice action (if parents are able to rig up such an electronic system).

PLAYTHINGS FOR SIX TO TWELVE MONTHS

When infants begin to crawl, the number of people, things, and events they must adapt to and assimilate increases. As a baby's seeing world enlarges, the desire to reach and touch everything within sight becomes overpowering. This stage of growth puts most parents in a state of frenzy.

The infant's need to touch and handle everything often results in a table-cloth pulled down, a small end table overturned, a filled ashtray dumped onto a rug, and objects being explored by mouth—all of which offend the sense of order and cleanliness of most parents and other adults.

Proper Environment for Crawlers

Preparing an interesting but safe environment for the crawler is the parents' responsibility. The crawler loves to hide under tables, under bottom shelves, in closets, and in corners. He pulls at accessible drawers and often gets stuck between a table and chair legs.

There is need for "peekaboo houses," contoured surfaces with "nests" in which one can cuddle up, and floor and manipulative play boards with programmed challenges. Parents might make a vari-textured carpet for the playpen. An unbreakable metal mirror may be hung low enough for the baby to see himself.

Intention and Goal-seeking Behavior

At this stage, infants begin to demonstrate intention and goal seeking. Motions are no longer completely haphazard. They pull a knob because they know this will cause a bell to ring. They drop something on the floor because they want to hear the noise or make a parent come running. Infants construct a sensorimotor intelligence whereby actions are "lived" rather than thought about. It is the kind of intelligence that comes from a fixed succession of static images, each connected with an action.

Manipulating the Environment

During the sixth-to-twelfth-month period, infants begin to grasp elementary ideas through countless actions and manipulations on the environment. With their hands, mouth, feet, arms, and body, they explore a vast variety of play experiences and develop notions of size, shape, texture, weight, volume, density, distance, speed, and altitude.

At five months, if an adult drops an object nearby, an infant will not react. However, at six months when a baby holds an object, lets it fall, and hears it drop, he will search for it with his eyes. After many holding and dropping experiments, the infant will have a schema for searching the floor for every object dropped. The existence of an object to a six-month-old always is directly related to seeing and holding it. Physical acts provide a sense of object permanency.

363

What Toys Exist That Help Build Relationship Thinking in the Early Years?

There are matching toys (with one-to-one correspondence) wherein a cup is matched with a saucer, etc. Or a soft ball or cuddly teddy bear is handled and the mother labels it "soft" or "furry." There are toys for eye-hand co-ordination whereby four blocks are fitted onto an upright peg or mixing bowls are nested in order of size. Once mastered, the process is repeated over and over again with satisfaction and delight in achievement.

Here are other toy recommendations:

Nesting Buckets	(Childcraft)
Walk-a-Bye	(Questor)
Bath Harbor	(Childcraft)
Soft Vinyl Animals	(Childcraft)
Ticking Clock	
Plastic Balls and Blocks	(Childcraft)
Transparent Music Box	(Creative)
Busy Box, Busy Bath, Busy Gym	(Kohner Bros.)
See-a-Sound, Squeeze Please, Big Bead Bus	(Questor)
Rattle Pals, Turn and Touch, Flip Book	(Questor)

Also check Fisher-Price, Playskool, Kenner Products, Childcraft, and Hasbro for new infant toys.

PLAY WITH YOUR BABY

"Play with your baby whenever you want to" is obviously an inadequate guideline for most parents today. Parents need to know *how*. Playing with baby is vital. The games babies play help them learn in a pleasurable way many of the essentials of life.

We have only recently begun to learn from psychologists, pediatricians, and educators that stimulation from the environment greatly influences a child's development. Parents who play, handle, imitate, smile, and talk to their babies, who provide things for their infants to look at, listen to, and explore with their mouths and hands have babies who become

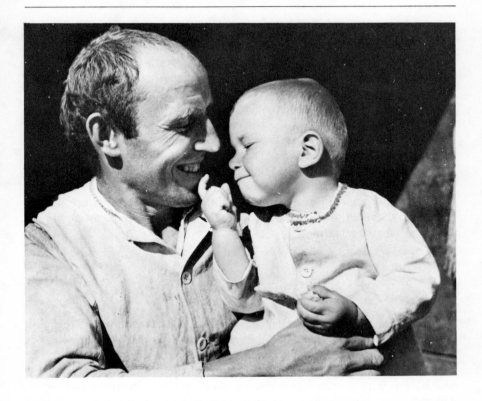

advanced in attentiveness, visual pursuit, and co-ordinated movements. More important, they tend to carry their early advantage into later life.

Dr. Leon Yarrow, Chief of the Social and Behavioral Sciences Branch of the National Institute of Child Health and Human Development, comments: "Perhaps the most striking finding is the extent to which mother's stimulation influences developmental progress during the first six months. Its amount and quality are highly related to her baby's IQ. These data suggest that mothers who give much and intense stimulation and encouragement to practice of developmental skills tend to be successful in producing infants who make rapid developmental progress."

Coughing Game

Games are a wonderful means to mutual fun, excitement, learning, and encouragement for baby and parent. Take the coughting game. As early as two months after the baby's birth date, a parent may imitate baby's cough. At first the cough and smile only attract the baby's attention, but eventually she coughs in return and starts an exchange. (The cough sounds like a smoker's dry hack.) Later the baby initiates the game by coughing and smiling when the parent least expects it. The game's value increases as the baby realizes that her cough can bring parents rushing. Parents often credit the baby with inventing the game, but recognizing authorship matters less than the parents' awareness of the coughing game as a real learning device. The baby learns about human communication and that vocal sounds (tongue clicks, coughs, etc.) are very effective initiators of social exchange. A baby learns quickly that her behavior can affect the environment positively, something very important for every baby to know. Above all, infants learn how to imitate oral sounds, an ability essential to language learning.

Peekaboo Game

Peekaboo, a game that appears about the beginning of the fifth month, is in the same class. Its first version involves the parent hiding her face with her hands, then removing them much to the baby's delight. The baby soon learns to cover his own face. The game is so instinctive that a healthy infant may draw other relatives into the fun. Brothers and sisters will play the game more vigorously than parents; leaping from behind chairs and roaring and yelling. All variants will probably enchant a baby.

Within weeks of its appearance, the infant may want to invent variations. Try setting a diaper lightly over the baby's face, then removing it. You might ask, "Where is ———?" After a few runs, take the baby's hand in yours as you snatch away the veil. In time he may draw the diaper over his face, chuckle, and call to you. If you remain quiet too long, the baby may vocalize again and kick anxiously, then remove the diaper from a startled little face to check on your whereabouts.

Peekaboo may be a first token of humor. Baby has played a trick on someone and has decided beforehand that she intends to do so. Clearly the game indicates that she is intrigued with human faces and the discrepancies offered by their partial concealment. Later on the game means that baby has a memory of someone she loves and the image is fixed enough in her feelings for the baby to try a short separation under her control. She has a sense of mother's permanence, as well as that of objects, and even anticipates the joy of recalling her.

Come-and-get-me Game

Around the crawling stage, the baby will assay separations in other ways. The "come-and-get-me" game requires a pursuing parent and a scrambling, frantically pushing baby. The game should not be curtailed too quickly unless the parent desires a furious, fussing infant. Several runs before abducting baby to something as run-of-the-mill as a meal or diaper change will promote a more resigned capitulation.

Pick-up-the-things-I-drop Game

At about the same age, babies may begin to look over the edge of their chairs at objects they have dropped to the floor. This is the "pick-up-the-things-I-drop" game. A variant during feeding times is dropping spoons and cups overboard as they avoid the spoonful of food you offer. When all droppable items are gone, they will probably cry for parent or sibling to retrieve them.

Like peekaboo, this game demonstrates that the baby is beginning to have a concept of self. She is separate from other people and objects and can influence them through actions that she has selected, for example, dropping an object. In a more general sense, baby's initiating a game relates to her growing capacity to formulate a goal, figure out and take the necessary actions to attain it, distinguish a desired from an undesired result, and respond appropriately to both. Intent matched with a plan that will achieve that intent is nothing short of intelligent behavior. (See Chapter 9 for further discussion on learning.)

PLAYTHINGS FOR TWELVE TO TWENTY-FOUR MONTHS

Physical development and learning go forward at twelve to twenty-four months because of the maturation of the large and small muscles and the development of locomotion and linguistic powers.

In a series of experiments at a Middle East orphanage, Dr. Wayne Dennis found that infants given adequate physical care, but no playthings (and no opportunity to play with adults) were retarded in mastering physical skills. Between the ages of one and two, fewer than half these children could sit unsupported; none could walk. When these backward babies were given a variety of objects to look at and handle, they made great leaps ahead physically and socially (four times the average gain as a result of play experience).

Somewhere from eighteen to twenty-four months a child's large muscles develop sufficiently to enable her to walk. Learning to walk represents important maturing of the nervous system. Now that she can locomote, she can explore more freely. Dependence upon parents for survival lessens somewhat.

Walking makes available a wider array of perceptual and tactile experiences. Toddlers interact with more people than those in their immediate family. To succeed in interpersonal relations in a widening world, they have to communicate—to talk and make themselves understood. No longer can they point to something and expect a hovering parent to understand their non-verbal communication. They develop words and then sentences and proper emotional tone when dealing with strangers.

This is the time to provide toys that encourage children to practice conversation with their peers and with adults other than members of their family. Fit-together toys enable a parent to label parts that are "bigger than," "smaller than," or "the smallest," "the largest," and so on. Toys that embody placement problems teach concepts and words, such as "over," "under," "in," "out," "more," "the same," etc. Hammer-and-peg toys now feature pegs in varying geometrical shapes that allow parents to name the pegs their children are to hammer: "Now hit the round peg," "the square one," "the star shape."

This is a prime time for introducing beginner storybooks with touch experiences—"Pat the bunny's fur," "Feel Daddy's scratchy beard"—and cloth self-help books with zippers to slide open and shut, buttons to unbutton, laces to tie, and so forth ("All by Herself" or "All by Himself," for example). Play with finger puppets encourages conversation. Identifying rubber or wood farm and zoo animals and listening and dancing to repetitive folk and rhythmic music are also satisfying activities.

Play Intervention and Intelligence

Most toys evoke verbal response, but it takes sensitive parents to help their offspring expand her vocabulary by subtly intervening with new ways to use playthings and posing fresh problem-solving situations. As children play with their toys, they establish the "inner speech and imagery" they need for reflective thinking and the mobilization of memory. Parental intervention with appropriate toys and activities for verbal interaction can be an influential contribution to forwarding a child's mental capacities.

Some Toys for Twelve- to Twenty-four-month Children

PUSH AND PULL TOYS

Heavy-based child-sized carriage	(Community)
Double-wheel wheelbarrow	(Community)
Interlocking train and boat sets	(Childcraft)
Walker-Wagon	(Creative)
Indoor Gym House, Infant Gym	(Creative)
Pull Cubes, Large Beads to String	(Childcraft)
Rocking Horse	
Taylor Tot	(local juvenile shop)
Toddler Truck	(Playskool)
Double-wheel Kiddie Car	(Community)
or	
Tyke Bike	(Playskool)
Little Tyke Wagon	(Rotodyne)

ACTIVE THINGS TO MANIPULATE

Walk-a-Bye	(Questor)
Nesting Blocks, Drum	(Childcraft)
Shape Sorting Box	(Creative)
Giant Nesting Buckets	(Childcraft)
Pounding Bench	(Playskool)
Bean Bags	(make them yourself)
Large Color Cone	(Playskool)
Stacking Discs	(Childcraft)
Small Rocking Chair	(Thayer, Community, Workbench)
Shape Stacker	(Questor)

DRAMATIC PLAY

Child-sized Wood Cradle, Bed	(Community, Creative)
Jiffy Playhouse	(Childcraft)
Cardboard Playhouses	(Childcraft)
Large Pocketbook	(ask grandma)
Soft Cuddly Animals	(Creative)
Rubber Dolls	(Childcraft)
Cloth Dolls	(Fisher-Price)
Tea Sets	(Creative, Childcraft)
Wood Telephone	(Community)

FINE ARTS, MUSIC, BOOKS

Wrist Bells, Music Box	(Childcraft)
Water Toys, Harbor Set	(Childcraft)
Books: Cloth and Hardboard Picture Books	(Western Publishing)
Cloth Book: *What's in My Pocket?*	(Fisher-Price)
Pat the Bunny, a participation book	(Childcraft)
Cloth Books: *All by Herself, All by Himself*	(Hoover Products)
Rhythm Band Instruments	(Creative)
Oversized non-toxic, water-soluble Crayons, Unused Newsprint Paper	

Explore also the Fisher-Price and Playskool lines.

PLAY FOR THE TWO- TO THREE-YEAR-OLD

The most uninhibited period in children's lives during which they can build their ego is the two- to three-year age level. For this group, play is the major means of building self-image. They have to be the center of every play situation. Toddlers want to play the mother, father, or the baby. They are not yet ready to allow dolls or play people to be the characters.

Toddlers Are Egocentric

Sometime during the second year, toddlers begin to develop a conception of themselves as people. Parents can be sure of this when their two-year-old calls himself by his name or says "me" or "I." The toddler is completely egocentric. He is unable to take the point of view of others. His play themes involve his self-image and proving and showing off his own powers to others.

If children did not have this period of ego play, motivation, drive, and will power would be adversely affected in their adulthood.

370

Toddlers Are Independent

Walking opens up fresh vistas. Two-year-olds are into everything and always on the go. They have attained mobile use of their bodies and are determined to exploit this fabulous power to the maximum. They have reached the full-bodied age of wonderful toddlerdom and savor to the full their growing sense of independence. To the toddler, everything is physical. Perpetually in motion, toddlers lug, tug, pull, push, dump, drag, and pound. They try to maneuver anything and everything within reach—a chair, table, lamp—even if their strength is not up to it. They will carry packages, open doors, try to button up their coats. This is the "me-do-it" age that requires infinite patience and tact on the part of parents.

The Walker-Runner Stage

How to provide exciting, satisfying, but reasonable activities and play equipment for these dynamos is the test of a good parent. Toddlers need playthings and equipment that are engineered to their size and current capabilities so that instead of feeling more helpless, they get to be more and more self-reliant. Small wonder the toys children this age most enjoy are those that add to their feelings of bigness and independence. Playthings that make big noises, such as drums or pounding benches, rank high because noisemaking is one way for little children to feel strong and powerful. Hammering is also a test of strength and getting the wooden pegs banged down is a real physical accomplishment.

Dr. James L. Hymes, Jr., retired professor of childhood education at the University of Maryland, in his book, *The Child Under Six,* puts it this way: "Often we buy toys to show love. This doesn't work. But toys that are right for one-to-two-year-olds stand a chance of giving a child a sense of power. The youngster learning to walk is the world's most eager 'pusher.' A baby carriage, a toy lawn mower, anything on wheels that he can hold on to for support means both good walking and good feeling. A little later the slightly more skilled walker is the world's most eager 'puller.' He toddles along pulling his wagon, sometimes empty or sometimes loaded . . . but feeling as big as all-get-out."

Outdoor Equipment

Preschoolers live dangerously in their push for bigness. Therefore, parents need to guard against providing them with playground equipment they cannot reasonably manage. Slides should not be too high, because great heights do not deter some toddlers and they can be dangerous. Children will even slide down head first! Playground equipment must be well designed, well constructed, and suitably scaled to the abilities and limitations of its users.

Some concerned toy manufacturers are now producing sturdy, safe toddler versions of large outdoor equipment in the form of a rocky boat, climb-around, jungle gym, and low slide. These items look so much like the older children's models that two- and three-year-olds conceive of them as being equal to what the "big boys" and "big girls" use. The rocky boat, longtime nursery school favorite, provides rocking motion to enthrall one to four small children when turned on one of its sides; turned on its other side, a small child can run up the stairs to a raised platform and then scamper down.

As soon as they are able to climb stairs, children enjoy sliding down a stairway slide. The toddler's gym has steps, a slide, and a hiding area under its platform. Toddlers express their burgeoning bigness by driving large ride 'em trucks, trains, oversized furry animals, and carriages on free-wheeling casters. Casters are most successful because toddlers can make them go where they want them to, whereas wheels restrict a toddler's ability to move a plaything. As they scoot about on their vehicles, foot and leg muscles are being exercised and strengthened.

Two-to-three-year-olds adore kiddie cars, pedal cars, and later the ever-favorite tricycle. Seeing how fast they can go, how sharply they can turn, how to bring their trikes to an abrupt halt—these are some of the exciting physical activities every toddler wants and needs. Tricycle manufacturers have lowered the seats so that toddlers are now closer to the floor, thereby minimizing falls. When children have appropriate physical equipment and play challenges, they can affirm their confidence in themselves while fully developing all their body skills.

Some Toys for Twenty-four- to Thirty-six-month-old Children

QUIET AND MANIPULATIVE PLAY

Books and toys with buttoning, lacing, etc.	(Western Publishing)
Dress-Me Dolls, Color Cubes	(Playskool)
Self-Help Cloth Books	(any store)
Beads to String, Junior Lock Box, Hammer and Peg Toy	(Creative, Childcraft)
Simple Puzzles and Lotto Games	(Creative, Playskool, Judy Co.)

SOCIAL PLAY—MAKE-BELIEVE

Mini Kitchen	(Creative)
Pots and Pans	(Creative)
Tea Set	(Creative, Childcraft)
Housecleaning Set	(Community, Childcraft)
Large Doll Bed	(Community)
Rag Dolls, Rubber Dolls, Animals	(Childcraft)
Hardwood Unit Building Blocks	(Childcraft, Creative)
Solid Wood Transportation Toys	(Childcraft, Creative)
Wood Telephone	(Childcraft, Creative)
Jiffy Playhouse	(Childcraft)
Giant Link	(Childcraft)
Dress-up Clothes	(your castaways)
Large Mirror, Hand Mirror	

ACTIVE PLAY

Double-wheel Kiddie Car	(Childcraft)
Bent Plywood Carriage	(Creative)
Indoor Gym House	(Creative, Childcraft)
Rocking Beauty (Rocking Horse)	(Creative)
Ride 'em Truck	(Creative)
Variplay House Gym and Slide	(Community)
Push Broom (Street Cleaner Type)	(any hardware store)
Sand Box	(Community)
Big-Eye, Little-Eye Lenses	(Creative)

Also explore Fisher-Price, Playskool, Questor, and Child Guidance Toys.

STRUCTURED VERSUS UNSTRUCTURED PLAY MATERIAL

Dr. Mary Ann Pulaski reports (in Jerome Singer's *The Child's World of Make Believe*) that the structure of the toys available to a child has a profound effect on the level of his make-believe play and creativity. One of the characteristics that distinguishes human from animal play in childhood is the capacity for make-believe. Dr. Pulaski worries that in today's society there are less and less opportunities for our children to exercise fantasy. Through movies, television, and their toys, children are provided with the utmost in prefabricated fantasy materials. "Dolls as well dressed and sophisticated as Vogue models, and war toys so realistic as often to be

374

gruesome. Nothing is left to the imagination, thus it is conceivable that imagination and fantasy may decline in some groups for lack of practice."

Fantasy, A Preferred Activity

There has been much agreement among child educators and researchers that promoting fantasy in children is of paramount importance. Researchers in creativity, including C. W. Taylor (1964), E. Paul Torrance (1962), and M. Wallach, and Jerome Kagan (1967), seem to be seeking ways to increase imagination and divergent thinking. Dr. Pulaski conducted a test on the type of toys high-fantasy children would choose.

Her results suggested that these children chose less structured play material: nursery school building blocks, wooden and rag dolls, paints, clay, dress-up materials, pipe cleaners, cotton balls—while low-fantasy children chose more structured toys: costumes, clay molds, character dolls, and carefully detailed cars. High-fantasy children showed greater concentration in their play and less structured toys evoked more play themes.

Unstructured Versus Structured Play

What is the difference between structured and unstructured toys? Generally, structured playthings have more detail, lack multipurpose, and can be used for one situation only. They are less flexible in a play setting. Most are designed for a specific play use; for example, a milk truck designed with great detail can be used only for milk delivery. However, a block on wheels or a cab and trailer shape with no detail can be used in all floor play situations.

A child has more play choices with unstructured play materials in which the reward lies in the excitement of discovery and in the play activity itself. There are no preconceived goals engineered into unstructured playthings, no adult-imposed objectives. Most often such toys are the raw materials of play and include nursery school unit building blocks, clay, sand, finger paints, water, poster paints, brushes, paper of all kinds, pegs and pegboards, design cubes, collage material, scissors, and paste, for which there are no blueprints to follow.

Initially the child "fools around" with the material. She sets the blocks in long roads or stands them up on end and topples them. She tries filling a piece of paper with broad brushstrokes of paint. While no one can foretell exactly what the end result of such free play will be, we know that a child gains pleasure and a sense of confidence in herself every time she masters the elements in her play world.

Unstructured play materials are not necessarily pliant or art materials only. They can take finished form. An electrical invention for nine-year-olds, for instance, provides buzzers, bells, sockets, wire, switches, and a dry-cell battery. It comes without limiting instructions while providing the raw material needed for safe electrical experimentation. The child discovers and tests out his own circuits and circuit breakers. Before too long, he will have hooked up a burglar alarm system or a Morse code transmitter. The results are limited only by the child's imagination and dedication. Provide a set of instructions with such play material and you have a "structured plaything," one that requires precise following of electrical plans formulated in the instruction sheets.

The Popularity of Unstructured Playthings

What makes unstructured playthings so popular and why do they involve children over long periods of time? Anyone watching a child playing with such materials will observe that they lend themselves to trial-and-error activity. There can be no failure and no disapproval if a project is not finished according to adult standards. Because there are no set goals or restraints, a child will try out new ideas again and again. These materials say to the child: "Here are things that lend themselves to the creation of any of your fantasies. You are in full command. You can manipulate them freely. You can make anything you wish with blocks or paint or clay. You can roll clay into balls, the balls into snakes, the snakes into pots, and the pots into people, if you wish. You can make your blocks form roads, your roads form fences, and your fences become a town."

We associate a quality of "pliancy" with unstructured playthings; that is, they can be more easily manipulated or a child can make them do his bidding more readily. The same pliancy can be given to more structured toys, such as dolls, community figures, construction sets, and so on. If a doll or community figure has a wire armature so that it can bend easily and its feet are weighted to stand firmly, this would enhance the toy's play possibilities. A child could make such a figure do exactly what she wanted it to: stand, sit, bend, kneel, climb, or even hold a baby doll.

Here are some examples of unstructured versus structured play materials:

Unstructured	*Structured*
Skaneateles Wood Train and Tracks Set (*Child pushes train;* train can come off track via a ramp)	Electric Train has little active participation for young child

Unstructured	Structured
Put-together Abstract Doll House, Solid-block Wood Furniture, Wired Standpatter Dolls, Floor Plan Dollhouse	Dollhouse and Dolls with intricate detail and open front: hard to get at in rear spaces
Play Pipes (a xylophone of metal pipes of various sizes placed on foam-formed base; can be interchanged)	Xylophone (metal keys permanently attached to wood base)
Abstract, Solid Wood Unpainted Trucks on Wheels, Interlocking Boats, Floor Trains Without Wheels	Molded Plastic Milk Truck or Garbage Truck with great detail
Liquid or Dry Poster Paints, Long-handled Brushes, 18"×24" Paper	Coloring Books, painting by numbers, etc.
Caroline Pratt Unit Building Blocks to make Houses, Barns, Airports, Garages, etc.	Finished, fully detailed Houses, Barns, Airports, Marinas, etc. (Fisher-Price, etc.)

CAROLINE PRATT UNIT BUILDING BLOCKS

Caroline Pratt, teacher of woodcrafts and founder-principal of the innovative preschool in New York City, the City and Country School, was also one of the pioneer educational toymakers in our country.

Secret of Good Playthings

Miss Pratt knew that the secret of good toys is multiple usage, freedom from frustrating details, and ease in manipulation. She created wedge-shaped people, six-inch-high wood cutouts of everyday community workers and family figures wide at the bottom and thin at the top so that they stood without toppling. She experimented with trucks and cars that were free of wheels for easy maneuvering. She developed long, interlocking floor trains without wheels, but with extra flatcars for carrying freight.

Miss Pratt also designed playground equipment for physical and dramatic play, the now famous hollow blocks, so large (5½"×11"×22") that they required the use of a child's back muscles and full physical energy to carry about and build with; as well as the three-way wood ladder,

378

ladder box, wood barrels, walking plank and sawhorse, platform truck, oversized wood packing crate—all of which were exciting, movable playground items that called for co-operative action on the part of the children.

We believe her finest accomplishment is her set of unit building blocks. These floor play blocks consist of many matched units: the unit block (5½"×3¾"×1⅜") the square or half-unit (2¾" long), the double unit (11" long), and the quadruple unit (22" long). Also included are curves, cylinders, ramps, triangles, and pillars. The smooth, accurately engineered blocks of natural-finished hardwood (birch and maple) are easily handled by children and can be put to an infinite variety of uses.

Miss Pratt thought that blocks were suited perfectly to children's play purposes because a simple geometrical shape could become any number of things to a child: a house, truck, plane, boat, railroad, car, barn, or skyscraper. Building with blocks starts out at about two years of age as an individual play activity. Co-operative block play begins at about four or five years of age, when plans and constructions grow increasingly more complicated.

Although parents are attracted by the many exciting shapes available (quarter-round, half-round gothic arch, double and single unit triangles, etc.), no child can build unless he has at least twenty to forty double units and twenty to forty units. Make sure you know the contents of prepackaged block sets. Ask if you can buy them by the piece and select your own. If your department store and/or toy shop do not sell blocks by the piece, try the school supply house listed in your yellow pages directory. Here are our recommendations for age-graded block sets:

379

Starter Block Set	*Intermediate Block Set*
2 years	*4 to 8 years*

10 squares (2¾")	10 squares (2¾")
16 units (5½")	24 units (5½")
16 double units (11")	24 double units (11")
2 columns (5½")	8 roof boards (11")
4 triangles (5½")	2 ramps (5½")
	4 floor boards (22")
3 years	2 quarter-circles
10 squares (2¾")	1 large switch and gothic door
20 units (5½")	4 triangles (5½")
20 double units (11")	
4 triangles (5½")	
2 ramps (5½")	

To add to these sets, buy blocks by the piece; more units and double units, floor boards, ramps, and then other shapes. Keep adding to a starter set each month until your child has enough blocks to build a structure as big as she is. Do not worry about their expense; *you can always resell them.* After your children have used them daily for ten years, you will be able to sell them as desirable "seconds" to schools or other parents. You will be amazed at the prices people pay for these hardwood block sets twenty years later. So beg, borrow, or budget the money; it will be your best toy investment!

PCI recommends that you buy your building blocks from a reputable kindergarten supplier (Community Playthings in Rifton, New York; Childcraft Education Corp. in New York City; Creative Playthings in New York, Los Angeles, Cranbury, N.J.) Blocks are hard to make at home because of the need for precise measuring and heavy-duty cutting tools.

Bendable or wedge-shaped play people in proper scale (one inch to one foot), assorted animals, and cars and trucks expand the play possibilities of unit building blocks. Parents or teachers who watch a city or country scene unfold can accelerate learning and encourage imagination by introducing signs to identify streets and buildings, and ferries and barges for food and other waterway transport. They can intervene with suitable stories and trips to local places of interest to keep curiosity alive and perking.

However, intervention is a role that all parents and teachers need to play with great care. Children relish interchange of playfulness with adults, but only when it is not heavy-handed. There is real imprinting on creativeness in later life if a child has enjoyed adult support for his early play fantasies and efforts. The right suggestion, the right word can deepen and enrich each play experience.

PCI Point of View

Parents are reluctant to buy hardwood building blocks because they are so expensive yet they turn around and buy many other toy community buildings (barn, garage, airport, house, etc.) at a combined price equal to two sets of unit blocks. With blocks, all of these and other community buildings can be built by the child. We are not criticizing toy industry designers. They have done a magnificent job in finally (after thirty years) discovering that children need "here and now" play tools and "real" play people—mother, father, policeman, fireman (not Mickey Mouse)—to carry on the dramatic play of building a community.

FANTASY

A child playing mommy with her dolls, two children playing spacemen using a kitchen chair as a launch pad, a child pretending to be chased by a growling bear—this is what fantasy or imaginative play looks like.

Fantasy play takes many forms, according to British psychologist Susanna Millar in her book *The Psychology of Play*. Through fantasy, a child may explore his feelings in an imaginary situation (being chased by a wild animal); he may re-enact some event that made a strong impression on him (going to the hospital); he may act out something puzzling to him in an effort to understand how it works (a windshield wiper), or he may "rehearse" some past experience (going to the store or to school).

Between the ages of two and nine, children normally engage in many types of fantasy play. Through such play, they work to make sense out of the puzzling adult world in which they live.

The Value of Imaginative Play

While the experts have different reasons for valuing imaginative play, the idea that such play is important seems undisputed. Sigmund Freud believed play was valuable for its cathartic effect, for the "letting loose" of pent-up aggressions. Erik Erikson hold that through play children gain a sense of their own capabilities. Jean Piaget believes fantasy play fosters intellectual development in the young child. Frank and Theresa Caplan

381

maintain that unless children have experiences with fantasy in early life, they will be incapable of imagination or creativity in their adult lives.

What Children Learn in Imaginative Play

Fantasy play has been defended as an important part of childhood since the time of the Greeks. However, it is only recently that studies have been undertaken to determine just what children learn through such play. In 1968, Dr. S. Smilansky trained a group of Israeli children in role playing and imaginative play. As a result of the training, he found the children better able to verbalize, more sensitive to their peers, more spontaneous in using play materials creatively, more organized in their play, and better able to think before reacting to unpleasant situations. Similar studies have shown almost identical results.

How Parents Can Stimulate Imaginative Play

Jerome Singer encourages parents to enjoy imaginative play with their children. He suggests introducing make-believe games and providing materials that lend themselves to dramatic play, such as dress-up clothes, building materials, house play equipment, toy people and animals, cars and trucks, etc. Frank and Theresa Caplan stress that toys should be as simple as possible since too much detail will confine a young child's imagination.

Glorianna Wittes and Norma Radin in their *Learning Through Play Approach,* recommend pantomime games and encouraging the child to pretend to use something that is not actually present, such as pouring pretend tea from a pretend teapot. They also suggest having the child try to remember what past experiences felt like, for example, eating chocolate or spilling paint. The parent can help the child plan the dramatic play by suggesting he play "milkman," for instance, and then ask what props he thinks he will need. The play itself might on occasion be followed by evaluation whereby the parent helps her child look at how he carried out the "job."

Through perceptive intervening in group play, parents can often redirect negative play. (As a dramatic game of battleships deteriorates into the throwing of block "bombs," the parent interjects and shouts, "Yo ho, I see a whale!" Soon the play content turns to underwater animals.) The parent might stretch this new interest by visits to an aquarium, books, painting, etc.

Children should be encouraged to change roles in their play; if the child is playing daddy, ask him why the baby is crying and suggest he be the baby to find out why he is crying.

Just as important as subtle parental involvement in and acceptance of imaginative play is time alone for the child. Children need time by themselves to explore and practice the many events and feelings they are trying to understand so they will be able later to incorporate these into dramatic group play at home and at school. (See Chapter 6 for discussion of Imaginary Playmates.)

TOY SAFETY

All concerned parents guard against illness and injury to their children. They feel their responsibility keenly and become familiar with the symptoms of illness, but many are unaware of the hazards that some toys present. National hospitals report that less than 5 per cent of over 120,000 reported injuries in and around the home that require hospital attention are caused by toys—not a very large number perhaps, but using a hospital is a big step for most parents to take. There may be millions of unreported cuts, bruises, and burns because they are not severe enough to require hospital attention. Fifteen per cent of all home accidents are the result of live animals, personal-use items, and environmental factors.

Carol Young, a staff writer for the Federal Drug Administration, has indicated that bicycles are involved in the majority of the toy-associated injury cases. Other vehicle-type toys—roller skates, tricycles, etc.—are linked to most of the injuries.

Five seems to be the most accident-prone age. However, children of all ages can get hurt if they are given a toy inappropriate to their age or agility or if the toy presents a hazard.

Today's children are lucky because of the activity of consumer groups desirous of keeping them from getting injured by their toys. The Bureau of Product Safety, an agency of the Department of Health, Education, and Welfare, provides one important means of assuring that the toys in your favorite toy store are safe. This agency inspects existing toys and almost all new ones for safety hazards.

The Bureau of Product Safety has the power to require that unsafe toys be removed from stores, according to Public Law 91-113, which passed the House and the Senate in November of 1969. This law is the Federal Substances Act that protects children from toys and other articles intended for their use; for example, spray adhesives that are dangerous due to the presence of electrical, mechanical, or thermal hazards.

Section 15 of this act is particularly interesting. "In case of any article or substance sold by its manufacturer, distributor, or dealer which is a banned hazardous substance (whether or not it was such at the time of its sale), such article or substance shall, in accordance with regulation of the Secretary, be repurchased . . . by the manufacturer, the person should be refunded his money and the person should be reimbursed for any expense involved in the return of the hazardous toy. This reimbursement applies to all retailers and importers."

Section 15 suggests that if you purchase a toy and it is later banned as hazardous, it may be returned to the store where purchased for reimbursement. Stores have been a bit unco-operative about this in the past because consumers have not been keeping their sales slips. It may be necessary to return the toy to the manufacturer and hope its consumer department is aware of Section 15. At best, this is a difficult area in which to get action.

The U. S. Consumer Product Safety Commission in Washington, D.C. has an extremely difficult job reviewing and testing all the toys that are manufactured. The law is very specific regarding what is dangerous, but new products are constantly being manufactured so new acts must continually be added to make the law completely up-to-date.

If you know of a toy that presents a hazard, let the Consumer Product Safety Commission know by writing to them. Include the following information: name of the article and brief description, stock or code numbers on article or package, country of origin, where and when the article was purchased, what is hazardous about the item, if there were any "close calls," describe them, and give your name, address, and telephone number.

Another aspect of this law is that any manufacturer or retailer who knowingly sells a banned product is subject to civil and/or criminal prosecution. The Consumer Product Safety Commission issues a list of all banned products to aid the manufacturer and consumer in choosing safe toys for children and to aid the retailer in promptly removing all items banned as hazardous.

The U. S. Department of Health, Education, and Welfare, FDA Product Safety Division, publishes a consumer's booklet ten times a year alerting the public to possible hazards in baby furniture, toys, and other child-oriented products. You may wish to write to the Government Printing Office, Superintendent of Documents, Washington, D.C. 20402 and ask for information about "FDA Consumer."

Other sources of information regarding toy safety are the countless booklets published by the HEW Office of Child Development and the Children's Bureau that are available at minimal cost. One booklet is called "Toy Safety" and presents the following warnings about toys found in most homes today: Baby bouncers are potentially dangerous and can cause finger amputation unless the "X" part of the frame is covered by guards. Squeaker toys and other noisemakers have small metal parts that can be swallowed. Over two hundred such toys are listed on the banned list. Pins, sharp barbs, and easily exposed nails or tacks are often hidden in doll shoes, ribbons, etc. (The Alexander Doll Co. in New York City had eighteen dolls banned as a result of using straight pins to fasten on buttons and ribbons.)

Parents should avoid toys with internal spikes or wires that could cut or pierce a child if the toys should break. Breakable rattles are dangerous because the beads inside could be swallowed. Hundreds of roly-poly toys, rattles, and other musical toys have been placed on the banned list.

Toys that break easily, give off heat, and are covered in plastics that are not flame-retardant should be gotten rid of. Swing sets, tricyles, and bicycles should be constantly checked for sharp points, loosening of screws, and any other broken parts.

TOYS OF WAR AND VIOLENCE

Violence is a condition of our lives. No matter how much talking is done about love of humankind and regardless of our efforts at fellowship with our neighbors, we cannot escape the fact that our society tolerates violence and that acts of aggression and violence are a sad part of our lives. Even though we have become somewhat immune to living under these conditions, we are still shocked when we are made aware of assassinations, wars, and strikes.

Living as we do in a violent world, it would be incredibly naïve of us to believe that our children live in a different world; to assume that their world consists of "sugar and spice and everything nice," including their toys. Along with the reassuring solidity of toys from Community Playthings, Creative Playthings, and Childcraft Education Corp. and the chic sophistication of F. A. O. Schwarz's exclusive offerings, we have other companies flooding the market with G. I. Joes, Create-a-Monster kits, and the like.

What the Experts Say About Toys of Violence

Dr. Joseph Church, in *Understanding Your Child from Birth to Three,* says we must avoid war toys at all costs, indicating that "they themselves will not make your child a killer, but they help create an atmosphere in which military and violent solutions come to be taken for granted."

In *Your Child's Play,* Arnold Arnold states that "toys, like anything else, reflect the tenor of the times . . . It is not surprising, therefore, that in our time, when violence is glorified in comics and on TV, that toys tend to mirror those elements of culture to which children are exposed." Mr. Arnold feels that the more innocuous forms of war play, such as toy soldiers, are not harmful. However, he reminds us that three-year-olds can say, "Bang, bang; you're dead!" just as effectively with a stick as with a plastic replica of an atomic weapon.

Parents need to be very selective in screening toys, TV shows, and experiences that further violence and brutality. Since parents cannot and should not shelter their children from all forms of rough play, they must help their youngsters understand that play pretense and reality are not the same. They must set sane and humane standards if they desire their children to react with disaffection to those aspects of society that merit it.

For many years, Dr. Spock emphasized that gun play is harmless, labeling it as a useful way of expressing aggressive and hostile feelings. However, in the 1968 edition of his *Baby and Child Care,* he revises his previously held opinion and encourages parents to guide their children away from violence. He states, "To me, it seems very clear that in order to have a more stable and civilized national life we should bring up the next generation of Americans with a greater respect for law and for other people's rights and sensibilities than in the past. There are many ways in which we could and should teach these attitudes. One simple opportunity we could utilize in the first half of childhood is to show our disapproval of lawlessness and violence in television programs and in children's pistol play."

We believe that children must be taught early that cruelty is never acceptable behavior—whether it is make-believe or reality.

In *The Power of Play,* Frank and Theresa Caplan indicate that there is a relationship between a nation's character and the play of its children. Although it has not been proved, they feel that frequent play with miniature war toys (soldiers, knights, generals, weapons, forts, castles, etc.) might just be encouraging a striving for world domination in adult life. In previous centuries and even today, minuscule war toys have been especially popular in Germany, France, and England. The Caplans note that whether due to the miniature size of the toys or their subject matter of mock war play, there seems to be too close a parallel between childhood play with metal soldiers and the real wars still being waged around the world. It evokes considerable uneasiness about the relationship between playing at war and the real thing. Whether wars come from economic causes or a desire to practice early childhood play fantasies, we leave to future historians. Suffice it to say, parents would do well to question overemphasis on miniatures and on war play. (See section in Chapter 11 on Aggression and Frustration.)

PCI Point of View

It is apparent that all child-rearing specialists are against toys of violence and war to a greater or lesser degree. Just about every parent would concur. PCI maintains that such toys have no place in our children's lives and that the efforts and vigilance of all parents are needed to counteract advertising, store displays, and pressure from our youngsters' peers. Almost anything can be structured into a child's play materials. Provide a child with toys that make sense and he will get the message in no time. Essentially the parents must decide what message the children should receive.

EQUIPPING THE PLAYROOM

Early in a child's life, certain *essential* equipment for dramatic, art, quiet, movement, and music play should be added to every playroom.

Double Easel

A double adjustable painting easel allows two children to paint at one time without getting in each other's way. Good ones are made by Community Playthings (Rifton, N.Y. 12471), Childcraft Education Corp. (20 Kilmer Road, Edison, N.J. 08817), and Creative Playthings (at better toy and department stores). Easel boards should be large (37"×25") to hold 18"×24" sheets of newsprint paper. Each board is attached to two frames by wing nuts. A series of holes make it possible to adjust the easel to the size of a growing child. The easel paint trays have open holes for six to ten two-ounce or half-pint jars of paint. For drying pictures, a collapsible clothes dryer can be used.

Bulletin Board

Every playroom should have a large bulletin board (4'×8') to display art work. Burlap-covered, soft Cellutex boards make excellent bulletin boards. Burlap can be purchased by the yard in assorted colors. Tack holes do not show. Sliding hardboard doors with baked enamel finishes

387

work well as washable chalk boards (use wax crayoffs). Painted steel boards hold magnetic letters, etc., and are sold in most variety stores.

Another popular approach today is the use of "do-it-yourself" cork board squares. These give tremendous flexibility since they can be cut to fit any wall space available and can be tacked and retacked without making holes.

Exercise Equipment for the Playroom

All children need opportunities to exercise, especially on rainy days. At sporting goods stores or good toy shops you will find gyms that clamp onto a doorway that have a chinning bar, seat swing, rings, etc. Gym mats for preschoolers who like to turn somersaults or wrestle are usually available at school supply or sporting goods houses.

Table, Chairs, and Rockers

Every two-year-old (and older) child needs a washable work table. A Formica top will make it impervious to water, wet clay, finger paints, etc. Most playroom tables come as 24"×48" rectangles or 30" to 36" rounds. Preferred are those with legs that can be removed so the table will grow with the child. A one-and-a-half-year-old child needs a table from 18" to 20" high; 20" to 22" high will serve three- to six-year-olds; 24" to 30" high are for preteens and adults. Chairs come in 10", 12", 14", 16", and 18" heights from seat to floor. Allow an 8" to 10" height difference from top of table to top of seat for a toddler; 10" to 12" for school-age children and adults. If you purchase more than two chairs, order stacking ones to save floor space. School supply or seating firms carry stacking furniture in all sizes.

Every playroom should have a rocker. A good bentwood rocker from Poland is sold by the Work Bench and other fine wood furniture shops. A slatted rocker from Appalachia is more reasonable and sturdy (Community Playthings carries this rocker). Most school supply houses are good centers for tables, chairs, and rockers, (Consult the yellow pages of your telephone directory for their locations.)

Work Benches

Adults as well as young children welcome a good work bench with screw clamps and storage for tools. Make sure that the top is heavy enough (at least 22"×42"×1¾" thick) to withstand hammering. A butcher block top is ideal. Make sure the height is between 24" and 27" to serve the growing child from kindergarten through high school. Get one with two vises if you plan to have two or more children. You may have to put up a pegboard storage unit to hold tools. Pegboard hardware is sold in every hardware shop and holds any tool. Lumber can be scraps from a lumberyard.

At first a child likes just to hammer nails into soft wood. Later boys and girls learn how to cut, sand, and construct crude boats, trains, doll houses, etc. Buy adult tools—do not waste money on "toy" tools. (Of course, adult supervision is essential until the children are skillful enough.)

Clay Storage

A ceramic crock with cover (five gallons or less) will hold twenty-five to fifty pounds of moist clay. Covered with a wet towel, the clay will remain pliant and usable for long periods. Although wet clay is considered messy, its use becomes an especially important release for a child living in a spotless environment.

Props for Dramatic Play

If the playroom is large, you will want to enclose areas where two or more children can play quietly. School supply houses make a variety of upright or folding pegboard screens that can be used to separate block play from housekeeping play.

Props for dramatic play include a Foldaway Play Store and puppet stage, a doll house, and a cardboard playhouse.

To build self-image, a large mirror in the playroom makes sense.

Homemaking Corner for Social Play

Sooner or later, a loving grandparent or good friend will give your preschooler a child-sized play stove, cupboard, or sink; also a wood ironing board, tea table, pots, pans, and silverware, housecleaning set, etc. Resolve to make room for the highly social and dramatic play this equipment makes possible.

Setting apart this corner with a foldaway or stationary screen results in a quiet intimacy that is so important to dramatic social play. Boys and girls enjoy this type of play and visiting children quickly become active participants.

389

Those who like woodworking will find that making child-sized doll carriages, doll beds, and foldaway doll houses is fun. There are excellent books on the market that provide blueprints for such equipment. One of the better ones is *How to Make Children's Furniture & Play Equipment* by Mario Del Fabbro, published by McGraw-Hill.

Parents will question this total repetition in the home of the equipment usually found in the better nursery schools. Nursery schools usually are run on a half-day program. The hours spent at home are longer than those in the preschool center. Moreover, children work in groups at these centers and there is little time for individuals to work by themselves. At home, a child has time to work out new block-building or dramatic play ideas that she will try out in school the next day.

Build a Play World Scaled to the Child

In all the equipment mentioned we have stressed the words *child-sized*. Much of a child's environment is giant-sized and frustrating. Imagine yourself in a world where a giant had to lift you onto a chair; where you had to stand on tiptoes to see what was being served for lunch, etc. It is pretty hard to change the adult world, but parents can provide a few corners where the furnishings are child-sized. In such an environment social and fantasy play is pleasurably and profitably practiced—and ego blossoms.

THE CHILD WHO DOES NOT PLAY: PLAY THERAPY

Childhood appears to be a trial run, when children are given the time they need to find out about themselves, other people, and the world in which they live. In the course of growing up some children develop different kinds of emotional problems: fears of many kinds, feelings of hostility, aggressive behaviors, lack of self-esteem, anxieties, poor social adjustment, intense jealousy, shyness, showing off, and withdrawal being the most prominent among them. A disturbed child usually also suffers from unconscious feelings of guilt.

Since it is impossible to determine exactly what goes on in a child's mind or to get children to talk like adults, specialists who work with distressed children have found that much can be learned about them from watching them at play, during which most children are able to reveal both their imaginary and real life. Because play is the young child's most natural form of expression, it can also expose his inner conflicts and immaturity.

One of the most striking characteristics of an anxious child is a strong inhibition of play activity. Often such a child is not able to play at all. When in a well-equipped nursery school, she may remain tense and incapable of doing anything with any of the playthings. Other traits of the neurotic child are her lack of constructiveness and an overpowering, persistent impulse to destroy. The disturbed child, whether emotionally ill or mentally retarded, when she does play acts as if she were younger than her chronological years.

If a child of six with an enriched environmental background were to spend a whole hour just filling a box with sand and emptying it endlessly, it would signify some immaturity worthy of further investigation. Constant reversion to an earlier level and the compulsion to use materials that are charged with symbolic significance (sand, water, or fire) might well signify some early, unresolved conflict or overly strict home training.

The nature of a child's play can indicate the type of disturbance that underlies it. Children who are meticulously clean and avoid "dirty" or "messy" play, who arrange toys in neat patterns only, who dislike painting and shun finger painting, whose drawings are "dominated by rulers and compasses," who play silently and alone, or keep up a constant chatter to hide their deepest feelings through their obsessional play indicate a rigidity that can mask a serious problem.

The child who aimlessly handles every toy in a playroom without playing with any one thing and who initiates half a dozen games only to drop each one moments later also is indicating some grave problems. The child whose play is accompanied by explosive excitement and who loses control of whatever he may be doing, for example, throws clay about wildly or destroys the constructions of his playmates, may well suffer from hyperactivity because of deeply buried inner turmoil. Such conflicts can only be uncovered by careful professional observation and analysis of the child as he is helped to play and to talk in the ameliorating atmosphere of the play therapy room or clinic.

It was Dr. Anna Freud, one of the pioneers of psychoanalysis for young children and the use of play therapy, who recognized that "the day dreams of children and activity of their fantasy in play is equivalent to the free associations of adults in analysis."

The denial of reality is one of the particular features of play in general and especially in games of make-believe. The elements for constructing a pleasurable world of fantasy and play are readily available to the child. The task of the child analyst is to get the emotionally disturbed child to separate fantasy from fact and to help him assimilate reality into his personal scheme of things. Fantasy is the name given to a kind of daydreaming that is the opposite of controlled thought.

Every small child recreates a world of fantasy for herself at some time. Some children, however, sink too deeply into the world of their own thoughts and feelings and so lose contact with reality. At some point the healthy child gets to grasp the difference between fantasy and reality and at eight and nine years of age becomes involved in explorations of the world of real people, things, and situations. She wants to understand herself and the adult world. The disturbed child cannot make this transition.

Play Therapy

This is a professional method of using play with non-threatening play materials to discover what is troubling a child and to help her attain better accommodation to herself and her life. Because verbal communication with a very young emotionally disturbed or mentally retarded child is very difficult, such a child is closely watched by the therapist while she is at play.

For children from three to twelve years of age, regular visits to a play therapist have proved effective in relieving them of emotional conflicts that often find expression in such manifestations as temper tantrums, bed-wetting, withdrawal, or general destructiveness. By bringing out into the open fears or anxieties that are distressing and immobilizing to a child and his sharing them with a tolerant grown-up (the play therapist), his terrors become less terrifying.

"Lack of ability to play is not natural and is not an inborn characteristic," writes Dr. Margaret Lowenfeld in her book *Play in Childhood.* "It is a neurosis and should be reckoned with as such. Children who fail in their ability to play with their fellows are children with characteristics that will make them unable to combine with their fellows in later life." She goes on to say, "Play is an essential function of the passage from immaturity to emotional maturity. Any individual without the opportunities for adequate play in early life will go on seeking them in the stuff of adult life."

PCI Point of View

Parents are urged to learn to understand their children's play activities —or lack of play. Play is a direct line to the child's inner world. Do not assume that isolated anti-social acts indicate serious problems; some "acting-out" activities are normal and to be encouraged. In fact, most adults could benefit from this type of activity.

11
Personality Formation

INTRODUCTION BY ROBERT J. HARMON, M.D., AND LEON YARROW, PH.D.*

Personality is one of the most difficult concepts to define, because it refers to the central core of the person—his uniqueness. It deals with how a child sees himself and how he responds to other people. It is concerned with his anxieties, fears, and fantasies; his ways of approaching problems; his likes and dislikes; and how he handles anger and hostility. Personality also deals with an individual's constructive behavior, how he acts on the environment to exert control, to master it, and to have an impact on it. Part of personality is the child's acquisition of values and his development of controls, how he learns to postpone gratification, and how he reconciles reality and fantasy.

Very young infants in the first days and weeks of life differ in many characteristics—in how active they are, how easily they become upset, the intensity of their irritation, and how readily they are soothed. They differ in their sensitivity to stimuli and the vigor with which they respond. All these facets of temperament combine and interact in different ways to give the distinctive flavor of each child's personality.

Personality develops through the child interacting with the environment. How much the child brings with her and how much she is molded by her environment probably differs for each child. We know much more about the effects of the development of grossly depriving or

* Dr. Robert J. Harmon and Dr. Leon Yarrow are research colleagues at the federal government's National Institute of Child Health and Human Development (NICHD). Robert J. Harmon, M.D. (Research Associate) and Leon Yarrow, Ph.D. (Chief of the Social Behavioral Science Division of NICHD) have as a team written many scholarly articles on child behavior and psychiatry for textbooks and professional magazines.

Dr. Yarrow, in association with the Children's Bureau, has been engaged in longitudinal (follow-up in adulthood) studies of adopted children. Dr. Harmon, in addition to his research, is clinical instructor in behavior and psychiatry at the George Washington School of Medicine.

traumatic experiences than we know about the effects of subtle variations within the normal range of experience.

Infants have been thought of in the past as simply objects to be fed, diapered, bathed, and put in their cribs; essentially to be made comfortable and satisfied. It is now clear that in addition to having their biological needs met, babies need and seek a variety of stimulation from their environment. Parents can provide a varied environment for their children in natural ways—by talking and smiling to their infants, making bathing and feeding times for play, and giving them a variety of colorful and responsive objects to handle and manipulate. All infants do not require the same amount of stimulation, nor do they all respond equally to being rocked or talked to. Some infants prefer more modulated stimulation; others learn best by looking at and being exposed to a variety of objects; others seem to prefer to be talked to. Whatever an infant's needs may be, parents have to keep in mind that they are the primary source of sustenance for the young child. Nourishing the infant means more, however, than providing him with appropriate amounts and kinds of stimulation. The infant needs to be held and played with, talked to, rocked, and bounced. He also needs to be responded to sensitively, not only when he is unhappy and obviously needs soothing, but when he is smiling and vocalizing.

Infants are strongly motivated to obtain feedback from people and objects in their environment. They need to manipulate a variety of objects that change shapes and make sounds. They enjoy peekaboo games, the changing inflections and tones in people's voices, and being smiled at in response to their smiles. Obtaining responses from people and objects gives them a sense of having an impact on their environment, which in turn leads to a sense that they can handle their environment, a precursor of feelings of mastery and effectiveness. Being responded to sensitively also helps the infant feel that what he does is important, that he is loved.

Almost from the very first days of life the infant begins to exert influence on his mother and to affect her behavior. This is the beginning of a very finely tuned symphony between a mother and her infant. At first the infant is most interested in survival and in having his basic physiological needs met. Gradually he learns to discriminate his mother from other people and soon is responding in a very special way to her. As his dependency on her becomes more focused, he primarily wants his mother. When his mother leaves him he may become frantic and protest vehemently. This is an expression of love.

396

Some mothers become very disturbed at this high degree of dependency and do not know how to handle it. Those who recognize it as the first overt expression of affection can more easily tolerate the infant's demands on them. They gradually build on this positive relationship so that the infant in time feels sufficiently secure to be separate from his mother and begins to establish relationships with other people. The infant's insecurity about being separated from his loved one is often the beginning of a difficult period for both mother and baby. Recognizing it as an expression of an immature organism's dependence helps the mother respond appropriately. In this process the infant gradually dilutes the intensity of his bond with his mother, although the latter remains one of the most important people in his life.

Young infants can form relationships with more than one person. Very early the father, too, becomes a special person for the infant. His role and importance have traditionally been neglected, but his influence on the development of young children is nonetheless very significant. The father not only has a direct influence on the child, but also has an indirect effect through his relationship with the mother.

With increasing frequency many children are having other caretakers assume varying degrees of responsibility for them. In those cases it is important to have a *regular* care giver assume responsibility for the child. It is also important that some one person, usually the mother, see herself or himself as the primary care giver, the person on whom the child knows he can always depend. We can recall that not too long ago the extended family still was part of our pattern of child rearing. Infants in extended families would often develop focused relationships with their grandparents, aunts, and uncles. Today, some people feel that it may, in fact, not be desirable for the child to have his attachments limited to one or two people.

As she grows into her second year, the infant begins to experiment with her independence, using her mother as a secure base from which to move out in the world and to explore it. As she becomes capable of independent locomotion, she is able to move away from her mother, to venture forth and explore her world. This is a very important further step in the assertion of herself as an individual, in the expression of autonomy.

She is also beginning to use her newly acquired language skills to further her individuation from mother. She begins to say "no." Only by saying "no" can she prove to herself and her mother that she is a separate person. If she were to acquiesce in everything, it might be easier for the mother, but she would not learn to assert her individuality. She

397

would still be "fused" with the mother, rather than establishing an independent existence.

This may be a trying time for many parents, but it can also be seen as a challenge to their ingenuity and patience. It is best for parents not to become involved in battles with their child over his sallies at independent action. Hopefully, they can keep in perspective what is going on with the child and recognize that this is a positive move toward self-sufficiency. It is important to keep the negativism from becoming tied in with other developmental issues and expressed in conflicts regarding toilet training, eating, or going to bed. Parents responding to the child's negativism may become overly sensitive to it and they may ignore the many instances of co-operative behavior. Positive behavior should be responded to promptly and praised. Even within a pattern of negative behavior there are positive elements to which parents can be sensitive and reinforcing. Telling the child that he must do some things, but giving him a choice between two or three alternative ways of doing them is often helpful. One should not demean the child when he goes ahead and does the thing that the parents wanted him to do, but which he said he did not want to. One should simply accept the fact that he may say "no," but then accept the ice cream cone anyway. There is no need to make an issue of it.

There is much misunderstanding about what discipline really is and great controversy about permissiveness and strictness. Too often "discipline" is associated with spanking or other forms of physical punishment. The main goal of discipline is to help the child gain control of his behavior so that he does not hurt himself or harm others and their property. The essence is setting limits that are appropriate for the child's developmental level and that are adapted to each particular situation. Not all situations require the same degree of strictness, but some consistency across similar situations is desirable. This is basic to the development of a sense of reality and predictability.

We should keep clearly in mind what the goals of discipline are. They are not to develop an automaton responding mechanically to our commands, but a child who has gradually learned to internalize controls while feeling free to express herself. A child whose discipline is too strict will feel inhibited in her attempts to express herself for fear of reprisal. On the other hand, a child who has had no limits set on her behavior may feel basically anxious about her own omnipotence and may express her need for controls by escalating her behavior in attempts to have limits set for her.

398

During normal development there are often many acute developmental crises that concern the parent, but which are usually transient and seem to resolve themselves with time. In some cases they may present real difficulty in the management of the child, but eventually they do pass. Some children seem to be harder to manage than others in this regard. Such problems as food jags, negativism, difficulties with toilet training, and thumb-sucking are just a few of these transient disturbances that are a part of normal development.

There are, however, more severe difficulties that do not seem to pass simply with time. These disturbances may require professional intervention. One of the most common problems seen during the first three years of life is hyperactivity. The hyperactivity itself is a symptom and may be the result of such causes as constitutional factors, birth trauma, or it may be largely psychogenic. The etiology of hyperactivity needs to be understood so that the most effective intervention may occur. There is a great deal of evidence to suggest that much of such behavior is due at least in part to organic factors.

Mothers describe very active infants in utero who come into the world kicking and screaming and are very difficult babies with whom to cope. In later years, some of these children seem to be prone to difficulties in learning and reading, have a short attention span, have difficulty in concentrating on tasks, and poor motor co-ordination. This group needs guidance from the family pediatrician or other professionals to lessen the likelihood of later serious problems.

Some children are born with physical handicaps, such as blindness, deafness, mental retardation, cerebral palsy, etc., that present unique adaptational challenges for that child and his parents. There is no reason to believe, however, that these children cannot have reasonably normal emotional growth within their particular limitations. While parents should be aware of their child's problems, they should not so completely focus on any disability that they fail to recognize his other areas of normality and strength and so fail to help him develop them.

The personality is growing and changing throughout life. It is not merely formed in infancy and set at age three or five. There is a core of continuity in everyone. Certain characteristic ways of responding may establish a kind of continuity through eliciting reinforcing responses from others. Within this core of continuity there is a wide range of variation in behavior patterns. These diverse aspects of functioning are co-ordinated and patterned in many ways and come to-

399

gether to give each child her uniqueness. How parents respond to this uniqueness in trying to socialize the child, in making her aware of other people's needs and feelings, and how the child learns socially acceptable ways of expressing her uniqueness cannot be spelled out; it is an art.

INDIVIDUAL DIFFERENCES

"Every newborn varies infinitely from every other—in looks, feelings, movements, reactions to stimulation, and in his effect on his mother." This quote from the Princeton Center's *The First Twelve Months of Life* sums up current thinking on the differences between babies.

It is recognized today that even at birth babies are individuals, with varying temperaments, physiques, and reactions to the stresses of labor and birth, and that the mother must study her own child to find the happiest method of handling his needs. A corollary to this difference is the effect each child has on his parents—a baby who is difficult to pacify evokes a different response than does a placid baby. Recent research has shown that the parent responds to a child's characteristics and sensitivities; his demands elicit their responses. Thus the baby molds his parents as much as they mold him.

It is in the second month that the baby's personality becomes more evident. The baby may be a "gulper," taking food with enormous gusto, anxious for attention; she may be quiet, take pleasure in gentle play, and be discerning about her foods; or she may fit in somewhere between these two extremes, all of which can be considered normal.

One of the most reassuring texts for the new mother is Dr. T. Berry Brazelton's *Infants and Mothers,* which illustrates at length three widely different types of babies, their mothers' reactions to them, and how the babies respond. In a composite description of babies, Dr. Brazelton discusses the *"average,"* the *quiet,* and the *active* baby and shows that within the range considered normal there are enormous differences of temperament.

The average two-month-old has achieved a routine of feeding, sleeping, playing, and fussing. He can engage his family's attention by responding to their playfulness. He has begun to integrate into the family group. The quiet baby, by contrast, may worry his parents by his seeming aloofness and his passive acceptance of feeding, though he may show a

401

quiet determination, for instance, to sleep on a favorite side and nurse from the preferred breast. While he may respond to gentle stimulation, he can shut out excess sound or attention by turning his head or closing his eyes. The active baby may by now go through his day like a small dynamo, sucking his thumb vigorously, flailing his arms and legs, fussing loudly. Although he may be exhausting to care for and even to watch, this baby gives a great deal of feedback to the mother and can be emotionally satisfying through his obvious curiosity and zest.

The quiet baby, paradoxically, may be cared for easily physically, even waiting quietly for food, yet exhaust her mother emotionally by the lack of feedback she gives. All of the mother's time and attention may appear at this stage to be just politely accepted. Therefore, this mother may need more support from her pediatrician than do other mothers. Sometimes a situation occurs that is problematic because there is a mismatch between infant and parent, e.g., a vigorous, fast-moving mother and a quiet, passive baby—and this may lead to puzzling baby behavior, e.g., withdrawal, irritability, etc.

Harmonizing the Temperaments of Parents and Babies

A child's personality development is the result of the interplay between her genetic make-up and her environment. As the child's individual characteristics unfold, her parents might at some point feel disappointed. Perhaps the father looked forward to roughhousing baby and discovered instead that his was a placid little one. The father will have to alter his expectations and plans somewhat and in time the baby will also learn to modify somewhat her moods and natural temperament. This is what is meant by harmonizing temperaments of parents and baby.

As every married couple knows, moods and feelings change frequently and husbands and wives learn to recognize and relate to these changes in each other when they occur. Sensitive parents and sensitive children can also learn how to "tune in" to each other. It takes a great deal of practice and imitation for young children (and many adults as well) to develop empathy, the ability to put oneself in another person's shoes.

PCI Point of View

The gist of current research in individual differences in small babies has departed from the earlier concept of the newborn as a blank slate who can be formed wholly by his environment. The fetus is individual even before birth. Parents need to study and respond to the varied needs of their offspring. Far from imposing a personality on their baby, their proper handling will in fact help in shaping his innate characteristics.

FEELINGS OF LOVE AND AFFECTION

Love is a reciprocal feeling that is learned by parents and children. A newborn baby depends upon her parents to satisfy her needs. They feed her and make sure she is warm and dry. Infants begin to recognize their parents' faces at about the second month and start to smile at them. This is one of their ways of communicating affection.

Early in the first year infants smile at anyone's face. However, between six and twelve months, they may not smile at any but the most familiar faces. Often they may respond to strangers, particularly in a new situation, by turning away from them, assuming a sober expression, sometimes by crying. When an infant is in unfamiliar situations, when she is hurt or frightened, she turns to her parents to be held and cuddled, showing that she relies on them for a sense of security and a feeling of being loved. In turn, this evokes in the parents a special feeling of love for the infant. The feeling of exclusiveness is important in the development of love.

The oft-quoted studies by René Spitz of babies raised in institutions emphasize the importance of the infant's special relationship with a mother figure. In spite of a hygienic environment and adequate nutrition, many of the infants in these institutions died from unknown causes. There were no consistent and responsive caretakers and the environment was a sterile, unstimulating one. Although these infants showed normal early development, during the second half of the first year they did not develop focused relationships.

These babies exhibited speech retardation and a limited ability for abstract thinking, as well as inferior physical development. They did not gain weight properly and slept poorly. They were unable to form stable human bonds of love and affection. Other studies suggest that children reared in similar institutional environments often become adults who have severe difficulties in establishing and maintaining close personal relationships.

At the Primate Laboratory of the University of Wisconsin, research suggests that bodily contact plays an important role in the origin of the infant's love for his mother. Using rhesus monkeys, Dr. Harry Harlow showed that it did not matter if the baby monkeys were breast fed or bottle fed as long as intimate physical closeness was present. Other types of stimulation, such as motion, do appear to enhance affection. We know that rocking a baby often quiets him and promotes his well-being. The mother

403

who nurses her baby and the mother who holds her infant while feeding him his bottle will achieve an intimacy not possible with a baby who is fed with a propped bottle. Bodily contact, say the researchers, is very important.

SELF-CONCEPT

One of the most important aspects of a healthy personality is self-concept. The mental picture one has of oneself influences one's behaviors and reactions to the surrounding world. Certainly a person with a positive self-concept will react differently to life's challenges and frustrations than someone who has a negative self-concept.

The foundation of a strong and healthy self-concept is *trust*. In this regard that little bundle who you think is merely sleeping and eating the time away, from the very first day of infancy, is acquiring basic feelings about what it means to be alive. Depending upon the environment provided, either a basic sense of trust and happiness, or of distrust and unhappiness is being formed. The stage of psychological development from birth to walking is so very crucial because the human infant is entirely dependent upon his parents and the environment they help create for him.

Creating a Favorable Environment

By fulfilling the baby's physical, emotional, and intellectual needs, an environment favorable to the development of a healthy self-concept may be created. A summary of the infant's most important basic needs follows:

1. *Need for food.* Babies have their own internal hunger clocks that should be respected. If they are fed when they are hungry, they are more likely to feel that the world is a safe and satisfying place. If parents can accept their children as individuals right from infancy, respecting their patterns of eating and sleeping, accepting their babyish temperaments and moods, it will be much easier to give them the freedom to be their own individual selves throughout their later stages of development.

2. *Contact need.* Lots of love expressed in many different ways is needed (rocking, singing, cuddling, kissing, etc.). Expressing your love through physical contact in a natural way is recommended. The baby will not be "spoiled."

3. *Need for sensory stimulation.* Providing adequate sensory stimulation can aid in cognitive and motivational development.

Why Self-concept Is Important

A positive self-concept may give a child in later life the courage to "try" new projects, to accept criticism, to play with ideas; to be creative and venturesome. A strong self-concept is developed through countless interactions between the child and her environment.

Competency and a Positive Self-concept

The growth of personality is not an isolated happening, but a structured process that is closely tied to the maturation of the body and nervous system. The growth of a sense of self is intricately bound to this physical development. With the maturation of vision and hearing, infants can

405

begin disengaging themselves from their surroundings. Around the age of four months, a new behavior pattern emerges when the infant gradually becomes able to co-ordinate vision with reaching and grasping objects. This connection launches the four-month-old into a world to be explored and manipulated.

When infants learn they can do things that affect their environments, they become much more aware of themselves as beings truly separate from their surroundings. If they try to do things that are difficult for them and succeed, their self-confidence increases and they gradually begin to see themselves as independent beings who can have an effect on their environment.

Having integrated the findings from studies of both children and animals engaging in playful, exploratory activites, Burton L. White and his colleagues at Harvard conclude in their book, *Experience and Environment,* Vol. I, that more than just a random flow of activity is involved. They believe that children have an active tendency to influence and gain mastery over the environment and a tendency to discover reality. Reality is not passively received, even by the infant. It is slowly constructed through active, varied, and persistent exploration. What is learned about reality is how to deal with it—"what actions produce what effects on what objects."

DEPENDENCE-INDEPENDENCE IN THE FIRST YEAR

Dependence

Parents need to bear in mind that it is normal for human beings throughout their lives to maintain some form of dependency. In *Understanding Your Child from Birth to Three,* Dr. Joseph Church describes our need for friends, mates, and advisors. The "totally self-sufficient person" who requires little contact or relationships with others is most atypical. The love and praise we seek as adults are even more pronounced in children. Their dependency is normal and healthy and should be recognized.

Parents know that a baby needs shelter and food. Equally important is his requirement for love and acceptance. The early bond formed between parent and infant gives the child a sense of security that enhances his positive development as a human being. According to Dr. Lee Salk and Rita Kramer, in *How to Raise a Human Being,* studies have shown that babies who are grossly deprived of warmth and responsiveness can become damaged emotionally and intellectually.

In the early months, infants learn to recognize the voice, face, and touch of their parents. They learn that when they cry to be fed or held, their parents will satisfy their needs. *They cry for a reason.* Parents should try to find out what it is their baby is crying about.

Erik Erikson emphasizes the importance of the development of "basic trust." Babies develop trust by learning that their parents will meet their needs. Trust in parents commences at birth and is developed very strongly in the first year. Trust in oneself is more subtle. It begins when babies realize their own abilities and strive for independence.

Independence

There is no one moment when an infant suddenly becomes totally independent. Children will waver between their need for their parents and their desire to express themselves as individuals. By about six months, infants begin to realize that they can do some things by themselves. They have developed some motor skills, such as rolling over, sitting, or crawling. Some six-month-olds may become impatient with too much cuddling during feeding. Quite often a baby will want to sit up rather than be held; she may want to hold her own bottle. These are healthy, normal signs of a first assertion of independence. This is the beginning of the infant's awareness that she can have an impact on her environment.

Allowing the baby to do things by himself faciliates the development of independence. Place a bright ribbon around his foot and encourage baby to pull it off. Give your baby praise not only if he accomplishes the task, but also for trying to do it. It is a small feat, but to the infant it presents a great challenge to his growing sense of ability. You can also place a ball on the floor. If your baby attempts to get it, but struggles, allow him to struggle. Although it may take him a long time to reach it, he will have learned to do it independently. If you quickly retrieve the ball, your baby will not experience the effort and will not learn how to do things independently. Always remember to praise his efforts, because this makes the expenditure of his effort easier for him.

Independent yet Dependent

Although the child is gradually becoming independent, she still has needs for which she must depend on her parents. The baby may crawl about and wish to explore, but as soon as the mother (or mother figure)

407

leaves the room, may cry and carry on. Although the baby may crawl away from the mother to explore, the separation is her choice. When separation is forced on her by the mother, the infant may become upset. She still needs her mother, but not so constantly. She is building her independence by using her mother as a secure base. Part of her courage comes from knowing she can rely on her mother to help her when she needs her.

Independence Comes from Security and Freedom

When the child is in his playpen playing and you leave the room, often he will cry. Tell him you will be back and speak to him from the other room. The voice contact may be comforting. In the first year, the baby should have the security of knowing that if he needs his parent, the parent will be there. It has been pointed out in *The First Twelve Months of Life* that even babies who have a good relationship with their mothers may be unhappy with separations.

However, babies have to learn to accept temporary unavailability of the mother. This is a long learning process. When you leave your child with a caretaker (preferably the same one), tell her in advance that you are going out tonight and "Mary will take care of you." Explain that you will be back and try to give her some idea of when in terms she can understand. "I'll be back to have breakfast with you," for instance.

Forcing Independence

Encouraging independence is not the same as forcing it. Presenting the infant with a task that is too difficult will only frustrate him and elicit dependency responses. If he shows signs of readiness, presenting him with reasonable challenges will help him to develop. One cannot "train" independence. Keeping a crying child alone in a room for long periods of time when he needs and desires company is not teaching him anything positive.

The opposite of forcing independence is overprotecting a child by doing everything for her and not allowing her to develop her skills. Admittedly, she must be watched and protected in the beginning, but she must also have ample opportunity to try things on her own. Growth toward independence is a slow, long process. It can be fostered but never rushed!

FROM DEPENDENCE TO INDEPENDENCE IN THE SECOND AND THIRD YEARS

Your Baby at Twenty-four Months

At about the time your infant becomes a toddler, your attitude toward her undergoes a subtle change. You are no longer able to think of her as only a baby; she becomes a real person able to take on increasing responsibility. Your attitude and understanding of her abilities, as well as your willingness to let her experiment, will greatly affect how she fares in becoming a competent person.

At this stage in your baby's physical development, she is probably walking, feeding herself, and attempting to dress herself. She may be in the process of toilet training. All these accomplishments are composed of many steps that are milestones in her march toward self-determination.

409

Goals

Hopefully a climate will be established in your home that will encourage your child to develop a wholesome personality and a sense of confidence and self-sufficiency. You want your child to learn not to cling, to learn to pick up his toys and amuse himself, to explore and try, and eventually to be able to take care of himself.

NORMAL FEARS

As babies grow older they become more and more aware of their environment. They have some appreciation of size and depth and realize that their parents are big and they are little. As their awareness of the environment increases, they also become more sensitive to new and strange objects and people and to unanticipated changes in everyday occurrences. They may startle at sudden, loud noises, at changes in temperature when they are bathed, at sudden approaches by children or adults. Because mother has become someone very special, they may become unhappy if she leaves them with a stranger. These are normal fears and almost all children experience at least some of them.

Without some fear, a child might injure herself. Fear seems to alert children that some things are dangerous; for example, a moving automobile will alert them to cross the street carefully. Yet we do not want children to become so fearful that they will not cross the street at all. Fear has a specific object—a danger we can identify. When we have a vague, fearful feeling that we cannot connect with a specific object, we feel anxiety. Fears are relatively easy to deal with; anxieties are not.

Newborn babies do not fear the dark, but by the age of two to three months, many babies show distress if they are left in a dark room. This can be explained in part by their ever developing awareness of themselves.

Fear of heights is a common fear. It serves a definite function. In an experiment undertaken by Richard Walk and Eleanor Gibson, babies would stop themselves from dropping if a drop were more than a few inches. In this experiment, the drops were perceptual rather than actual; even so the babies would stop. However, never assume that young babies will not fall from a high place, such as a changing table or bed. Indeed, babies should never be left alone on an elevated surface lest they fall off.

There are other fears that serve no useful function, e.g., fear of the vacuum cleaner, among others. You can help your child recognize the fear and overcome it. Pick your baby up and carry her around while you vac-

410

uum. Let the baby turn it on and off while you are reassuring her with soothing words and by holding her. This approach may not work the first or even the fifth time, but eventully it should. Since the fear of a vacuum cleaner is often connected with its loud noise, other fears of noises may be overcome in similar ways through your supportive understanding.

Toddlers also have a variety of fears that develop along with their expanding imagination; make-believe creatures, such as ogres, boogiemen, giants, and monsters, are especially prominent. These creatures represent in a concrete way a child's undefinable fears and anxieties.

Dr. Church notes that children this age are also apt to develop fears about "intactness." Some children are afraid of or refuse to have anything to do with broken toys or broken cookies because they have a sympathetic reaction to such brokenness; that is, "if it happened to the cookie, it might happen to me."

Fantasy Enlarges Fear

The world as perceived by a child is full of magical possibilities; as a result the young child's thinking is not restricted to what is or is not possible. There could be something under his bed; he reasons, his cat goes under there all the time, maybe other animals do, too. The obvious next step is to imagine something like a tiger under the bed. Children react differently to this imaginary fear. One child might stay awake all night to be ready for the tiger if he should come out; another might cling to mother and scream frantically at bedtime; one might stalk the imaginary tiger during the day; another might have fear of all animals.

How Children Cope with Fear

Every child is equipped to deal with his own fears. Fear may lead a child to learn more about the frightening object or situation. As an example of a positive response to a fear of noise there is the two-year-old child who disassembled the vacuum cleaner in his search for the source of the noise.

Imagination can be used by children to cope with their fears. Selma Fraiberg, in *The Magic Years,* tells of two-year-old Jan, who created a playmate she named Laughing Tiger. By stalking and conquering her imaginary enemy under the dining room table, Jan worked through her fears. Young children develop a variety of defenses against fear. Some children totally withdraw from threatening situations, an example being the nursery school child who stands in a corner with her coat on, day after

411

day. Other children regress to babyhood by going back to the bottle, baby talk, and bladder and bowel accidents.

The child who cannot deal with his fears may claim that a frightening event never happened, for example, that his pet did not die. Children who are afraid of admitting something "bad" about themselves may blame the badness on someone or something else. It is natural to use defenses like these and sometimes they are helpful, but their persistent use as a way of avoiding facing reality is a sign that the child is overly anxious.

Children have their own way of dealing with their fears, but it is up to the parents to help them by encouraging positive attempts to overcome fears.

Fostering Independence

Give your toddler as much leeway as she can handle while you supervise her daily routine. Dr. Lloyd Rowland, editor of the magazine *Pierre the Pelican,* notes that a test of a good parent is one who establishes the habit of letting the child do what she can do for herself and stands by to help only when necessary.

Not all toddlers take the initiative in independent play. They need patient encouragement and reassurance to help them develop the ability to play on their own. Many may return to their parents from time to time to have their emotional batteries recharged. The development of independence in such areas as toileting, eating, and dressing will not be steady and progress may slip from time to time. Normally many toddlers alternate between babyish timidity and courageous venturing into new areas. Dr. Church says, "There is nothing to be done about growth ambivalence except to recognize it, tolerate it, and lend the toddler your finger to get him over the rough spots."

It is advisable not to encourage independence in more than one area at a time. If your child is in the midst of toilet training, it is not a good time to get him to give up his pacifier. If a new baby is expected in the family, it is wise to postpone toilet training since your firstborn will have enough to cope with for a while. Common sense dictates that if a child is permitted to face one challenge at a time, the satisfaction gained from each achievement will make the next goal that much easier to attain.

Developmental Disorders

You may recognize an attitude in your toddler that might result in a lag in his or her development of independence. Timid children may let themselves get pushed around or whine. They need experience in playing with other children. Parents should encourage these children to work out their problems by themselves; then they will learn to stand up for themselves.

Your child may be slower in developing independence due to under-stimulation and over-restriction. Parents should play with their children and provide them with sight, sound, and movement activities that aid learning and development. However, parents must not respond to their child so quickly that she does not have a chance to indicate what she wants or to do it independently.

PCI Point of View

Parents need to be aware of their own and their children's ambivalent feelings during the various stages of development. Dr. Church describes this dual ambivalence simply: "When a child is ready to move forward, the parents hold him back and when the child wants to hold back, the parents press him ahead." Being aware of this can help parents cope better with this normal predicament.

PCI would like to emphasize the importance of a relaxed, happy attitude in dealing with the charming but demanding stage of toddlerdom. It is up to the parents to provide a climate that stimulates learning and development. They should concentrate on letting each child do as much for himself as he can and interfering only when necessary.

HELPING CHILDREN DEAL WITH FEAR

When adults seek to help children learn to cope with fear, they need above all to have accepting attitudes that enable them to watch, listen, and wait. There is no use in saying, "There is nothing to be afraid of" without knowing what is behind the fear. The parent can help the child by:

1. Explaining the situation. The parent should tell the child what is happening, answer any objections, and present a clear idea of the events. The child will know things are all right when the parent thinks they are, but the parent has to be realistic in explaining the situation. He or she can say that there is no need to be afraid of the puppy, but at the same time the adult should not try to convince the child that "dogs don't do any harm," because this is not always true.

2. Setting an example of calmness. A parent can look at the lightning and wait with a smile for the thunder that follows it, thus reassuring the child of the foreseen and natural event.

3. Listen to the child's account of her feelings and encourage her to talk about them. The child can be told that fears are natural, that there are times when everyone is afraid of something. The parent can help the child distinguish between what is real and what is imagined. If a four-year-old thinks there is a bear in the closet, she needs to be shown that there is no bear instead of being told that the parent is going to drive the bear out.

4. Trying to effect "positive reconditioning" by replacing the feared stimulus with an attractive one. You can give a child a cookie or pat her head reassuringly when she is looking at a dog, gradually bringing her to watch the dog from shorter distances.

5. Limit his behavior when it causes discomfort to others or threatens danger to himself. Sometimes a firm hand on the television switch is needed when the program depicts violent scenes that a specific child (not every child is influenced to the same degree) might take as real and so react with fear.

6. The child's use of dramatic play should be encouraged, as should her interest in exploring and understanding new objects and situations. Explanations should be reassuring, but straightforward. Robertson and Wood note that when children develop a sense of independence and competence in their own play, they tend to be less fearful. Children learn from their own falls and scrapes rather than from barrages of "be careful!"

It is not helpful to force a child into the feared situation. When this is done before the child is mature enough to understand the situation and to handle it, it merely increases the fear. We often hear of a father urging his son to fight a neighborhood playmate or forcing him to approach a barking dog. Both are negative approaches that should not be practiced.

Ridiculing or punishing a child for being afraid is not recommended. Some parents view their children's fear as a sign of weakness, and tell them, "Big boys like you shouldn't be afraid of the dark. Even Mary, who is younger than you, isn't afraid." Other parents may become angry with the child, which causes the youngster to deny his fears. These adult reactions do not help a child overcome his fears.

Parents should not constantly ignore fears. If parents remain unaware of their children's fears or are indifferent to them, the fears tend to pile up because the children do not get the reassurance they may require to help them gain understanding of them.

Dealing with Specific Fears

1. *Fear of animals*. If growing up with pets, the child will come to understand that there is nothing to be afraid of. Watching animals, explain-

ing how they live, what they eat, going to the zoo—all these can be of help.

2. *Fear about the body.* Reassure your child that the doctor's periodic checkups of her development will help keep her in good health. Do not be overconcerned about her physical condition, nor be overly anxious when she feels a little under par on occasion.

3. *Anxiety due to separation.* Always help and encourage your child to do those things that he can and should do by himself. Parents should tell their child when they have to go out and let him know when they expect to return. Parents should not surrender to their child's dependence; nevertheless, they need to respect his need for reassurance.

4. *Nightmares.* If nightmares occur frequently, it may mean that a child is wrestling with upsetting feelings. Sometimes they can stem from outside events, like moving to a new house or the birth of a new baby. Usually turning on the light to let the child see that she is in a familiar place is enough. You can talk with her a little to make her forget the frightening dream. If nightmares persist for a long time, the doctor's advice can be helpful.

5. *Dealing with family crises.* In her new book *Teaching Your Child to Cope with Crisis,* Suzanne Ramos describes, according to subject, just how children react to many *possibly* stressful situations and, based on

415

numerous interviews with practicing experts, suggests ways of helping children adjust and cope emotionally so that long-term damage is avoided. The chapter headings of her book speak for themselves: death, hospital, separation and divorce, remarriage, parental traumas, adoption, moving, sex, financial stress, children's emotional problems, school, race and religion, siblings, separation and work. It is a sensible, simple book worth reading. (See also Chapter 12, sections on Divorce and Separation, Adoption, Explaining Death to a Child, and Moving.)

AGGRESSION AND FRUSTRATION

Aggression in babies seems to be universal. That thought may worry some parents as they look at their peacefully sleeping newborn.

Present-day riots and wars have made parents think more about things they can do to prevent violence as they raise their children. Aggression may express hostility, but assertive behavior can also be a sign of growing independence in young children. It is the violent forms of aggression that we seek to understand in order to channel them into acceptable behavior. (See Chapter 10, section on Toys of War and Violence.)

An aggressive reaction takes place when a baby is frustrated and unable to obtain immediate gratification of his own needs. How we react to the baby's pugnacity will determine how that behavior will develop.

First and most important, we must understand that aggressive feelings are natural. We want to help the baby control her feelings in order to use them constructively as she grows into a healthy, mature individual. What we want to do is help each child learn to cope with this natural emotion so that it does not become too much for her to handle.

Biological Factors

It is not completely clear how we get our hostile feelings. Feelings of hate and aggression appear to be a natural counterpart of feelings of love and tenderness. Feelings of love and hate are learned after birth; frustrating experiences become associated with anger and pleasant experiences become associated with love.

It may be that sex differences in the expression of aggression have a biological basis. Although it is unclear whether the particular human traits of aggression are inborn or acquired, parents frequently tolerate certain aggressive characteristics in their sons that they tend to squelch in their daughters. We do know that many differences in the intensity and form of aggressive expression are molded by society as represented by the family.

416

The constitutional make-up of a child also influences his activity level, which in turn is related to the child's aggression. Active children are apt to encounter more frustrating experiences as they are continually on the go.

Growth of Hostility

In examining the emotions of the newborn, childhood specialists have been able to isolate only two states of feeling—"pleasant" and "unpleasant." The infant is relaxed and in a pleasant state when she is full, dry, and warm. When a baby is hungry, cold, or in pain, she is in an unpleasant state and shows distress in no uncertain terms.

The number of times a baby is hurt, uncomfortable, or angry, how long these feelings last, and how the parents react to these feelings all help determine what his attitude toward himself will be, what he will expect from others, what feelings of hostility will develop as he matures, and how he will handle those feelings. The child learns to feel and show affection to those things or people who make him feel pleasant and anger at situations that frustrate him.

A baby's first anger seems to be aroused in relation to feeding. When he wakes up hungry he often screams violently until fed. Several months later he shows anger when his activity is restricted. To quote Dr. Fraiberg, "The desire to look, to touch, to handle is as urgent for the baby as hunger and as necessary for his intellectual growth as the books we will give him later on. Too many restrictions on mobility create irritability, temper outbursts and conflicts between the baby and family which require much time to undo and are often easily avoided through practical approaches to the child's needs."

As a baby learns to crawl and then walk she needs many opportunities to practice this activity. For a time you can childproof your house or apartment by putting away breakable or dangerous objects so the baby has an opportunity to explore the environment without too many "no-nos." At this age it is better to try to avoid as many contests with the baby as possible. If the baby finds her environment too frustrating she may lose her curiosity and initiative for learning.

How to Handle Hostility in the One-year-old

Under the age of one year, an infant is unable to keep from showing his feelings. For example, some parents mistakenly feel that temper tantrums are under the child's control and so react with anger that may distress the baby even more. Other parents react with a great deal of sympa-

417

thy, whereupon the baby probably learns that the best way to get affection and care is with a good loud scream. If parents recognize this first violent behavior for what it is—a blind, uncontrollable rage—they will feel neither the need to fight back nor to run scared.

Babies do need comforting when angry or distressed. The parent who remains relatively calm and undisturbed is in the best position to help the baby overcome her uncomfortable feeling quickly. Sometimes it is wise to wait a minute, take a deep breath, and perhaps by that time the baby will have overcome the frustrating situation herself.

PCI Point of View

In this first year of growth, there are going to be many frustrations that the baby will react to with aggressive behavior. In the lives of everyone there are many frustrations, some of which are reacted to with anger. It is not the *feelings* that must be controlled, but the hostile *actions* that must be curbed. Since children learn from parents both consciously and unconsciously, you might examine your own reactions to frustrations. If you behave violently, your baby will probably do likewise.

AGGRESSIVE BEHAVIOR

In the course of maturing, a child has a natural tendency to bring his aggressiveness more and more under control, but in the toddler stage he is still growing in his awareness of how the world operates. He is learning to feel and show affection for people and situations that make him feel pleasant and anger at those that frustrate him.

Most young children engage in a little fighting, biting, and hitting as they learn to get along with others. If a child constantly resorts to these actions in her day-to-day relationships and persists in hurting other children over an extended period of time, then perhaps it is a sign that she may require special help. Usually, like many other problems of childhood, this is a passing phase and can be handled by the child and observant parent.

From a practical point of view, a parent may ask, "How far should I permit my two-year-old to go?" "Should he be permitted to hit, bite, and scratch other children?" The answer, of course, is no. He must learn how to get along with other people and to respect their feelings and rights. The parent must help the child to understand that hurting others cannot be allowed. It is also important for him to know that there is someone who loves him, but will not permit him to hurt others. To find that there are limits beyond which he cannot go is very reassuring to a toddler.

In handling the situation, parents should try not to think in terms of "punishment to fit the crime." Instead, they need to think of *what will help their child*. Try not to use words that give her guilt feelings of being bad or wicked. It is best to keep in control of yourself so that you can handle the situation in a way that would be most beneficial in teaching your child acceptable methods of handling frustrations. Remember to praise your child for the good things she does, thereby reinforcing her positive behavior.

Teach your child gradually that some things are socially acceptable and some are not; that when she does certain things, such as hurting others, people do not like it. Be sure, however, that in trying to get this point across, you do not let her build up a fear that she is not loved or that she will be loved *only* if she is a good girl.

If a child of two always seems to be a grabber, it does not necessarily mean he is going to become a bully. Since he is still too young to have much feeling for others, you should let him grab sometimes. However, if he is doing it constantly, it may help to let him play occasionally with older children who will stand up for their rights. If he seems to be intimidating a particular child, it might be better to keep them separate for a while. Sometimes just taking him away in a matter-of-fact manner and getting him interested in something else can be very helpful.

Sara Gilbert maintains that even though we should be firm in dealing with the two-year-old, we should never resort to severe punishment. We do not want to crush completely the child's newly found ability to assert herself because the child is going to need some of this behavior later on in life. What we really need to do is to help the child redirect the aggression into less harmful activities.

It is important to understand that our child's behavior depends largely on our own standards, our reactions to behavior, as well as our own behavior and the examples we set. Our personal feelings about misbehavior are influenced by many things, including the values stressed by our own parents and teachers, neighborhood practices, the standards our society strives to impose, and our position in that society.

Since even a young bully is expressing negative behavior, it is interesting to note that studies of aggression have indicated the importance of three factors that contribute to the instigation and learning of such behavior:

1. *Frustration, restrictiveness, and rejection.* The effects of punitiveness and restrictive child-rearing practices have been studied by psychologists. Many have found that the highest percentage of aggression was associated with high permissiveness and high punishment; the lowest with low permissiveness and low punishment. Parents who go to extremes by

permitting adverse or destructive behavior or by instituting severe punishments seem to be fostering childhood aggression.

2. *Modeling of aggressive figures in the environment.* The parents' use of punishment serves as a model for the learning of aggression. Its employment provides a living example of the use of aggression at the very moment parents are trying to teach the child not to be aggressive.

3. *Norms or reinforcement contingencies surrounding aggressive action.* The importance of reinforcement has been demonstrated as having a decided effect on the performance of aggressive behavior.

As you attempt to guide your two-year-old, it is important to keep in mind always that you are the parent and that you, not your child, must set the controls. It does your child no good if you deny your authority. The trend today is to set clear and consistent limits without forgetting love. As often as you can, establish limits without blowing up and then live by your decisions.

COMMON BEHAVIORS OF CONCERN TO PARENTS

Many behavior difficulties are normal reactions to growing up. Some behaviors of concern to parents include head banging, pica (non-food nibbling), the use of a security blanket, thumb-sucking, temper tantrums, breath holding, stuttering, shyness, destructiveness, and dawdling. These behaviors are nothing to be worried about and normally disappear within a few months. It is important for parents not to become unduly alarmed at their child's behavior and perhaps create a real problem out of what may be a normal occurrence at a particular age and stage. Parents can try to recognize some of the reasons for their child's behavior without resorting to labels, such as "stubborn" or "sloppy." In spotting and understanding the causes of behavior, parents can ease and sometimes remedy the situation for their child.

Head Banging, Head Rolling, and Jouncing

Toward the second half of the first year babies sometimes take to banging their heads hard and rhythmically against their crib, rolling their heads from side to side, or they may get on hands and knees and jounce against their heels in a steady rhythm.

Head banging is especially disturbing and frightening to parents. They are afraid that their baby will hurt herself and sometimes imagine that she is lacking in normal intelligence. Even when they are reassured that this

420

banging will not injure the brain and that it is not a sign of any kind of mental abnormality, they may find it nerve-racking to listen to the constant thudding.

Why do babies do this? No one seems to know for sure. Many babies do not go directly to sleep, but first seem to go through a short period of tenseness. Head banging, head rolling, and jouncing, like thumb-sucking, may be the baby's way of handling tension before falling asleep.

If your baby bangs his head, you can line the crib with quilted padding so he will not bruise himself. Try padding the outside of the crib if head banging causes the crib to thump against the wall. An infant who bangs his head may need more cuddling and stimulation than he is getting. Scolding the baby and/or trying to restrain him physically are likely only to make him more tense. It will probably not be long before he outgrows this behavior. Your baby may get over it even sooner if you can relax, cuddle, and generally enjoy him.

For head banging, you might try a radio tuned to an all-music station (if possible start with music that approximates the rhythm of the banging). The ticking of a metronome or the beat of music may satisfy your baby and eliminate head banging for a while anyway. Sometimes a warm bath right before bedtime will have the effect of relaxing your baby so that she will go right to sleep.

Tics

A tic is an uncontrollable, persistent muscle spasm, such as eye blinking, shoulder shrugging, facial grimacing, neck twisting, throat clearing, sniffing, dry coughing, etc. The motion always takes the same form. A tic may last on and off for weeks or months and go away for good or a new one may take its place.

Generally a tic develops as the result of some anxiety with which a child is unable to deal. For example, bottled-up resentment, too much pressure at home, reaction against constant disapproval. Tics seem to develop more commonly in tense children. A child may copy a tic from another child, but he would not have picked it up if he were not already tense.

A child should not be scolded or corrected on account of a tic. Since a tic is beyond the child's control, it cannot be reasoned or disciplined away. The remedy is to discover and try to relieve the basic cause of the child's anxiety. If no physical cause is found and the symptom persists after the parents have made every effort to make the child's home life relaxed and agreeable, her school and/or social life satisfying, and their own attitude undemanding, then consultation with a trained counselor is suggested.

Pica—Non-food Nibbling

Pica is a condition in which the child continually eats things that are generally considered inedible—paint, plaster, dirt, dust, paper, etc. Often pica is highly selective; one child will confine his nibbling to chips of paint while another child is partial to strands of wool from a blanket, still another will eat dirt from the back yard. Some of the substances are harmless, while others (paint and plaster, for example) are prominent causes of lead poisoning.

Pica is not too well understood. In some cases, the child may be trying to compensate for some lack in his diet or for an inability to utilize certain nutritional elements. It may merely be a habit that has persisted since infancy (when children will put practically anything into their mouths). In some cases, pica may be a sign of an emotional disturbance.

Pica usually does not go on beyond the age of five, but if you find that your child is an habitual non-food nibbler, she should be checked by her pediatrician for any damage the ingested material may have caused and to determine the cause of her behavior.

Security Objects

Many babies develop an attachment to a favorite blanket or toy. Such an object becomes a concrete security link for the child who is encountering new situations and should be made available. Most parents do not look upon this kind of attachment as being objectionable when they view it properly as fulfilling their child's emotional needs. (See Chapter 2, Security Objects.)

Thumb-sucking

Thumb-sucking is a normal reflex behavior. In fact, it has been proved that thumb-sucking occurs in utero. Some parents react negatively to this behavior because it mistakenly represents to them their failure to satisfy their child's basic needs. Current research suggests that contented, happy babies suck their thumbs and the habit usually is outgrown well before the age of four or five (thereby precluding damage to permanent teeth, which do not come in until about the age of five or six. (See Chapter 2, Thumb-sucking.)

Temper Tantrums and Breath Holding

These are common behavior patterns in one- to three-year-olds, but not as easily ignored or even tolerated as is thumb-sucking. Suddenly a child goes into a tantrum, performing usually in front of an audience. The causes are varied—fatigue, frustration, seeking attention, etc. Parents should try to "keep their cool" during these outbursts since adult screaming will only serve to reinforce the child's behavior. (See section in this chapter on Temper Tantrums.)

Stuttering

Stuttering (or stammering) is quite common in young children when they are first beginning to talk. At this time speaking is new to children and they cannot keep up with their thoughts. Often children become frustrated and tense as they grope for the words to express themselves, which then causes them to repeat phrases. In some instances, the reverse is true; these children talk faster then they can think, thus producing repetitions of words and letters until their thoughts catch up with their tongues. Sometimes stuttering develops when the child is under too much pressure or when there are anxieties with which he cannot deal, such as a move to a new home or the departure of a close relative. (See Chapter 8, Stuttering).

Shyness

Sometimes shyness bothers parents, but in young children occasional shyness is often a sign that the child has become more aware of the world around her and has learned that new things and situations should be examined carefully before fully accepting them. It is not good to force your child to accept a person or situation before she is ready to do so.

Some children are timid when playing with others, especially if they have had little opportunity for playmates. If your child is being pushed around by her peers, help her stand up for herself (without fighting her battles for her). Teach her how not to be browbeaten by other children. It may be desirable for you to stay with her at first to help her to verbalize her needs if she lacks the words to do it. If her toys are taken, suggest that she go and get them back, but do not get them for her. You might accompany her at first in her quest for lost toys. This way you are helping your child gain independence while letting her know that you are there for reassurance.

Destructiveness

Tearing things down and building things up are common practices for toddlers, who are discovering things around them. In a child's attempt to explore objects and discover their properties, he may take things apart or inadvertently break them. In addition, young children are somewhat clumsy. They usually are not able to manipulate objects precisely, so they may appear to be careless or destructive.

Some children, however, may destroy things purposefully for a variety of reasons. For example, the child may be angry at his parents and unable to express his anger in other ways. He may be upset over a parental separation or he may be seeking attention. An understanding of why he is behaving destructively helps you to know what to do.

Dawdling

With most children dawdling is merely a result of their imprecise notions of time. When they are absorbed in play, "five more minutes until cleanup time" does not mean much. Therefore, parents should compensate for the toddlers' distractibility by allowing more time than is necessary for the expected cleanup or other activity. Frequent reminders also help. (See section in this chapter on Negativism and "No.")

It is important to stress that the "problem" behaviors of toddlers described here may in fact be normal reactions to growing up. The parents' handling of their child may be an important factor as to whether their child's behavior will become a real problem or whether the child will pass through this stage of development and on to the next plateau of growth.

Childhood Tension

Dr. Brazelton points out (in the Boston Children's Hospital's *Child Health Encyclopedia*) that "tension in children can set the stage for psychosomatic disease later on. There is even recent evidence to suggest that susceptibility to infection may be associated with tension. This may take such forms as respiratory infection in small children, just as parents are about to go away on a trip or move to another city; or lowered resistance from tension in a household. More serious are the complaints associated with stress, such as asthma, eczema, stomach ulcers, and colitis."

The reaction to stress or stimulus takes so many psychological forms

425

that it is impossible to prescribe remedies. But there are certain age-determined physical and psychological symptoms that crop up regularly. By recognizing them as normal and passing signs of development, parents can avoid their becoming serious.

FIRST YEAR

Colic and crying—normally two to three hours a day in the first three months

Spitting up after feedings

Thumb- or finger-sucking

Infrequent bowel movements in a breast-fed baby

Constipation—hard bowel movements which can be softened by changes in diet

Waking at night just prior to developmental spurts

Feeding refusals associated with wanting to feed self at eight months or so

SECOND YEAR

Feeding aberrations—refusing one food after another, eating only one meal a day

Temper tantrums and breath-holding spells

Withholding stools and problems around toilet training—usually from too early and too much pressure to conform

If parents overreact to these symptoms and are punitive or overly strict, are overconcerned, or if they ignore the symptoms, the problem gets unreasonably worse. Doctors often dodge their responsibility by such advice as "He will grow out of it"—some prescribe aspirin. Parents need to establish close communication with their child by attentive listening and helping their child understand the reason for the symptom.

DISCIPLINE

One of the most widely written about topics in the field of child behavior concerns discipline techniques. Many years of research and study have gone into most professional opinions and total trial-and-error child rearing is being replaced by more developmental and humanistic approaches. Especially reassuring for new parents is the fact that the experts are in agreement in many important areas concerning developing good mental health and self-responsibility in children. They see discipline as training that corrects, molds, strengthens, or perfects. It is the child's ongoing learning of socially useful behavior. Discipline is something you do for and with the child, not *to* him.

Dr. Mary Ainsworth states that "the sensitive mother is able to see things from the baby's point of view." This is difficult for some parents, but an important accomplishment throughout their guidance of their offspring's toddlerhood and adolescence. How many disagreements between people (babies and children are included in this category) and nations (also people) could be avoided if each of the parties could "put himself or herself in the other person's shoes!"

Discipline at the Pre-verbal Stage

Can you imagine living in a giant's house where you could not speak the language, a house in which there was little required for you to do, and little you were allowed to do? You would probably do your best to find something to keep you from dying of boredom. Cupboards and drawers might contain something of interest. Pulling on a cord or cloth might bring taller objects down to your level. Maybe you would try climbing up to investigate—a truly intelligent way of approaching the situation.

According to Selma Fraiberg, an active baby should not be confined for long periods of time in a playpen, because it becomes a prison to her. It is important to note that an infant's vigorous interaction with and exploration of her environment can sometimes create problems for the parents; yet these behaviors are important to the baby's progress and growth. The very young child who begins to master her environment and try out her skills (throwing, messing in food in her first attempts to feed herself, pulling up to stand, climbing, walking, running) needs all the support that she can get. There are times, however, when she needs restriction. This, then, is the start of the long and demanding process of discipline.

Discipline is not synonymous with punishment. Many parents confuse these terms when dealing with children. Lee Salk states in *What Every Child Would Like His Parents to Know,* that "while punishment is basically different from discipline, its existence is implied in the concept of discipline. Punishment is a sort of fine, or price you pay, for deviating from the established rules and regulations."

Three important discipline techniques are anticipation, diversion, and substitution. Anticipation in a very young baby might mean simply changing his physical position before he gets weary of lying on his back. With a crawler or toddler, you know fragile vases or lamps are in peril, so remove them or adjust their placement. You may want to restrict your child to certain rooms so the whole house does not have to be babyproofed.

427

There are countless situations worthy of anticipation. A tote tray or bag of toys to take on an outing or errand is a worthwhile forethought. An extra-long nap before going to grandma's for the evening might make your child much happier. When you get to grandma's, anticipate that her prize flowering begonia is in great danger on the coffee table and ask her if you might change its location. It is hard to believe, but grandmothers and mothers sometimes forget just what needs to be done to babyproof a home.

Although diversion of attention is more difficult as the baby gets older, it certainly is a positive approach in avoiding discipline problems. Give the child something of interest that you would allow her to play with and take away from her the dangerous or undesirable object. Some situations may call for the removal of the object from the child or the reverse, removal of the child from the object.

Spanking

All the experts agree that only under the most extraordinary circumstances should a parent spank a child under one and most extend this to two and a half. A few say no spanking at all. A parent saying, "I told you *not* to hit," while administering blows to her child's bottom, seems incongruous. (However, with the older child and in certain other instances, some experts believe a good swat on the posterior may be what is called for.)

A more effective alternative to spanking is to reinforce positive behavior, to reward appropriate behavior, and to ignore or discourage inappropriate behavior. Praise your child when he does something you approve of or does something you have asked him to do. Within this framework parents need to establish reasonable and clearly defined limits that are understood by the child. Children should not be allowed to hurt other people or pets, destroy property, or harm themselves. Pertinent adult language has to be broken down for the child to the very simple "Use the crayons only on the paper" and "Friends are to play with, not hit."

Controlling the child's environment is also an indirect way to promote acceptable behavior—changing seating arrangements or removing a toy from the table are common examples. In addition, some rooms in the house and areas of the yard might be "off limits" to children in consideration of the needs of the parents. However, a child needs an area where he can pursue his own activities, such as a low cupboard in the kitchen for his playthings.

428

PCI Point of View

Parents must understand that suitable discipline is part of their expression of love and caring for their child. In reading the experts' opinions on discipline, one point comes shining through—using techniques to avoid the use of discipline is sounder and more conducive to happy family life and the mental well-being and positive self-concept of the child. However, it is the mother's and father's responsibility to provide their child with a clear concept of what is expected, what is permitted, and what is not acceptable.

NEGATIVISM AND "NO"

As children approach the age of two, you can expect them occasionally to exhibit a form of behavior that is frequently described as negativism. Some refer to it as the "terrible twos." During this stage children will respond with "no" to nearly every suggestion you make. This negativism is a transitional stage between babyhood and childhood. Dr. Dodson suggests that the parent should view it as a *positive* stage in the child's development. "Without it he would remain stuck in the equilibrium of babyhood."

During this period the child's contrary and contradictory behavior may leave the parents bewildered and annoyed. The child is often taking a stand for her own rights and trying to see how it feels and what the consequences are of making decisions on her own. In *Three Years to Grow* Sara Gilbert writes, "We shared the baby's delight when he discovered his hands and feet and his pride when he took his first step. 'No!' and 'Mine!' may be harder to take, but they are just as surely signs of progress toward independent selfhood."

The child at this age seems defiant of his parents and very inflexible. He seems to want to do everything immediately and insists that things be done in the same way every time. He will attempt to dominate his parents and make unreasonable demands of them. His mood will change frequently and his emotions will sometimes be violent, as displayed in a temper tantrum.

The child will often say "no" even to those things she wants to do. For instance, she may be loudly exclaiming, "No, I don't want to take a bath," even while climbing into the bathtub. It seems that to do just the opposite of what the parent wants strikes the child as being the very essence of her individuality. Parents need to take heart because this constancy of "no" is a natural part of each very young child's growth. Dr.

Brazelton explains that to the child being negative and saying "no" is "like standing, he must practice it day and night."

Parental Approach to This Stage

Often when the child is saying "no" he does not expect it to be taken seriously. However, there are times when he does mean what he says. Dr. Church, in *Understanding Your Child from Birth to Three,* states that "at such time, parental authority must prevail, but it doesn't have to explode. When the baby has a tantrum, adult calm is even more in order."

There are several methods for dealing with children during this stage. Keeping in mind what this negative behavior means, parents should try not to become angry with their children.

Lead your child rather than ask what he wants to do. Give him several options as to how a given activity can be done. For example, he can be given an opportunity to choose whether he wants a cheese or peanut butter sandwich or what color glass to drink from. Attempt to divert his attention by making games out of what you want him to do. Limit your commands to as few as possible. According to Dr. Church, "Insist upon obedience when it is absolutely necessary for your child's welfare and let him make the decisions in other matters."

Dawdling

Dawdling is a subdued form of negativism. You will find that your child will dawdle around the age of two or three. It will seem that she is taking forever to eat dinner or take her bath. Your child should be allowed extra time for such tasks as dressing herself, washing, and eating. The idea is to get things done without causing disruptions.

A parent's exasperation with a child's dawdling may also be shared by the child. Dr. Church explains that "the child's life is lived to the refrain of NOT NOW, SOON, LATER or IN A LITTLE WHILE. These adult stallings and delays are probably well justified, but to the child they seem just like dawdling."

At about this time your child may begin to pick up swear words and unpleasant expressions from other children. If you act shocked and surprised at hearing these words, your child will be delighted with his power over you. Threats to your child demanding that he immediately stop using these words is the same as "handing him a full-size cannon and telling him, 'For goodness sake, don't set it off,'" says Dr. Spock. It is best just to ignore his language. However, if it persists you may have to tell him firmly that you do not like that kind of language and you do not want him to use it.

Dr. Dodson tells us that at this stage of development the child is learning self-identity versus social conformity. He thinks that a child's rebellion against his parents is one of the ways in which he tries to establish his individual sense of identity.

Happily for all concerned, the toddler does not spend all her time being negative. This is a period during which she experiences joy and intoxication with her new relationship to reality. According to Selma Fraiberg, "It is a kind of declaration of independence, but there is no intention to unseat the government." A child will stage a full-scale rebellion only if she is subjected to too much pressure or forceful methods by her parents.

Disciplining Toddlers

Effective discipline must be based on an understanding of what can be expected of a child at different stages and the child's needs. Anticipation, diversion, and substitution work very well with babies and young children, but as children become three and four years old, their level of symbolic understanding increases along with their physical and social boundaries. Parents should always attempt to encourage acceptable behavior. When misbehavior occurs, however, parental action should be prompt, consistent, and firm.

According to Dr. Rudolf Dreikurs, the parent can remain an ally of the child rather than his opponent through a method of "logical consequences." For example, a child breaks a window with his baseball, after having been warned against playing near the house. His parents sympathize with him, but he still must pay for the new windowpane. The child who deliberately throws her cup of milk on the floor must not be hungry, so she has to clean up the mess she made and then go to her room while everyone else is still eating.

In these examples, mommy and daddy are *not* ogres because they are doling out discipline. Simply stated, children need to learn early that certain acts lead to pleasant consequences and other acts lead to unpleasant circumstances. In this manner, the parent is never forced into rejecting the child. Through the process of logical consequences, children are gradually being educated to consider their actions and the results of their actions beforehand. They are learning to think and act responsibly.

THE "TOO GOOD" CHILD

The child who is extremely eager to please, overly conscientious, diligent, and polite may not be a problem to his parents, but may be defending himself against inner anxieties. The child has to be especially good to avoid being what he considers bad. Parents can help their child by letting him know that his impulses are normal, encouraging him to understand them, and helping him to develop acceptable forms of behavior.

Behind the co-operative behavior of very young children may be the desire for special attention. Dr. Rudolf Dreikurs asserts that it is often difficult to distinguish between behavior for the sake of attention getting and co-operative behavior that stems from a genuine feeling of belongingness and willingness to contribute. He indicates that the child whose goal in attention getting is to be best or better than the other children is often a perfectionist; such a child is often very sensitive to criticism and fearful of failure.

Home is a place to be "bad," as well as "good." Young children need to let their feelings out. Anyone may feel hostile when frustrated and children experience frustration dozens of times a day. Drs. Freda Kehm and Joe Mini suggest that the parent can be helpful by teaching the child to release tension and express her feelings in an acceptable way. For example, strenuous outdoor play uses up tense energy. If children do not learn how to handle their hostilities, they may become behavior problems at home or at school. In order to be loved, some children repress all their hostile feelings, and this may lead to serious personality problems later.

Dr. Dodson also emphasizes that feelings cannot be ignored. Parents often attempt to repress their child's feelings, which can lead to severe problems. The child's feelings, even such negative feelings as rage, hate, anger, fear, etc., should be expressed. The expression of negative feelings can help a child move on to express positive feelings and to engage in constructive behavior.

The "Too Clean" Child

Children often get dirty. It is part of their attempt to learn about the world around them. Some parents can overdo a "fondness for cleanliness." They may want their young child to have white-white shoes, clean fingernails, mud-free overalls. They might even withhold love from a "dirty" child. The child may sense that the only way to get love is to be spotlessly clean. You can make a baby so uneasy that by the age of two, he will become frantic when he dirties his clothing or shoes. In order to accomplish neatness at this early age, parents may even resort to punishment, resulting in a worried, unhappy child.

The "Too Obedient" Child

When a child always meekly gives in, it is time for the parents to investigate the reason. Often the too obedient child has aggressive feelings, but is deeply afraid of expressing them. For countless, not always explainable reasons, a youngster who has every reason to feel loved and secure may be uncertain, shy, and timid. Instead of being alarmed, parents should feel relieved when one day their child fights for his rights or answers back instead of giving up. Children who never rebel need encouragement to speak up for what they want. A healthy aggressiveness need not always show itself as a readiness to fight physically or speak loudly. Some gentle, soft-spoken people are most effective in protecting their rights and opinions.

The Loner

Some young children prefer to spend an inordinate amount of time by themselves or with adult relatives. Solitary play or adult-associated play should not be totally condemned. According to Dr. George Gardner, the loner, through fear due to an unfortunate past experience or shyness, prefers to be alone. She may lack basic social skills and experience to reach out to others and needs to be encouraged to be with her peers. On the other hand, there are some children, usually firstborn, who genuinely enjoy solitary play, but will also participate in group activities. These children may not have any social problems at all. Parents should be sensitive to the child's feelings and try to introduce the child to her peers in situations where she feels most secure. Some aspects of personality growth and socialization can go forward only through satisfying relationships with other children. Two- and three-year-olds who appear very timid in the presence of their peers will learn by experience if they play near children regularly.

As parents you will learn to accept and respect the preferences of your child. One important goal is for parents and their children to form a harmonious pattern of family and social living. You should not feel threatened when the "socialization" standards of your child are different from your own.

PCI emphasizes the importance of understanding the "overcontrolled" child. Do not put too much emphasis on "good" habits only. Every young child needs opportunities to rebel on occasion and to assert more independence.

TEMPER TANTRUMS

Temper tantrums usually occur in children between one and three years of age. Often with apparently little or no provocation, the child may exhibit what appears to be completely illogical behavior. Some children use the "exhibitionist" approach—crying, shouting, screaming, throwing themselves on the floor, kicking, or flailing. A more exotic variation of this approach is the breath-holding spell. Then there are those children who utilize the more "activist" approach. They employ such tactics as hitting, pinching, kicking, or biting. Of course, any combination of these actions may be utilized.

Causes

Believe it or not, this mode of behavior is common and expected in this age group. There is nothing inherently "wrong" with a child who displays such behavior.

Dr. Dreikurs, in *Coping with Children's Misbehavior,* tells parents that a display of temper does not mean that the child has a nervous problem or a hereditary defect. If a member of the family does have a temper and is effective in getting what he or she wants when displaying it, the child may merely be imitating the distressing behavior.

Often someone in the family history had a temper. After the first emotional outburst by the child, the parent assumes he "inherited" it. Apprehension by the parent may merely encourage the child in his displays of anger. As the tantrums continue, the problem is not one of inheritance, but of unconscious fostering by the parent.

There are overt causes that may not seem so obvious when a child is screaming and kicking. She may be overtired or hungry, her daily routine may have been disturbed to fit the needs of the parent rather than the child or maybe the child has been overstimulated by too much activity and excitement.

One of the major causes is frustration. Too many "don'ts" can eventually build up in a child; even something seemingly as minute as the child wanting a cookie and not getting it. Constantly telling the child what to do rather than occasionally asking, or limiting the child's freedom to release energy may be other causes. There is also the possibility that the child could be sick.

The parent must remember that the child is learning to exert his independence. He may not be very verbal and thus not know how to express his anger in words when his independence is thwarted. The result could be a temper tantrum.

What to Do

The parent must first realize that each child is different. What can be effective with one child may have no effect on another. Parents are also different and their different approaches may be equally effective.

In *How to Parent,* Dr. Dodson tells of some parents who "can stand there and say nothing and wait until the tantrum runs down of its own accord. Others will want to say: 'I know you're frustrated and mad, but you'll need to go to your room until you've finished crying. Then when you're through, I have something interesting to show you.' Others will say sternly: 'Go to your room.'"

As is true in all aspects of child rearing, there is no magic formula here. The primary goal to work toward is preventing the child from hurting himself or others and/or going out of control. It is important not to give in to temper tantrums, because the child may learn to associate this behavior with getting his own way. If the parent gives in, then the child has found an effective method for getting what he wants. He then may have temper tantrums whenever he wants to control the parent.

Carl Williams, in his article entitled "The Elimination of Tantrum Behavior by Extinction Procedures," discusses a twenty-one-month-old child who had been ill for the first eighteen months of life. His health had improved, but the child still desired the special attention he had previously received. At bedtime the child would have a "tyrant-like" tantrum if the parents left the room before he fell asleep. This carrying-on continued every night. Finally, the parents left the room at bedtime and closed the door. The child screamed the first time, screamed a little less the next night, and then accepted the situation and went peacefully to sleep alone. This case is an extreme example of a child using temper tantrums to control a parent. Once the parent does not reinforce the child's behavior by giving in, there is no gain on the child's part for the emotional outbursts.

Trying to remain calm is most often easier said than done. At all times, nonetheless, parents need to remember that they are adults dealing with a child. Shaking, spanking, or screaming at a child bring parents down to child level. Parents soon learn that they will never win an argument with a child by behaving like one. Strong anger and physical punishment usually make the child even angrier.

Try to ignore the tantrum. With some children, leaving them alone may be effective. If there is no audience, there is less incentive to cry. However, a child should never be allowed to hurt himself or others during a tantrum. Occasionally a temper tantrum may occur in a public place, such as a supermarket. Dr. Virginia Pomeranz and Dodi Schultz, in *The First Five Years,* indicate that the basic principles are the same—remain calm and do not give in to your child. You may be embarrassed, but many of the people around have gone through the same experience. Trying to reason with a child who is screaming is most ineffective and frustrating. Wait until your child calms down and then try to talk to her.

Be consistent while still trying to understand in each situation the basis for the child's anger. Whatever method proves effective with your child, try to maintain consistency each time the temper tantrum occurs. Eventually she will realize that she is gaining no ground by her outbursts.

When your child finally calms down, comfort him. Even though you may feel mentally and physically drained, the experience is also very traumatic for your child. Dr. Brazelton, in *Infants and Mothers,* discusses the child's inner turmoil. "The turmoil is based on his developing attempts to sort out 'yes' from 'no,' 'out' from 'in,' 'his' from 'not his.' These are struggles that must be mastered by the child himself."

Can a Tantrum Be Avoided?

Can parents avert a temper tantrum? Parents would be unnatural if they could always maintain their patience. Since most children do go through this stage, it is difficult to avoid. Like all stages the child has gone through so far, the parents should again question how they can help their child with this one.

Sometimes a parent can see "it" coming. Ask yourself if your child is tired, overstimulated, or having her routine broken. Consider whether she is being treated like a baby with no thought or will of her own. By examining each situation the parent might be able to understand the child's temper tantrums and perhaps even avoid some of them.

HOW A CONSCIENCE IS BUILT

The conscience is generally defined as a set of standards of acceptable behavior and prohibitions adopted by the personality that governs behavior from within and results in guilt when violated. Your growing child exhibits his developing conscience when his behavior, formerly so daring and extreme, becomes more cautious and prudent. As Hamlet put it, "Conscience doth make cowards of us all."

Most researchers agree that an internal system of standards that functions without the need of an external policeman does not emerge until about the fifth or sixth year. What immediate relevance, then, has a discussion of conscience to parents of preschoolers?

Selma Fraiberg comments that the modes of parental control that are established in the earliest years of life serve as the patterns of conscience in later years. Thus we can speak of conscience building in the early years before a conscience has appeared.

Dr. Sigmund Freud regarded the development of conscience to be a product of identification. Most authorities view conscience as developing through a youngster's relationship with other people whom she loves, depends on, and takes on as models—usually the parents.

Understanding of the origins and workings of a conscience and an awareness of their own attitudes will enable parents to facilitate the development of a sound conscience in their children.

A child develops a conscience as he incorporates the customs and values of his family, his neighborhood, and his culture into his own inner monitor. Dr. George Gardner, in *The Emerging Personality,* explains, "We can think of the superego or conscience as that process of our inner self which reviews our primitive impulses and evaluates them against the demands of our society."

Values vary in different periods of history, dissimilar cultures, and in disparate groups within each culture. As a result, children grow up with varied external forces molding the shape their developing conscience may take. For example, we are now encouraged to love ourselves, "hangups" and all. Behavior of this sort would have produced guilt a century ago, when great stock was put in self-denial.

Children attain a reliable conscience at different ages. A conscience may be solid in one situation, but shaky or nonexistent in another. Vacillation is to be expected. The preschooler's conscience is similar to a microscopic form of life that after bulging in one direction tends to shrink in another.

Most values are instilled through the small child's observation of the manner in which his or her parents handle situations in their own lives. Tolerance for the feelings and views of others, for instance, grows out of seeing and identifying with the tolerant behavior of the parent during and *after* an encounter with someone whose beliefs are different than those of the family. The development of a healthy conscience is facilitated by the example of adults who carry out their responsibilities without preaching about doing so.

Sometimes small children in their efforts to cope with a confusing world become burdened with guilt over trivial or nonexistent matters. Parents can help their child most if they can diminish such feelings of guilt, yet support her conscience by not making her feel foolish. Statements such as "You did something you feel sorry about and it's okay now" and "Now that you have talked about it, you will feel better," make the child feel both unburdened of guilt and respected for her attempts at trying out her budding conscience.

The following are some ways in which parents can be of definite help in the stages of their child's conscience building. Show faith in her ability to take a new step and become more grown-up. Be reasonably consistent in discipline. Take mistakes in stride. Do not be "preachy," self-righteous, or excessively moralistic when the child has made a mistake or done something of which you do not approve. Avoid an impasse over truthfulness by preventing situations in which untruthfulness would be all too easy. Encourage a realistic inner monitor. Trust your own judgment and gear your expectations to match your child's ability to handle them realistically.

THE CHILD WHO "LIES AND STEALS"

Lying and taking things that belong to others are two common negative behaviors that require sympathetic but firm parental guidance. For preschoolers, these experiences are often a prelude to the incorporation of honesty into their evolving consciences. Like all the other values that collectively make up an inner system of control, honesty is an abstract concept that a young child *gradually* internalizes through his interaction with the world around him. The process of conscience building cannot be rushed. It will take all of the first five years of your child's life before you will see signs of an internal government in his personality.

Only so much can be expected of a child at any point in the process. Imposing a complex code of honesty on a child who is not mature enough to grasp it is like forcing a plant to bloom too early. In dealing with untruthfulness and taking things, parents need to gear their guidance to what the child is realistically capable of understanding.

Ashley Montagu, in his book *On Being Human,* gives the following example: At the age of three, a child may be able to understand the distinction between what belongs to him and what belongs to others, but this does not mean that he really understands honesty. Knowing that a new ball is his sister's does not decrease his desire for it; acquiring it in any way he can is likely to be more important to him than any abstract ideas about honesty.

It would be helpful to look at how a child's view of "honesty" changes as her conscience develops in order to put your expectations into a realistic perspective. At first, a child sees "good" and "bad" solely in terms of herself with no awareness of the needs and rights of others. Whatever gives her pleasure is good and what gives her pain is bad. As the child begins to learn a more advanced code of behavior, she may know that certain acts are "right" or "wrong" because of the approval or disapproval of the parents. However, the child does not yet understand the broader implications of good or bad behavior. Around age four, the child's growing inquisitiveness, characterized by her favorite word "why" sets the stage for her becoming aware of the reasons for the behavior expected of her. Between five and six, she begins to learn ethical behavior at a somewhat abstract level.

The Preschool Years

Pediatricians and child psychologists maintain that when small children of one, two, and three years take things that do not belong to them, it is not stealing. They just take them because they want them very much and they do not have a clear sense beyond this. "A 4-year-old is no more a thief than he is a liar," states Dr. Fitzhugh Dodson. "The 4-year-old has no sense of property rights except for his quaint belief that everything he sees is his property. At this age, possession is ownership."

How should parents approach this situation? Most authorities agree that this is the opportunity to teach the child in a firm, pleasant manner that she is not permitted to take things that do not belong to her. Making the child feel "wicked" is inappropriate and may be harmful.

To separate the "real" from the "pretend" is often all but impossible for a small child. Usually when a child of three or four tells a made-up story, he is not lying. His imagination is vivid to him. You need not jump on him, make him feel guilty, or even be concerned yourself. If, however, these stories make up a major part of his life, it raises the question of whether the child's real life is satisfying enough. Perhaps the remedy will be to help him enjoy companionship with children his own age and with his parents.

Reasons for deviating from the truth are varied. Sometimes what appears to be a falsehood merely reflects a lack of vocabulary. A deeper cause is described by Edith Neisser, in *Primer for Parents of Preschoolers,* when fantasy may be the result of an "overactive" conscience. Children sometimes attribute magical power to their thoughts. As a result of their "bad" wishes or thoughts, children may anticipate that punishment will descend on them, perhaps in the form of an ogre or large animal that "comes in the room at night." Sometimes an explanation of the difference between wishing things and doing things reassures a child and eases his primitive conscience.

PCI Point of View

Probably no one approach can expand conscience during the early years to the point where it will always be strong enough to resist the temptation to take another's possessions or to lie. Occasional lapses will most likely occur. A combination of good example, establishing self-respect, and supplying sufficient parental affection and acceptance will usually produce a reliable conscience.

12

Today's Family

INTRODUCTION BY BELLE PARMET
AND MORRIS PARMET, M.D.*

The nuclear family in contemporary society is under attack and at risk. Certainly the mass media are replete with material describing the family as repressive, cumbersome, and obsolete. The re-echoing chorus underscores the presence of change and upheaval.

Family, being defined as a biological unit that involves a parent or parents caring for offspring, has appeared in every culture and also in non-human species. On the human level this interaction between man and woman and parents and children is not only physical or biological, but simultaneously provides for the development of an integrated person capable of living in society.

It should be noted that the study of the human family in various cultures and in different historical periods teaches us that there is no absolute standard of family function that is universally natural or normal. This perspective should be helpful to us when the voices of doom decry the end of the nuclear family. Our own point of view is that there are many potential strengths within the family that allow for change, innovation, and even radical alteration.

If we view the family as a social system whose function requires

* The Parmets, as a practicing team, have been studying the results of changing family life-styles for over twenty-five years.

Dr. Morris Parmet, a child psychiatrist and associate clinical professor in child psychiatry at Bellevue, New York University, and Rutgers Medical School, has frequently encountered the needs of disturbed children and their parents. In Princeton, New Jersey, he served as consultant to numerous child guidance clinics and schools and has been a president of the New Jersey Mental Health Association. He has published many papers and articles on child psychiatry.

Belle Parmet is a social worker with an M.A. degree from Bryn Mawr. Early in her career she was associated with family service organizations in Philadelphia and Allentown, Pennsylvania. For ten years she was director of psychiatric social work at the Carrier Clinic in Belle Mead, New Jersey. Since 1966, she and her husband have been in private practice as licensed marriage and family counselors and therapists.

boundaries, role definitions, and successful patterns of interaction to maintain its equilibrium, then it is clear that there are societal pressures that affect this stability. Increased urbanization and geographical change, isolation from the extended family, demands for success in a materialistic world, and the concomitant striving for upward social mobility are a few illustrations of this. Even more significant is the whole movement for maximal development of human potential.

In this striving for self-actualization there is considerable consequent social upheaval. Thus currently one out of every three marriages ends in divorce and in 80 per cent of these divorces both partners will remarry. More than ten million children now live with one parent. Multiple styles of family life have come into being that involve one-parent families and two-parent families in which both parents are gainfully employed and share responsibilities of child rearing. Families also encompass biological parents, stepparents, half-siblings, and multiple grandparents. In addition, numerous children are being reared in social arrangements of some impermanence, such as in transient communal groups.

One of the important questions still unanswered involves the cumulative effects on children of their exposure to greater numbers of significant caretakers with varying degrees of emotional depth ranging all the way from meaningful daily encounters with child-care workers to occasional visits with one of their biological parents. In other words, are multiple parent figures positive or negative experiences in the child's psychosocial development?

In this whirlwind of social and personal change, the process of parenthood, the very choice of bearing a child contains an implicit commitment to provide the requisites of appropriate nurture. These include material support, physical protection, as well as the experiences of interaction with significant others in a variety of gradated growth experiences in a supporting, accepting environment. On the other hand, parenthood can also be seen as a developmental process for the parents—with continual personal growth, ego satisfaction, rewards, and disappointments occurring simultaneously with the developmental pattern of the child.

When we speak of the need for stability and continuity in child rearing we speak on behalf of the parent as well as the child. There is no other relationship that requires of a human being such continuous investment in the needs of another. For parents to be capable and comfortable in this role they must have been well nurtured themselves. If there is any rationale for the nuclear family, it is that parents can be nurturing to one another and subsequently to their offspring. Both pleasures and pains, based on primitive and sophisticated needs, can be mutually experienced.

Ideally, in the process of child rearing, a family group will emerge that can meet the individual needs of children and parents in an atmosphere of creative tension. This means in a practical sense that biological, psychological, and social functions will take place on the basis of age-related needs. Finding a balance and a value system that includes individualization and participation, identity and fusion, a system of negotiation of differences, and the provision of affection without exploitation is a very complex task.

Significant questions are emerging that affect these day-to-day issues. As role and sex stereotypes change, as emotional needs are frequently met outside the family, as the time necessary to work out these complicated processes is diminished because of the lessened continuity of parental ties, we need to rethink ways of enabling parents through social supports to receive emotional nurture for themselves so that they do not attempt to work out their own unresolved conflicts through their children.

A system of professional or co-operative child-care services is a beginning requirement. Institutionalized ways of providing surrogate family members, that is, artificial extended families, are being attempted in conjunction with public housing in some communities. Day-care and infant-care programs are being attempted more and more. It has also been our own experience that the process of divorce and remarriage has within it some heretofore unrecognized potentials for positive contributions to the lives of families. The addition of significant and not necessarily blood-related family members often develops for a child a wide range of experiences with people of differing backgrounds, interest, and styles of life. To maximize this potential involves careful attention to arrangements of custody and visitation. It also calls for mature handling of the inevitable rancors of divorce and remarriage that have too often overburdened children with conflicts, guilt, and confusion of loyalties.

There is developing in our own professions a new direction in therapy that likewise has within it the potential for enormous supports for distressed parents and children. This trend involves a proliferation of the family therapies. In contrast to the usual therapeutic focus on individual psychodynamics, there is now a conceptual revolution that involves a view of the family and its discord as a multi-person or a transactional system. Family therapy may occur as a process of intervention at a time of crisis to minimize the destructive sequelae of upheaval. It may also provide an ongoing learning system that deals with the existential reality of the ongoing group process rather than viewing the effect of this process on one individual family member at a time.

Essentially family therapy can bring together the experience of the individual, past and present, and his current functioning with his intimate, ongoing family relationships. But it is more than an information-gathering process. It can be most effective as it facilitates change in this intricate interlocking social system and brings various members of the family into more comfortable equilibrium with one another, underscoring those strengths that the family itself contains.

Is the nuclear family obsolete, repressive, and cumbersome? It appears to be viable, but in the throes of transition. There are many positives on the current scene. More people are entering marriage with greater self-understanding. In the flow toward personal fulfillment, we have greater openness, and more honest and less exploitative relationships. There may be fewer children born, but hopefully they will be cherished rather than abused. Marital partners will be deeply aware of the obligations of childbearing and consciously commit the necessary time and energy to child rearing. We recognize the value for a child of close relationships with adults of each gender. We are beginning to consider the provision of social supports if the family itself cannot provide this opportunity.

As men and women struggle with new ways of validating their own identities, as they achieve a greater sense of personal value, it is perhaps not too utopian to project a time when self-sharing with another can include the experience of nurturing a child. For parenthood, though filled at times with frustrations, disappointments, and unhappiness, is also a time of great personal growth, one of those indefinable peak experiences. The humanity that is developed in this way has no other similar source.

BIRTH ORDER IN THE FAMILY

The term "family constellation" is used to indicate the characteristic relationship of each member of the family to one another. A family with children includes a mother, father, and baby, and among these three a pattern develops with the baby receiving a great deal of attention from the parents. When a second baby arrives, the position of each member changes. Baby is no longer the baby and must establish himself in a new position.

The new baby of the family soon discovers her place as the "baby," but this position has a different meaning to the second child, because now there is an older sibling. If a third child arrives, positions shift once again, and the family constellation develops new interactions and new meanings. As the constellation evolves, each child will find her place in her own way.

Birth Position Myths

OLDEST CHILD

A "man's man"—aggressive, assertive, in control. A higher achiever who leans toward conservatism, is orderly and perfectionistic, accepts authority, and exhibits patterns of dependency. Given a great deal of responsibility for the younger sibling, he chooses a career as a manager or administrator.

MIDDLE CHILD

More outgoing and more overtly competitive and openly aggressive than the big brother or sister the middle child always has to contend with. In performance middle children do not fare so well and do not set quite so high goals for themselves.

447

YOUNGEST CHILD

Daring, imaginative, creative, uneven in performance, and spoiled. The youngest child assumes a privileged position by being born last and clings to it.

THE ONLY CHILD

Much has been written about the only child and usually it is unfavorable, one disadvantage being that he has no siblings and, therefore, does not learn to establish relationships with his peers. He may strive constantly

448

to please adults while trying to reach an adult level or may become an eternal baby always inferior to others. In general, an only child receives much parental attention and may come to expect this attention from others.

However, if you are the parents of an only child, you can encourage group activities, especially those that require give and take with other children. Allow and encourage overnight friends. Do not let your child get used to constant undivided attention. While there is no sibling rivalry for an only child, similar feelings may occur in relation to parents. An only child may align herself with the parent of the same sex for the attention and affection of the other parent.

On the positive side, only children who have had a reasonable balance, who are not kept isolated, can have enrichening experiences in time spent alone. They have the opportunity to learn that being alone can be a rewarding rather than a lonely experience. They may develop more individuality and be less bound to constant outer stimulation.

PCI Point of View

As far as is known, birth order does not limit or define a child's development. It is likely that size and socioeconomic status of the family and the education and occupation of the parents are more influental factors since they do directly relate to child-rearing values and attitudes. When attempting to apply the few tentative findings that exist regarding birth order to one's own family, the following must be taken into consideration: first, the entire family constellation as an interactive unit; second, the sex of each child; and, third, parental attitudes and child-rearing practices.

SIBLING'S REACTIONS TO THE NEW BABY

The Older Child Feels Jealous and Displaced

It is natural for parents to be anxious about the effect of a new baby on their older child. Psychiatrist Alfred Adler formalized the notion of sibling rivalry and the "dethroning" of the first child. While jealousy is the accepted reaction to a sibling, your older child's feelings are probably more complex. In many cases he has been waiting for a long time for a baby brother or sister to play with and instead is presented with a tiny,

wrinkled, red-faced bundle that cannot do much. His disappointment might be heightened if he has been waiting for a brother and instead he now has a sister. At the same time he may experience a feeling of loss. Though he has been prepared for the new arrival, he cannot help but resent sharing your time and energies. He is probably angry at you for getting someone to take his place. Being afraid to show his anger lest he lose you altogether, he directs his anger at his new sibling.

These feelings are the rule and they will find some way of expressing themselves, either in outright physical assaults on the baby (when gentle pats become hits and squeezes) or more subtly in suggestions that the baby be returned to the hospital. Frequently the older child regresses to earlier infant ways in order to compete with the baby on the baby's level. If you want a baby, she will be it. Then, too, she may become noisy and aggressive in her demands for attention or withdraw into silence in order to hide her hurt and angry feelings.

Preparing Your Child

Much of this resentment can be minimized if you begin ahead of time to prepare your child for the new baby's arrival. Your firstborn's life should be uprooted as little as possible. Preparation should be for physical as well as psychological change.

Furniture and room changes should take place several months ahead of time so she feels she is moving on rather than being pushed out of her place.

How you prepare your child depends on her age, understanding, and temperament. Children have a hazy concept of time. At two, your child has little sense of the future. If she is older, she may become bored and disappointed by unending references to the coming event. If she is old enough, it is best to include her in discussions and plans. Thus the baby will become the family's baby. (However, do not tell her before you are ready for the neighborhood to know. You cannot expect a toddler to keep this good news to herself.)

How Do Babies Grow?

Experts agree that it is a good idea for a child to know that the baby is growing inside his mother and to feel it move. If your child asks questions, answer him truthfully and simply. You need not be too graphic with two- or three-year-olds. You might say, "Mommies have a special place

451

inside where babies grow until they are ready to be born," and add that a doctor usually helps a baby get born.

Separation

In addition, it is wise to prepare your child for your stay at the hospital. This is an especially difficult time for the first child. The current trend in hospitals is to keep mother and new baby a minimum of time, and some permit the older child to visit. It is suggested that a friend, relative, or housekeeper be available for this period of time so that the older child's normal routines are maintained.

Bringing the Baby Home

The new baby will take up a good deal of your time. One psychologist prepared his child for a new sibling by accenting the negative; the child would have less time with his parents, there would be much crying, and he would be needed to help in caring for the baby. A couple of weeks after the baby came home the child announced that having a baby around was not nearly so bad as he had expected.

Bringing the baby home is an exciting and joyous occasion for the entire family and while some feel it would be easier for you if your older child were not at home, the Princeton Center feels that he *should* play a part at this time.

From the start, help the older child to get to know the newborn. Let her touch, unwrap, and hold the baby (with help) if she wants to. A toddler can help bathe and dry a baby and rock the baby to sleep. You will quickly discover that newborns do not break easily. By allowing the older child to help, you are doing things together and encouraging her to feel grown-up.

Visitors

Sometimes visitors, especially grandparents, unknowingly hurt your older child. They are eager to see the new baby and bring presents. Some are thoughtful enough to bring something for your older child, but if they do not, it is a good idea to have small gifts on hand. If conversation seems exclusively about the baby, it is up to you to draw your older child into the conversation.

Treat Firstborns as Individuals

Firstborns need the help of the parents to realize that even though there is a baby in the house and they now have to share the parents, they are not less loved. They have a special place in the family as the older one and the baby can never take this place.

Hard as it is, it is best to play down the new baby. When possible tend to your baby's needs when your older child is at school or outside playing. See that your firstborn's established interests and companions are maintained. Do not put off his reasonable requests with a steady "In a minute," "Later," "I'm busy with the baby." Arrange time for just taking him to places the baby is too young for.

Avoid Comparisons

Each child is different and develops in his own way. This is a principle to be followed throughout your child's growing up. When you make comparisons someone always loses.

If the Older Child Regresses

You should tolerate lapses into baby behavior. If your firstborn wants a bottle, too, there is no harm in indulging her. It will not last. Nor will toilet-training accidents. You can help by rewarding mature behavior so your child will want to be herself again—not the baby. However, you should not tolerate overt resentment in the form of hitting, grabbing, or pulling the baby. Reassure your older child that you love her very much, but will not let her hurt the baby.

Siblings Teach Babies

All the research points to the fact that children learn with great efficiency and ease from their peers. Schools are capitalizing on this, to wit, the open classroom. Observant parents have always known this to be so. Little ones exhibit long attention spans when it is their older sibling who is reading or singing to them. They watch intently in order to join in the song. The older child enjoys being idolized—smiled at, etc.—and eventually comes to love and regard the little one as a part-time playmate.

PCI Point of View

You must take cues from your child to help him overcome negative reactions. While you can help, he will have to come to terms with the baby himself. As your children grow they will work out their own relationship. If you do not constantly interfere, it is likely that they will work out a partnership rather than a rivalry.

TWINS

Parental attitude toward twins is the most important factor in developing their individuality, meeting their specific needs, and coping with the extra physical work involved in raising twins. Twins' physical care both in infancy and early childhood is something that should be governed not by regulation, but by common sense. A most essential ingredient is a husband who is patient and understanding and not afraid of a wet diaper or doing the dishes. As with anything else, one's attitude on approaching a situation more or less defines the situation. If twins can be viewed as a cheerful, joint effort, much of the trauma they usually generate will be diminished.

During the infancy of their twins, many parents are so overwhelmed by the work load and the exhaustion they encounter trying to keep up with it that they often feel consumed. Dr. Spock offers a comprehensive list of suggestions for coping with this problem in his *Baby and Child Care* book. The recurring theme in his discussion of twins is *shortcuts*.

The Twin Mothers' Club of Bergen County, New Jersey, agrees with Dr. Spock (in their book *And Then There Were Two*) not only about devices, but also with regard to saving energy. Housecleaning, an example cited in both books, need not be done as meticulously as perhaps it once was, nor as often. The Twin Mothers are mindful that "there will always be dust. They won't always be babies." A relaxed, rested mother is far more important than an empty ironing basket or a freshly waxed floor!

Development

Twins, both identical and fraternal, are individuals and have different growth rates. One twin may crawl and walk earlier; the other may talk earlier. This has important implications for the parents of twins. They need to recognize and work with these differences.

Most of the studies done on twin development have concentrated on identical twins, dismissing fraternal twins as merely two siblings who happen to have been born at the same time. However, authors Vincent and Margaret Gaddis point out in their book *The Curious World of Twins* that two out of every three sets of twins born are fraternal.

In their book *Child Behavior,* Dr. Frances L. Ilg and Louise Bates Ames write about sibling rivalry, a problem of special importance when twins are of the opposite sex and maturing at different rates. Here language and individuality are compounded by a usually dominant, more rapidly developing girl. (Non-twin females usually develop faster than male children, too.)

Individuality

Emphasis on individuality is the most important aspect of twin development. Experts in child rearing do not recommend rhyming names, identical clothes and toys, or shared classrooms. Twins will have different mannerisms, abilities, likes, dislikes, and friends, and parents need to encourage this. It is important that each child develop positive feelings of uniqueness. Parents should react to each child as a separate entity and avoid viewing their twins as a set.

THE WORKING MOTHER

To work or not to work, that is the question facing so many young mothers today. Increasing numbers of young mothers are choosing employment. For some, there is no choice; their income may either supplement or completely support the family financially. But for many others, the need to find employment outside the home is an emotional one. The young mother may feel cut off from interaction with other adults; that she is wasting her years of higher education and varied talents by staying at home; or she may feel frustrated by her daily child-rearing and house-keeping chores. A mother should review her reasons for working, but she should not feel guilty about recognizing her own needs as an individual.

A 1973 study of the effects of maternal employment on children confirmed that mothers who are satisfied with their roles—whether working or not—have the best-adjusted children. The idea of a mother having a career besides motherhood is gaining ever increasing popularity. The Women's Rights Movement has given expression to the varied needs of women to find fulfillment. Mothers who resent or get boxed in on full-time child care should not stay home out of a sense of guilt or fear of short-changing their children. Dissatisfaction with one's life gets transmitted to the child and can be of greater potential damage than mother's absence.

Sara Gilbert states, "If a mother must or strongly wants to work outside the home, there is no reason why, for the baby's sake, she shouldn't, as long as she plans for his needs with the same loving, intelligent interest she would give those needs if she were at home."

Baby's Needs

The foremost consideration, of course, is the baby's need for a consistently dependable mothering figure. Pediatricians and child psychologists agree that there must be one constant person for the baby to rely on for help, comfort, learning, and attachment. According to *The First Twelve Months of Life.* "A baby is less likely to form a strong, close bond with another human being if no one has ever had one with him." Studies of attachment behavior in infants and preschoolers indicate that strength of at-

456

tachment to the mother is a result of the *quality* and *intensity* of mother–child interactions rather than the sheer availability of the mother or the number of caretakers.

In his new book *The Natural Way to Raise a Healthy Child,* psycho-analyst Hiag Akmakjian discusses all the common child-rearing topics, including the working mother, from a mental health point of view. It is Dr. Akmakjian's opinion that the mother should stay home during the first two years of her baby's life. He bases this advice on psychological principles. Growing babies need the dependable closeness that only the mother can provide. He writes, "Babies care deeply to have their mother at their side most of the time." The working mother (no matter who her substitute is) is depriving her baby of a relationship that is intense and deep and critical to her baby's future security.

Unless it is necessary for financial reasons, it seems desirable that a mother should not take on an outside job during the first two years of her baby's life. However, if this is necessary, a substitute mother is needed: one individual, loving person on whom baby can depend for the personal, special care she has the right to expect. The mother substitute should concern herself not only with the baby's physical well-being, but also with her mental and social progress.

The baby learns so many basics between the third and twelfth months that mother's absence at this time can be damaging to the baby's development. The mother substitute must be competent, dependable, warm, and loving, but also have verbal capacities and training to further the infant's language acquisition and his self-image.

If you have decided to return to work, then consider all aspects carefully:

1. Return gradually—part-time—and, if possible, build up your hours away from home gradually.

2. If your husband works out of the community, you should work nearby, so that if necessary you can be reached and available.

3. Hire a permanent baby-sitter.

4. Some experts suggest that you postpone returning to work when the baby is between fifteen and eighteen months (a normal period of separation anxiety) or if the family has recently undergone a crisis (divorce, illness, death).

5. Special problems to be dealt with:
Children's vacations
Children's illness
Children's resentment

Look for symptoms such as withdrawal, overaggressiveness, depression, and not eating in preschoolers. Older children can directly tell you how they feel. Sensitive parents will alter their schedules to assure that their children's needs are met.

Child Care

There are many possibilities for good child care. One obvious choice is the father. If he is self-employed or has a flexible work schedule, or would prefer taking care of the children, the child-care problem may be solved.

Another obvious choice is grandparents or other relatives if they are living nearby and are eager and able to cope physically and emotionally. Grandparents can provide warmth, security, and loving care for a baby. However, some grandparents might not be a good choice if they strongly disapprove of the mother's working, use unacceptable discipline methods, or criticize the parents' methods of child rearing.

Day care for infants is available in some communities, although frequently only older, "toilet-trained" children are eligible. Sometimes there are long waiting lists to contend with. Often the working mother can find another mother who truly delights in child care and who is willing to care for another infant or child, in addition to her own. Arranging for good child care is a challenge, but not an insurmountable obstacle.

Effects of Maternal Employment on Older Children

The effects of maternal employment on infants and preschoolers are related to the provision of stable and stimulating caretaking arrangements. No clear-cut evidence has emerged to discourage mothers of school-age children from working provided good child-care arrangements can be made. Older children of working women tend to have more household responsibilities; there are few differences in the leisure activities of children with working and non-working mothers; mothers in professional occupations tend to have highly achieving children. Educational aspirations generally are higher among both sons and daughters of working mothers.

In the opinion of Dr. Joseph Church, "Children of school age . . . are likely to benefit from having a working mother . . . During the school years, the child can take an increasing share in the actual running of the house. We are coming back to a realization that for many years middle-class childhood was a period of regal self-indulgence and over-indulgence, which is not good preparation for life; we are rediscovering that giving children responsibilities that they can manage—and for all their seeming incompetence they can manage quite a few—benefits them."

Financial Considerations

Another consideration of the working mother is simply a financial one. Will the salary earned cover the cost she incurs? First, there is the cost of child care and possibly help with the housework. Dr. Joseph Church states, "Skilled day-care workers cannot be had for a song . . . nor can the physical facilities needed for a sound operation—ample quarters, good climate control, the right kinds of bathrooms and kitchens, the right sorts of play equipment and toys, the necessary safety measures, access to outdoor play areas. Harassed and underpaid workers are not likely to be good for your child, and even capable workers cannot do much without adequate facilities. Thus, if you are counting on a day-care center to play substitute mother while you work, please be aware that good day care is almost certain to be expensive."

Other financial considerations include the cost of transportation, clothing, and meals away from home. After these expenses, will there be enough money left over to make working worthwhile? Consider, too, whether the income earned will put your family in a higher tax bracket, thus defeating any financial gain you may have made.

Managing Household Tasks

There are many popular books and articles related to streamlining household tasks and efficient household management for working mothers. A real asset, however, is a co-operative, encouraging husband, willing to share responsibilities. Helpful children also contribute a great deal. The working mother should be wary of attempting to do all the housework, shopping, and laundry herself out of any sense of guilt or subconscious role expectation. Co-operation and planning are obviously important factors for the success and happiness of the working mother.

PCI Point of View

We would encourage you to stay at home for the first two years of your baby's life and become a full-time professional parent. When your child is over two, you may resume your former career, if you so desire, and you will not experience debilitating feelings of doubt and guilt once you do make this decision.

BABY-SITTERS

Baby-sitters are people most parents have to contend with at some time in our modern world. Whether they are a treasure or a trial depends on the care we put into their selection and the way we communicate our expectations to them. With the increased mobility of families, parents may be forced to rely upon unfamiliar baby-sitters. When you know your baby is in good hands you can enjoy yourself and return home with more enthusiasm to cope with your everyday routines.

Dr. Brazelton writes the following about the three-month-old baby: "This is a time for some 'sitting' help. A mother needs a chance to get out of the house and both parents need to feel together again. This is a common time for fathers to pull away. They tire of their wives' involvement in the infant. Each parent could be refueled with a little pleasure together, which is now important to their lives as a family."

How to Select a Good Sitter

"Sitter" is really a misnomer, because the best sitters do not sit. You want a person with some understanding of your baby's needs. Almost anyone can take care of physical needs, but you will want a warm, understanding person to take care of his emotional needs as well.

In some neighborhoods parents can easily observe young teen-agers and select one who is mature and well-adjusted. Personal recommendations from your friends and neighbors are other guidelines to use. Age and sex are not the important criteria; the individual's personality and maturity are. A fine sitter can be eighty years old or a terrific sixth grader. Some of the youngest sitters are thrilled with the opportunity to hold and care for a baby, whereas their older sisters or brothers may be somewhat bored with the whole thing.

461

Although children's needs differ at various ages, some basic qualities are necessary in all sitters: (1) maturity and competence (this includes the ability to handle emergencies), (2) reliability, (3) patience, (4) flexibility and imagination, (5) ease in handling children. You may find it helpful in evaluating a sitter to invite him or her to come and play with your children while you are at home.

Some parents find good sitters by calling the offices of nursing schools or colleges in their area. Some cities have professional baby-sitting services, although these usually charge a high fee.

There are baby-sitters who care for children in their own homes. Different states have their own licensing procedures for these homes ranging from no laws to strict regulations. This situation should be checked out carefully for all ages, but especially in the case of a baby or toddler. You should evaluate the home atmosphere, the play and rest areas, how many other children will be cared for, and any potential safety hazards.

Your Responsibilities to the Baby-sitter and the Sitter's Obligations to You

When you leave the baby, you should instill in the mind of the sitter that his safety is the major responsibility. The National Safety Council reports that home accidents kill more children than all the childhood diseases combined. In 1969, 5,700 children under fifteen years of age died due to home accidents. These most frequently happen to impetuous children who are not watched closely and those who are tired, hungry, or emotionally upset. Allow enough time for the sitter and your baby to become acquainted and for the sitter to become acquainted with the house. Some parents whose babies put up a great deal of fuss when they leave mistakenly feel their exit will be smoother if the baby is already in bed. However, if the baby should awaken and find a stranger in your place, he may associate going off to sleep with losing you. Even when a baby is too young to know the difference, it is good to get into the habit of introductions, a kiss, and a "bye-bye."

Let the sitter know: (1) Where you can be reached in case of an emergency or the telephone number of a close neighbor who could be of some assistance. (2) The telephone number of your doctor and the fire department. (3) What and when to feed the baby. Try to anticipate any problems that could arise and suggest possible solutions. (4) Specific details about your house—where things are kept, how to adjust the thermostat, how to lock the doors and windows, and *not* to unlock the door to strangers under any circumstances. (5) When you will return. Especially when you hire teen-age baby-sitters, you should inquire what hour they are expected home, for they have parents who worry, too. (6) What food is available for them to eat. Important reminders should be written down. Even the most astute mind can be confused by a lot of last-minute instructions.

PCI Point of View

This section has dealt mainly with temporary or part-time sitters, not those who will provide the major care of your baby. If you need a permanent caretaker, you will want to investigate more thoroughly before you hire her so the baby will not have to make a series of adjustments to new sitters. You will want to make sure that the sitter's basic child-rearing beliefs agree with yours. Even in the case of a part-time sitter, it is wise to limit yourself to one or two special people as regular sitters. They will get to know the special needs of your baby and respond to them. An older woman can be a substitute grandmother.

CHILD-CARE ALTERNATIVES: PLAY GROUPS AND BABY-SITTING POOLS

Play Groups

Many parents are currently experimenting with a relatively new idea in child care—the play group. The play group can be highly structured or very informal, but it is used as an alternative or precursor to the nursery school and is carefully planned by the parents so a regular schedule will be maintained.

The purpose of a play group is to provide the two-, three-, or four-year-old with companions her own age to interact and play with. Most parents recognize that as their children mature they display increasing curiosity about other children and actively seek out peers with whom to play. They also discover that household chores or other responsibilities often interfere with their supervision of spontaneous play groups that may form in their own back yards.

The Formal Play Group

Parents carefully organize this play group before it begins. A supervisor is selected to co-ordinate activities and mediate problems should they occur. She handles problems of illness and special projects. All the parents discuss what activities should be stressed, safety, snacks, accidents, toys, materials, frequency of the play group meetings, and transportation. A formal play group attempts to provide an atmosphere similar to the one the children would encounter in the standard nursery school.

The informal play group may have many similarities to the formal play group, except the purpose is to provide as much free play as possible. The informal play group may have less "teacher (parent)-structured" activities, such as cooking, crafts, etc., whereas the formal play group has "teacher" supervision as a regulatory factor almost all the time.

The laws pertaining to play groups in your area should be checked by calling a local agency (Social Services, for example) or by calling a lawyer. Often state licensing is required if you have more than five children in your house at one time on a regular basis.

Unlike the nursery school that has many teachers and children, the ideal number of children for a play group seems to be five or six in one house under the supervision of one parent.

Parents who have participated in a play group feel that the five children should be approximately the same age so the types of play and art work made available can be enriching to all the children. They also feel twice a week for two to three hours is plenty.

How the play group is organized depends on the people involved, but the play group does provide playmates for your children and if you take the play group for two days one week, you are free those same mornings for the four following weeks.

Harriet M. Watts, in her book *How to Start Your Own Preschool Playgroup* presents many helpful hints about how to get started without making a lot of mistakes. She shares with you her ideas about what activities are appropriate for different age levels and outlines the basic organization of one play group in which she was active.

Some Hints for Play Groups

1. *Transportation:* Each parent would drive her child to the destination (or a car pool could be formed); the parent in charge would drive them back; that way the session would terminate promptly without waiting for latecomers.

2. *Health:* Never take a sick child to the play group. Children of preschool age are highly susceptible to each other's germs. In case your child should become sick while at the play group, you should always leave the telephone of your child's doctor, and where you can be reached.

3. *Equipment:* Before the play group begins, make sure you have a low table where all five can sit comfortably, plenty of transportation vehicles, crayons, blocks, puzzles, paper, glue, paints, scissors, etc.

4. *Discipline:* Discuss this beforehand with all the adults. A good rule to follow is "Scold and let scold," each in her own way. It is often good for a young child to be exposed to different methods of discipline.

5. *Snacks:* The supervisor can provide a light snack midway through the session or each child can bring his own. Find out if there are any allergies.

6. *First Aid:* A refresher first aid course is highly recommended.

Baby-sitting Pools

If you have decided your child is too young for a play group, or perhaps you have an infant and you need or want some free time during the week, a baby-sitting pool might be the answer for you. Many parents find it impossible to find a sitter during the day. Why not take turns?

Once again it is a good idea to have a supervisor to keep track of the hours you all baby-sit for each other. A list with each member's name, address, and telephone number is given to each participant and she is free to call anyone on the list. When one sits so many hours, she calls and reports to the supervisor, who, for this service, gets so many free hours of baby-sitting. She might also recommend people to call; someone who owes a lot of hours, for example.

Hints For Operating a Baby-sitting Pool

1. Each parent takes her baby to the baby-sitter's house.

2. Never leave a sick baby.

3. Give explicit instructions for care and provide all food, diapers, and toys.

4. Outline exactly where you can be reached the whole time and if you change your mind about your destination, be sure to report it to the baby-sitter.

5. Give spouse's office and work phone numbers and the number of the baby's doctor.

6. A refresher first aid course for all involved is highly recommended.

7. If it works during the day, it can also work in the evenings.

If you need ideas for related projects or wish to review child care, your local library has many books to help you. The play group and baby-sitting pool are two alternatives to the standard nursery school and pay-as-you-go baby-sitter. The former are free, provide valuable stimulation for your preschooler, and give you some precious time to yourself.

SELECTING A DAY-CARE CENTER

If parents accept the reality that each preschool child requires constant individual attention and daily routines which overburdened mothers or working parents cannot always supply, then quality day-care centers can contribute greatly to strengthening family life. They can fulfill the needs of both the children and the family.

A day-care center is as good as the caretaker who works there. She must earn the trust of her charges by being sensitive to their moods, feelings, and needs. She must always be conscious of how the children respond to what she does with them.

Parental participation is fundamental to a successful operation. Parents and teachers need to exchange information about the child's behavior, his likes and dislikes, and his health on a regular basis.

We have learned at least two things from Head Start: remedial programs must begin before the child is three years of age and the parents must be involved in these programs. A day-care center that provides the child with a good initial learning experience and social stimulation is offering an opportunity that many children would not receive from their mothers. Even if the mother were at home and had the time available, chances are she would not have the educational background to offer her child the stimulation he needs.

Should a mother feel guilty about wanting to send her toddler to a day-care center? Is a day-care center as good as home care? Is day care *only* for working mothers? Dr. Bruno Bettelheim, a distinguished child psychiatrist, disagrees. "I feel that it is too narrow to think of Day Care Centers merely for mothers who have to work or as therapeutic centers for underprivileged children. Day Care can do a vital job for *all* mothers and *all* children. There is no doubt that mother is the most important person for a child but we are aware of too intense a mother–child attachment. . . . We need to find a better balance between home care and day care. . . . A child feels much better about himself and the world if he spends part of the day in a planned setting that exists only for him."

The real difficulty with day-care centers is not that they separate mother and child, but that there are so few good ones. The modern mother has considerable need for time by herself. If she has her own time, she can more easily and happily relate to her child. A child, too, needs to go his own way.

Syracuse University has set up a day-care center for children beginning at six months of age. The center began as an experiment to show how "culturally determined mental retardation" could be prevented among children from disadvantaged areas. It deliberately tried to stimulate the child's intellectual development by offering a highly individualized type of care. The experiment proved that the children thrive and that their IQ score increased with time (rather than the reverse, which usually happens with these children).

The study also demonstrated that early day-care experience with its attendant separation from the mother does not lead to emotional insecurity. Conversely, inadequate day care may be harmful and nothing is worse than a series of caretakers. A child needs one person to identify with as the mothering figure.

Educators agree that in addition to complying with local safety regulations, a good day-care center should have a cheerful environment, good equipment, and well-trained, loving teachers, as well as:

1. Forty to fifty square feet of indoor space per child.
2. One hundred square feet of enclosed outdoor space per child.
3. A nourishing lunch and frequent snacks available.
4. A place to nap with privacy and a cot for each child.
5. Medical attention at the center, as well as home care when the child is too sick to attend class.
6. Diapers and changing tables.
7. Furniture and toilet facilities adapted to the child's height.
8. Two to three adults available to each group of eight to ten children.
9. Ample storage space for the child's clothes and toys.
10. Mandatory parent participation.

Day Care and Early Education, an informative magazine presenting a broad range of topics to the concerned working mother, is available by writing 2852 Broadway, New York, N.Y. 10025 ($1.50 an issue or $9.00 a subscription).

Private industry is beginning to enter the day-care field, realizing that providing day care increases their available work force and aids in retaining their employees. Day-care facilities cut down on expensive absenteeism and permit a woman to work full time instead of part time. Without day-care centers, many mothers could not work and as a result would be on welfare.

Expense

Providing good day-care service is expensive, but what better opportunity do we have for offering children of low-income families educational and health facilities where they are most needed?

The federal government makes funds available to state public welfare agencies under Title IV of the Social Security Act. Other funds may be obtained from state and local public welfare agencies.

PCI Point of View

Children who are taught how to learn, to use their senses to their best advantage, and to express themselves in their early years are more likely to function successfully in any classroom. In fact, day-care services should be available to all families so a child can have experiences that supplement the ones provided by the home. Our children are our best investment and richest resources!

HOW TO SELECT A PRESCHOOL

In selecting a preschool, parents are sometimes bewildered by the variety of different programs available, as well as the differences in methods, materials, and goals. Many preschools have no "formal information sheets" describing their educational philosophies, so the astute parent must visit the various programs and observe the classes in session. Before making a final selection, you should discuss the program in detail with the teacher. You should not hesitate to ask questions. It is much better to ask questions than to enroll your child in a program you are not comfortable with.

Matching a Preschool Program to Your Child

First of all, the preschool program you select for your child should not conflict greatly with your own philosophy of child rearing. If you tend to be a "permissive" parent, you probably would not choose to enroll your child in a structured preschool program. If you encourage independence, self-discipline, and responsibility, you probably would be unhappy to have your child in a very "permissive" or "anything-is-okay" school. Similarly, you must consider your child's personality and tendencies.

Also, you should consider the number of children in the class, their ages, and the child–adult ratio. How much individual attention does your child need? Most nursery schools use chronological age grouping while many Montessori schools use mixed-age grouping.

In evaluating a preschool, you should look carefully at its program. Is there a daily routine followed by allotted time periods for free play, snack, story time, rest time, etc. or is most of the time unstructured?

Does the teacher insist that all the children join the group during certain activities—group singing, story time or snack time? What is included in the *content* of the curriculum? (Are there science experiments, nature study, animals, pre-reading and pre-math activities, etc.?) Can you judge how much pre-planning takes place? How many new projects are planned and how many trips are taken? Is the program organized into units (farms, community workers, foods, etc.)? Does the program incorporate special events and special visitors?

Are there special teachers to enrich the program (music, science, art, foreign language)? What is the music program: singing, rhythm instruments, Montessori sensory training, Orff and Kodály music methods? What is the structure of the program, formal or informal, i.e., do the teachers instruct the class as a whole? Is a great deal of spontaneous learning taking place?

What are the opportunities for group interaction and for dramatic and social play? This varies with the goals of the particular preschool. Are there opportunities for individual play and concentration? How is snack time handled, as a group social time (everyone altogether) or individually at any time during the preschool day, as in many Montessori programs? How is rest time handled and moving from one activity to the next?

What *values* are stressed in the program: sharing, co-operation, cleanliness, routines, etc.? Are the children encouraged to learn to do things for themselves? Finally, are fathers encouraged to become involved in the program in any way?

The Staff

It is important that you feel some rapport with your child's potential teachers. You should feel comfortable with the way the teachers are handling the children. You should feel satisfied with their "education approach" and their competency.

Do they in any way seem "overwhelmed" by the classroom situation? What are their methods of "discipline," of modifying the unacceptable behavior of a child? How well do they handle disputes among the children?

Do the teachers interact with the children as individuals or is the majority of their time spent dealing with small groups of children? Are teachers tuned in to the "room as a whole," as well as individual children? Are they warm without "smothering" them with affection? Are they genuine with the children? How do the children respond to the staff?

Discipline and Behavior

What kinds of behavior are encouraged and what are the limits on a child's behavior? How is discipline handled and how effective does it seem? How much pressure is put on the child "conforming," joining the group, and learning to "get along" with the group? Does the teacher allow for a child's individuality? How are the children helped to grow? Do the teachers encourage the children to learn to do things by and for themselves? Do the teachers genuinely listen to the children when they are talking or are they busy "getting something ready" for the next project?

How do the children interact with one another?

Atmosphere

How would you describe the atmosphere in the classroom? Is it chaotic, spontaneous, controlled, or stilted? Do the children seem happy? Do you feel their social, cognitive, and affective needs are being met? Do the children seem bored, restless, or overstimulated by the program?

Physical Equipment and Surroundings

Look carefully at the physical surroundings. Are they clean and inviting? Are the children learning to handle the equipment with respect or are they behaving destructively? Are the books and puzzles accessible and attractive? Are the children encouraged to clean up after themselves; to put their own toys, books, and materials back on the shelves? Is there enough of a *variety* of stimulating materials accessible to meet the changing interests of the children? Are the materials varied during the school year?

Outdoors, is the equipment safe, supervised, adequately spaced, and attractive? Are the children able to move freely from indoors to out or does the group as a whole have an "indoor time" and an "outdoor time"?

Indoors and outdoors, is there opportunity for sand play, water play, and other "messy" activities? Is there a variety of art materials available at all times or only during art "lessons"? Are the art "projects" appropriate for the preschool child or are they teacher-designed to "take home and

470

impress mama and papa"? Is there enough physical space inside, as well as some indoor provision for rainy day, large-muscle exercise and play?

What is the physical arrangement of the room? Are there activity areas: a doll corner, a housekeeping corner, an art area, a place for water and sand play, toys, blocks, puzzles, a workbench, a comfortable book corner, records, child-sized tables and chairs?

No two preschool programs will ever be exactly alike. The most important variable is the teacher. You should feel she is genuinely enjoying her work with young children. You should see whether she acts as a caretaker or as a sensitive person who enters into the play life of the group and enhances the learning. The second most important variable is the physical space and equipment.

COMPARING PRESCHOOL CURRICULUMS

During the 1960s, the idea that mental growth and intelligence depend in part on early intellectual stimulation led to an increased cognitive emphasis in early childhood education. The "child development-type" nursery school, with its emphasis on social-emotional growth through play and the creative arts, was criticized and parents began to explore other preschool alternatives. Today there are probably a variety of preschool curriculums in your neighborhood. Familiarity with the goals, methods, and materials of these programs will help you select the "right" preschool experience for your child.

However, an important point to keep in mind is that although schools may share a common name (e.g., Montessori), stated goals, or certain materials, they may have very different "atmospheres." This results from the variety of teachers and their individual methods and philosophies of education. There is *no* typical Montessori school or typical nursery school. It is essential, therefore, to visit the specific programs you are considering, spend some time observing the groups of children during a session, and discuss the program with the teacher afterward.

Many preschool curriculums share similar long-range goals. For example, both Montessori and more traditional nursery schools are philosophically dedicated to the optimum development of the individual child. Although both share this goal, their materials and methods are quite different.

This child in a Montessori class is working with cylinders which, when shaken, produce sounds varying from loud to soft. The aim is to help the child refine auditory discrimination.

The Montessori Preschool

A world-renowned innovator in education, Maria Montessori was born in Chiaravalle, Italy, in 1870, the only child of cultivated parents. She spent her life observing children and developing a system of manipulative materials that enables a child to master increasingly difficult sensory tasks, such as sequencing, matching, ordering, counting, fine motor development, etc. Dr. Montessori designed materials to prepare children for present and future learning. The materials isolate sensory attributes and permit the child's progress from the simple to the complex. They are self-correcting and thereby eliminate the need for outside evaluation.

Visitors to Montessori classrooms are often impressed with the "prepared" environment. Children are usually working very intently individually or in small groups and are free to work with a material as long as they choose. Then they return the material to its proper place. The environment is aesthetically attractive and ordered. The role of the Montessori directress is not to teach, but carefully and scientifically to observe the child and introduce materials when he is ready for them. She serves as a resource person and a catalyst.

One aspect of Maria Montessori's pedagogical understanding and contribution to learning is her recognition of and respect for individual differences. The Montessori classroom is a "prepared environment" in which each child is free to learn. The Montessori method seeks to develop an inner discipline that comes from interaction with a wide assortment of "self-corrective" learning materials and tasks that provide a physical "manipulative" base for grasping number concepts, mastering shape, form and color, experimentation with musical tone bars and sound, and so on. There are some parents who have mistakenly interpreted these materials as "early academics" instead of recognizing them as sensory challenges and experiences.

Other important aspects of the Montessori method include:

1. Heterogeneous grouping by age.
2. Emphasis on reality (as opposed to fantasy).
3. A respect for nature.
4. Emphasis on structure and order.
5. The co-ordination of motor and mental activity.
6. Clearly set limits against destructive and asocial actions.
7. Daily life exercises (physical care of child and surroundings), sensorial exercises, and academic exercises.
8. Correlation between "sensitive periods" of learning and maturation of bodily skills.

Traditional Nursery School

By comparison, "free, imaginative, fantasy play" is usually the most important activity in the traditional nursery school. Social and emotional growth through play has been its primary goal. Building a positive self-image comes from construction play with blocks; creativity, from painting, clay work, collage, and dancing in the traditional nursery school.

However, in response to criticism of a lack of cognitive stimulation and academic preparation, many nursery schools are now redefining their goals, restructuring their programs, and attempting to provide more learning stimulation. In addition to the now familiar activity areas (a housekeeping and doll corner, an art area with double easels, blocks, an outside play area with hollow blocks, a sandbox, jungle gym, tricycles, etc.), there may be a puzzle and game table and an inviting book corner. Some nursery schools even have Montessori materials available.

Many nursery schools have more specific and planned curriculums that include learning about community workers, animals, the seasons, nature, etc. Still other nursery schools have become "prekindergarten" programs with reading readiness, workbooks, etc.

In general, nursery schools have:

1. Chronological age grouping and an emphasis on maturational development (age norms).

2. Emphasis on *process* (process of playing, process of experimenting with art materials, etc.).

3. Physical space divided into "activity centers" or zones (i.e., doll corner, dress-up corner, etc.).

4. Emphasis on vigorous, unstructured "free" dramatic play and self-expression.

5. Emphasis on socialization and affective growth.

6. Emphasis on peer group interaction and emotional ties to the teacher.

7. Some teacher-directed activities (group singing and games, community trips, and storytelling, etc.).

8. Concern with large-muscle development.

The major differences in the two approaches are:

1. The Montessori program puts less stress on play and more on structured sensory exercises and achievements.

2. The Montessori method allows the child to move into early reading and writing at his own pace. Most nursery schools have reading readiness materials, but do not include formal reading activities.

Another completely different approach to preschool education is that of Carl Bereiter and Siegfried Engelmann. Their emphasis is on improving language skills and they employ a strict drill-and-rote approach. Although their program was originally designed for "disadvantaged" children, it is receiving attention in middle-class areas as well.

PCI Point of View

As more parents are becoming informed, interested, and involved in preschool education, preschool programs are enriching their curriculums to meet more of the needs of the preschool child. This diversity of programs is stimulating and permits parents to be more selective in the preschool education of their children.

SINGLE-PARENT FAMILIES

Single-parent families are a result of adoption, separation, divorce, death, and unwed parenthood. Being a single parent offers special challenges and special rewards; you have complete freedom to choose and control the influences that affect your child's development.

The Child's Needs

A STRONG, CONSISTENT HOME LIFE

One of the first challenges that must be dealt with is the attitude of your friends, relatives, and other associates toward you and your child's special status. Overindulgent, overprotective, and apologetic attitudes do not provide a strong foundation for a well-adjusted individual, adult or child. Although these attitudes will be encountered by your child from time to time, it is important for your child's well-being that they not be indulged in at home.

Growing up with two parents can and often does have some built-in hazards and few professionals will say that children of single-parent families will be particularly handicapped psychologically. A good relationship with one parent is better than growing up with two discontented parents.

REALISTIC HUMAN ATTITUDES

Embittered single parents who harbor deep feelings of resentment toward their former partners can do irreparable damage to a child if their hurt and anger are directed to everyone of the opposite sex. A child has not yet developed an understanding of the complex problems and emotions that occur during adulthood. You are the closest and most trusted person your child has, so in the formative years your opinions and emotions have a profound effect on her development. Therefore, you must constantly be in control of adverse emotions directed to the opposite sex so that the proper perspective of male/female relationships is developed.

Once your child is of an age to be aware of the world outside your immediate home, you should anticipate innumerable questions concerning your status. These questions should be answered at a level your child can understand, simply, honestly, and with understanding of his inquiry, but without undue emotion. Do not be impatient if your child asks the same question in a different way at different times. Questioning is the most important part of the learning process and *you* are your child's first teacher.

RELATIONSHIPS WITH ADULTS OF THE OPPOSITE SEX

Significant relationships with people of the opposite sex from the parent are important to the single-parent child's sexual development. This relationship can be with a friend, a member of your family, or someone who is paid to look after your child and your home, but it should be with someone who will provide some continuity in the association. Of course, it is important that this person share your basic philosophy of child rearing, or confusion and your loss of control will result.

The Parent's Needs

As a single parent, you need a good sense of self-identification and ego in order to allow your child to develop into an independent person. It is important to remember that you are first an individual with feelings, desires, needs, and responsibilities, and second, by choice or circumstance, you are a single parent with obligations to another person—your child.

ORGANIZATIONS

If your single-parent status is relatively new, you may feel a strong need to talk to someone about how other single parents handle their problems. Perhaps there is an organization in your area that is devoted to single parents, for example, Parents Without Partners. (The national address of Parents Without Partners is 7910 Woodmont Avenue, Suite 1000, Washington, D.C. 20014.) A similar group is the Momma League, a national single-female parent organization that includes activities relating to programming for children in which mothers develop social arrangements that compensate for the absence of siblings and fathers. This organization encourages modes of child-rearing practices unique to the single-female mother.

All problems seem more manageable when you realize that they are encountered by others and you have a chance to discuss them and find possible solutions. In addition, almost every community has various clubs or organizations that cater to adult interests and you may meet another single parent among the membership. These organizations are also an easy way for you to meet people who share your enthusiasm for a particular sport, craft, or endeavor.

If there are no such groups in your community, do not overlook the possibility of creating one with the help of your local community services organizations. You and your child will benefit from the endeavor.

THE SINGLE FATHER

There are many single-parent families in which the parent is the father. Situations such as death, acute mental breakdown, and divorce are common precipitators. The age of the child, the nature of father's work, and his personality are significant factors, but there are several general guidelines that apply to all new single-father families.

1. A period of transition will occur. All children and their fathers will undergo a painful period of adjustment to what can only be called a major loss.

2. The father takes on tremendous emotional importance to the child. At a time when he can least afford the extra demands, his time and energies will be at a premium at home. He will have to establish a normal home routine, maintain his professional life, and also meet the time-consuming emotional needs of his child.

3. Some children go through a period of regression sometimes characterized by withdrawal and a rigid desire to please. Others act out, developing temper tantrums and other rebellious and negative behavior patterns. Father's time spent in playing with the child will greatly aid in eliminating these symptoms.

It cannot be overemphasized that this transitional period of adjustment is inevitable, just how difficult and long-lasting it will be varies. Eventually the family develops its own cohesive patterns and then, as occurs in all families, new problems with attendant adjustments crop up. For example, usually at the time when things are proceeding in a stable way, father starts to relax a little and experiences feelings of loneliness and resentment. As soon as he makes any attempts to establish a personal life, there are repercussions at home, which should not discourage father. On the contrary, there is a life for him to live apart from child rearing and breadwinning. However, it is recommended that any new relationships be developed *very slowly*.

SINGLE MOTHER

Many of the stresses and strains already alluded to in the above section on single fathers apply equally to single mothers. In one very specific way the mother has an additional adjustment to make. She will most likely work, either because she financially has to or because she needs to go beyond the four walls of a home and live on another level. Once her initial adjustment problems subside, the single mother should not make the mistake of narrowly confining her life to child care. She must work at developing a personal life for herself (and in the 1970s it remains harder for a woman to do so than it is for her male counterpart). Clubs, athletics, and both male and female relationships should be sought. These interests will add balance and also enrich the family's life-style.

DIVORCE AND SEPARATION

If separation or divorce occurs in a family, it is natural for the child to react adversely. The home and parents are the center of a child's world. A drastic change is occurring and the child feels that his security and love are being threatened. Mary Hoover, in *The Responsive Parent,* indicates that the greatest threat for the child is that he will be left alone with no one to love and take of him. Proper parental guidance during and after a divorce is vital if the child is to develop into a normal, healthy adult.

Divorce? Yes and No

Some parents hesitate to separate "because of the children." Most authorities agree that this idea can arouse many problems. It is not the divorce itself that can hurt a child; it is the harmful relationship between the parents that preceded it. An atmosphere of constant tension is harmful. Some parents rationalize, thinking, "My child is too young to understand." Actually children, even very young children, are quite capable of comprehending the emotional state of their parents.

Newly divorced parents mention the negative reactions their children experience following their divorce. According to Dr. J. Louise Despert in *Children of Divorce,* these children have been reacting negatively for a long time, unnoticed by their troubled parents. In many instances, separation or divorce results in a healthier climate for all concerned.

Child's Reactions to Divorce

Obviously not all children react the same way when they realize that their parents will no longer live together. Feelings and attitudes will depend upon the child's age, emotional and physical needs, and sex.

If separation or divorce occurs during pregnancy or early in the baby's life, the mother may be too emotionally upset to adequately care for her child. Since all infants need love and physical attention, especially from the mother, the result can be a nervous, irritable baby with difficulties in sleeping and eating. The opposite problem can also occur. As the child gets a little older, the mother may transfer to him the love and affection that previously she gave her husband. She can become overprotective and impede her child's development.

Dr. Graham Blaine, in *Are Parents Bad for Children?,* concludes that the father generally plays a minor role during infancy. Studies have shown that the non-verbal infant–mother relationship is of prime importance. The father–child relationship develops most strongly as the child gets older. A child of three or four, especially a girl, may find separation or divorce (with the father leaving home) a very traumatic experience.

There is other research available that specifically points to the importance of the father's availability for his child's later adjustment. Some single-parent families succeed. Some two-parent families fail. Actually, just what is meant by "failure" or "success" is yet to be scientifically defined.

Early in her preschool years, a child may falter in her new motor and emotional achievements, resulting in bed-wetting, temper tantrums, or other regressions. Two questions are raised in parents' minds: (1) How can I help my child through this? (2) What do I do if the regression persists? Dr. Despert puts it this way: "If a parent can understand that such regression is a child's way of expressing anxiety and grief he feels but is not able to verbalize, it will help him not to compound the problem by punishing the child for his babyish behavior and thereby increase his sense of alienation from the parent with whom he is living. Since the child is responding not only to a loss, but to a break in routine, he will usually regain the controls he has temporarily lost."

As the child approaches later preschool age, divorce may precipitate psychological problems because he is now concerned with "good" versus "bad," birth, death, and sex differences. The child labels his parents "good" or "bad." depending on the situation. If one parent is absent, the young child may assume that the parent is dead or that he has been a bad boy and, therefore, his parent has gone away.

The most important thing a child needs to understand is that neither his mother nor his father has abandoned him—that though marriage is broken by divorce, parenthood isn't.

Parental Guidelines That Help a Child Adjust to Divorce

The following are some of the mistakes divorced parents make:

Trying to hide the fact that they have decided to divorce, parents delay in telling the child. Since the child eventually learns this, it is better if he is told as early as possible so he can gradually accept it. Of course the amount of detail depends on the youngster's age. The child needs to be helped to accept the fact that he still has two parents who love him, even though they are no longer in love with each other.

A major problem that results from separation or divorce is a child's feelings of guilt. A small child may have made a wish in anger that one parent would go away. Four- and five-year-olds develop a strong tie to the parent of the opposite sex and often believe that they are competing with one parent for the affections of the other. In such cases, the child often feels that he caused the divorce.

Constant bickering in front of a child can be more harmful than the divorce itself. A child's sense of security is threatened by perpetual tension.

The parent should try not to criticize the other parent to the child. To refrain from attacking the other parent is one of the hardest, yet most essential things divorced parents must do. It is essential to a child's sound development to feel free to love and respect both parents.

Avoid making your child take sides; this can only confuse and upset him.

Do not change your child's routine. He needs the continuity of his customary daily life for his sense of security. When considering custody, the welfare of the child rather than the personal satisfaction of the parents is of paramount importance.

With regard to visitation rights, parents should not use the child as a pawn during each visit. In their book *Uncoupling,* N. Sheresky and M. Mannes explain that as children grow, situations change and parents need to realize that visitation rights may also have to change.

It is important for the visiting parent to keep appointments. If the child is continually disappointed, she may find it difficult to accept the parent's word that he or she loves him. The result can be very damaging to their relationship.

480

The Parent Who Abandons

What if a mother or father suddenly leaves the family and does not return? The remaining parent should be honest and truthful, even though it may require telling the child that the parent may not return. Although the child may be upset initially, honesty will pay off as he gets older.

PCI Point of View

The entire family unit experiences a separation or divorce and undergoes radical, unhappy changes. Understanding is the first step in the process of adjustment! First, the children must understand and accept the events as objective reality and then be helped to face attendant problems. Second, the parents must learn how to respond appropriately to their children's new needs and anxieties. Third, professional help is available and should on occasion be sought.

ADOPTION

Availability of Children

In 1970, the Child Welfare League of America declared a change in adoption: "Children waiting for adoption are children of black and mixed racial heritage, school-aged children, sibling groups and youngsters with physical, emotional, and intellectual problems." The "white, blond, blue-eyed" infant was gone from the adoptive market.

The present adoptive process is affected by the drop in the birth rate due to such factors as newly enacted federal legislation liberalizing abortion laws, easy access to birth control devices, and an increasing number of white unwed mothers deciding to keep their babies. Current adoption agency requirements regarding age, race, and religion, and even the necessity of two parents, have been greatly relaxed.

Agency Versus Independent Adoptions

At present, the most frequent path to adoption is the traditional one, an approved public or private adoption agency. Which agency to choose is a question that can be answered by the Bureau of Children's Services operating in most states as part of the Department of Institutions and Agencies.

The adoption process is a detailed, but simple one in which a trained caseworker assesses applicants while they in turn learn about adoption in general and a great deal about themselves. Rather than an atmosphere of "putting your best foot forward" or "selling yourself," the focus is always on matching the needs of a waiting child with the needs of applicants. No one passes or fails; he or she either fits or does not fit. A formal application is required, necessitating some medical history and a doctor's signature.

The next step is acceptance of applicants, indicating their eligibility, followed finally by adoption. Ruth Carson, author of the pamphlet *So You Want to Adopt a Child,* asserts, "No child will ever be urged upon you. You may want more than one meeting to decide. There will be no obligation built up. And there will be plenty of opportunity for you and the child to get acquainted before you make your decision." The final steps: state laws usually require six months to a year before an adoption may become legal. When the adoption becomes legal, a new birth certificate is issued with the child's new name and your name as parents. The original birth certificate is sealed and filed and may only be opened by the state registrar under very special circumstances and by court order. (There is a movement afoot to liberalize the revelation procedure. Florence Fisher, an adult adoptee, has founded The Adoptees Liberty Movement Association [ALMA] to help adoptees find their biological parents.)

Another way to adopt a child is through independent, or "gray market," adoptions that are arranged by third parties, usually doctors or lawyers. These placements are not made for profit, the fees paid are for services (legal and medical) connected with the adoptive process. No fee is paid for the baby and the adoption is legal.

"Black market" adoptions, where placement is totally indiscriminate and dependent only on a "customer's readiness to pay," are to be avoided.

Colette Taube Dyasuk, an adoptive parent herself, has written an excellent book, *Adoption—Is It for You?* It is an objective treatment of the subject and will help you with your questions about adoption.

What Age Child Should You Adopt?

When adopting a child, early placement of a newborn is, of course, closest to bearing one's own. On the other hand, adopting an older child means that detailed background information and aspects such as appearance and alertness, can be ascertained beforehand. Also, adopting parents and child are free to meet and "choose" each other.

Bringing home an older baby is a joyous occasion for you, but be prepared for his negative reaction. According to a study by Dr. Yarrow (Public Health Paper No. 24, 1964), many babies as young as three months show disturbance when moved from foster to adoptive homes; 86 per cent of all six-month-olds and almost all seven-month-olds were clearly disturbed by this change. In some ways you should welcome this reaction. Your child could be reacting to the loss of a loving figure, showing that he was well cared for. It is a good sign, too, that your child is reacting to his surroundings. With your love and attention, he will gain emotional stability, this time with you.

The Family with Adopted and Biological Children

If yours is a home with both biological and adopted children, *you* know that your love is not influenced by how the child came into the family. However, children themselves are not always sure of this. The adopted child frequently feels "second best." You have to stress to him or her that what was important to you was having children, not where they came from. Your biological child may resent your "choosing" another and tease your adopted child about not being wanted. In this instance, you must make it clear that both children were equally wanted and are equally loved.

Telling Your Child About Adoption

All people experienced in adoption agree that the child should know. Since you are not ashamed of it, why hide it? From the beginning let the fact that he is adopted come openly into conversation within the family and with friends. The first time you tell someone that your child is adopted you may feel uncomfortable, but as you become more accepting of the circumstances, discussing adoption becomes natural.

When you tell your very young child, it may not have much meaning for her but it is good practice. You will be discussing it with her many times and as she grows older, different aspects of the process will concern her.

Dr. Edward M. Schwartz, a child psychologist, explains that the adopted child has the same curiosity about his biological parents as anyone has about great-grandparents they have never seen. Withholding information when your young child asks for it encourages his fantasizing about his biological parents.

483

PCI Point of View

It is the caring not the bearing that counts. Perhaps the most important preparation for adoption is coming to terms with your own feelings. If you feel that you are comfortable with the idea and go through the adoptive process, you will find your adopted child is as much your child as if she had been born to you instead of for you.

EXPLAINING DEATH TO A CHILD

Children cannot be protected from learning about death, but what and how they learn are greatly influenced by the parents' feelings about the subject. The impact and meaning of death will vary with the child's age and the depth of the relationship. For example, the death of a beloved pet may be of much greater significance to a young child than the death of a distant grandparent.

Anger and guilt are normal reactions of the young child to the death of a parent. Under the weight of such intense feelings, he needs continual reassurance and emotional support from his surviving parent and family members. New York child psychiatrist Dr. Gilbert Kilman indicates that following the death of a close relative or friend, children frequently become afraid of dying themselves or of losing their parents. The child who has lost his mother may become afraid to get attached to another adult for fear of losing him or her also.

The behavior that results from these intense feelings will vary considerably from child to child. Some children will revert to babyish behavior; others will become aggressive. Some will ask questions repeatedly about death, while others will work hard to understand death (by becoming interested in dead bugs and beetles, for instance).

Each child has her own way of coping with her feelings and needs to act out her feelings in a way that is helpful to her, even though it may be an unconventional type of mourning. It is the child who withdraws, who refuses to talk about her feelings who may need special help.

Ways to Help Children Deal with Death

For the young child with no previous understanding of death, facing the loss of someone close can be devastating. Children should gradually get used to the idea that death is a normal part of the life cycle. When a pet dies or when the child finds a dead bird in the park, he should be encouraged to mourn and bury it. Do not rush to replace the pet, because to do so is to demean the child's love for it and also cuts short the important mourning period.

In *Helping Your Child to Understand Death,* Anna Wolf recommends preparing children for the death of someone terminally ill. Tell him, "Daddy is very sick and may not be able to be with us always." At the same time, Dr. Gilbert Kilman urges parents to be alert to hidden fears. A child learning that his grandfather died in the hospital may believe hospitals "mean" death. Explain the circumstances of the death; that the person had an unusual sickness; and that it is not likely to happen to the child.

Most important of all is that you, as parents, come to terms with death. If parents go into a deep depression, the child will suffer a double loss, but if they accept the inevitability of death, they will be able to help their child. Grief should be shared with the child, as should cherished memories of the deceased, but a child should never be overburdened with her parents' grief. She needs assurance that the loved one did not want to leave her and that she is still very important to the family.

If a sibling or parent is dying, the child should be permitted to visit daily and also be educated to the severity of the illness. Hospital procedures should be flexible in this instance. Children should be encouraged to talk about their feelings—of sadness, of anger over losing a parent and loss of attention, and their fears of abandonment, and dying themselves. Children over the age of eight should attend funerals and other mourning rituals, according to Suzanne Ramos in *Teaching Your Child to Cope with Crisis.* Four- to eight-year-olds should be exposed if the scene will not be extremely hysterical and fearful. Those under four should experience mourning, but the funeral and the very concept of death are still too abstract for them.

Anticipate reactions such as regressive behavior and a general mistrustfulness to occur. The child is waiting for the other shoe to fall. If "the child withdraws, if the parent is too upset to talk and listen at length to his child, if there is a history of mental illness in the family; or if there has been an accidental death of a sibling or parent," it would be well for the parents to consult a professional, according to Ms. Ramos.

PCI Point of View

Inasmuch as one out of every twenty children loses a mother or father before the youngster is finished with elementary school, there is no time like the *present* to discuss death with our children. The death of a relative or friend or a pet presents the opportunity to introduce the subject. If there were no *other* reason than this to have a pet (and, of course, there are many), the PCI strongly recommends pets for young children. Much more than responsibility is attached to owning and caring for a tiger cat or mutt; a deep attachment develops and the loss and sadness that accompany the death of the pet will provide a very positive experience of a loss in a rather small dose.

Children should be told the truth in all crisis situations, in a matter-of-fact way, and in an atmosphere of support. Contrary to traditional theories of "shielding" or "protecting" the child, all experts agree that helping children face reality is a prime parental responsibility.

MOVING: CHANGES IN THE FAMILY

Over two million American families will move this year. Whether you are moving across town, to another state, or around the world, moving is a bittersweet affair.

Your Feelings and the Move

The reason for moving affects a family most. If the parents welcome the change because it represents a promotion or a return to the old home-town, the feelings they convey to their children will be positive and happy. However, if the move results from a job loss, death, or divorce, both the parents and children will be troubled.

Because a move is difficult under the best of circumstances, there is a tendency for children to be shoved aside. Preoccupied with a myriad of details, parents frequently do not take the time to discuss the move with their children. If not invited to talk about the move, children feel isolation and fear just when they most need a supportive sense of family.

Reservations about the move are natural and you need not hide them. There is comfort and consolation for your child in knowing that you have qualms about moving just as he does. When he hears you admit that you will miss your friends, or job, or favorite park, he will realize that you understand the feelings he is struggling with. If you have the conviction that the move is the right step for the whole family and that all will work out well, your children will be more likely to accept the change with greater equanimity.

How the Move Will Affect a Toddler

The infant is least affected by a move. A baby could not care less where she is going as long as she is comfortable and cared for and her routine is not disrupted too much.

It is the eighteen-month- to three-year-old who has the greatest struggle to hold onto her sense of self. Much of her identity is tied to her mother, her accustomed surroundings, and a few favorite objects: a teddy, her crib, a beloved blanket. Deny her these vital personal possessions and she might become upset.

In the confusion of moving, the toddler may get the feeling that she is losing everything that is "her." She sees her toys being packed away, her crib dismantled, and wonders if she will ever see them again. During the hubbub of moving day, she may even fear that she will be abandoned.

Minimizing Fears and Upsets

Include your toddler on the trip to select your new home or apartment. If that is not feasible, return home with pictures of the house. A few snapshots of the park, neighborhood children, and nursery school will do much to help him look forward to the move while realizing that life will continue much as before.

Use the colorful booklets provided by the moving company for story time and as a basis for discussing the move. Familiarize your child with the moving men and van. Moving day can be played with dolls, a few empty cartons, and a wagon, so that the whole process of packing, loading, unloading, and setting up can be enacted.

Now is not the time to throw out your toddler's old and scruffy toys. Pack his possessions last and be sure to leave a box of his favorites to accompany you in the car. This will help him overcome his sense of dislocation and strangeness.

Although the temptation may be great, do *not* send your toddler to grandma during the move. It will do more for your child's peace of mind if she can stay with you. A toddler who had spent moving day with relatives came to her mother a month after the move and tearfully asked, "When are we going home?" When a child actually sees the family's belongings going into the van and reappearing later in a different house, she is more likely to accept the new house as home.

On moving day you will want to accept help from friends with meals and watching the children. Be sure to set aside luggage, food, toys, and other items that will accompany you. Ask the moving men to load your toddler's things last, unload them first, and label them accordingly. This will help you re-establish your child's surroundings quickly.

After your arrival, do not be in too great a rush to set the whole house in order. Concentrate on the major necessities. With your child or children in tow, explore the new neighborhood, find the park, the library, and the shopping center, and treat your family and yourself to dinner out.

Go slowly with any major changes in household arrangement or routine. If your toddler previously shared a room with an older brother or sister and there is now a room of his own, introduce it slowly. Let the new room serve as a playroom at first and only present it as sleeping quarters when family life has returned to normal.

Do not be upset if you notice changes in your toddler's sleeping habits or if she clings a little closer to you than before. She may ask for old friends. It is best not to underestimate her feelings and to deal with them openly. Now is the ideal time for you to admit that you miss your friends, too. Before long your child will be mixing the names of new friends with the old. Then you will know that you all really are "home."

OPTIMUM FAMILY SIZE

The Right Number of Children for You

The greatest feeling in the world is to be pregnant with a baby *you want at the time you want it*. Sound impossible? It is not!

Today couples can plan their families in advance with a rather startling degree of accuracy, so that their family life can be richer, healthier, and more rewarding. You are lucky. You can have the number of children you want spaced the way you want them. Your grandparents and perhaps your parents were not so lucky. There was no really foolproof way to plan a pregnancy.

Doctors agree that both mothers and babies will be healthier if children are not born too close together. After the baby is born, the mother's body needs time to rest and regain its strength. Also, with the cost of living what it is and with college tuitions going up, couples may wish to limit the size of their families. They are free to make a choice. They can decide if and how many children they want and when they want to have them.

No Children

People with traditional upbringings often have children by virtue of religious dogma, biological accidents, or social pressures toward conformity. In contrast, many modern young adults do not get married in order to bear or rear children. They view marriage as an emotional commitment, couched in "legalese," as culturally defined. This group's attitude toward having children is "We'll wait until we're ready, or choose not to have children at all."

There are just as many good reasons to decide in favor of children. First, there are currently many opportunities for both parents to share child-rearing responsibilities; second, reproducing oneself is contributing to society and may be a deeply satisfying personal experience; third, the children are a source of great love and an outlet for love.

Family Planning Center

Now that you have decided to plan your family's size, where do you go to find out how?

The Planned Parenthood Association provides a clinic where one can get advice on birth planning regardless of marital status or income. Its main purpose is to educate people about the needs of children and the family's responsibility to the child and to the world. The clinic offers a discussion of birth control methods and counsels on family planning. There is a doctor's examination that includes a simple cancer check and breast exam and a venereal disease test, after which birth control supplies are provided. A small fee is charged for these services. The National Office of Planned Parenthood-World Population is located at 810 Seventh Avenue, New York, N.Y. 10019. Write for their literature and local office address.

Zero Population Growth

In 1968, an organization was formed for a single purpose: to stop the population explosion first in the United States and then in the rest of the world. It is called Zero Population Growth. It concentrates on educating the general public of the population problem. Its main goal is for each couple to limit its family to no more than two biological children. The central office of ZPG is 330 Second Street, Los Altos, Calif. 94022.

Methods of controlling family size include a myriad of contraception, sterilization, and abortion techniques.

PCI Point of View

The right number of children for a family depends on the kinds of parents and the kinds of children in the family. For the few who delight in or are capable of managing any number of children, any number of children is "right." In line with world overpopulation, some parents are turning to adoption as a means of having a large family. For most parents who have average limits on the amount of love, stamina, and emotional resources they can muster, perhaps one or two children is "right." For those couples who do not really want children, but who feel pressured to have them for other reasons—to please their parents, because of the pressure of convention, to save a poor marriage—the "right" number of children is *zero.*

THE RIGHTS OF CHILDREN

A growing field of social reform is emerging on the American scene, that of children's rights. Child advocates are making it clear through their consciousness-raising efforts that the needs and interests of children do not always coincide with those of their parents or the state. Laws and policies that allow adults to decide what are a child's best interests are proving inadequate in achieving beneficial ends.

In our society, there is a division of rights between children and adults supported by a "powerful social consensus that parents should dominate children," writes Hillary Rodham of the Children's Defense Fund. It is based on the assumption that (1) America is a family-oriented, child-centered society in which parents are responsible for their own children, (2) the state will assume responsibility for the child if parents cannot, (3) in a child-loving society, non-parents, the state, and other adults will do what is best for the child, (4) children need not or should not participate with the family and the state in making decisions that affect their lives.

Failures Prove Need for Change

The law, therefore, presumes that parents or state (as parent) know what is best for children. Both parents and the state have failed too often, however, to indicate that they are equipped to determine what is best for the physical and psychological welfare and development of children.

Present custody laws, for example, are supposed to protect the child's needs and best interests. According to authors Joseph Goldstein, et al. in

490

their book *Beyond the Best Interests of the Child,* the laws serve either the parents, the courts, or the social welfare agencies. The authors recommend that, instead, the laws should focus on all needs of children, and especially their psychological well-being. Too often the emphasis has been solely on their physical well-being. Understanding a child's psychological needs from infancy, therefore, is paramount to forming any legal guidelines.

The authors above discuss three areas that should be explored by decision makers in determining the placement of children: the child's need for continuity of relationships, the child's subjective built-in sense of time based on emotional needs, and the limitations of the law.

When we realize the child's need for continuity in her relationship with her "psychological" parents and her special concept of time, as discussed by Goldstein, Freud, and Solnit, then certain conclusions regarding the law follow. Adoption, like a birth certificate, should be unconditional and final the moment a child is placed with her new parents. It should deny any legal rights to biological parents. There should be no waiting period for adoption. It should begin at birth so that there are no interruptions of continuity between parent and child.

Adoption should be final, with no trial periods to threaten the emotional commitment of the parents. Foster parents should be given children with the idea that they will become psychological parents with the right of adoption. While there exists the legal right to remove the child at any time, there exists the lack of commitment on the part of the parents and a feeling of insecurity for the child. Decisions in custody suits in cases of divorce or separation should be final. The parent given custody and the court should make all further decisions about the child's life.

Children's Rights as Human Rights

When we talk about children's rights, we are really talking about human rights. John Holt, in his book *Escape from Childhood,* describes the needs of children as those of adults. Dr. Richard Farson of the California Esalen Institute proposes a similar children's liberation movement to free children and adults from the attitude that age is a barrier to human rights. Both Holt and Farson propose a host of children's rights that would automatically flow from treating children as persons under the law.

In the present social context, however, many of these rights would be unworkable. Take, for example, due process, concerning which Holt claims, "No society is likely to give to young people the right to equal treatment before the law if it denies this right to adult women or to members of racial or other minority groups."

Children's Rights and the Future

The movement toward achieving children's rights is in a consciousness-raising stage. Groups such as the Children's Defense Fund are beginning to organize (as of 1974). In general, however, the child rights movement is advancing very slowly due to lack of funds and support.

For the present, society must deal with the question of how the state and the adult public should regard children in a society marked by turbulent political, social, and economic change and a high degree of geographical and social mobility. Only when society agrees on what kind of future it wants for its children can it seek ways to achieve it.

13
Clothing and Equipment

INTRODUCTION BY FREDELLE MAYNARD, PH.D.*

Bringing up babies is easier than it used to be—and a lot more fun. A generation ago, for instance, the atmosphere surrounding child care could best be described as awesome. During the 1950s the final authority on babies was the U. S. Department of Labor pamphlet *Infant Care*. (Dr. Spock's more benign influence was just beginning to make itself felt.) *Infant Care* made it plain that babies were Serious Business. I was a young mother then and I remember how I trembled over its pages. "Don't let anyone lean over a baby's crib," the section on health warned. "Don't let anyone—not even your own mother—pick up the baby without first washing her hands."

Infants, it seemed, were terribly fragile. They had to be bundled in a formidable array of garments—abdominal bands, undershirts, diapers, knitted "soakers." Baby boys wore rompers; baby girls wore dresses. ("The baby's dress can be worn without a slip," the writer added in a rare moment of relaxation. "It is not *necessary* to iron diapers, though they may be ironed if the mother wishes.")

Food for babies, we were told, required clinical standards of sanitation. *Infant Care* devoted twenty-five pages to formula preparation alone. It was not only that the milk had to be boiled, but it had to be precisely timed. All utensils coming in contact with the milk had also to be sterilized—bottles, nipples, caps, funnel, strainer, spoon. Babies had to be guarded against a frightening list of "Common Disorders" —impetigo, scabies, scurvy, rickets, pellagra. So they were handled as

---

* Fredelle Bruser Maynard is a recognized writer in the field of child development. Her two books on childhood, *Raisins and Almonds* and, more recently, *Guiding Your Child to a More Creative Life,* have won wide critical acclaim; in 1973, she won a Penney-Missouri Award for Women's Journalism in the field of family life. Dr. Maynard received a Ph.D. from Harvard University and is currently giving lectures and workshops on the preservation and encouragement of creativity and originality in children. "And," in her own words, "I am the mother of two notably creative children, both writers."

little as possible, fed quickly, and returned to their immaculate cribs to await the next sterile meal. Traveling with babies was to be avoided. Contact with strangers was to be avoided. In fact, it seemed real life was to be avoided until the child, at three or so, became strong enough to cope.

All this is now happily changed. We dress infants far more simply and sensibly, in unisex garments such as the snapped or zippered stretch suit, and with a minimum of bundling. (One eminent pediatrician urges parents to forgo the long sacred undershirt. "I have never seen any need for a child to wear an undershirt under whatever else he is wearing," insists Dr. Virginia E. Pomeranz, "and no parent of an undershirted child has ever been able to explain to me why his or her child was wearing one.") High boots for babies have pretty much vanished, as well as stockings and those decorative knit booties that never stayed on. Girl and boy toddlers wear much the same clothes, the best of which are now sturdy, practical wash-and-wear garments that feel free and look great worn straight off the line.

Along with freedom in dress has come a relaxed attitude toward the child-in-the-world. Infants, as we now know, need stimulation and variety. It has been shown that newborns discriminate between various odors and sounds. They respond more vividly to a representation of the human face than to random shapes. Since we have also learned that the first few years are crucial for the child's intellectual and emotional development, emphasis has shifted from "Keep him clean and safe" to "Give him an enriched environment." A typical invention of the 1940s was B. F. Skinner's "air crib," a large, air-conditioned, temperature-controlled, germ-free, soundproof glass box in which a baby could sleep and play. A typical invention of the 1960s is the infant crawler, a contoured, plastic body support on wheels that allows a baby of six months or so to move about on the floor. The rigid playpen with slatted sides (cage-like) has given way to the soft-sided playpen, the movable expandable playpen, or most often to a quilted pad that can be laid down whenever and wherever baby joins the family group. We hang mobiles above cribs now, paint shapes on the ceiling, and suspend graspable objects from crib sides so that even lying prone the baby has something interesting to see and do.

Perhaps no single item of baby equipment has so revolutionized child care as the molded infant seat. Supported in an infant seat, even tiny babies can share in the rhythm of family life. Time was when the five-month-old baby spent most of the day flat on her back in crib, carriage, or playpen—now she goes where the action is. Carriages, bulky and cumbersome, have largely given way to light, collapsible strollers and to baby carriers. There are carriers of all sorts available —slings that hold an infant against the breast or over one hip and frames to fit the back. (These are new to Americans but, of course, babies in primitive societies the world over have always traveled this way, snug against a parent's body, but with a view of the world.)

These new styles of transportation—and the boon of disposable bottles and diapers—have made traveling with infants practical and fun. Small children go camping now and nobody worries about boiling formula. Where once pediatricians cautioned against upsetting infant routines, now most authorities favor at least occasional changes in the interest of the baby's developing resilience and adaptability. Where once we revered the antiseptic world, we now celebrate warmth, closeness, touching, and joyful activity as essential to a baby's growth.

I think that as a nation we are becoming more child-centered in the best sense of the word, by which I mean not more indulgent, but truly more aware of the child as a person with his own rights and dignity. We dress the young in overalls so they can play, climb, jump, run —not in the starched pinafores and little-man suits that gave such charming effects. We buy them child-sized blocks and cooking sets rather than miniatures. We arrange their possessions with accessibility, not color schemes in mind. We do not treat children as "cute" imitations of adults, but as real people—which they are.

LAYETTE AND CLOTHING FOR THE FIRST YEAR

A Basic Layette

3–4 dozen diapers
safety diaper pins
3–6 undershirts
3 sacque sets (newborn size)
4 nightgowns (newborn size)
4 kimonos (newborn size)
4 stretch suits (second size, or larger)

2 sweaters (machine washable)
3 small bibs
4 plastic pants
1 sleeping bag or bunting
2 bonnets
booties

Your baby's clothing should always be comfortable and washable. When choosing garments, remember that a baby grows very quickly. If you buy something that fits her just right, she'll be out of it in a few weeks. Another matter to consider is fabric content. Cotton and cotton blends shrink when washed; the higher the percentage of cotton in a garment, the more shrinkage you should expect.

Keep in mind that you will be receiving baby gifts, so concentrate on necessities and allow friends and relatives to provide the extras.

Once your baby starts to crawl on the floor, which is cooler than his crib and inevitably less clean, he will need sturdier clothing. Be sure that all clothing goes on and off easily. For example, polo shirts with snap openings at the neck are easy to pull over the baby's head. All overalls or stretch suits should have snap crotches or zipper fronts for easy diaper changing; otherwise you will find yourself undressing your baby every time you have to change his diaper.

Underwear

If your baby uses plastic pants, be sure there is no elastic binding around legs or waist to interfere with circulation. Undershirts can be purchased in three basic styles—snap fronts, lap shoulders, and slip-ons. Snap fronts are especially good with small babies since they do not have to be pulled over the head. Lap shoulders are similar to slip-ons except that the shoulder seams are opened, thus allowing for easier dressing. All three come in short and long sleeve styles and sleeveless slip-ons may be purchased too.

Booties, Socks, and Shoes

Indoors, your baby needs nothing on her feet until she starts walking. A baby's feet and hands should feel cool; otherwise she is dressed too warmly. For outings on cold days, knitted booties are ideal if you can find a pair that do not slip off. Corduroy booties that tie under the ankle bone seem to stay on the feet best. Ankle socks always slip off. For warmth, you would be better off using stretch knee socks that fit snugly and cover more leg area or stretch tights that go up to the waist.

Babies do *not* need shoes until they can walk well by themselves.

Gowns

Cotton knit nightgowns, kimonos, and sacque sets are the most convenient attire for a new baby. For the first month or so, a baby wears them continually.

Stretch Suits

After the first month, terry cloth stretch suits may be worn night and day. They keep the baby well covered and the snap opening that extends from neck to toe makes for easy dressing and changing.

Pants and Overalls

Overalls are wonderful for the crawling baby. They protect his knees, and can be worn with or without a shirt depending on the temperature. Length can usually be adjusted a couple of inches just by moving the buttons on the shoulders. Coveralls or jump suits are similar except that they

499

do not adjust to the growing child as overalls do. Both are better for crawlers than are dresses or shirts and pants. There will be time enough once your child is walking for more sophisticated costumes.

Shirts

To ease pulling the shirt over your baby's head, try to get shirts that have some opening around the neck. When dressing the baby, slip the shirt first over the back of the baby's head, then forward, stretching it forward as you bring it down past his forehead and nose. To take it off, gently pull the baby's arms out first, raise the front part of the shirt up past his nose and forehead, then slip it off toward the back of his head.

Bibs

Get bibs with plastic backings so spills will not soak through to clothing. Do not get too many small bibs. As soon as you start giving your baby finger foods she will need large bibs to cover all her clothing. These will be of use right through toddlerhood and serve double duty as painting smocks.

Outerwear

Be sure everything is washable. Sweaters and jackets with hoods are invaluable. Knitted caps should cover the ears and will stay on better if they tie under the chin. The warmest, most convenient snowsuits are one-piece models with attached hoods and a *very* long zipper.

Try not to overdress your child. Put the same amount of clothing on him or her as you would on yourself.

CLOTHING FOR CREEPERS AND WALKERS

The second year of life introduces new clothing requirements. Infants are well provided for as long as they are kept warm and dry. Toddlers need clothes that allow them free movement and lend themselves to speedy dressing and undressing. Since children are more mobile and may be toilet trained during the second year of life, they need more and different kinds of clothes.

Once toddlers master the art of walking, climbing, and running, they

will need warmer and sturdier clothes. They will get dirtier too, so look for fabrics that will take hard scrubbing. Corduroy and stretch synthetic knits, although not so warm as some other fabrics, wash well and are sturdy. Remember that dark colors do not show dirt, spills, or repairs as much as light colors. In buying pants, look for reinforced knees. Buy them longer than you need and hem them; then they will last for more than one season. Coveralls are good for rough outside play and indoor dirty play, but some-

501

thing of a nuisance if a child is being toilet trained.

As children grow older, they will want to learn how to dress and undress themselves. You can help by choosing pants with elastic waists and shirts with necks that permit the head to slide in and out easily.

Waterproof Clothing

Since playing outside becomes increasingly important during the second year, children should have waterproof clothing and an inexpensive raincoat and boots. They will certainly want to walk through puddles and may fall in the mud, but if properly dressed, a tumble need not be a disaster. In fact, it usually is fun. For winter, choose a one-piece snowsuit, warmly lined, with a long zipper for convenience and rapid undressing. Add boots, mittens, and a wool hat and your toddler is prepared for snow and even freezing weather.

Underwear

Toddlers should continue to wear undershirts. Buy them large enough and they will last a long time. When your child is ready for training pants, be sure to buy good quality garments since they will be washed and bleached constantly. Some pants have foam between the layers of fabric, a real aid in keeping a child dry whose control is uncertain. As for how many pairs of training pants you will need, they may have to be changed several times a day. (Incidentally, these pants can be worn as regular underpants after training is completed.)

Sleepwear

Since a child's bedroom should be cool (a temperature of 68 to 70 degrees is recommended, and most young children are unable to keep blankets on them during the night, it is practical to buy at least two pairs of footed sleepers. These will keep your child warm and also eliminate the need for slippers. What you buy, how much you spend, and what items you choose are personal preferences, but we do have a few recommendations.

Brand names (Carter's, Health-Tex, Sears, Danskin, etc.) are reliable as to size, construction, and washability and most mothers feel that money spent on these items is a good investment. Some clothes, if bought large enough, will last a whole year, but generally growth is so rapid that garments are outgrown rather than worn out.

Mittens should be attached to snowsuits with clips or knitted chains; otherwise they are easily lost.

Two or three outfits for play and one "good" outfit for special occasions seem to be enough for this age.

Children's skin should be protected with sun hats and shirts during the summer to avoid sunburn.

Sizes

Many consumer groups are working toward standardization of size in children's clothing. Lack of uniformity at the present time means that one brand's Size 2 may fit and another Size 2 may not. To avoid this problem, try to find a brand you like and keep using it. Discount store bargains are often a waste of money; cheaply made garments shrink, stretch, fade, or rip easily.

Flammability of Children's Clothing

Flammability of children's clothing has long been a matter of concern. As of July 1973, there was a complete ban, according to federal regulations, on flammable sleepwear in sizes up to 6x. All sleepwear today must be marked as to whether it is flame-resistant or not, so read labels carefully. Acrylic fibers do not readily burst into flame, but they do melt and can cause severe burns.

Consumer Concerns

Labels must also tell you what fibers are used in the clothing and how they should be washed. Follow the directions carefully to ensure long-lasting wear.

The pamphlets below are available through Consumer Information, Public Documents Distribution Center, Pueblo, Colo. 81009:

Clothing and Fabric Care Labeling, 036 A, free
Clothing Repairs, 037 A, 25¢
Fibers and Fabrics, 038 A, 25¢
Removing Stains from Fabrics, 040 A, 20¢
Sanitation in Home Laundering, 041 A, 10¢
Soaps and Detergents for Home Laundering, 042 A, 10¢

In a recent survey, mothers asked what they would do differently when buying clothes today for the twelve- to twenty-four-month-old child said they would buy fewer items, would stick to name brands, and would resist compulsive spending for "cute" items.

SHOES

Shoes—When to Buy the First Pair

Since manufacturers make conflicting claims and even doctors disagree, parents are often confused about when to buy their infant's first pair of shoes. It is safe to say that shoes are unnecessary until a child walks alone, after which they serve to protect the feet from rough surfaces, rocks, sharp objects, and cold weather. Normally a baby's feet stay warm in the same way as his hands do. During the first year, therefore, no footwear at all is required unless the house or floor is unusually cold. Of course, if the baby wears stretch suits, he is snugly covered from neck to toe. Around the sixth month, some mothers buy expensive shoes to support their infant's feet "in case" he should begin to stand or walk. But shoes will not make children walk any sooner than they would otherwise have done. In fact, very stiff shoes with slippery soles can make it harder for them to balance on some surfaces.

Value of Going Barefoot

Even after babies are walking, there is a real value in leaving them barefoot most of the time. Initially a baby's arches are relatively flat. By vigorous use in standing and walking, the arches are built up and the ankles strengthened. Furthermore, walking barefoot on an uneven or rough surface fosters the use of the foot and leg muscles. If a baby walks only on smooth surfaces and wears shoes continually (particularly stiff-soled shoes), he is encouraged to relax his foot muscles and walk flat-footed.

Buying Shoes

During the rapid growth of the first years, a baby outgrows shoes at a discouraging rate. Between the ages of eight to fifteen months, your baby will probably need a new pair of shoes every four to six weeks. Between fifteen months and two years, she will probably need a new pair every two to three months. Consequently, it is unwise to buy overly expensive shoes.

Form the habit of feeling your baby's shoes every few weeks to make sure they are still large enough. Examine her feet regularly to see if there is any swelling or thickening of the skin or spots (pink, red, or darkened places) that reveal pressure.

Although you should rely on a salesman skilled in fitting children, the following information will be helpful in choosing the right shoe:

1. Look for a firm sole that is flexible at the widest part. If it is too stiff, the foot muscles will not develop properly.

2. The upper part of the shoe should be made of soft, porous leather to control sweating.

3. The shoes should be big enough so that the toes are not cramped, but not so big that they almost slip off.

4. There must be more than just enough space for the toes, because as the child walks, the toes are squeezed up into the front of the shoe with each step. There should be at least half an inch (thumb's width) between the tip of the toes and the edge of the sole. (The child should be standing when you make this test.)

5. The shoes should be comfortably wide, too. When the baby puts his weight on his foot, the sides of the shoe should be full, but not bulging.

6. The shoes should be snug-fitting in the heel.

7. The shoes should be no higher in the heel than the thickness of the sole.

Frequently mothers are encouraged to buy shoes that are too large so the baby's feet "will have room to grow." This is bad advice. First of all, an active baby will wear out the shoes before she can grow into them. Second, when shoes are too long, a baby will accentuate the way she usually walks, throwing her feet in or out to avoid the extra toe space and possibly developing an abnormal gait. Finally, tripping is much worse and more frequent in shoes that are too big.

Do not buy shoes for the baby without trying them on. (Occasionally mothers simply purchase new shoes one size larger than the old pair, but the baby's feet may have grown more than one size larger.) Never pass on an outgrown pair of shoes to another child. After shoes are worn for a while, they take on the shape of an individual's feet. Each child wears shoes differently. Wearing someone else's shoes may cause permanent deformity.

To avoid accidents, scrape the soles of a new pair of shoes before letting your child wear them. If a floor is too highly waxed and slippery and the child takes a fall, he may be discouraged from practicing standing and walking.

If you observe anything unusual in the way your baby stands or walks, you should consult your doctor. Special shoes and/or corrective exercises may be necessary.

High-top Shoes

Although some doctors claim that high-top shoes support the ankles, others argue that a child's feet and ankles need no support. It is true, though, that since baby feet are pudgy, high shoes sometimes stay on better than low-cut ones. The decision depends on the individual child and rests with the parents.

Sneakers

According to Dr. H. L. Duvries, writing in *Today's Health,* "The statement that canvas shoes can hurt a child's feet is a myth. It's dead wrong. Actually, canvas shoes may be the best thing you can buy for your child because they're soft, more elastic than leather and may give the feet more room to develop." The one problem with sneakers is that they may cause excessive sweating.

Socks

Just as important as the fit of your baby's shoes is the fit of her socks. (A baby's socks should always extend a quarter inch beyond her toes.) Remember that babies outgrow socks, too. If the socks are too tight, they will curl and cramp the baby's toes.

BASIC EQUIPMENT FOR INFANTS

Planning your baby's nursery will happily occupy much of your thought and require several shopping trips. Ideally, your baby should have his own room, an arrangement that will help him build better sleeping habits and give you more rest.

Below are basic items of equipment for your baby. Some will be used for a matter of months; some, for a couple of years. Regardless of the period of service involved, examine all equipment carefully for safety. Always keep in mind that the first two years of your baby's life are extremely important as far as stimulating his five senses are concerned.

Bassinet, Cradle, and Portable Cribs

For baby's first bed, a bassinet on wheels is convenient since it can be taken anywhere in the house. However, a cradle, portable crib, or even a

506

well-padded drawer will serve as well. If you can locate a transparent plastic bassinet, it will serve even better. Whatever temporary bed you use, be sure it is ample enough to allow for lots of kicking and wriggling.

Cribs

Full-size cribs come in every shape. There are traditional, rectangular wooden cribs and canopy cribs with frilly organdy tops. Some manufacturers, taking advantage of new infant research, employ large transparent Plexiglas windows either in front and back crib boards or in up-and-down crib sides.

A baby spends a lot of time in a crib—before she falls asleep, while she is sleeping, and after she wakes up. As she gets older, her waking periods become longer, increasing the time during which she is constantly observing and moving. So she should be provided with bright objects to observe and plenty of room to reach out and wriggle about. Forget about the delicate pastels traditionally used for the very young; give your baby color and patterns, too. (Designs on crib sheets, for example, usually fascinate babies. These designs are close enough to the baby so that she can distinguish the details of the patterns.) Forget about "interior decorating" when it comes to your baby's room, otherwise you will find yourself paying more attention to matching colors than to creating a stimulating environment.

There are safety regulations regarding cribs that you should know about before you make your purchase. The Consumer Safety Division of the Food and Drug Administration has set forth these new safety specifications for all cribs produced after February 1, 1974:

1. The posts on all full-sized cribs ($28'' \times 53''$) will be not more than $2\frac{3}{8}''$ apart when a 20-lb. wedge test is applied. This means that thin spokes that give way too easily and allow a baby to get his arm or head through will not be permitted.

2. The distance between the bottom of the mattress and top of the side panels in up position will be $26''$. A $6''$ mattress should be used. If an $8''$ mattress is used, the side panels must be $28''$ or $29''$ high. There must be a minimum of $20''$ from top of mattress to top of side panels in up position. This new regulation takes into account safety for larger babies.

3. When side panels are in down position, the top of the panels to top of mattress will be $9''$ to prevent a child from rolling off.

4. No horizontal members that allow infants a toehold to climb over the top of the crib will be permissible. All paint will be free of lead or other poisonous substances.

507

5. Side release mechanism will have double action (two kicks) to foil dogs and older children from dropping the side.

Do not borrow a friend's or relative's used crib if it lacks the safety features described above.

Mattress

If there are allergies in your family, be sure to get a foam mattress or a hypoallergenic type. A mattress should be firm with a waterproof covering and not more than six inches thick or the child may tumble over the side of the crib. If you are planning a large family, you may want to buy an innerspring mattress.

Sheets

Even if the mattress you buy is covered with waterproof flannel sheeting, cover it completely with another rubber sheet. Have at least two rubber sheets for convenience in laundering. Smaller squares of rubber sheeting or quilted pads are useful to put under the baby in the crib and on your lap as you hold her. Your baby should not lie directly on rubber or plastic. *Never* use thin plastic bags to cover sheet or mattress!

Pillows and Blankets

Neither is necessary. An infant should never sleep with his head on a pillow. As for blankets, if it is cold in your baby's room, he would be warmer in a sleeping bag or wearing a footed stretch suit. Tucking blankets in may be a danger since the baby can slip back underneath the covering. If you feel you must use a blanket, use a thermal or knitted one that is porous, allowing air to pass through, and lessening any danger of suffocation.

Storage Furniture

The fewer pieces of furniture you have in your baby's room, the more floor area she will have to play on. If you can, store her clothing in a closet. (You may need to add a few shelves.) Toys should be easily accessible. Open cubes, open shelves, or roomy plastic baskets make good containers. Toy boxes with lids, on the other hand, can easily hurt little fingers. In addition, they encourage breakage and the jumbling of toys.

Changing Table

This should be high enough to work at comfortably during changing and dressing. Whatever arrangement you choose, never leave your baby unattended, even if strapped to the table. Make sure all changing tables have six-to eight-inch sides to prevent roll-over falls.

Rocking Chair

This traditional nursery item has become more popular in recent years. Rocking a restless baby often soothes him and gives you a rest at the same time. It is a good idea to have a small, stable serving table at the side of your chair to hold items needed during a feeding.

Carriage

Some carriages convert into strollers and have lift-out top sections that can be used as car beds. Consider these models if you have need for their extra functions. Most carriages have solid interiors that are visually not very interesting for baby. Cut out colorful designs of various textures or use bathtub appliqués and put them around the inside of the carriage for visual and tactile stimulation. Hang colorful toys across the inside of the carriage for your baby to watch and play with as she rides. Look for carriages that give the maximum seeing area outside the carriage. Some newer models have "see-through" sections.

Stroller

There are many variations of the stroller on the market today. If you will be walking outdoors often, you will need something that is comfortable and provides protection against wind and rain. If you are in and out of your car a great deal, you will probably find the new fold-up, lightweight strollers best. These are also popular in metropolitan areas because they require minimum storage space and are easily carried about. Whichever you use, do not forget to use a harness around your baby. Babies move quickly and are very curious; they can easily pull themselves over the sides of a stroller.

Carriers

Babies should be close to their mothers. For the first three months of life, you can carry your baby with you in a sling-type front carrier. After that, the baby can be carried in a backpack-type carrier that fits around your shoulders and leaves your arms free. Infant seats allow even a very young baby to sit up and take part in family life. They are also convenient to use for feeding an infant before he can sit in a high chair, and for carrying him short distances, or about the house. Be sure the seat is deep, so that when you raise it to a more upright position your baby will not slip out.

For babies who are able to sit up well, there are bicycle carriers. The safest carrier for good balance fits on the back of an adult bicycle. Some are molded plastic; others are metal-framed with cushioned seats. The molded seats offer side protection and good coverage over the wheels so that the baby's feet will not get caught. A waist belt is not always sufficient to keep a wriggling baby secure on the seat; a harness is much more effective.

High Chairs

To avoid accidents, be sure your high chair has a broad base so that it does not tip over easily. *Always harness your baby into the seat. Never leave him alone in it.* You may want to consider getting a convertible chair that will serve as a high chair on some occasions and a low chair on others. Low feeding tables are very safe and offer a play surface, as well as an eating place. But they have certain disadvantages; you will have to bend over to feed your baby unless you sit on a very low chair. The baby also misses out being a part of the family table at mealtimes in a low chair since he is far below eye level. You might want to explore baby seats that fit at the edge of the table and permit your child to be truly a part of the family meal.

Car Seats

The federal government has established very rigid standards for the construction of car seats. Since 1973, manufacturers have not been permitted to market any car seat not up to these standards. A good car seat is expensive, but well worth the price for both baby's safety and your own peace of mind.

The most dangerous position a child can be in when a car accident

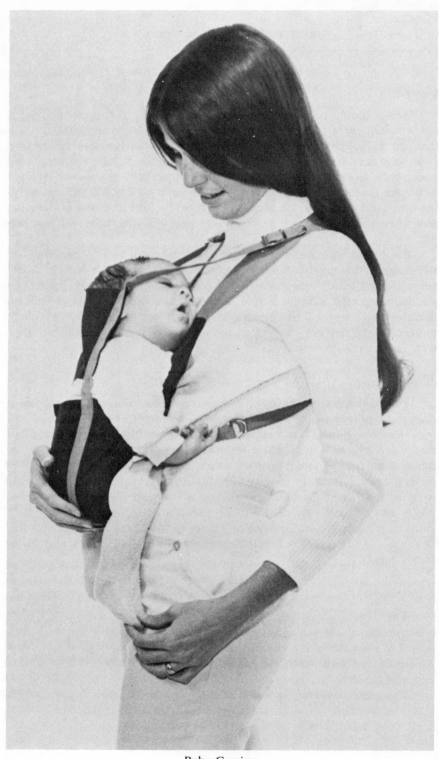

Baby Carrier.

Car Seats.

occurs is in an adult's lap. Restraining carriers are a safety necessity for your infant and child. The American Academy of Pediatrics recommends an infant carrier (like the GM Infant Love Seat) for infants up to twelve pounds as the most protective device available. For children twelve to twenty-four pounds, a toddler car seat (such as the GM Child Love Seat, Peterson's Car Seat, or the Ford Tot Guard Seat), or a restraining harness with both pelvic and chest straps is recommended. At fifty pounds a child can begin to use an adult lap belt.

Parents should be aware of the following safety information when traveling with their children:

1. The safest seat in the car is the center rear. The most dangerous is the right front.

2. The most dangerous way for an infant to travel is in mother's lap.

3. Remove all sharp and heavy objects from the rear car shelf or seat since they become flying missiles on a sudden stop.

4. Always lock all car doors.

5. Do not allow a child to play with door handles, window knobs, instrument panels, or the steering wheel.

6. Do not allow the child to stick his hands or head out the window.

7. Avoid horseplay in the car.

8. Do not discipline your child in a moving car; draw to the curb for such action.

9. Never leave a child alone in the car.

10. Fasten all seat belts before beginning a trip.

PLANNING YOUR CHILD'S BEDROOM

A growing, playing child needs as large a room as you can provide. While adults use a bedroom mainly for sleeping, a child needs ample floor space for many vigorous activities, and so you might consider giving up your bedroom to the child (keeping a smaller room for yourself). Or if you have a large basement, how about converting it into a play center?

A child's room should reflect in decor and play materials the needs and interests of her particular stage of development.

While an infant needs a crib, diaper changing table, storage unit, rocking chair, and so forth, the preschooler requires considerable floor and storage space for a large set of school-type building blocks, trucks, toy animals and people, puzzles, and dolls. A school-aged child should have alcove space for a play stove and cupboard, a crock of clay, a double easel, and art supplies. In addition to her own bed, she will enjoy an extra bed or cot for an overnight visitor.

A child's room is his castle, not your showcase. It should be a place where he can explore, and learn, and grow.

Where Will Baby Sleep?

If at all possible, a baby should have his or her own room. It is true that during the early months a child is not likely to be affected by sharing a room with parents, but it is a rare parent who is not disturbed by the small cries and stirrings from a bedside crib. Certainly by six or seven months, an infant should be out of his parents' room. The presence of a child may inhibit sexual expression. Furthermore, as the child becomes more aware, there is a real danger that he will overhear—and be upset by —his parents' lovemaking. (To a two-year-old, sexual intercourse may seem an alarming struggle.) At the very least, a child who sleeps in his parents' bedroom will crawl into bed with mommy and daddy, a habit hard to break.

If you cannot manage a separate room for your baby, try to arrange a separate place. Perhaps a section of the dining room, hall, or kitchen could be set aside for the crib. With a little imagination, bookcases or decorative screens can be made to function as room dividers. Do not be concerned about the problem of normal household noises or diffused light; infants become easily accustomed to these. Another alternative is to have the baby use her parents' bedroom during the day and then wheel the crib out at night.

What Temperature Should Baby's Room Be?

A room temperature of 68 to 70 degrees is healthy for a baby (as it is for the rest of the family). Since dry heat takes needed moisture out of baby's nose and mouth membranes, you should take pains to ensure adequate humidity. Individual humidifiers, pans of water near a radiator, and other devices may be used to increase the moisture content of the air. Cross ventilation in warm weather is important, too. Keep your baby's bed out of a draft by using ventilators or cloth screens in open windows.

Room Planning for Infants and Toddlers

Since children grow and change so rapidly, it is foolish to lock yourself into a decorating scheme geared only to a nursery. The soft pinks and blues traditionally thought appropriate for an infant can seem much too tame for a lively three-year-old. So it is a good idea to postpone a costly decorating scheme until your child is at least three years old. Meantime, since an infant's and toddler's sensory and physical powers need lots of practice, be sure you provide encouragement for looking, touching, sucking, crawling, and walking.

For seeing, brighten the wall with colorful pictures and posters; hang mobiles from the ceiling. A phonograph and tick-tock clock for hearing; a texture rug for feeling; a bulletin board on which to stick different soft plastic, hand-painted decorations or storytelling graphics—all these are basic equipment.

When your baby is three to eight months old, she can be made independently mobile by means of a body-shaped crawler complete with casters. (This works best on a bare floor.) When your baby begins to crawl, provide maximum floor space (and put breakable or dangerous objects out of reach). When she stands, you may want to provide low balancing bars and furniture with which she can practice walking. When she is eighteen to twenty-four months old, she is ready for a step-up infant gym and other body-building and climbing equipment.

FLOOR SURFACES

The best floors are resilient and easy to clean. Asphalt, vinyl, vinyl asbestos, linoleum, rubber plastic, and cork floor coverings provide washable surfaces well suited to the tremendous amount of floor play that goes on in early childhood. One section of the floor might be carpeted with a variety of textures for crawlers to *feel*. Furry nylon rugs in whimsical shapes are another cheerful addition. Or you might cover the entire floor in sturdy indoor-outdoor nylon carpeting that can be purchased in nine-by-twelve-foot sizes or in twelve-inch self-adhesive tiles.

WALL COVERINGS

You will need a finish that is washable and durable. Glossy paints are good; so is vinyl wallpaper that comes in bright colors and motifs specifically designed for children. You can make large bulletin boards out of corkboard or fiberboard and a smooth wall can be converted into a writing and drawing surface if you give it a coat of "blackboard" paint.

SLEEPING SPACE

A bed is usually the biggest piece of furniture in a child's room. If floor space is limited, consider the use of bunk beds or fold-up beds. (Check the room's ventilation before you decide; sleeping on the top bunk may be too warm for good health.) The great advantage of bunk beds is, of course, that they increase the amount of available play space.

Sleeping space for two is a great convenience even if you have only one child. The extra bed will come in handy for an overnight baby-sitter, guest, and for parents during a child's illness if they want to be close by during the night. Trundle beds offer a compact, efficient way of sleeping two in the day space of one bed. Still another idea: one bed can be fastened to a wall and dropped down into place when a visitor comes.

Many parents, decorating a room for a first child, fail to make allowances for changes and additions that will be necessary when a second child arrives. A canopy bed might be lovely for a first small daughter, but can you duplicate it if you should end up with two girls in one room? If not, a simpler choice is also a wiser one.

WORK SPACE

A table, desk, or counters will be needed later when children work on hobbies, art projects, or school work. If the room must be shared, each child should have his own work area. Putting a folding table on either side of the double bunk beds is one way to divide up available space. If the room is large enough, it might be well to put a folding screen in the middle so that each child has his own private place.

STORAGE SPACE

Toy bins and wood or fiber tote boxes on casters are good for transporting large building blocks, but very poor for storage since the toy a child wants may be buried at the bottom of the bin. Open, adjustable shelves (12″×12″×36″) or 12″×12″×12″ wood cubes are the best way to store children's possessions. Everything is then on display, can be easily found, and easily put away. 12″×12″×12″ wood boxes can be fastened to studs on the wall or left free. These cubes can double as open shelves, seating, and so forth. Put four boxes together and they can become a dollhouse.

Toy bins can be stored under cushioned window seats. Closed bins (with hinged tops) should be no higher than 12″ to 15″ so that small toys can be readily retrieved. Many toys or doll collections can be stored on compartmented shelves (2½′×4′). Wall-hung 3½″-deep shelves are ideal for displaying toys, dolls, horses, and other childhood collections. Sliding glass cases are good for older children anxious to protect (and show off) prized possessions.

If you are living in your own permanent home, consider customizing the closet and building in a storage wall. This is a good way to store those much loved but rather unsightly toys your child still wants to keep.

14

Enrichment Activities

INTRODUCTION BY FREDELLE MAYNARD, PH.D.

The inclusion of a chapter on Enrichment suggests an important step forward in child rearing. Up until recently, books on the first years of life might mention toys, but would certainly not have concerned themselves with clay, paper, and paints. Those were for children old enough to work neatly and turn out creditable products. Now our interest is in process rather than product in the arts as a mode of self-expression and self-realization. We give a two-year-old finger paint not so that she may produce a picture suitable for framing, but because the act of painting, the spontaneous swirling and patting and dabbling, is in itself a delight.

Modern mothers are more willing, I think, than mothers of my generation to tolerate mess; they understand that at certain stages of their development children *need* to be messy. A child being toilet trained, trying to obey those mysterious new imperatives about dry pants, may very much need to splash water and punch clay. A child just entering kindergarten may have no way to express his anxieties except through paint.

One other theme in these pages deserves mention—the awareness that the best entertainment for the young is simple entertainment in which they themselves play an active part. You do not have to take your children to Disneyland to amuse them; a trip to the local fire station or the library will do just as well, perhaps even better. You do not have to buy musical instruments; you and your child can make them, because in the long run there is no real division between "kiddie pleasures" and adult pleasures—there only are pleasures. If you enjoy a visit to an art gallery or a walk through the woods, your three-year-old will enjoy it, too—partly because you do and partly because to him, do not forget, it is all new, all wonderful.

Some of the advice in these pages is "expert" and some is commonsense suggestion based on the experience of ordinary parents. None should be viewed as absolute.

Your child is a unique individual. Never since the world began has there been anybody just like him or her. Respect the individuality of your child. Have faith in your own intuitions; you know this child better than anyone. And do not worry about making mistakes. Everyone makes mistakes. If you show that you love and accept your child, if you make him feel that the world is a good place, if you give him both support and the freedom to explore, then he is well launched on the road to happy, confident adult life.

TRAVELING AND VISITING WITH CHILDREN

Americans are a people on the go and increasingly they are taking their children along on trips and visits. Families are traveling together by car, plane, train, or bus. Restaurants and motels are catering more to their needs. Although traveling and visiting with a child does present certain problems, advance planning and some simple precautions will enable you to avoid difficulties and enjoy even the most ambitious outing.

Traveling with Baby

A small baby usually travels well. If she is kept dry, fed regularly, given sufficient opportunity to sleep, and receives the usual warmth and attention from her parents, she will scarcely notice any change in her environment. The key to your happiness and hers is *simplicity*. Avoid the temptation to cart along every piece of nursery equipment you own.

A carriage or stroller that converts into a car bed will satisfy all his sleeping needs; an infant seat will keep him in touch with the world while you visit and provide for comfortable feeding; a backpack or sling will keep him as mobile as you are. Remember that motels and restaurants provide baby equipment, usually without charge. If you are visiting relatives or friends for an extended stay, most necessary items can be borrowed or rented inexpensively.

With infants, the biggest problem is formula. If you are nursing the baby, accustom her to an occasional bottle in case your milk supply fluctuates during the trip. Let your doctor advise you. By far the easiest formulas to use while traveling are the fully prepared "nursettes." They are easily purchased and require no refrigeration or further sterilization.

Other feeding methods are less expensive and less convenient, but will work nicely. Consider purchasing a nursing unit with disposable "bottle bags" to be used in conjunction with individual cans of fully prepared formula. Sterilized nipples and a can opener can be carried in separate plastic bags.

If your baby is on a sweetened formula, you can substitute ordinary sugar for Karo, usually in the same amount. Little packets of sugar served in restaurants are handy to carry and easy to obtain. This substitution should also be tried out in advance.

Diapers are no longer a problem. The disposable ones, with accompanying plastic garbage bags, are a real boon to the traveler. Continue to use them if you are a houseguest. It is a convenience for you and a courtesy to your hostess. Be sure, however, to ask where to dispose of them. Your hosts will appreciate your thoughtfulness if you use a rubberized pad under baby at changing time.

For general cleanliness en route, tissues, lotion, a dampened washcloth in a plastic bag, and moist towelettes are helpful. There are prepared travel kits of baby products that you might find handy. For convenience, set aside one tote bag for all your baby's needs.

The Older Baby

At about eight months, a baby becomes more aware of her surroundings and it may take more time to settle her in an unfamiliar room. It is wise, therefore, to take along some of her favorite toys. Feeding should be no problem. Baby food is available everywhere and can be eaten at room temperature. Simply feed your baby from the jar and throw away any leftovers. Prepared cereal mixes up into a nice meal at the table.

Teething biscuits, toast, crackers, and other familiar table food will keep baby content while you eat. If you are traveling by plane, try to secure a "bassinet" or bulkhead position. The number of these roomy seats is limited, so speak to the stewardess before boarding. For the car, a sturdy car seat or harness is a must and for other outings a folding "umbrella"-style stroller will accompany your backpack nicely.

The Toddler

The toddler is by nature an explorer. A wonderful companion and adventurer, he is apt to become bored when required to sit for long periods. Allow for ample running time in your schedule. Look for motels with playgrounds, parks, and waysides on the highway, and open spaces at plane and train terminals. If you are driving, it is a good idea to stop a half hour for every two hours in the car and find accommodations for the night in the late afternoon.

Always carry plenty of food. Fruit, crackers, raisins, dry cereal, and sandwiches are easy to carry and can make the difference between a good trip and a miserable one.

Toys will occupy some of the toddler's time. Old favorites are important, but a new little toy hidden away can be a wonderful surprise when the child begins to get restless. Storybooks, pads of paper, crayons, and other simple activity toys are worthwhile additions.

Arranging the passengers in the car can be important. If the parents take turns driving, one can sit in the back with the toddler, who will enjoy the company. A harness will give him freedom to sit, stand, or lie down while keeping him safe.

If you have traveled and visited often with your child, bedtime should present no problem, but if this is a first outing, be prepared for possible upset. By all means, bring with you any security item your child prefers to her other toys and be hesitant to leave a stranger in the role of baby-sitter in a strange house, at least for the first night or so.

PCI Point of View

Traveling and visiting with a child is like most human activities: the more you do it the more accomplished you become and the easier it is for all concerned. Children who have been taken on outings since infancy learn to adapt to new surroundings with adult aplomb and a zest for adventure, while stay-at-home babies become set in their ways and difficult travelers.

LOCAL TRIPS

Until your child reaches the teen years, few pleasures match the joy of a special family outing. To be special, the outing need not be extraordinary. In her book *Guiding Your Child to a More Creative Life,* Dr. Maynard relates the great effort she and her husband made to show their three-year-old daughter a real circus. After a long, hot drive, and the noisy confusion of the big tent, the child seemed more dazed than delighted. She was puzzled by the clowns, frightened by the lions; finally she lost interest and settled into weary boredom. Then, just as her mother was about to suggest that they leave, the little girl came to life: "Oh, Mummy, look! There's a man feeding a horse!"

The Maynards' circus fiasco points out a fact we often forget; to a child the most ordinary things can be remarkable, while what we consider exciting may be only confusing and frightening. Sights adults take for granted (a window washer on a tall building or a road repair crew, for example), children find fascinating. Often the most thrilling excursion involves no more than a short walk or ride from home.

The following suggested outings should be reasonably accessible to all:

Fire Station

Telephone first to find a good visiting hour. If the firemen are not busy, they may let the children climb up on the truck, polish some chrome, and try on a jacket or hat.

Police Station

This is a good way to introduce a small child to an important future source of assistance.

Post Office

Prepare for this trip with a letter-writing or picture-making session at home. The letters can then be mailed at the Post Office. Be sure to include one item addressed to your own home. If you visit at a time when employees are not too busy, you may find someone willing to show you just what happens after an envelope drops through the slot.

Greenhouse

If you go before the summer rush, you will find a lush variety of plants and workers happy to show you around. Children enjoy smelling flowers, observing plants in various stages of growth, and watching soil preparation and potting activities. Purchasing a small plant to take home is a good idea.

Other local activities to consider are a visit to a bakery, a lumberyard, an auto body repair shop, and an artist's studio. One frequently overlooked outing in this age of the automobile is a bus ride. If you have a car, leave it at home one day and take the bus. Your child will love it.

Aquarium

Children usually are fascinated by the large turtles, whales, and a dolphin or seal show.

Botanical Gardens

Your visit to the greenhouse will prepare your children for this outing. In most cities, the gardens are an outdoor affair, but in St. Louis, for example, there are two indoor botanical extravaganzas. Few children can resist the excitement of walking through a real rain forest or watching bananas and orchids grow in their natural setting.

Airport

Drive around first so the children get a sense of the total area. Show them the ticket counters, baggage handling system, and security procedures. Go up to the observation deck to see planes landing and taking off. Point out the importance of the control tower and the ground crews.

A Factory

Ideally, your visit should be to a chocolate or cereal factory full of delicious smells, fascinating operations, and a tasty free sample at the end of the tour. Inasmuch as all processes are interesting to children, do not be deterred by the fact that neither Hershey's nor Kellogg's is within reach.

The University Campus

If you live near a major university with a college of agriculture, you are very fortunate. Such an institution offers a myriad of free activities fascinating to children. Children love to visit the *apple orchard* and *animal barns* and the agriculture students who work there are usually eager to show them around. Many large campuses have an *observatory, aviary,* and *arboretum,* all open to the general public. The *campus bell tower* can also be visited for concerts and demonstrations.

Cultural Activities

MUSIC

Many symphony orchestras offer a series of "kinder concerts." These are a wonderful introduction to the world of good music. Take advantage of outdoor band concerts in the park, group song fests, musical demonstrations, and the high school band's outdoor practice sessions.

DANCING

Probably nothing could compete with the color and excitement of a ballet like *The Nutcracker Suite,* but there are simpler ways to introduce your child to dancing. There are folk dance and square dance groups at community centers, as well as creative movement and rhythm classes that welcome small visitors.

THEATER

Even small communities now offer numerous theatrical activities for young children. Marionette and puppet shows are always fun, but nothing takes the place of live actors. Look for a group of good amateur adults who specialize in performing for children; or you may find professionals (part of a local repertory or regional theater) who produce a regular children's season. Call in advance to determine each production's intended age level. You might prepare your child in advance by reading or discussing the play together. Do not be surprised if your little one turns out to be a real first-nighter. Television has made this generation very sophisticated theatergoers.

CAMPING WITH INFANTS AND TODDLERS

Today many young families are discovering family camping as an ideal, inexpensive means of vacationing. A weekend or several days spent in the out-of-doors can be a refreshing experience for the entire family. There is no need to wait until your child is older to enjoy camping; even the youngest infant can be made part of the outing.

The key to successful camping is *preparation.* This is especially important when you are camping with your infant or toddler. Campgrounds vary greatly in facilities. Some offer raised platforms, hot showers, and flush toilets. Others may be much more primitive. (Most campgrounds have telephones and physicians within easy call.) You should check ahead with a campground if facilities are important to you.

If you feel apprehensive about camping out with your young child, start with an overnight "trial run" in your back yard if you have one. This experience will allay your fears and help you gain confidence about your child's adaptability. It will also give you an opportunity to double-check your routines, equipment, and supplies.

528

Basic Equipment

The most basic piece of equipment is a tent or tarpaulin to sleep under. Second, for your infant or young child, you must have some sort of bassinet, basket, portable crib, or his own (washable, waterproof) sleeping bag. Since children are restless sleepers, sharing your sleeping bag will not do. With a ground cloth and warm sleep wear (zipped one-piece blanket sleepers are ideal), your littlest camper will be warm, dry, and comfortable.

The next most important piece of equipment is a backpack child carrier. If you are walking or hiking, your infant can nap en route. The backpack is also useful as a feeding chair or—with rope tied to a tree—as a baby swing. A backpack carrier enables you to get off the beaten path and gives you much more freedom to enjoy the out-of-doors than do carriages or strollers (which are not practical for most campgrounds).

Diapers, Clothing, and Food

Disposable diapers are ideal for camping. If your infant is sensitive to paper diapers when used for extended periods, you may consider buying from a diaper service clean, "used" cloth diapers that are worn out and frayed. Often they can be purchased in bulk at a price comparable to paper ones and then disposed of after use.

If you are nursing your baby, a sterile source of milk is assured. However, if you are bottle feeding, do not despair. Either the powdered formula mixed with bottled water and poured into disposable bottles or the premixed formula in sterilized ready-to-use bottles (that do not require refrigeration) will be safe and convenient. If your toddler is drinking regular milk, you may either keep a small quantity of fresh milk in an ice chest at your campsite or, preferably, use canned evaporated milk or dry milk powder. "Bottled" sterilized water is recommended to avoid any possible digestive upsets.

Commercial baby foods are the most convenient way to feed your baby while camping. A word of caution about food: fresh air stimulates the appetite, so take plenty of food and do not be surprised if your baby demands grown-up portions!

Clothing depends on *where* and *when* you are camping. A good rule of thumb is to bring plenty of warm articles (long-sleeved shirts or turtleneck pullovers, for example), some clothing that "breathes," and some that is water-repellent. You may be surprised at how cool camping can be unless you are prepared.

Routines

Do not be surprised if your baby wakes earlier than usual. She may find the unfamiliar outdoor noises and early morning light a stimulant. If you find yourself tired from early rising, take a nap later on when she does, or alternate early morning risings with your husband.

Be psychologically prepared to see a grubbier child. All children love to play in the dirt and little campers are no exception.

If your toddler is beginning to be toilet trained, get him used to "potting" behind the bushes before your trip so he will not be too surprised to find no potty in the woods.

If you are hiking, as mentioned above, your infant may nap in the backpack carrier or you can make a little "nest" for him to take a nap in when you all stop for a rest. Even a reluctant napper will probably rest if you tell him how "all little animals cuddle down in their little nests for a rest . . ."

COMMUNITY RESOURCES

Whether you live in a small town or a large city, you can enlarge your children's horizons, develop their imagination, awareness, and knowledge by making good use of community resources.

The Public Library

To begin with, visit your public library regularly. Modern librarians are service-oriented, anxious to make the library a learning center for the entire community. Many libraries have lending collections of films, cassettes, tapes, posters, sculpture, and art prints to be checked out, taken home, and enjoyed. Most also have family film programs, as well as toddler and school-aged story hours. The reference collection has all sorts of directories for information sources and will be helpful in planning vacation trips, locating museums of special interest, providing information about the fees, accommodations, and services in national parks, and identifying community services. (The reference librarian, usually stationed at a desk nearby, knows which books will be most helpful to you. Do not be shy about asking.)

Get to know your library, its staff, and resources. Let the staff know what additional services you would like to see offered. (Talks by local craftsmen and artists perhaps? Puppet shows in the children's room?) If your library has a Friends of the Library group, join it. The membership fee is small and this is a good way to influence community resources.

Museums

Many museums have gift shops that sell reproductions of lovely art objects in their collection or in the collections of other museums at reasonable prices. (Museum shop catalogues are generally available by mail on request.) When visiting art museums, a stop at the postcard counter for postcards of reproductions of the collection makes possible recreating the visit on rainy indoor days. Buy two of each. They are inexpensive and a way to make up picture-matching games to teach "art appreciation." When you take a child to a museum, keep the visit brief. Choose a few special things to look at—some you have seen before, and a few unfamiliar pictures or sculptures each time. In that way, children acquire old favorites in the museum and develop new ones.

Check your community for children's museums. These are not merely display centers, but active organizations that involve children in living and learning activities in science, art, music, and the language arts. The small annual fee for membership is a good investment if you can afford it; it will bring you notices of special shows, the monthly informative newsletter most museums publish, and the satisfaction of knowing you and your children are supporting a life-enriching community endeavor.

Posters

In addition to art reproductions, consider the use of posters as wall decorations in your children's rooms (and throughout your house). Posters are particularly good as a source of visual stimulation for babies; they are colorful, easy to hang, and readily available. Furthermore, they are so inexpensive that you can probably afford a sizable poster collection, changing your decor from time to time. Some of the commercial sources for posters and art reproductions suitable for young children are:

Harlem Book Company
221 Park Avenue South
New York, N.Y. 10003

Friends of the Earth
c/o Western Service
350 Paul Ave.
San Francisco, Calif. 94124

The Postermakers, Inc.
7519 Melrose Ave.
Los Angeles, Calif. 90046

Travel posters (often free) are another attractive possibility. These can be obtained from travel agencies, airline companies, and the embassies and consulates of foreign nations located in Washington, D.C., and New York City. Check the phone book of nearby large cities for the addresses of the consulates of countries that interest you. For games, songs, stories, posters, and pictures of children's cultural activities in other lands write to:

The United States Committee for UNICEF
331 East 38th Street
New York, N.Y. 10016

Music

What about music for the young? If you live in a community where live music is available, your children are especially lucky. Recordings and radio and television programs are all very well, but there is no substitute for the concert hall, where children can see, as well as hear the music making. Look for benefit concerts at your local private schools, museums, and other non-profit institutions; such organizations often sponsor folk music concerts for children as fund-raising activities.

Children who have had the opportunity to see musical instruments being played may wish to acquire their own. In that case, a family collection of simple rhythm instruments, recorders, an Autoharp, and other easy-to-learn instruments will provide a fine accompaniment for singing (and one in which the youngest children can join in).

Rhythm instruments are available as sets or singly from:

Childcraft Education Corporation
21 Kilmer Road
Edison, N.J. 08817

Children's Music Center, Inc.
5373 Pico Boulevard
Los Angeles, Calif. 90019

Creative Playthings, Inc.
Edenburg Road
Cranbury, N.J. 08512

Music Shops (Ask for low-priced cymbals, 5"–6", maracas, tambourines, triangle and striker, rhythm sticks, and tone blocks and bells.)

BOOKS FOR BABIES AND PRESCHOOLERS

A love of books can begin as early as nine months, when a baby begins to sit up, babble, and respond happily to the rhythmic beat of nursery rhymes. During this early period of language development, books can and should play an important part.

Hold your baby in your lap and look at the pictures with her, talking, naming objects, and making appropriate sounds. (Although there are picture books designed to be tied between the spokes of the crib so that a baby can "read" by herself, nothing can substitute for the closeness of sharing a book with an interested adult at this early stage.)

Some books should be made of cloth or heavy cardboard so the baby can touch and handle them. Others, to be shared with an adult, need not be chew and tear resistant. The first books should contain colorful pictures of familiar objects, things the child has touched or seen. Text is unimportant. (You may prefer to supply your own, appropriate to your baby.) A baby is often impatient to get on to the next page or next picture, so keep your comments simple and brief. Do not be surprised if your baby begins to imitate, "reading" the book along with you.

All babies enjoy books that provide touching-feeling experiences. Good examples of this type are Dorothy Kunhardt's *Pat the Bunny* and Margaret Wise Brown's *Little Fur Book*. As the child begins to talk, you can introduce a more elaborate commentary and also ask questions about the pictures. ("What is the kitty doing? Where is the little boy's Mummy?")

Early books with words or stories should have lots of repetition, a pleasing rhythm, and clear bright pictures. Margaret Wise Brown's *Good Night Moon* is strong in all these qualities and is generally adored by young children.

A Word of Caution

Avoid the pop-up books, Color Form Stick-On Books, the four-foot-high giant books, the "smell" books, and other varieties of toy books. They are more costly than good quality standard books and are often poorly written and designed. Pop-ups, for example, tear easily and end up frustrating instead of amusing.

Be wary of children's books illustrated in a highly abstract "modern" manner. Such books appeal more to adults than to children. Most important, be sure the picture really illustrates the text. It is very confusing for a child just beginning to understand language if the story describes a red ball and the pictures show a green one.

Picture books for the toddler should deal with the familiar, everyday world and include animals, vehicles, and people in his world of experience (mothers, fathers, children, policemen, mailmen, and so on). Lois Lenski's stories for young children—*The Little Auto, Policeman Small,* and *Papa Small*—are just right for these early reading experiences and are now available in paperback editions. Children have always valued the concrete pictures and simple narrative language of these books.

Leave folk and fairy tales (such as "Goldilocks and the Three Bears," "Cinderella," "Little Red Riding Hood") for a much later time, when the child is able to distinguish between reality and fantasy. Little children are apt to be terrified by the wolf that eats up grandmother or the three bears who frighten Goldilocks.

Of course, no baby is too young for Mother Goose; the rhymes are perfect for singing, reciting, dancing, and clapping. Never mind whether your child understands the words; the rhythms and sounds are enough. Who can resist joining in "Goosey, goosey gander/Whither shall I wander?/Upstairs, downstairs,/ Through my lady's chamber" or "Tom, Tom, the piper's son,/ Stole a pig and away he run . . ."? Children love alliteration in poetry—"Susie's galoshes make splishes and sploshes . . ."

A good collection of Mother Goose, an anthology of poetry, and a guide to children's literature on the bookshelf will help a family to develop a reading program and provide many hours of shared joy and enrichment.

MUSIC

Music is a first language for all children. An infant of four months plays with sounds as she babbles. At nine months, she gets considerable pleasure out of beating a pot with a spoon, clashing pot covers as ardently as the percussion player in the orchestra. By eighteen months, she sings and dances rhythmically along with her records. Music needs to be part of an infant's experiences from the very beginning of life. Children enjoy all kinds of music, classical as well as folk, jazz, and rock.

Singing

Children are musical beings. Even in the womb, a child will respond to musical stimulus. (Between the sixth and ninth months of pregnancy, the fetus may be stimulated by loud music into vigorous kicking.) A newborn responds to his mother's voice and will turn his head to hear the household noises. Five-month-old babies babble and coo (a first form of singing) for the sheer joy of trying to get out sounds. Six- to nine-month-old babies react positively to mother's songs and body games. Toddlers hum and sing as they go about their play.

Even the adult who claims to have no ear, no musical knowledge, probably knows dozens of songs with strong rhythmical patterns and repeated melodies that make them especially suitable for children. "Row, Row, Row Your Boat," "Yankee Doodle," "Old McDonald Had a Farm," "Pop Goes the Weasel," "Where, Oh, Where Has My Little Dog Gone?" "Swing Low, Sweet Chariot," "Oh! Susanna"—all these songs are simple, direct, and rhythmical (and suggest lively accompanying actions). Repeated words and lilting rhymes are popular with children of all ages— and their parents, too.

To make songs more meaningful, parents can personalize by introducing the child's given name into the song. In "Oh! Dear! What Can the Matter Be?" forget about "Johnny and the Fair" and substitute "Mary (or John or Jack) is so slow with her lunch." Action songs, such as "Here We Go Round the Mulberry Bush," can be adapted to any situation. Also, "This is the way we wash our hands—brush our teeth—eat our peas," etc.

Every home should have a collection of recorded songs (folk, ethnic, and traditional) and as many song books as possible. Since your child will most likely want the same songs played repeatedly, you will find music time more enjoyable if you do not confine yourself to children's records. Broaden your child's musical taste. Try everything from classical guitar to Indian sitar. Even better is to take the young child to live folk singing concerts. Parents with some flair for instruments might master playing a guitar or Autoharp to accompany the singing at home.

ART SUPPLIES TO HAVE ON HAND

Experts agree that the kind and quality of art experiences you give your preschool child will have a deep and lasting effect on his abilities, perceptions, and personality. They affect his powers of observation, his emotional health, his confidence, and his ability to express himself.

The years between two and five are particularly significant in terms of creative growth. To guide your child's artistic development during this period, you do not have to be an artist yourself. All you need is sympathetic interest, some understanding of the developmental stages children pass through in art expression, and a willingness to provide suitable materials.

Stay away from coloring books and prepackaged "art kits"; they undermine a child's confidence in his own creative abilities because they substitute someone else's symbols for his own.

The natural beginning stage of artistic development is scribbling, so your child should be encouraged to scribble freely. She is ready for this as soon as she can hold a crayon in her hand and demonstrates an interest in making marks on paper or on a blackboard. This can be as early as fifteen to eighteen months. Give your child large, 18"×24" sheets of newsprint paper. After much practice in scribbling, she will eventually develop line control, then shape control, and finally will arrive at the stage of *naming* her scribbles. Around the fourth year (although this varies greatly), she will begin to make recognizable symbols—her symbol for a man, a house, the sun, etc.

Understanding this sequence will help you appreciate your child's efforts (and save you unreasonable disappointment when the "man" he draws at age three is not recognizably human). Acceptance and respect for what your child creates are fundamental. Do not attempt to show him how to draw "a real house" or "a real car." What he draws is real to him.

Do not make disparaging comments, such as "That doesn't look like a fire engine!" or "What's that?" If you cannot figure out what he is drawing (and even if you can), a good safe observation is "Oh, I like your picture. Tell me about it." You can talk about colors, shapes, and textures. Together you can begin collecting interesting materials for collages and other simple constructions.

Soft, moist clay and/or Play-Doh are other good art materials for very young children. Again, do not expect representational creations, but encourage your child's sensuous pleasure as she experiments with the material.

In addition to being appropriate to your child's developmental level, art materials should be readily accessible, on open shelves if possible. If she can set up and put away these materials by herself, the young painter's independence will grow along with her artistry. An "art area" is ideal, even if it is only a corner of your kitchen.

A parent's role in the child's art activities should be helpful, but never intrusive. It is all right to make simple suggestions—"The paint's gotten thick. Shall we add some water?"—but do not offer advice unless requested. You should, of course, feel free to play with art materials yourself if the impulse strikes. Do not, however, accept the invitaton to "draw something" for your child when he asks; rather, encourage him to draw his *own* version by talking about how an object looks and feels, its size, color, shape, and so forth.

Finally, remember to display examples of your child's finished art work. This is one way of letting her know that what she is doing is important.

PETS (FROM GERBILS TO BUDGIES)

Pets and Small Children

It is a rare child who does not long for a pet of his very own. The range of possible domestic pets is very wide, including not only the common mammals and birds, but also assorted reptiles, insects, and fish. (A few people go in for exotic creatures, such as tiger cubs, but here we consider only some of those animals that can be humanely cared for in the home. Wild animals belong in their own natural habitats.)

Children and Pets

If you decide to get a puppy or kitten for your child, remember that new puppies and kittens need a great deal of care, including periodic examinations and shots by a veterinarian. If you have a pet, you will have to teach your child to treat it humanely, not pull the kitten's tail or poke the puppy's eyes. In many cases, this training is not possible until three or four years of age. (Which is also the time when a child is ready to relate emotionally to a pet.)

A child of three or older may see a new pet much as she would see a new baby, reacting with rivalry and regression. Behavior of this sort should be handled with gentle firmness. Assure her that she is still and always will be special to you. Give her an opportunity to share in the responsibilities of raising her pet, even if her "job" is no more than filling the water dish.

Do not expect a child under the age of nine or ten years to be totally responsible for a pet. If, however, a small child gradually assumes small responsibilities, he learns how dependent his pet is on proper food and care (and, incidentally, comes to understand the responsibilities that parents have for their young). With a pet, your child can also share in the joys and sorrows of mating, pregnancy, birth, and even death. No book, no verbal explanation can ever take the place of this actual learning experience.

For some children, a pet takes the place of an imaginary friend to whom secrets, angers, hopes, and fears can be safely confided. A pet has some advantages over parents (it never scolds or punishes) and indeed over real-life friends (since it is less likely to shift allegiance).

Choosing a Pet

If you want a pedigreed dog, locate a reputable breeding kennel. If you want a mongrel, try the pound. Since there are so many homeless cats, why not adopt one from your local animal shelter?

Before you acquire a dog or cat, make sure your child is not allergic to animal fur. Let her handle the pet; if her face turns red or if she has a sudden coughing spell, you may have an allergic child. In that case, wait an hour or so to see if the symptoms persist. If you are in any doubt, consult with your doctor before buying a pet.

Rodents are easily cared for and are clean and docile enough to be handled. They require less care than cats or dogs, are soft and warm, and make good companions for children. Their food requirements are simple: rabbits, guinea pigs, hamsters, mice and gerbils eat prepared food pellets, seeds, fruits, and vegetables.

Rabbits are very gentle and love to be held and stroked. Indoors, their cage should be all-wire with a removable metal tray-type bottom for easy cleaning. If your rabbit is kept outdoors, it should live in a hutch constructed of wood, with a wire mesh floor and door, and an enclosed section that offers protection from severe weather conditions.

Guinea pigs and mice are social animals; several of these can be caged together without fear of their fighting except during and right after pregnancy and birth. Watch the newborns carefully since the parents will often eat or abuse them. Metal cages, with a wooden shelf for the guinea pigs to rest their feet on, are easy to keep.

Guinea pigs like to be taken out of their cages for exercise and play and can be allowed to roam (with supervision) around a room. Mice, kept in plastic or glass communal cages, are fun to watch. Put swings, a platform ladder, and an exercise wheel in to keep them busy. Mice are very gentle and make excellent pets for children, but should not be over-handled.

Gerbils and hamsters are best kept alone since they tend to fight. Gerbils can be kept in mouse cages or in aquariums with wire mesh tops. Gentle, daily handling of a young hamster will ensure that he remains tame. Hamsters are nocturnal, so *do not* keep them in a bedroom at night!

Parrakeets (sometimes known as budgies) and canaries are the most popular pet birds in America. Both must be cared for devotedly since they cannot survive even twenty-four hours without proper food and water.

Any child will enjoy teaching a parrakeet to speak or letting the bird perch on his shoulder as he plays. Male canaries sing beautifully but canaries should not be handled very much and make less suitable pets than do parrakeets.

Fish are ideal pets for all ages, fun to watch, and easy to breed. Guppies and mollies, which reproduce rapidly, provide a fascinating life cycle for infants and children to watch. (Creative Playthings, Inc., makes a plastic tank that fits over the side rail of the crib. Filled with fish, it is an exciting living "mobile" for babies.)

Reptiles and amphibians can be kept easily in a natural environment if you have a terrarium. Your child will enjoy helping you assemble the terrarium. Chameleons, frogs, and snakes also make good terrarium pets. Avoid turtles, though; they are disease carriers.

PCI Point of View

No matter which pet you choose to have in your home, the emotional and factual learning on your child's part will be very great, well worth the effort of remembering to clean the cage or set out the dog's food.

TELEVISION AND YOUR CHILD

Children look at television because their parents do and for much the same reasons. It provides opportunities for entertainment and escape and also is a great source of information. To the busy mother, TV offers an attractive solution to the question of how to keep the little ones occupied. Too much reliance on this constantly available "electronic mother," though, may create problems later on. Television's endless stimulation and excitement may make everyday life look insipid by comparison. Unfortunately, TV has a seductive power to hold and attract regardless of quality.

Originally greeted as a device that would encourage family life by keeping the family at home together, television is often, instead, an intruder, an uninvited guest, disrupting conversations, and creating areas of conflict between parent and child. (If dad wants the football game and the children want "Sesame Street," who wins? What about noisy commercials that set children clamoring for unsuitable toys? How much watching is too much?)

What Are the Positive Values of Television Viewing?

An important value of television viewing is the amount of knowledge effortlessly acquired. Children learn about letters and numbers from "Sesame Street," about words from "Electric Company," about interesting things to do from "Zoom." They gain an increased awareness of the world about them through television's coverage of news events. They learn about space explorations (and also, unfortunately, about wars and killings). Television enables young children to view official celebrations, helps them develop a sense of heritage, and respect for the achievements of outstanding scientists, athletes, and artists. Broadcasts about animals and the world they live in, visits under the sea with Jacques Cousteau—all these expand a child's knowledge.

Television can also be a positive family activity, providing occasions for relaxed sociability. (At nursery school, when a young child was asked what she liked best about television, she said, "I get to sit on my daddy's lap.")

What About Television Is Cause for Concern?

A constant barrage of entertainment leads the small child to expect that she will be continually entertained. She becomes a passive listener, seldom paying full attention to what she hears. Later on, when she goes to school, she may be unable to follow directions, unlikely to exert initiative.

Another important concern is that television takes time away from other important activities necessary to the child's proper physical and social development. TV has decreased the *amount* of playing time and apparently has affected the *quality* of imaginative play in the preschool child. The knowledge children gain through television is largely vicarious; young children do *not* distinguish clearly between fantasy and reality. Children, especially two- and three-year-olds, need to see and hear about animals; they need to touch and smell them, too. They need not only to see and hear about forms and shapes, they need to manipulate them. Even such a fine TV program as "Sesame Street" has come under attack from psychiatrists, such as Dr. Werner Halpern of a Mental Health Center in Rochester, New York. After noticing an increase in the number of two-year-old patients with compulsive frantic behavior and discovering that they were regular viewers of "Sesame Street," Dr. Halpern became a viewer himself. His conclusion: the program's pulsating, insistent visual and auditory stimulation can act as an assault on the nervous system of young children with immature neurological and perceptual development. The two-year-old patient's pressured speech, constant movement, frantic reactions, and compulsion to recite and identify numbers and letters could be the result of "sensory overkill" produced by the show's overheated teaching techniques. Dr. Halpern asserts that the exhausting stimuli on TV can lead to emotional instability.

Finally, most parents are concerned over the amount and kinds of violence pictured on TV. The Surgeon General's Committee on Television and Social Behavior recently demonstrated a causal link between violence watched on television and some forms of aggression and violent behavior. As far as is known, scenes of violence should have no permanent ill effects on the well-adjusted child. But for the child frustrated in other aspects of his life or for the aggressive child, violence pictured on TV can serve as a stimulant. Of course, common sense tells us that programs full of horror and brutality and gruesome and morbid presentations have no place in a young child's life.

Action for Children's Television

Concerned with the effect violence on TV might be having on children and on society as a whole, a group of parents in suburban Boston organized as ACT (Action for Children's Television) to discuss the problem. These parents studied what was being offered children on television and discussed ways of making television a creative and constructive force in children's lives.

After several meetings, they came to the conclusion that violence was featured on children's television programs because it sold products. As long as broadcasters believe that violent programs attract more viewers and, therefore, more revenue from advertising, they will continue to schedule such material. ACT's objective is to make children's TV a public service area, responsive to the needs of the child rather than the pressures of the advertiser.

Some of ACT's accomplishments: They have influenced broadcasters to appoint vice-presidents in charge of children's programming, pushed through the elimination of vitamin advertising on children's TV programs, begun ATAC (Advice on Toys at Christmas) to help parents cope with the pressures of Christmas selling on TV, encouraged some different programing on Saturday morning—CBS "News Spots," CBS "Children's Film Festival"—some local programs, and the ABC "After-School Special" for children during the week.

Probably ACT's biggest accomplishment has been a general "consciousness-raising" about children's TV. In July 1974, ACT published a guidebook, in co-operation with the American Academy of Pediatrics, to help parents decide which programs are good for children, which might harm them, and which have too much violence. Written by Evelyn Kaye,

The Family Guide to Children's Television—What to Watch, What to Miss, What to Change and How to Do It will be helpful to any parent concerned about children's TV viewing. Its contents include advice on which shows are good, cartoons, violence, commercials, and a workbook section for children that can be used to rate favorites.

Maximizing the Values of Television

Some parents are so concerned about the dangers of television that they have refused to have a set in the house. This is surely an extreme position. Television is an important tool of modern man, to be used with understanding and judgment.

Television can be an asset in a child's life or it can be a liability. It is up to the parents to see that its influence is positive and wholesome. Children need some entertainment and much television entertainment is first-class. Musical shows, for example, can increase a child's musical appreciation, family shows (the Waltons, for instance) can provide them with warm, reassuring images of family life. However, all children need quiet times, too. Parents should refuse to let children spend hours glued to the set.

PCI Point of View

You should be familiar with the programs your child watches, not only to see if they are suitable, but to explain where necessary the differences between what is real and what is pure fantasy. You might consider delaying your child's introduction to TV until she can begin to differentiate between reality and fantasy. If you see what your child is seeing you can work to improve the quality of programming available. Having a supply of stamped postcards on hand enables you to write immediately—both compliments and complaints—to sponsors and stations while the matter is fresh in your mind. Letters do affect programming decisions, but too many parents forget to write and then wonder why the quality of programs does not improve.

Bibliography

Ainsworth, Mary D. *Infancy in Uganda*. Baltimore: Johns Hopkins Univ. Press, 1967.

———. "Patterns of Attachment Behavior Shown by the Infant in Interaction with His Mother," *Merrill-Palmer Quarterly*, 10, 51–58 (1964).

———; Bell, Silvia M.; and Stayton, Donelda J. "Individual Differences in the Development of Some Attachment Behaviors," *Merrill-Palmer Quarterly*, 18 (1972).

Akmakjian, Hiag. *The Natural Way to Raise a Healthy Child*. New York: Praeger, 1975.

Alexander, G., and Williams, Daniel C. "Maternal Facilitation of Sucking Drive in Newborn Lambs," *Science*, 146, October 1964.

American Dental Association, Chicago, Ill. *Accepted Dental Therapeutics*, 1973.

———. *Parents Want to Help*, 1970.

———. *Your Child's Teeth*, 1967.

American National Red Cross. *Advanced First Aid and Emergency Care*. Garden City, N.Y.: Doubleday, 1973.

Ames, L. B., and Ilg, F. L. *Child Behavior*. New York: Harper, 1955.

Anderson, David C. *Children of Special Value*. New York: St. Martin's, 1971.

Andry, Andrew, and Schepp, Steven. *How Babies Are Made*. New York: Time-Life, 1968.

Apgar, Virginia. *Is My Baby All Right*. New York: Pocket Bks., 1974.

Arms, Suzanne. *Immaculate Deception*. Boston: Houghton, 1975.

Arnold, Arnold. *Teaching Your Child to Learn from Birth to School Age*. Englewood Cliffs, N.J.: Prentice-Hall, 1971.

———. *Your Child's Play*. New York: Simon & Schuster, 1955.

Atkin, Edith, et al. *The Complete Book of Mothercraft*. New York: Greystone, 1952.

Azrin, Nathan H., and Foxx, Richard M., Ph.D. *Toilet Training in Less Than a Day*. New York: Simon & Schuster, 1974.

Bandura, Albert; Ross, Dorothea; and Ross, Sheila A. "A Comparative Test of the Status Envy, Social Power, and Secondary Reinforcement Theories of Identificatory Learning," *Journal of Abnormal and Social Psychology*, 67 (1963), 527–34.

Banks, A. J., and Grambs, J. D. *Black Self-concept*. New York: McGraw, 1972.

543

Barnard, Kathryn A., Ph.D. "A Program of Stimulation for Infants Born Prematurely." Unpublished paper presented at meeting of the Society for Research in Child Development, Philadelphia, Spring 1973.

Baughman, E. Earl. *Black Americans.* New York: Academic Press, 1971.

Bayley, Nancy. *Bayley Scales of Infant Development.* New York: Psychological Corp., 1969.

Bean, Constance. *Methods of Childbirth.* Garden City, N.Y.: Doubleday, 1972.

Beck, Joan. *How to Raise a Brighter Child.* New York: Trident Press, 1967.

Beckwith, Leila. "Relationships Between Infants' Social Behavior and Their Mothers' Behavior," *Child Development,* 1972.

Bereiter, Carl, and Engelmann, Siegfried. *Teaching Disadvantaged Children in the Preschool.* Englewood Cliffs, N.J.: Prentice-Hall, 1966.

Berman, Claire. *We Take This Child.* Garden City, N.Y.: Doubleday, 1974.

Berrill, N. J. *The Person in the Womb.* New York: Dodd, 1968.

Berry, M., and Eisenson, J. *Speech Disorders.* New York: Appleton, 1956.

Biller, Henry, Ph.D., and Meredith, Dennis. *Father Power.* New York: McKay, 1974.

Bing, Elizabeth. *The Adventure of Birth.* New York: Simon & Schuster, 1970.

———. *Six Practical Lessons for an Easier Childbirth.* New York: Bantam Bks., 1969.

Birch, William G., M.D. *A Doctor Discusses Pregnancy.* Chicago: Budlong Press, 1972.

Birns, Beverly, Ph.D.; Blank, Marion, Ph.D.; and Bridger, Wagner H., Ph.D. "The Effectiveness of Various Soothing Techniques on Human Neonates," *Psychosomatic Medicine,* 28, 1966.

Blaine, Graham. *Are Parents Bad for Children: Why the Modern American Family Is in Danger.* New York: Coward, McCann & Geoghegan, 1973.

Bland, Jane Cooper. *Art of the Young Child.* New York: Mus. of Modern Art, 1968.

Blomfield, J. M., and Douglas, J. W. B. *Children Under Five.* London: Allen, 1958.

Bloom, Benjamin S. *Stability and Change in Human Characteristics.* New York: Wiley, 1974.

Boston Children's Medical Center and Feinbloom, Richard I., M.D., et al. *Child Health Encyclopedia: The Complete Guide for Parents.* New York: Delacorte Press, 1975.

———, and Gregg, Elizabeth. *What to Do When There Is Nothing to Do.* New York: Dell, 1967.

Boston Women's Health Book Collective. *Our Bodies, Ourselves.* New York: Simon & Schuster, 1973.

Bowlby, John. *Separation, Anxiety, and Anger.* New York: Basic Bks., 1970.

Brackbill, Yvonne. "Cumulative Effects of Continuous Stimulation on Arousal Level in Infants," *Child Development,* 1971.

———, and Thompson, George, eds. *Behavior in Infancy and Early Childhood.* New York: Free Press, 1967.

Brainerd, Charles J. "The Origins of Number Concepts," *Scientific American,* March 1973.

Braun, Samuel J., and Edwards, Esther P. *History and Theory of Early Childhood Education.* Belmont, Calif.: Wadsworth Pub., 1972.

Brazelton, T. Berry, M.D. *Infants and Mothers*. New York: Delacorte Press, 1972.

———. *Toddlers and Parents*. New York: Delacorte Press, 1974.

Broadribb, V., and Lee, H. F. *The Modern Parents' Guide to Baby and Child Care*. Philadelphia: Lippincott, 1973.

Brody, Sylvia. *Patterns of Mothering*. New York: Int. Univs. Press, 1972.

Bronshtein, A. I., and Petrova, E. P. "The Auditory Analyzer in Young Infants," in *Behavior in Infancy and Early Childhood*. New York: Free Press, 1967, 163–72.

Bruner, Jerome, Ph.D. "Play Is Serious Business," *Psychology Today*, January 1975.

Buktencia, Norman A. *Visual Learning*. San Rafael, Calif.: Dimensions Pub., 1968.

Calderone, Mary S., ed. *Manual of Family Planning and Contraceptive Practice*. Baltimore: Williams & Wilkins, 1970.

Callahan, Daniel. *Abortion: Law, Choice and Morality*. New York: Macmillan, 1972.

Callahan, Sidney. *Parenting: The Principles and Politics of Parenthood*. Garden City, N.Y.: Doubleday, 1973.

Callaway, W. Ragan, Jr., Ph.D. *Modes of Biological Adaptation and Their Role in Intellectual Development*, Perceptual-Cognitive Development Monograph Series, Vol. 1, No. 1, 1970.

Caplan, Frank, and Caplan, Theresa. *The Power of Play*. Garden City, N.Y.: Doubleday, Anchor Bks., 1973.

Carmichael, Leonard. *Manual of Child Psychology*. New York: Wiley, 1946.

Carson, Ruth. *So You Want to Adopt a Child*. New York: Public Affairs Pamphlet No. 173-A.

Chabon, Irwin. *Awake and Aware*. New York: Dell, 1973.

Cherry, Sheldon H. *Understanding Pregnancy and Child Birth*. Indianapolis: Bobbs, 1974.

Child Health Centers of America. *Your Child: Keeping Him Healthy*. Jackson, Tenn.: 1971.

Child Study Association of America. *What to Tell Your Child About Sex*. New York: Pocket Bks., 1974.

Chrystie, Frances N. *Pets*. New York: Little, 1974.

Church, Joseph. *Understanding Your Child from Birth to Three*. New York: Random, 1973.

Cohen, Dorothy. "Is TV a Pied Piper?" *Young Children*, November 1974.

Committee on Nutrition. "Obesity in Childhood," *Pediatrics*, 1967.

Corcoran, Gertrude B. *Language Arts in the Elementary School*. New York: Ronald Press, 1970.

Davis, Adelle. *Let's Have Healthy Children*. New York: Signet, 1972.

DeCaire, Theresa. *The Infant's Reaction to Strangers*. New York: Int. Univs. Press, 1974.

DeLucia, Leonore D. "Stimulus Preference and Discrimination Learning," edited by J. F. Rosenblith, et al., in *The Causes of Behavior*, 3rd ed. Boston: Allyn & Bacon, 1972.

Dennis, Wayne, and Najarian, P. *Infant Development Under Environmental Handicap*. Psychological Monograph No. 7, 1971.

Despert, J. Louise. *Children of Divorce*. Garden City, N.Y.: Doubleday, Dolphin Bks., 1962.

Dick-Read, Grantly. *Childbirth Without Fear*. New York: Harper, 1970.

DiCyan, Erwin, and Hessman, Lawrence. *Without Prescription*. New York: Simon & Schuster, 1972.

Dodson, Fitzhugh. *How to Father*. Los Angeles: Nash Pub. Corp., 1974.

———. *How to Parent*. New York: Signet Bks., 1971.

Dreikurs, Rudolf. *Coping with Children's Misbehavior*. New York: Hawthorn Bks., 1972.

Duffy, J. K., and Irwin, J. J. *Speech and Hearing Hurdles*. Columbus, Ohio: School & College Services, 1951.

Dyasuk, Colette T. *Adoption—Is It for You?* New York: Harper, 1973.

Edelman, Marian W. "Seeking Effective Child Advocacy," *Young Children,* July 1974.

Ehrlich, Shirley. "The Psychological Impact of New Parenthood," in *Pregnancy, Birth, and the Newborn*. New York: Delacorte Press, 1972.

Engelmann, Siegfried, and Engelmann, Therese. *Give Your Child a Superior Mind*. New York: Simon & Schuster, 1966.

English, O. S., and Foster, C. J. *A Guide to Successful Fatherhood*. Chicago: Science Res. Assocs., 1954.

Engstrom, George. "Motor Development," *Baby Talk,* March 1970.

Erikson, Erik. *Childhood and Society*. New York: Norton, 1963.

Etaugh, Claire. "Effects of Maternal Employment on Children, a Review of Recent Research," *Merrill-Palmer Quarterly,* 20 (1974).

Falkner, Frank, M.D. "Key Issues in Infant Mortality." Bethesda: National Institute of Child Health, 1969.

Family Publication's Center. *Pierre the Pelican*. New Orleans, 1967.

Fantz, Robert L., M.D. "Visual Perception from Birth," *Annals,* New York Academy of Sciences, 118 (1965), 793–814.

Farb, Peter. *Word Play*. New York: Knopf, 1974.

Farson, Richard. *Birthrights*. New York: Macmillan, 1974.

Feinbloom, Richard I., M.D., et al. *Pregnancy, Birth, and the Newborn Baby*. New York: Delacorte Press, 1972.

Fitzpatrick, Elise, et al. *Maternity Nursing*. Philadelphia: Lippincott, 1966.

Fraiberg, Selma. *The Magic Years*. New York: Scribner, 1959.

Frank, Lawrence K. *On the Importance of Infancy*. New York: Random, 1966.

Freud, Anna. *Normality and Pathology in Childhood*. New York: Int. Univs. Press, 1965.

Fromme, Allan. *The Parent's Handbook*. New York: Simon & Schuster, 1956.

Gaddis, Vincent, and Gaddis, Margaret. *The Curious World of Twins*. New York: Warner Paperback Lib., 1973.

Gardner, George. *The Emerging Personality*. New York: Delacorte Press, 1970.

Gersh, Marvin. *How to Raise Children at Home in Your Spare Time*. New York: Stein & Day, 1973.

Gesell, Arnold, M.D., and Ilg, Frances, M.D. *Infant and Child in the Culture of Today*. New York: Harper, 1943.

Gilbert, Sara D. *Three Years to Grow.* New York: Parents' Mag. Press, 1972.

Ginott, Haim G. *Between Parent and Child.* New York: Macmillan, 1965.

Giovanni, Nikki. *Spin a Soft Black Song.* New York: Hill & Wang, 1971.

Goldstein, Joseph, et al. *Beyond the Best Interests of the Child.* New York: Free Press, 1973.

Goodrich, Frederick W., Jr., M.D. *Preparing for Childbirth: A Manual for Expectant Parents.* Englewood Cliffs, N.J.: Prentice-Hall, 1966.

Gordon, Ira; Guinach, Garry; and Jester, R. Emile. *Child Learning Through Child Play.* New York: St. Martin's, 1972.

Gordon, Thomas. *P.E.T., Parent Effectiveness Training.* New York: New Am. Lib., 1975.

Gornick, V., and Moran, B. K. *Women in Sexist Society.* New York: Mentor Bks., 1971.

Graham, George, M.D., and Adrianzen, Blanca, M.D. "Late 'Catch-up' Growth After Severe Infantile Malnutrition," *Johns Hopkins Medical Journal,* 131 (1972).

Grimstad, Kirsten, and Rennie, Susan, eds. *The New Woman's Survival Catalog.* New York: Coward, McCann & Geoghegan, 1974.

Gruenberg, Sidonie, ed. *The New Encyclopedia of Child Care and Guidance.* Garden City, N.Y.: Doubleday, 1968.

Gunther, Mavis, M.D. *Infant Feeding.* Chicago: Regnery, 1970.

Guttmacher, Alan, M.D. *Pregnancy and Birth.* New York: Signet Bks., 1962.

Hadfield, J. A. *Childhood and Adolescence.* Middlesex, England: Penguin, 1969.

Hadley, Leila. *Fielding's Guide to Traveling with Children in Europe.* New York: Fielding Publications and Morrow, 1972.

Hammett, Frederick S. "Studies of the Thyroid Apparatus: V," *Endocrinology,* 6 (1922).

Harlow, Harry. "Love in Infant Monkeys," *Scientific American,* June 1959.

————, and Harlow, M. "Social Deprivation in Monkeys," *Scientific American,* November 1962.

Hartley, Ruth, and Goldenson, Robert. *The Complete Book of Children's Play.* New York: Crowell, 1963.

Hawkins, Robert P. "It's Time We Taught the Young How to Become Good Parents," *Psychology Today,* November 1972.

Hellyer, David. *Your Child and You.* New York: Delacorte Press, 1966.

Henderson, Neil C., M.D. *Emergency Medical Guide.* New York: McGraw, 1973.

————. *How to Understand and Treat Your Child's Symptoms.* New York: Award Bks., 1971.

Hole, J., and Levine, E. *Rebirth of Feminism,* New York: Quadrangle/The N. Y. Times Bk. Co., 1971.

Holt, John. *Escape from Childhood.* New York: Dutton, 1974.

Homan, William E. *Child Sense.* New York: Basic Bks., 1969.

Hoover, Mary. *The Responsive Parent.* New York: Parents' Mag. Press, 1972.

Huizinga, Johan. *Homo Ludens.* Boston: Beacon Press, 1964.

Hunt, W.; Clarke, Frances; and Hunt, Edna. "From the Moro Reflex to the Mature Startle Pattern," in *Behavior in Infancy and Early Childhood,* New York: Free Press, 1967.

Hymes, James L., Ph.D. *Teaching the Child Under Six.* Columbus, Ohio: Merrill, 1974.

Ilg, Frances L., M.D., and Ames, Louise B., Ph.D. *Child Behavior.* New York: Harper, 1955.

Inhelder, Barbel, and Piaget, Jean, M.D. *The Growth of Logical Thinking,* New York: Basic Bks., 1958.

——. *The Psychology of the Child.* New York: Basic Bks., 1969.

Isaac, Jean Rael. *Adopting a Child Today.* New York: Harper, 1965.

Janov, Arthur. *The Feeling Child.* New York: Simon & Schuster, 1973.

Kagan, Jerome. "Do Infants Think?" *Scientific American,* March 1972.

Kagelman, I. Newton. *Wisdom with Children.* New York: Day, 1965.

Karelitz, Samuel, M.D. *When Your Child Is Ill.* New York: Random House, 1969.

Karmel, Marjorie. *Thank You, Dr. Lamaze.* Garden City, N.Y.: Doubleday, 1959.

Katz, Sanford N. *When Parents Fail.* Boston: Beacon Press, 1971.

Kaye, Evelyn. *The Family Guide to Children's Television.* New York: Pantheon Bks., 1974.

Kehm, Freda, and Mini, Joe. *Let Children Be Children.* New York: Associated Press, 1968.

Kelley, Marguerite, and Parson, Elia. *The Mother's Almanac.* Garden City, N.Y.: Doubleday, 1975.

Kenda, M. E., and Williams, P. S. *The Natural Baby Food Cookbook.* New York: Avon Bks., 1972.

Kent, Saul. "Perinatology: New Science of Childbirth," *Saturday Review/ World,* July 1974.

Kidd, Aline, and Kidd, Rivoire. *Perceptual Development in Children.* New York: Int. Univs. Press, 1966.

Kippley, Sheila. *Breast Feeding and Natural Child Spacing.* New York: Penguin, 1975.

Kitzinger, Sheila. *Giving Birth: The Parent's Emotions in Childbirth.* New York: Taplinger, 1971.

Klaus, Marshall H., M.D., et al. "Human Maternal Behavior at the First Contact with Her Young," *Pediatrics,* 46 (1970).

Korner, Anneliese, and Grobstein, Rose. "Visual Alertness as Related to Soothing in Neonates: Implications for Maternal Stimulation and Early Deprivation," *Child Development,* 45 (1974).

La Leche League International, Inc. *Breast Feeding and the Premature Baby.* Franklin Park, Ill., 1971.

——. *The Womanly Art of Breast Feeding.* Franklin Park, Ill., 1963.

Lamaze, Fernand, M.D. *Painless Childbirth: The Lamaze Method.* New York: Pocket Bks., 1972.

Leboyer, Frederick, M.D. *Birth Without Violence.* New York: Knopf, 1975.

Lenneberg, Eric H., et al. "The Vocalization of Infants Born to Deaf and to Hearing Parents," *Human Development,* 6 (1965).

Liley, H. N. I., with Day, Beth. *Modern Motherhood.* New York: Random House, 1969.

Lipsitt, Lewis, Ph.D., et al. *Learning Capacities of the Human Infant.* New York: Academic Press, 1969.

Lowenfeld, Margaret, *Play in Childhood*. New York: Wiley, 1967.
Lowenfeld, Viktor, and Brittain, W. Lambert. *Creative and Mental Growth*. New York: Macmillan, 1964.
McCall, Robert B. "Exploratory Manipulation and Play in the Human Infant," *Monograph* of Society for Research in Child Development, Vol. 39, No. 2. Chicago: Univ. of Chicago Press, July 1974.
McCleary, Elliott. *New Miracles of Childbirth*. New York: McKay, 1974.
McGraw, Myrtle. *Neuro-muscular Maturation of the Infant*. New York: Columbia Univ. Press, 1943.
————. "Swimming Behavior of the Human Infant," *Journal of Pediatrics,* April 1939.
Marzollo, Jean. *9 Months, 1 Day, 1 Year*. New York: Harper, 1975.
————, and Lloyd, Janice. *Learning Through Play*. New York: Harper, 1972.
Maynard, Fredelle. *Guiding Your Child to a More Creative Life*. Garden City, N.Y.: Doubleday, 1973.
Mead, Margaret. *Sex and Temperament in Three Primitive Societies*. New York: Mentor Bks., 1950.
Meier, John H., Ph.D. *Systems for Open Learning*. Denver, Colo.: Child Development Center, Denver Medical School, 1973.
Metraux, Ruth W. "Speech Profiles of the Preschool Child," *Journal of Speech and Hearing Disorders*, Vol. 15, No. 1 (1950).
Millar, Susanna. *The Psychology of Play*. Baltimore: Penguin, 1968.
Miller, John Seldon, M.D. *Childbirth*. New York: Atheneum, 1962.
Mohr, George. *When Children Face Crises*. Chicago: Science Res. Assocs., 1952.
Montagu, Ashley, Ph.D. *The Direction of Human Development*. New York: Hawthorn, 1968.
————. *On Being Human*. New York: Hawthorn, 1967.
————. *Prenatal Influences*. Springfield, Ill.: C. C. Thomas, 1962.
————. *Touching*. New York: Harper, 1972.
Moore, A. Ulric, M.D. "Effects of Modified Maternal Care in the Sheep and Goat," in *Early Experience and Behavior*. Springfield, Ill.: Thomas, 1968.
Mussen, Paul H.; Conger, John J.; and Kagan, Jerome. *Child Development and Personality*. 3rd ed. New York: Harper, 1969.
Navarra, John G. *The Development of Scientific Concepts in a Young Child*. Westport, Conn.: Greenwood, 1973.
Neisser, Edith. *Primer for Parents of Preschoolers*. New York: Parents' Mag. Press, 1972.
Newman, James, and Newman, Barbara. *Family Camping Guide*. New York: Grosset, 1972.
Newman, Virginia Hunt. *Teaching an Infant to Swim*. New York: Harcourt, 1972.
Newton, Grant, Ph.D., & Levine, Seymour, Ph.D., ed. *Early Experience and Behavior*. Springfield, Ill.: Thomas, 1968.
Newton, Niles Anne, Ph.D. *Family Book of Child Care*. New York: Harper, 1957.
Nilsson, L., and Ingelman-Sundberg, A. *A Child Is Born: The Drama of Life Before Birth*. New York: Dell, 1971.
Painter, Genevieve. *Teach Your Baby*. New York: Simon & Schuster, 1971.

Paulson, Conrad G. "The Legal Rights of Children," *Childhood Education,* April/May 1974.

Piaget, Jean. *The Construction of Reality in the Child.* New York: Basic Bks., 1954.

———. *The Origins of Intelligence in Children.* New York: Int. Univs. Press, 1952.

———. *Play, Dreams and Imitation in Childhood.* New York: Norton, 1962.

Pines, Maya. *Revolution in Learning.* New York: Harper, 1970.

Pomeranz, Virginia, M.D., and Schultz, Dodi, *The First Five Years.* Garden City, N.Y.: Doubleday, 1973.

Pomeroy, Wardell. *Your Child and Sex.* New York: Delacorte Press, 1974.

Prenatal Care. U. S. Department of Health, Education, and Welfare, Children's Bureau Publication No. 4, 1962.

Princeton Center for Infancy. *The First Twelve Months of Life.* New York: Grosset, 1973.

Ramos, Suzanne. *Teaching Your Child to Cope with Crisis.* New York: McKay, 1975.

Rheingold, H.; Gewirtz, J.; Ross, H. "Social Conditioning of Vocalizations in the Infant," *Journal for Comparative and Physiological Psychology,* 1959.

Rheingold, Harriet L., and Samuels, Helen R. "Maintaining the Positive Behavior of Infants by Increased Stimulation," *Developmental Psychology,* 1 (1969).

Ribble, Margaret. *Rights of Infants.* New York: Columbia Univ. Press, 1965.

Robertson, Elizabeth, and Wood, Margaret. *Today's Child.* New York: Scribner, 1974.

Rodham, Hillary. "Children Under the Law," *Harvard Educational Review,* November 1973.

Salk, Lee, Ph.D. *Preparing for Parenthood.* New York: McKay, 1974.

———. *What Every Child Would Like His Parents to Know,* New York: McKay, 1972.

———, and Kramer, Rita. *How to Raise a Human Being.* New York: McKay, 1972.

Sasmor, Jeanette. *What Every Husband Should Know About Having a Baby.* Chicago: Nelson-Hall, 1972.

Shapp, Charles; Shapp, Martha; and Shepard, Sylvia. *Let's Find Out About Babies.* New York: Watts, 1969.

Sharp, Evelyn. *Thinking Is Child's Play.* New York: Dutton, 1969.

Sheffield, Margaret. *Where Do Babies Come From.* New York: Knopf, 1972.

Sheresky, N., and Mannes, M. *Uncoupling.* New York: Dell, 1973.

Shiller, Jack, M.D. *Childhood Illness.* New York: Stein & Day, 1973.

Showers, Paul, and Showers, Kay. *Before You Were a Baby.* New York: Crowell, 1968.

Simner, Marvin L. *Newborn Response to Cry.* New York: American Psychological Association, 1971.

Singer, Jerome L. *The Child's World of Make Believe.* New York: Academic Press, 1973.

Skelsey, Alice, and Huckaby, Gloria. *Growing Up Green.* New York: Workman Pub., 1973.

Smilansky, S. *See* Singer, Jerome.

Soman, Shirley C. *Let's Stop Destroying Our Children*. New York: Hawthorn, 1974.

Sparkman, Brandon, and Carmichael, Ann. *Blueprint for a Brighter Child*. New York: McGraw, 1973.

Spock, Benjamin, M.D. *Baby and Child Care*. Rev. ed. New York: Pocket Bks., 1972.

———. *Problems of Parents*. Cambridge, Mass.: Houghton, 1962.

———, and Lowenberg, Miriam E. *Feeding Your Baby and Child*. New York: Pocket Bks., 1956.

Steptoe, John. *Stevie*. New York: Harper, 1969.

Toy Safety. Bureau of Product Safety, U. S. Department of Health, Education, and Welfare Pub. No. 73–7009.

Turner, Mary D., and Turner, James S. *Making Your Own Baby Food*. New York: Bantam Bks., 1972.

Twardoz, S.; Cataldo, M. F.; and Risoly, T. R. "Infants' Use of Crib Toys," *Young Children*, July 1974.

Twin Mothers' Club of Bergen County, N.J. *And Then There Were Two: A Handbook of Mothers and Fathers of Twins*. New York: Child Study Association of America, 1971.

U. S. Government Book of Infant Care. New York: Award Bks., 1968.

Van Riper, Charles. *Speech Corrections*. Englewood Cliffs, N.J.: Prentice-Hall, 1972.

Vygotsky, Lev. *Thought and Language*. Cambridge, Mass.: MIT Press, 1962.

Warren, Jonathan R. "Birth Order and Social Behavior," *Psychological Bulletin*, 65 (1966).

Watts, Harriet M. *How to Start Your Own Preschool Playgroup*. New York: Universe Bks., 1973.

Weisberg, Paul. *Social and Non-social Conditioning of Infants' Vocalizations*. New York: Free Press, 1967.

Weiser, Eric. *Pregnancy, Conception and Heredity*. New York: Blaisdell Pub., 1965.

White, Burton L., et al. *Experience and Environment*. Vol. 1. Englewood Cliffs, N.J.: Prentice-Hall, 1973.

Williams, Carl. "The Elimination of Tantrum Behavior by Extinction Procedures," *Journal of Abnormal and Social Psychology*, 1959.

Winick, Mariann. *Before the 3 R's*. New York: McKay, 1971.

Wittes, Glorianna, and Radin, Norma. *The Learning Through Play Approach*. San Rafael, Calif.: Dimensions Pub., 1969.

Wolf, Anna. *Helping Your Child to Understand Death*. Child Study Association of America, 1973.

Wolf, Stein. *The One Parent Family*. New York: Public Affairs Pamphlet No. 287, 1973.

Yarrow, Leon J. "Measurement and Specification of the Early Infant Environment," *Public Health Paper* No. 24 (1964).

———, and Goodwin, Marion S. "Some Conceptual Issues in the Study of Mother-Infant Interaction," *American Journal of Orthopsychiatry*, 35 (1965).

Index

552

555